SYSTEM SIMULATION IN WATER RESOURCES

IFIP Working Conference on
Biosystems Simulation in Water Resources and Waste Problems
Bruges, Belgium, September 3-5, 1975

organized and sponsored by
IFIP Technical Committee 7, Optimization
International Federation for Information Processing

NORTH-HOLLAND PUBLISHING COMPANY
AMSTERDAM · OXFORD · NEW YORK

SYSTEM SIMULATION
IN WATER RESOURCES

Proceedings of the
IFIP Working Conference on
Biosystems Simulation in Water Resources and Waste Problems

edited by

G.C. VANSTEENKISTE

Professor of Engineering
Universities of Ghent and Brussels, Belgium

1976

NORTH-HOLLAND PUBLISHING COMPANY
AMSTERDAM - OXFORD - NEW YORK

North-Holland: ISBN 07204 0453 3
American Elsevier ISBN: 0444 11093 3

Published by:
NORTH-HOLLAND PUBLISHING COMPANY - AMSTERDAM, NEW YORK, OXFORD

Distributors for the U.S.A. and Canada:
American Elsevier Publishing Company, Inc.
52 Vanderbilt Avenue
New York, N.Y. 10017

PRINTED IN THE NETHERLANDS

FOREWORD

This book on "SYSTEM SIMULATION IN WATER RESOURCES" reports the proceedings of the IFIP Technical Committee on Optimization (TC-7) 1975 Working Conference of the Modeling and Simulation Group WG-7.1. This international symposium was held in Bruges - Belgium from September 3 to 5 on the topic "Biosystems Simulation in Water Resources and Waste Problems".

The aim of the Working Conference was to review the state of the art of modeling and estimation techniques applied to water resources systems and waste problems, with special emphasis on biological aspects, water quality and surface water systems. Due to the most efficient discussions and the large amount of interest in the first meeting organized July 30 - August 2, 1974 in Ghent (proceedings edited as "Computer Simulation of Water Resources Systems" by North-Holland Publishing Company - Amsterdam), it was felt necessary to organize a similar meeting including waste problems in 1975. A very important task of the 1975 meeting was to hold active discussions to assess the relevance of systems engineering methodology and simulation techniques to typical problems in the proposed environmental area, as well as to stimulate interdisciplinary research in this field.

The organizing committee was composed of the following members : J. Andrews (Houston, U.S.A.), A.V. Balakrishnan (Los Angeles, U.S.A.), B. Davidson (New Brunswick, U.S.A.), M. De Boodt (Ghent, Belgium), W. Gardner (Madison, U.S.A.), D. Hillel (Rehovot, Israël), W.J. Karplus (Los Angeles, U.S.A.), J.R. Philip (Canberra, Australia), G. Vachaud (Grenoble, France), G.C. Vansteenkiste (Ghent, Belgium), R. Vichnevetsky (New Brunswick, U.S.A.), S. Wajc (Brussels, Belgium), P.C. Young (Cambridge, England). The conference was sponsored by the IFIP Working Group on Modeling and Simulation (WG-7.1), the Belgian National Science Research Foundation, the Free University of Brussels and the State University of Ghent.

Survey papers were presented by M.B. BECK, W.J. KARPLUS, S.P. NEUMAN and G. VACHAUD. Almost fifty specialists in the identification and physically oriented area from twelve different countries attended the three day round table discussion. Also a panel session on "Credibility and validation of water resources simulation" chaired by R. CROSBIE, was included in the program. The introductory paper on "System simulation in the testing role" presented by G.C. VANSTEENKISTE, reviews the conclusions of the conference as well as the general lay-out of this book in the scope of its topic : system simulation techniques applied to water resources research.

September 1975

Ghislain C. Vansteenkiste
Ghent - Belgium

Vice Chairman IFIP-WG 7.1
"Modeling and Simulation"

CONTENTS [*]

_____

[*] The papers were presented in the order indicated by the numbers

PART THREE

ON THE USE OF DEDUCTIVE INFORMATION IN QUANTITY MODELS
OF WATER RESOURCES SYSTEMS

PART FOUR

ON THE USE OF DEDUCTIVE INFORMATION IN QUALITY MODELS
OF WATER RESOURCES SYSTEMS

PART ONE

SYSTEM SIMULATION IN WATER RESOURCES - STATE OF THE ART

System Simulation in Water Resources, ed. G.C. VANSTEENKISTE
1976, North-Holland Publishing Company

SYSTEM SIMULATION IN THE TESTING ROLE

Ghislain C. Vansteenkiste
Professor of Engineering
University of Ghent and Brussels, Belgium

INTRODUCTION

The relationship of water resources systems to the natural
and biological area as well as to the economical and institutional
domain creates complicated and complex systems. Their analysis and
understanding necessitate the construction of mathematical models.
This illustrates the multi-disciplinary aspect of water resources
development, utilization and conservation. Such analysis has been
advanced through the growing tendency toward interfacing the environment oriented approach and the systems engineering orientation. It
is the purpose of this introductory paper to report on some of the
difficulties water resources models are affected with, to show how
simulation techniques are adapted to build such models, and to stress
on the role of water resources models in environmental research.
The ideas reflect results from panel and round table discussions
during the first and second working conference devoted to this topic.
In the text, reference is made to participants of both meetings.
The paper also surveys the lay-out of the content of this book on
SYSTEM SIMULATION IN WATER RESOURCES.

FACING WATER RESOURCES SYSTEMS

The very nature of environmental processes leads to such a
complex of interconnections of subsystems, that isolation of a portion of the system in order to separate input and output information,
may destroy its natural function and thus lead to identification of
a purely hypothetical process. Many systems are too complicated for
any reasonable model to include all the factors that might be important, leading to complaints of incorrectness and incompleteness.
On the other hand, a model which does include most of the relevant
factors may be too complex to be optimized by the existing techniques.
No criteria of completedness for an environmental model can be stated.
The model does not meet the criterion of "best-fit".

The validity of water resources modeling is mostly blurred
by the *low quality of experimental data*, much more than by the incompleteness of the equations involved. It is the acquisition of
truly representative field data that sets the identification of
environmental processes, somewhat apart from the average industrial
process simulation problem. As every experimenter knows, systems
related to nature exhibit great variability of the data, such that
parameters obtained from identification techniques applied to ensemble averaged raw data may have little or no significance for the
user and therefore be suspect. This variability may result from
nature itself as well as from the available instrumentation and
measuring techniques. Environmental systems display an interaction
of dynamic processes in different time scales with time constants
ranging from milliseconds to years, so that measurement time which
is required to obtain consistent parameter estimates may be so long
that stationarity can no longer be assumed and requires time isolation

3

for measurement purposes. Local constraints, sometimes with an institutional character, prevent uniformity of experimental results. In
several water resources studies, only natural excitation of the process dynamics can be observed in general and artificial disturbances
are precluded. So normal operational records exhibit just one particular mode of process behaviour, deviations from the steady state
may even be insignificant, blocking all information about the dynamics. This again entails a low signal to noise ratio.

SIMULATION PROBLEM IN WATER RESOURCES STUDIES

        System analysis of physical research problems can be subdi-
vided into three aspects called *inverse problems, direct problems
and control problems*. In water resources studies, simulation meets
a partly inverse, partly direct problem situation and has a control
problem as final goal. This is illustrated in figure 1. The content
of this book on *"SYSTEM SIMULATION IN WATER RESOURCES"* follows this
classification :
- *Part two* describes the inverse synthesis problem aspect of water
  resources simulation (called inductive modeling by W. KARPLUS).
  Excitation-response combinations are given and the description of
  the system has to be determined.

- *Parts three, four and five* show how partly deductive information,
  the basis for direct (analysis) problems, is utilized. System structure and excitation are partly known as a physical description or
  in mathematical form, solutions can be computed. System structure
  is gradually less determined moving from part three to five. The
  structure is best specified in the quantity models in water resources studies from part three ; far less specified in the quality
  models of part four, but worst of all determined in the quality
  models involving biosystems as discussed in part five.

- *Part six* shows briefly how water resources models can be used as
  an aid for control purposes ; a lot of illustrative examples can
  be found in the proceedings of the previous working conference [1].
  Looking at the environmental model from a control standpoint, system and desired response are formulated and the input control variables have to be calculated.

        Starting from a synthesis point of view with known excitation
response (input - output) combinations, the first step in the derivation of a water resources model is the system characterization
stage where a specification of the mathematical structure of the
model governing the system is made. The input - output data may be
used either directly or indirectly in determining the structure.
In the indirect approach a structure is postulated from a set of
feasible structures. After parameter identification on the postulated
model, the structure will be accepted or rejected according to a
verification procedure : if rejected, a new structure is postulated
and the determination is repeated. This method does not necessarily
converge to a correct model [2]. In contrast, a direct approach
attempts to determine a structure immediately from the observations
without identifying the parameters [3]. Parameter identification
can be accomplished either implicitly or explicitly. In the implicit
case numerical values are determined minimizing a certain criterion
function of the error between model and system. Techniques like
least squares, generalized least squares, maximum likelihood, instrumental variable and correlation and least squares are sufficiently
described in the literature. In the explicit method mathematical
relationships between system input and output result in the parameter
values ; step response or pulse response measurements, frequency

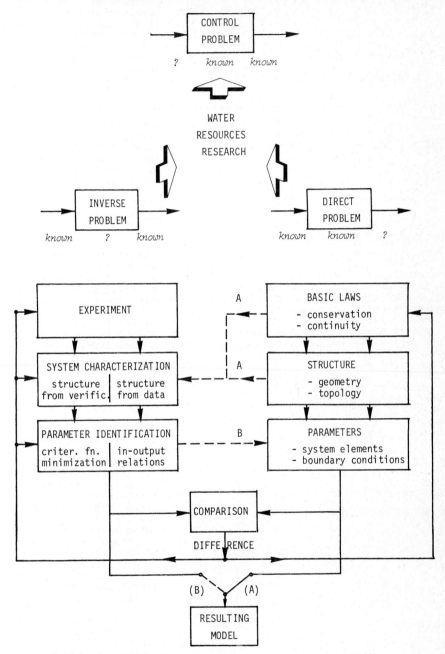

Figure 1 : Simulation techniques in water resources studies

response techniques, Fourier-, correlation- and spectral analysis techniques have to be used in this case.

Ion exchange and movement in soils for instance, are based on mass-flow, diffusion and dispersion as governed by clay- and humus-content, cation exchange capacity and pore space. A general form of the mathematical expression of these phenomena is known a priori, but an explicit structure of the mathematical expression is lacking. This structure is to be inferred from input-output observations. This is the way how deductive information filters into the previous system characterization stage like indicated by the dotted lines A in figure 1. Balance equations, physical-chemical state equations, phenomenological equations and entropy balances are well known and understood in quantity models for water resources studies, resulting in a simulation technique having its gravity point far to the right side in figure 1 (models discussed in part three of this book).

In the water quality field different attempts have been made in order to link for instance N-transformations such as mineralization, nitrification, denitrification, ion-exchange and its transport to a water-flow model, predicting nitrate concentrations in tile-effluents as a function of farm management practices and climatic conditions. Here there is only an approximate knowledge of the physical-chemical state equations which underlie the physiological phenomena, resulting in simulation techniques which rely more upon inductively-derived information, hence their gravity point is more to the left side of figure 1 (models discussed in part four of this book).

Examinations of biosystems in quality models as there is in studies of the dynamic behaviour of activated sludge processes, aerobic digestions and DO-BOD-algae interactions in rivers, have only a very incomplete knowledge of the basic laws characterizing the generation and disappearance of the effects of water pollution. Furthermore this knowledge is blurred by a hostile environment in which system characteristics are changing in time in an unpredictable manner. Biosystems simulation techniques are therefore almost purely based on inverse modeling. This is the case for the contributions in part five of this book.

W. KARPLUS shows in his contribution how the *predictive validity* of the obtained water resources model is limited, proportionally to the amount of inductive thinking needed for its construction. Validity of a simulation is an objective attribute of the model. Validation asks whether the basic assumptions made about relationships between variables and values of system parameters are justified. According to R. CROSBIE it is not an easy task to do validation of water resources models in practice. It is difficult to get an idea of how reliable these data are - data used for calibration should not be used to establish the validity of the model. E. TODINI points out that validation should be done on the models as well as on the data ; examples of validation of models in surface hydrology for instance are rare in literature. Simpler models could replace the ones used if they could be validated in the sense that it cannot be proven that the simple models are worthless using statistical tests on the hypotheses made. G. de MARSILY points out the importance of defining validation in a quantitative way when trying out to assess efficiency in testing different theories to solve a problem. Constraints and conditions under which the obtained models are valid should be well established to allow evaluations through comparisons.

Credibility of a model is a more subjective factor and brings in, according to R. CROSBIE, a lot of psychological factors. The manner of presentation of the results (animated pictures, impressive graphics) can make a great deal of difference to whether the results are found credible or not ; the degree of involvement of the subject in the modeling process as well as the expectedness of the results are also important in this aspect.

As W. KARPLUS points out water resources models have to be made credible within their limitations. Every field has to make its own approach to make its models credible leading to its goal and utilization domain. It would be useful to get a sort of agreement to what point the models can be considered credible.

WATER RESOURCES SIMULATION FEEDBACK - A TESTING ROLE

The degree of refinement and the generality of the model required of a particular system depends quite definitely on the context and the purpose. The nature of the model should suit the nature of the problem. Analytical tools used in modeling water resources systems should be of sufficient flexibility to be in agreement with the validity of those models : excess refinement leads to deceptive simulations. Although the simulation task goes through definite stages of modeling, the way it is performed in reality gives the impression of not being standardized in methodology. Some rationalization of the approach and the avoidance of stretching a problem to fit the methods would make a lot of criticism worthless.

Figure 2 illustrates in a summarized form how the different water resources models described above should be utilized according to their validity. As was discussed the prediction power of water resources models is relatively low. Again in relation to the amount of decisions based on raw data utilized in the modeling process, quantity models should be oriented towards general experimentation under a set of different control strategies and towards decision purposes only on the long run ; while quality models based on physical laws should be used for testing theories and hypotheses. Models are ideal tools for insight and instruction purposes when biosystems are involved ; the different successive steps of the modeling activity, which means asking questions on each step, leads indeed to a better estimation, classification and understanding of the acting factors ; it is possible in the so-called sensitivity analysis to determine the most important parameters of the system.

On the other hand, as S. NEUMAN mentions the need of actually using the water resources models for prediction purposes is growing. This creates the important task of handling the data available at the present moment in the best way to bring the model to a state where it can predict in a credible way. This task relies partly upon the development of more efficient structure characterization algorithms. At the present state we don't really know how to validate our models in a way that they could create credibility for prediction purposes.

As illustrated in figure 2 water resources modeling effort should end up in the development of a more rational data collection scheme ; the interaction with the model should direct the search of additional data. This is an extremely important task. This goal is also stressed by S. NEUMAN. G. VACHAUD illustrates how involved the parameter linkage is in studies on water uptake by plants. Ten to fifteen years are necessary to know what parameters are the most

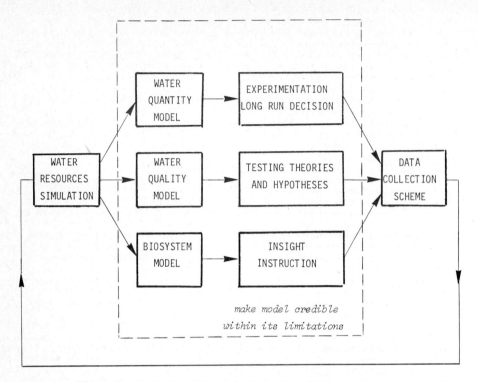

Figure 2 : Goal of models with limited predictive validity

important to follow ; sensitivity techniques applied to the water
uptake model will guide the selection of the parameters to be measured. P. WIERENGA indicates that you can keep measuring for thirty
years in a study on quality of irrigation return flow, whereas collecting data during a five year period might be sufficient for constructing the model and use its prediction capability to complete
for the remainder of the measurements. This is the important *testing
role of water resources simulation* : whenever data are collected one
should try to understand what is involved ; a good way to understand
is to try to model ; this step gives a feeling of the sensitivity of
the parameters which in turn direct the experimental design. This
explains the feedback loop in figure 2. Because the value of environmental data is so high, it is desirable that experimental work should
be well planned in advance so that the amount of information derived
can be maximized. Any a priori knowledge of the system's dynamic behaviour can be used to establish, for example, the relevant state
variables to be measured, the sampling rate at which measurements
should be made, the duration of the experiment, the desired nature
of the input forcing signals, etc.

    There are in addition three aspects of simulation which seem
to be difficult to substitute by any other method in environmental
studies. The first is cross checks between various types of readings
and technologies used. Environmental models can be used in collecting

and condensing information and in controlling the quality of additional information. The determination of the DO in water quality
models according to a wet analytical method on one hand and by means
of a dissolved oxygen electrode on the other hand, will lead to different results if no intercalibration has taken place between the
various laboratories. In other instances one finds that a large number of observations have been made and these are documented very
carefully, but the control over the ever-growing material has decreased with time ; mathematical models will help to condense data
material. When a descriptive and possibly a predictive model has
been formulated for conservative water constituents (like chloride
ions) and also for non-conservative substances (like BOD), it is
much simpler to check the quality and consistency of subsequently
gathered information.

A second aspect provided by simulation is the possibility of
measuring quantities in real systems which seem to be very difficult
to follow, or which require an unnumerable amount of samples, such
as seepage through dikes, acquifers, etc. This results in an inten-
sification and improvement of the monitoring system. A first model
inspection can show where due to a consistency of modeling results
and observed data, the frequency of data collection could be reduced.
Questions like : in which locations should continuously measuring
devices be installed, in what points will samples be taken to be
analyzed by laboratory means, what is the optimal sampling frequency,
what are the costs and possibly the benefits of additional information leading to increased precision of process behaviour, could be
checked out on the model.

Finally, a model permits predictions of responses to unusual
events and conditions and therefore might help or prepare decision-
making. The simple and condensed representation of all important
data describing the system under study in conjunction with the effects of certain measures upon the characteristics of the system is
in itself already an aid in decision-making.

CONCLUSION

The complexity of today's water resources systems makes it
almost mandatory that their management be achieved through the application of the technology of a variety of disciplines. In order to
formulate policies for future system development, an easy assessment
necessitates the use of computer simulation. It has been seen that
the development of such models depends on a close interaction with
the water resources specialist and in itself has a most important
testing role for the user. It is therefore of the utmost importance
that experts of both sides have dialogues in a proper atmosphere,
with mutual respect for each other. Both sides should appreciate
the ultimate limitations of their model and utilize it conformable
its validity.

REFERENCES

[1] Proceedings of the IFIP Working Conference on Computer Simulation of Water Resources Systems, Ghent, 1974 - G.C. VANSTEENKISTE (ed.).

[2] Vachaud, G., Vauclin, M. and Haverkamp, R., "Towards a comprehensive simulation of transient water table flow problems", Proc. of the IFIP Working Conference on Computer Simulation of Water Resources Systems, Ghent, 1974 - G.C. VANSTEENKISTE (ed.).

[3] Karplus, W.J., "System identification and simulation - a pattern recognition approach", Proc. Fall Joint Comp. Conf. 1972, pp. 385-392, 1972.

System Simulation in Water Resources, ed. G.C. VANSTEENKISTE
1976, North-Holland Publishing Company

THE FUTURE OF MATHEMATICAL MODELS OF WATER RESOURCES SYSTEMS*

Walter J. Karplus
Computer Science Department
University of California, Los Angeles

INTRODUCTION

The past years have seen an intensive level of activity in the modeling
and simulation of water resources systems. In the United States alone there are
approximately one thousand government funded projects involving the modeling of
surface and underground hydrologic systems. If one adds to these the many projects currently under way in Europe, in Japan, in the Near East, and in other
parts of the world it becomes clear that a very large amount of money and effort
is being expended in this area. As a result, the modeling of water resources
systems is gradually assuming the proportions of an independent technical discipline. Nonetheless it appears pertinent and useful to view the modeling of water
resources systems in perspective as falling along a comprehensive spectrum of
mathematical models. This permits inferences based upon the experiences of other
application areas and facilitates the prediction of eventual levels of elegance
and validity to be expected from water resources models.

DEDUCTIVE VERSUS INDUCTIVE MODELING

A mathematical model is a set of equations which characterizes a real-life
system, the prototype system, in the sense that at least some of the excitation/
response relationships of the prototype system are correctly represented. A subset of all the prototype system inputs is expressed mathematically and serves as
the excitation of the mathematical model; the solution of the model equations
then constitutes the mathematical representations of the corresponding subset of
system responses; the better this representation, the more valid the model. The
ultimate objective of most modeling efforts is to predict responses to excitations
other than those utilized in constructing the model. It follows that the more
valid the model, the more reliable it is as a tool for prediction.

The construction of a mathematical model entails the utilization of two
types of information: deductive and inductive. Deduction is reasoning from
known principles to infer an unknown; it is reasoning from the general to the
specific. In modeling deductively, one derives the mathematical model analytically from knowledge or intuitions about the system. This analytical process
makes use of a series of progressively more specific concepts which may be broadly
categorized as: laws, structure and parameters. Laws are the basic concepts
which determine the general character of the equations characterizing the system.
In physical systems, these laws are usually expressions of the principles of
conservation and continuity. Structure refers to the geometry and topology of
the system, the manner in which its components are interconnected or the general
configuration of a distributed system. The parameters in a mathematical model
are the numerical values assigned to the various coefficients appearing in the
equations. These are related to the magnitudes of all of the elements comprising
the system as well as to the boundary and initial conditions. If the laws,
structure and parameters of a system are completely specified deductively, a
unique mathematical model can be derived.

Research in the mathematical modeling of physical systems at the University of
California, Los Angeles is supported by the National Science Foundation under
Grant GK 42774.

Inductive modeling, by contrast, makes use of experimental data constituting observed excitations and responses. This brings system characterization and parameter estimation techniques into play. Inverse problems such as the inductive modeling problem generally do not have a unique solution. That is, a valid model can generally not be constructed purely inductively from excitation/response observations, since an infinite number of models satisfy these relations.

In most instances, mathematical modeling entails a blending of deductive and inductive techniques. The modeler assembles all known facts about the system being modeled. This information includes the general equations characterizing the phenomena under study as well as descriptions of the specific system. When all sources of this type of information are exhausted, and only then, are system observations and experimental data brought into the picture. And it is the introduction of these inductive data, as well as the quality of the system observations, that circumscribe the ultimate validity of mathematical models. The more inductive the modeling process, the less reliable and valid the mathematical model.

BLACK BOXES AND GRAY BOXES

Inverse problems in general are often referred to as "black box" problems since the characterization of the system is initially unknown - hence black. In most mathematical modeling situations, however, the contents of the "black box" are not totally unknown. In fact, occasionally the entire contents are known, except perhaps for one or two element values. In other cases the assortment of elements within the box may be known, but not how they are interconnected. And in still other cases, there may be only a qualitative, intuitive insight into the behavior or certain components of the system. It therefore appears appropriate to extend the "black box" metaphor so as to provide for boxes of various "shades of gray" - the lighter the shade of gray, the more is known about the system prior to resorting to inductive modeling.

An examination of the modeling techniques utilized in any specific application discipline, reveals that the bulk of the models can be characterized as utilizing approximately the same proportion of deductive and inductive information. In fact, the entire modeling methodology and the eventual utilization of the models is attuned to the uncertainty existing about the mathematical representation of the system. It is possible therefore to arrange the various fields which utilize mathematical models according to the grayness of the "black box" problem which must be solved.

Figure 1 shows the spectrum of mathematical modeling problems as they arise in a variety of physical, life, and social science disciplines. It is recognized of course that there are many types of mathematical models in use in any specific application area, and that there may well be some overlaps in the shades of gray applicable to different fields.

Near one end of the spectrum, the "white box" end, we find the mathematical models arising in electric circuit theory. Here one usually knows the structure of the circuit and most, if not all, of the element values. Using Kirchhoff's laws and similar network theorems one can construct the mathematical model virtually without recourse to experimental data. Occasionally one or more parameter values remain to be identified, but this is a relatively simple and straightforward problem.

Proceeding along the spectrum we encounter the problems in mechanics such as aerospace vehicle control. Here most of the model is well known from basic mechanical principles and knowledge of the dimension and characteristics of the system. However, some parameters, for example certain aerodynamic functions, must be identified from actual flight experiments. This identification, using excitation/response relationships, is complicated by the presence of noise and by lack of control over certain experimental conditions. Proceeding further away from the white end of the spectrum we encounter the mathematical modeling problems in chemical process control. Here, the basic chemical reaction equations and reaction rates are provided. However, a considerable number of variables and parameters are not capable of being directly measured.

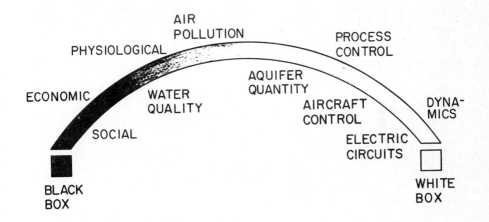

Figure 1

Moving still further into the dark region of the spectrum we encounter the models of socalled environmental systems. Here there is a general understanding of the physical and chemical processes involved (e.g., movement of water in underground reservoirs, diffusion of air pollutants, etc.). But the field within which these processes occur is not readily accessible to measurements; the phenomena being modeled therefore take place in a medium whose distributed properties are only very imprecisely known. Continuing further into the direction of darkness, a variety of life science models are encountered. Here there is only an approximate understanding of the physical and chemical laws which underlie the physiological phenomena, and furthermore the characteristics of the system being modeled are apt to change in time in an unpredictable manner.

Economic and social system models fall in the darkest region of the spectrum. Here even the basic laws governing the dynamic processes, not to mention the relevant constituents of the system, are open to question and controversy.

Water resources systems models are seen to fall near the central region of the spectrum of mathematical models. In the case of quantity models of underground water reservoirs, the basic equation characterizing fluid flow is well known and understood; the spatial distributions of the transmissibility and the

storage coefficient are known from core samples at a few locations in the field,
but must generally be inferred from system observations; the field boundaries are
usually a matter of guesswork and inductive inference as well. Water quality
models are generally of a darker shade of gray than aquifer quantity models since
they require a knowledge of the water flow rate throughout the system in addition
to the inductively-derived parameters and boundary configuration. Even further
in the direction of darkness are water quality models involving biological processes; here there is only very incomplete knowledge of the equations characterizing the generation and disappearance of the effects of water pollution. As a
result, models of water resources systems are not of sufficient predictive validity to permit their use for day to day forecasting. On the other hand, they are
considerably more reliable than the bulk of the model developed by social
scientists to characterize economic, sociological and political phenomena.

IMPROVEMENTS IN MODEL VALIDITY

An examination of the history of mathematical modeling in the various
application disciplines indicated in Figure 1 reveals a rather consistent sequence
of events. Initially all of the application areas were qualitative in their
approach to analysis and synthesis. Gradually each of the disciplines developed
a quantitative orientation as groups of creative practitioners began to develop
mathematical models. Eventually, the modeling and simulation of systems became
a formalized and recognized specialty within the field. The mathematical models
developed in that way gradually found their place along the spectrum of mathematical models according to the mix of deduction and induction involved in the
modeling process. As the use of models became more and more widespread, there
arose in each of the application disciplines the optimistic expectation that with
more intensive efforts there would take place a gradual shift away from the dark
end of the spectrum, so that models and simulations would become progressively
more and more valid. This hope was heightened by the advent of larger and more
powerful computers. Unfortunately, these expectations were doomed to disappointment in virtually every case.

In most application disciplines, a plot of the accuracy of models in predicting future events when plotted against time since the start of modeling
efforts within the discipline takes the form shown in Figure 2. As each discipline emerged from its qualitative period, the initial validity of models was
quite low. After the number of scientists and theoreticians active in quantitative modeling achieved a "critical mass", there commenced a period of rapid improvement in the quality of mathematical models. This in turn led to the application of the models to more and more challenging problems and more and more
"useful" investigations. Inevitably this period of improvement came to an end,
so that after a given time no significant increases in model validity occurred.

The curve of validity versus time invariably appears to have two break-
points, A and B, as shown in Figure 2. The elapsed time between A and B varies
considerably from discipline to discipline and is determined largely by the importance of the discipline to government and industry, which in turn determines the
amount of funds made available for the development of models. In recent years,
as more and more powerful computing systems have become available, the time period
between points A and B has become shorter and shorter. Thus each application
discipline appears to be anchored to its region along the spectrum of mathematical
models. That is, after a discipline reaches a certain maturity, efforts to improve the predictive validity of mathematical models can be expected to be relatively unproductive.

One explanation for this phenomena may be that the ultimate validity of
mathematical models, as represented by the asymptote of the curve of Figure 2,
does not depend upon the skill or intelligence of the modelers nor upon the
financial support, nor upon computational capabilities; rather the limit of model
validity in any discipline is imposed by nature. Fundamental to each application

discipline are the basic laws used to derive the characterizing equations. As one
moves to the darker regions of the spectrum, these laws become more and more uncertain and more and more obscured by "noise". The same applied to the deductive
methods involved in the specification of the structure and the parameters of the
system. Very soon after the commencement of concerted quantitative modeling
efforts all opportunities for improved deductive inference become exhausted, and
the proportion of deduction and induction involved in the modeling process becomes
fixed. The quality of models continues to improve for a time as more effective
methods for parameter identification are implemented, and as more accurate and
more complete system observations become available. These efforts soon reach a
point of diminishing returns however, and after a certain point in the life cycle
of any modeling activity, few basic improvements in the ultimate validity of mathematical models can be expected.

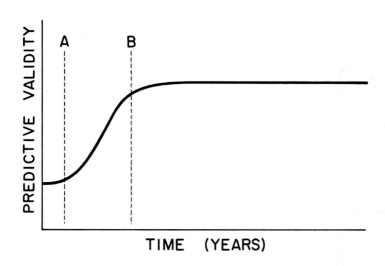

Figure 2

CONCLUSIONS

        It would appear that the life cycle of models of water resources systems
has well passed point B in Figure 2. In other words, the validity of water resources systems models is circumscribed by the very nature of these systems rather
than by the mathematical and technological skills of the modeling community. But
this does not call for a reduction in modeling efforts; rather it suggests the
need for changes in emphasis. In evaluating and in using mathematical models, it
is important to recognize that their ultimate mode of application, hence the
motivation for modeling, is largely determined by their "shade of gray". Models
near the light end of the spectrum serve primarily as tools for design. In the
slightly darker regions, models serve for performance prediction and detailed
forecasting. As one proceeds to the still darker regions of the spectrum, models
gradually assume more qualitative and less quantitative roles. Thus they may be
used for experimentation with control strategies, the testing of theories, the
gaining of insight into "counter-intuitive phenomena, or to influence public
opinion.

The important point is that the ultimate use of the model must conform to
its validity. Likewise, the analytical tools used in modeling and in simulation
should be of sufficient elegance to do justice to the validity of the model; excess refinement usually leads to excessively expensive and deceptive computations.
If one were to plot usefulness to the ultimate user of mathematical models in any
given discipline, a peak would usually be discerned a considerable number of years
after point B in Figure 2. Only when both the designers of models and their cus-
tomers appreciate the ultimate limitations of the models can full efforts be
brought to bear upon optimizing the models in terms of their usefulness.

In the water resources field, governmental water control agencies are only
beginning to realize the importance and the possibilities of mathematical models.
As in other application disciplines there has been some tendency to promise too
much and to call insufficient attention to the limitations of the mathematical
models. As a result there has been some disillusionment and disappointment with
the usefulness of mathematical models of water resources systems. Major emphasis
should now be placed upon the reconciliation of the needs and expectations of
water resources specialists with the ultimate capabilities and limitations of
mathematical models of water resources systems.

DISCUSSION

*It is difficult to accept that in water resources modeling we have reached
a peak. Perhaps in certain parts of water resources we have, but there is at least
one area where I can point to future contributions that might be important. That
is the process of how the water runs down from the surface to the water table.
I really have barely started to model this on a watershed scale. This is just an
example and I hope there might be a lot of progress in modeling for I'm not satisfied with what we have today. (NEUMAN)*

I would like to re-emphasize that within any of the disciplines there are
subdisciplines that may have life cycles that are offset from the curve of Figure
2. And there are of course many specific problems, within a larger discipline which
have not yet been touched. My contention is : the ultimate validity of your model
in each area is circumscribed by the considerations that I mentioned. (KARPLUS)

*I would surely agree with your estimation in your last statement, that the
communication with the general public or the authorities is one case where maybe
we are at the very start of the curve. Do you have a suggestion how to make our
results more acceptable in the eyes of the potential users ? (LOMEN)*

A part of the answer is humility. Within our own discipline we use words
like prediction, and we know what we mean ; but this word has a different meaning
to someone outside of mathematical modeling.
For example I had a conversation with an official of L.A. water control district.
He said, I just don't believe that the flow of water under ground is governed by
differential equations. We use words like "govern" in a very specialized way.
Perhaps we should try, when we are communicating to conform more to the general
terminology. And not to say "we are going to predict" in the sense of : we can
tell you what will happen tomorrow, when we really mean the forecasting of general
tendencies. (KARPLUS)

I have some experience with talking to the authorities in England, about applying some of the models. We found there was a great deal of scepticism as to what mathematical models do achieve in fact. I think a lot of it is based on papers on optimum control strategies, which really have no possible applications. They are dealing with problems where they cannot measure the variables, they have not got the money to build the systems. There is a basic communication gap between how to apply optimum schemes and the handling of very practical systems. (WHITEHEAD)

That is a very good observation. I think by virtue of the fact that in water resource modeling we are in the middle of the spectrum, we are in danger of being confused with either end.
On one side, we have the people who use very refined mathematics, which are not really all that helpful in water resources. On the other side, in the dark end of the spectrum, we have people who use models in a far more qualitative way.
Moreover in the management and business administration area, the word simulation is used to mean something quite different. On another point, I would say that we can "sell" mathematical models by pointing out that modeling is really inherent in virtually all intellectual activity. That anyone who makes a decision is in fact using a model that resides in his head, even if he has not formalized it or is not fully aware of its use. In modeling we are really just putting down on paper as completely as possible what is involved in reaching a decision. (KARPLUS)

What was your reasoning when you came to the conclusion that in water resources, we have reached a peak. What are the considerations behind this ? It is an important conclusion, and if it is time, we all have to take the consequences. (NEUMAN)

As I look to the various disciplines in the spectrum I am not aware of any breaktrough that has occured spontaneously after models became mature. There is a large body of scientists that rush to work in a new area that is promising, so that the problems get worked out rather quickly. Perhaps there are some surprises still to come, but I doubt it.   (KARPLUS)

There are a couple of things I just want to bring up. One is that there are two ways, at least, in which we use models. One is to organize our efforts to help us to better understand a complex system, without necessarily worrying too much about the precision of our predictions. The other way is to use the model to try to help, for example water engineers, in undertaking some complex task. In that latter situation, I think our experience has been that the people who are involved in developing the models have a great deal to gain from considering themselves as the manufacturers of a product and thinking about the consumer and what his constraints and requirements may be, and really developping the model with a very specific application in mind. (PECK)

This comes back to what I said about motivation of modeling. What you suggest is that even in an area in which we could use the model to determine general control strategies, we might settle for more qualitative type of result. (KARPLUS)

When you speak of the predictive validity of the model, I may agree with you. But when you look at the application of the model, I would not at all agree with the limitation of predictive validity of the given model, because with time, more data come from the problem you are studying, and each time the models can be made in better agreement to reality. Even if the mathematics are not better than it was before, the parameter values that you have may gain in validity. I do not see how you can fix a limit to this predictive validity. (DE MARSILY)

What I tried to show is the ultimate that we can reach. The best you can hope to do. Beyond this, the noise inherent in the system will restrict you

regardless how complete are the measurements. The curve in Figure 2 is intended
to indicate the validity of the best models than can be made at any given time in
the history of the modeling process. Of course specific models can be much worse,
if they are constructed with insufficient information. (KARPLUS)

*There may be at least one historical example to show that your abscissa
scale here is probably very short. That is the example of geometry. When we consider geometry as a mathematical model of reality, it is very remarkably that the
evolution of its predictive validity is characterized by some very discrete jumps,
as there were the development of the Euclidean system and the development of the
non-Euclidean geometry, many centuries later. So why couldn't we expect such a
second jump, once we reached the plateau ? (WAJC)*

There is a tendency these days to take nothing deductive for granted.
We say ultimately everything is empiric. But I used the term deductive in a specialized sense. I observed that the time between A and B on the curve got smaller and
smaller during the last century, because of the mass of people brought to bear on
any modeling area, and the computation tools that are made available. (KARPLUS)

*When the asymptotic region is reached is it possible to improve the model,
not by getting better results, but just using less expensive means, smaller amounts
of data, so getting models easier to be applied ? (TAVARES)*

Absolutely. We might even say that only when the knee of the curve of
Figure 2 is reached do people really seriously look for convenient tools, for
example simulation languages.   (KARPLUS)

*Do you mean by a model the basic set of partial differential equations that
we use, for example to model an aquifer, or do you mean the computing programs
that are used, because I think there is a difference. I may agree that the basic
set of partial differential equations are there to stay for quite some time, with
minor modifications here and there. What we do with these partial differential
equations may, I hope, still change drastically in the next few years, and my
question is : what do you mean by a model, do you mean the basic set of equations
or do you mean the computer programs ? (NEUMAN)*

The combination of the basic equations, the description of the system in
terms of what is it composed of, what are its boundary and initial conditions ;
i.e. what we call a complete mathematical specification of the problem. Certainly
there are improvements to be made in the numerical methods we employ to solve the
problem, and tremendous improvements are to be made in the utilisation of the
results. (KARPLUS)

System Simulation in Water Resources, ed. *G.C. VANSTEENKISTE*
1976, North-Holland Publishing Company

IDENTIFICATION AND PARAMETER ESTIMATION OF BIOLOGICAL
PROCESS MODELS

M.B. Beck[*]
Control Engineering Group
University Engineering Department
Mill Lane, Cambridge, England

Abstract

This paper deals with the application of system identification and parameter
estimation to problems of the dynamic modelling of biological processes in wastewater treatment and river water quality. The subject of identification and estimation is discussed in very broad terms and some of these ideas are then illustrated by case studies in which actual field data have been used. These case
studies include examinations of the dynamic behaviour of activated sludge processes, anaerobic digestion, and DO-BOD-algae interaction in a reach of river.

1. Introduction

The aim of this survey/tutorial paper is to give an introduction to the
methods and application of system identification and parameter estimation to
problems of modelling the dynamic behaviour of some biological processes in water
quality systems. The "survey" aspects are limited by the fact that very few publications have appeared in the literature which combine practical field data with
the use of identification/estimation methods for the derivation of the relevant
dynamic models. The "tutorial" aspects can be treated in greater depth. While
a basic minimum requirement is an understanding of system identification and parameter estimation, it is not intended that the paper should pursue the theoretical
background of the subject. Rather, from an engineering viewpoint, it is more
instructive to discuss how these techniques can be made to work in practice with
practical data from the real system. In order to illustrate these points we
present a number of case studies.
A water quality system may be defined, for our purposes, as the following
group of individual, but mutually interacting, subsystems: (i) potable water
abstraction, treatment, and supply; (ii) urban land runoff, consumer effluent,
and the sewer network; (iii) wastewater treatment plant; (iv) a reach of river.
We are concerned primarily with the identification of dynamic mathematical models
for the various component processes of the system (Beck(1975b)). We emphasise
the word "dynamic" since, although it may be desirable to operate a process at a
given steady-state, or reference, value, there is no guarantee that the input
disturbances to the processes are time invariant. Therefore, some form of
dynamic control must be exercised to maintain predetermined satisfactory output
product specifications, e.g. for effluent discharge, potable water supply. In
this paper control problems are not considered, but it should be borne in mind
that the ultimate goal of the dynamic model, other than for forecasting or planning purposes, will be its application in the synthesis and evaluation of control
schemes. It is also worthwhile to remember that almost all systems in the real
world are naturally both dynamic and stochastic.

After a general discussion of the subject, in which we point out some of the
advantages and disadvantages of the various model types and identification/estim-
ation schemes, a number of illustrative case studies are given. Firstly, the
problem of experimental design is discussed with respect to some proposed work on
the activated-sludge process of wastewater treatment. Secondly, results are

---

[*]Ernest Cook Trust Research Fellow in Environmental Sciences.

presented for a preliminary model of the anaerobic digestion process: this is
a complex process and, although a theoretical model is available, it is quite
difficult, yet very desirable, to establish some fundamental, simple cause-effect
relationships for the system.   Thirdly, we describe the identification of models
for the interaction between dissolved oxygen, biochemical oxygen demand, and algae
in a freshwater stream.   All three processes are biological in nature, they are
also multivariable, non-linear, and subject to severe limitations on data acquisition.

2. Biological processes in a water quality system.

Figure 1 gives a pictorial definition of the water quality system.   For the
purposes of this paper we are concerned only with the dynamic behaviour of some of
the biological processes of the system.   More specifically, the biological processes of subsystem (3), the wastewater treatment plant, and subsystem (4), a
reach of river, are discussed.   Of course, that is not to say that there are
no biological phenomena present in the other two subsystems.   For instance, the
storage of abstracted water prior to treatment may promote the growth of algae,
which are both a physical nuisance in the purification processes and a possible
health hazard in potable water supplies; it is also known that slimes of micro-organisms attached to slow sand filtration beds play an important role in the efficient
removal of organic material from potable water (STEEL (1953)47).   It is curious
to note, therefore, the absence of any qualitative or biological considerations in
one of the few recent studies of the dynamic control of potable water purification
plants (KLINCK (1975)25).
What particular problems attach to the dynamic modelling of biological processes?   As we have stated in the introduction, there is little published work
in the area of identification and parameter estimation of dynamic biological
process models from field data.   Some articles have appeared which treat these
problems with the use of synthetic data (e.g. KOIVO and PHILLIPS (1971)36), but
it is not constructive to use a model unless it has been shown to be a reasonable
description of the observed behaviour of the system.   Such a lack of the relevant
field data is understandable, since the intensity and duration of sampling and
monitoring required for the validation of a dynamic model is often prohibitive
(see section 3.2).   And, if the available manpower is limited, as is generally
the case, then only small portions of the system can be investigated in detail.
For in spite of the current focus of attention on environmental technology, which
is broadening the scope of commercial probes and instruments required for on-line
measurements and control (BRIGGS (1975)15), there continue to be difficulties in
developing the techniques for direct access to, or correlative measures of, some
of the most important biochemical and biological variables (OLSSON et al (1973)41).
The biochemical oxygen demand (BOD), one of the most widely used, and most fundamental, determinations of organic pollution levels, is a notoriously awkward
variable to measure, since it takes five days (or more) to carry out the test.
Indeed, almost by its very definition, it is a measurement which defies automation,
although recent results suggest that an alternative means of monitoring organic
pollution levels may soon be available for use in the field (BRIGGS (1975)15).
Yet the BOD is not the only measurement of biological variables with a claim to
notoriety (and we shall have more to say about in in section 4.4): there are many
other problems which surround the measurement of micro-organism and substrate
concentrations, for example, in the biological processes of activated sludge and
anaerobic digestion (see sections 4.1 and 4.2).
Moreover, these difficulties of process observation are compounded by a
hostile environment in which sensors are fouled rapidly and require frequent
calibration, cleaning, and maintenance in order that they retain the sensitivity
needed to monitor minute changes in the concentrations of dissolved and suspended
substances.   And, once a measurement is made, the receipt of that information
may be subject to the inadequacies and strain of planning an experimental study of
a river system which ranges over a wide geographical area.   Some telemetry
systems exist (BRIGGS (1975)15), but they are the exception rather than the rule.

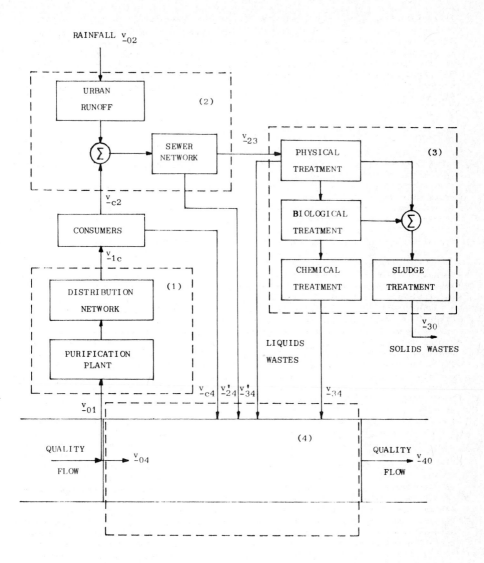

Figure 1   The water quality system

SUBSYSTEMS:

    (1) POTABLE WATER ABSTRACTION, PURIFICATION, AND SUPPLY NETWORK
    (2) URBAN LAND RUNOFF AND THE SEWER NETWORK
    (3) WASTEWATER TREATMENT PLANT
    (4) A STRETCH OF RIVER

In fact, it suffices to say that, in the majority of cases, the observation of
water quality variables is very much a labour-intensive affair of manual or
automatic sampling followed by laboratory analysis.

Thus, in answer to our earlier question, it is the acquisition of truly
representative field data that sets the identification of biological processes
somewhat apart from the average industrial process modelling problem.   The
observation of a biological system is an action which (given the present instrumentation) necessarily "prefilters", and possibly even distorts, the information
contained in the data about the dynamic behaviour of the process.   These features,
together with its inherent subtelties, make the biological process both especially
challenging and rewarding to the systems analyst.   After all, it is the data on
the observed dynamic (and stochastic) nature of a system which are the sustinence
of the model-builder and without them he should, by rights, be sorely pressed to
survive.

3.   System identification and parameter estimation.

The field of system identification and parameter estimation has developed
rapidly over the past decade.   Much of the large body of literature on the
subject suggests a multitude of methods for solving a multitude of problems However, this is only a superficial impression since, in effect, very similar techniques are being proposed to attack the same central questions.

Our purpose here is to outline a framework within which many of the modelling
aspects of the water quality system can be treated with a fair chance of success.
The concepts and procedures presented are an aggregate of those which have been
applied to the analysis of field data (section 4) and any comments made on them
are based upon practical experience rather than theoretical considerations.   In
view of this it is preferable to give an insight into the subject of system
identification without the confusion that might arise from a discussion of problems of a more theoretical nature.   Clearly, it is beyond the scope of this paper
to review the whole subject of identification and estimation.   For a more complete
presentation of the general underlying theoretical aspects we may refer to the
work of, for example, ÅSTRÖM and EYKHOFF (1971)5, EYKHOFF (1974)20 and ISERMANN
(1975)28; slightly more specialised treatments of certain topics are given by
BOX and JENKINS (1970)14 (time-series analysis), and YOUNG (1974)51 (recursive
spproaches to parameter estimation).

3.1.   Problem definition.

Let us define the context of system identification and parameter estimation
of biological process models as follows.   Assume that the component variables
of a system can be defined as in figure 2, which implies that a clear distinction
can be drawn between the system and its environment*.   Thus, given that the system
is subject to random disturbances, ξ, i.e. system noise, and that any measurements
of the systemvariables, y, are contaminated with random errors, η, i.e. measurement
noise, we are required to derive and validate a model which represents concisely,
according to some criterion function, the information contained in the data on the
observed dynamic behaviour of the system.   Let us also assume that these data are
obtained from an actual piece of process plant (i.e. they are not pilot plant or
synthesised data) and that we are considering only the class of parametric models.
Let us also not forget the purpose of the model-building exercise: in our case it
is generally either a desire for more insight into the system behaviour or the
need for a model with which a control scheme can be synthesised and evaluated.

---

*It seems reasonable to assume that this is possible for most biological processes,
although notice that the problem may be less straightforward in the case of socio-
economic models, for instance (GILLESPIE (1975)21).

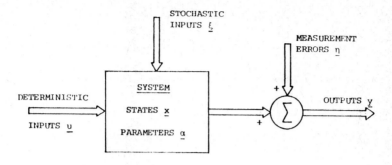

Figure 2   Schematic representation of the system variables

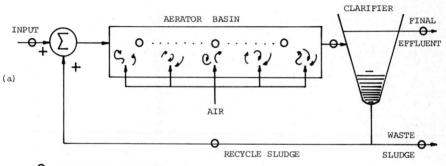

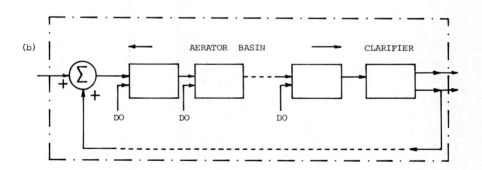

Figure 3   The activated sludge process with desirable points for
observation (a) and breakdown into subsystems for dynamic
model(s) analysis (b)

3.2. Experimental design.

A prerequisite for identification is a suitable record of the observed process dynamics.   Because the premium on biological process data is so high, it is
desirable that experimental work should be well planned in advance so that the
amount of information derived can be maximised.   Any a priori knowledge of the
system's dynamic behaviour is an advantage, since this knowledge can be used to
establish, for example, the relevant state variables to be measured, the sampling
rate at which measurements should be made, the duration of the experiment, and
the desired nature of the input forcing signals, u.   Most of these conditions
have been discussed fully elsewhere and, for the sake of brevity, we merely
refer to the work of GUSTAVSSON (1975)24.   There are, however, some points which
are pertinent to the discussion here.   If the forcing disturbances u can be manipulated artificially, e.g. step, pulse, pseudo-random binary sequence (PRBS)
testing, they must be constrained in order to retain process stability at all
times.   Unfortunately, it is a characteristic of the water quality system that
only natural excitation of the process dynamics can be observed in general and
artificial disturbances are precluded.   This tends to mean that normal operational records exhibit just one particular mode of process behaviour (worse still,
deviations from the steady state may be insignificant, thus giving no information
about the dynamics), there is a low signal/noise ratio, and the routine measurement sampling rate may obscure the effects of some of the most important time-
constants of the system.   Consequently, even when we can be sure of measuring
the desired process variables, it is probable that many current experimental
studies of biological systems will be inadequate, simply because there is so
little a priori information on the dynamic behaviour that we wish to examine.
Frequently, subsequent attempts at modelling show that the experiment should have
included measurements of additional state variables, in other words we may find
that the distinction between the system and its environment should be redrawn in
the light of later evidence.

3.3. Choice of Model.

It follows that with the retrieval of experimental data a model must be
chosen to represent the information in those data.   Broadly speaking, the choice
of parametric model is between two polarised forms:

(i)   a black box (or input/output) model

(ii)   an internally descriptive (or mechanistic) model.

A linear form of the black box (input/output, time-series) is given by the discrete
-time, difference equation,

$$y(k) = \frac{\sum_{i=1}^{m} B_i(z^{-1})}{A(z^{-1})} u_i(k) + \frac{D(z^{-1})}{C(z^{-1})} e(k) \qquad (1)$$

in which $u_i(k)$, i=1,2,...,m, and y(k) are respectively the observations of the
multiple (m) system inputs and the system output at the kth sampling instant; e(k)
is a sequence of independent, normal $(0,\lambda^2)$ random variables and z^{-1} is the backward shift operator, i.e.

$$z^{-1}(y(k)) = y(k-1) \text{ etc.}$$

$A(z^{-1})$, $B_i(z^{-1})$, $C(z^{-1})$, and $D(z^{-1})$ are the polynomials, of order n,

$$A(z^{-1}) = 1 + a_1 z^{-1} + \ldots + a_n z^{-n}$$

$$B_i(z^{-1}) = b_{i0} + b_{i1} z^{-1} + \ldots + b_{in} z^{-n} \; ; \; i=1,2,\ldots,m \qquad (2)$$

$$C(z^{-1}) = 1 + c_1 z^{-1} + \ldots + c_n z^{-n}$$
$$D(z^{-1}) - 1 + d_1 z^{-1} + \ldots + d_n z^{-n}$$

The essential feature of this type of model is that it assumes no knowledge of physical or internal relationships between the system's inputs and output other than that the inputs should produce observable responses in the output.   In other words, it is a time-series model in which the prediction of the output is a function of previous observations of that output and the inputs u_i, together with past realisations of the "lumped" stochastic noise sequence e, i.e. factors aris-ing both from measurement error and random disturbances of the system. (c.f. the system definition of figure 2).   The use of the model is particularly advantag-eous when a priori information on the physical phenomena governing the system dynamics is minimal;   in this case the black box is literally a fair reflection of our knowledge of the system and the model is a first attempt at elucidating any observed dynamical relationships.   Alternatively, where a mechanistic, or intern-ally descriptive, model is available, but its form is so complex that it requires the characterisation of too many parameters from an insufficient number of data, an input/output model can yield equally useful results in forecasting or control system synthesis applications.   The limitations of the model are that it is not, generally, a universal description of a system's dynamics, being specific to the sample data set from which it is derived, and it is not necessarily amenable to interpretations on the physical nature of the system .   Notice also that the model of eqn I is restricted to a single output system;   a feature which we shall discuss later.

In contrast, an internally descriptive type of model exploits much more, if not all, of the available a priori information on the physico-chemical, or biolog-ical phenomena governing the process dynamics.   This type of model may be repres-ented by the following continuous-time, linear, state vector differential equation,

$$\dot{\underline{x}}(t) = A\underline{x}(t) + B\underline{u}(t) + \underline{\xi}(t) \qquad\qquad (3a)$$

in which the dot notation refers to differentiation with respect to time t, $\underline{x}$ is the n-dimensional state vector, $\underline{u}$ is an m-dimensional vector of deterministic in-puts or forcing functions, and $\underline{\xi}$ is a p-dimensional vector of zero-mean "white" noise disturbances of the system.   A, and B are respectively nxn, nxm matrices containing the parameters that characterise the system.   In addition, consider that we have the set of q noisy, sampled observations $\underline{y}(k)$ of the outputs of the system given by

$$\underline{y}(k) = C\underline{x}(k) + \underline{n}(k) \qquad\qquad (3b)$$

at the instant of time k, where C is a qxn observation matrix and $\underline{n}$ is a vector of zero-mean, independent measurement error sequences (see figure 2).   Eqns (3) constitute a continuous-discrete version of the state space model with continuous-time dynamics and discrete-time observations.   The advantages of using this type of model are that it can give considerable insight into the physical nature, i.e. $\underline{x}$, $\underline{\alpha}$, of the system's dynamics and it has a greater potential for universal applic-ation than the black box model.   In addition, it is not restricted to a single output system and, at the same time, the noisy environment of the process is def-ined more closely by the separation of stochastic system disturbances $\underline{\xi}(t)$ from the output measurement errors $\underline{n}(k)$.   However, these latter advantages lead to certain added difficulties in the operation of the corresponding estimation and identification procedures, since the statistics of the noise processes must usually be specified a priori, for which several assumptions have to be made.
If a given internally descriptive model were a perfect representation of the system, we might call it a "white box" model.   And, taking this analogy further, we might also view the two representations as the extremes of a whole spectrum of models in which most models lie within a "grey box" band! (c.f. KARPLUS (1975)34).

   One further model merits attention here.   In some ways it is a model which
gives us a bridge between the concepts of a black box (single output) and an internally descriptive (multiple output) model.   If eqn (3) is integrated over the
interval k-1 to k (k-1 $\leq$ t $\leq$ k), and if the noise processes ξ and $\underline{n}$ are lumped together into a single noise vector $\underline{w}$, i.e. the process dynamics (eqn.3)) are considered as deterministic, a particular form of a discrete-time, state-space, internally descriptive model results (YOUNG and WHITEHEAD (1975)52),

$$\underline{x}(k) = \Phi \, \underline{x}(k-1) + \Gamma \, \underline{u}(k-1) \qquad\qquad\qquad (a) \; \Bigg\}$$
$$\underline{y}(k) = \underline{x}(k) + \underline{w}(k) \qquad\qquad\qquad\qquad\quad (b) \; \Bigg\} \; (4)$$

with Φ and Γ being matrices of appropriate dimensions.   While this model
requires certain assumptions to be made about the noise processes in the system,
it retains much of the simplicity of the black box models, since it requires only
the solution of difference equations as opposed to differential equations.   Yet
it is multivariable, it contains a considerable amount of a priori knowledge of
the system (as translated from the matrices A and B into Φ and Γ), and, like
the black box model, the identification of this model has the advantages of requ-
iring no a priori knowledge of the noise statistics (YOUNG and WHITEHEAD (1975)52).

3.4. Identification.

   Having chosen the model type, an identification stage in the analysis is
carried out in which the causal relationships between the inputs, states, and
outputs, together with the order and structure, of the model are established.
That is to say, for a black box model the order n of the polynomials of eqn (2)
is defined, and for the internally descriptive model the order n of the state
vector and the non-zero elements of the matrices A and B are specified.   The
separation of the identification and parameter estimation stages is essentially
one of concept.   Identification is frequently made on the basis of parameter
estimation results in which the analyst is more concerned with assessing the
adequacy of the model structure than with estimating the parameters accurately.
   The procedures for black box model identification are much more well defined:
they include   correlation analysis (see e.g. BOX and JENKINS (1970)14), statistical tests which indicate the significance, or otherwise, of increasing the order
n of the polynomials (ÅSTRÖM and EYKHOFF (1971)5), or it may simply be that certain parameter estimates have such large estimation errors that these parameters
may, to all intents and purposes, be set equal to zero.   In contrast, very few
hard and fast rules attach to the identification of internally descriptive models.
Generally, the analyst's own understanding of the physical system is fully exploited in the interpretation of the results (see e.g. BECK and YOUNG (1975b)12).
Despite the attempts to put the identification on a firm mathematical basis, the
choice of the final model structure remains very much an art.   Especially with
respect to biological processes, it is not a trivial problem to develop tractable
mathematical expressions which both describe the "anomalous" behaviour of the
system and do not distort the laws thought to govern such mechanisms.   In practice, part of the model identification may be specified a priori by the limited
number of variables which are measurable.   Notice too that it is extremely useful
to identify models whose inputs are control variables, i.e. bearing in mind the
application of the model, they can be manipulated to control the process outputs.

3.5.   Parameter estimation.*

   Given the identified model structure, the parameters that characterise that
model are now estimated according to any one of a number of procedures which fall

---

* To give the discussion a broader perspective, the parameter estimation problem
is also known by other titles; for instance, NEUMAN (1975)39 talks about the
inverse problem, which, in his case, is the estimation of parameters in an internally descriptive model of groundwater flow.

into the two categories of

    (i)   off-line methods

    (ii)   recursive (or on-line) methods

By off-line we mean the estimation of parameters by repeated updating of the estimates after each iteration through a given block of N data samples, whereas the
recursive methods adapt the estimates at each sampling instant k (where k = 1,2,
....N) within that set of N sampled values.   In this context the parameters $\underline{\alpha}$
that characterise the internally descriptive model of the system are the elements
a_{ij}, b_{ij}, c_{ij} of the matrices A, B, and C in eqn (3) (c.f. figure 1); the parameters of the black box model are the coefficients of the polynomials $A(q^{-1})$ B_i (q^{-1}),
$C(q^{-1})$, $D(q^{-1})$, in eqn (2), let us say Θ .   There exists a subtle distinction
between these two sets of parameters: whereas the estimated values of the parameters $\underline{\alpha}$ have meaningful interpretations for the nature of the physical system, there
are no such interpretations which can be placed on the estimates of Θ .   Neither
are the interpretations of the parameters $\underline{\Theta}'$, being the elements of the Φ and Γ
matrices in the model of eqn (4), always strictly meaningful in a physical sense.
    Recursive approaches, which have received less popular acclaim in the liter-
ature, are particularly useful for the identification phase of the analysis.
They offer an added insight into possible variations of the parameters with time,
and from a purely practical point of view, they require a smaller computational
effort in the treatment of the data.   These benefits, however, are gained for
the loss of some statistical efficiency and of many of the theoretical proofs for
convergence.   The crucial point in an applications context is that, while being
cognizant of such limitations, some of the statistical efficiency of the estimation procedure can afford to be lost without undue damage to the viability of the
model.
    One of the major problems of parameter estimation is the derivation of un-
biased estimates.   If the noise processes $\underline{\xi}$ and $\underline{\eta}$ are not independent of $\underline{u}$ and
$\underline{y}$, or if they are autocorrelated in time, then the simplest, and most fundamental,
method of least squares * (see e.g. ÅSTRÖM and EYKHOFF(1971)5) for the off-line
version, and YOUNG (1969)50 for a recursive version) gives biased estimates.   It
is from the solution of this problem that the aforementioned multiplicity of techniques has arisen, especially with respect to black box models (ÅSTRÖM and EYKHOFF
(1971)5).   Several comparative studies of the individual techniques are available
(GUSTAVSSON (1972)23, SARIDIS (1974)43, ISERMANN et al (1974)29).
    The estimation of black box model parameters is, once again, more straight-
forward than for the internally descriptive model.   In fact, the procedures for
the former have been refined to quite a high level of sophistication and several
interactive computer program packages are currently in use, e.g. SHELLSWELL (1972)
45), GUSTAVSSON et al (1973)25.

3.6.   Diagnostic checking of the validity of the model.

    When the final model and set of parameter estimates are obtained, their valid-
ity should be assessed by carrying out various statistical checks on the errors
between the observed system and model output responses.   This generally entails
the satisfaction of the assumptions about the noise processes in the models, e.g.
normality of distribution, and independence.   Essentially, the question must be
answered: does the model simulate the system adequately in accordance with the
objectives and proposed application of the model?   We might also ask the question:
are the estimated parameter values (of an internally descriptive model) physically
meaningful?   Yet in answering this second question, we must bear in mind the

---

* i.e. as with most estimation schemes, the criterion for "best" estimates is
taken to be the minimisation of some squared error function (ÅSTRÖM and EYKHOFF
(1971)5).

danger in comparing estimates of the parameters α obtained by applying parameter
estimation techniques to the set of "in-situ" field observations u,y,(as here)
with those obtained either from empirical relationships or from laboratory analyses of bottled river water (or effluent) samples.

4.   Applications to biological process modelling.

When considering the application of identification and parameter estimation
to biological process modelling, one problem which faces the systems analyst is
his level of understanding of the fundamental theories which govern these processes.   Indeed, it is a problem which recurs with embarrassing regularity.   But then
again, systems analysis is possibly an equally bewildering prospect for the biolog-
ist. Dynamic models are inherently more complex than any corresponding steady-
state models and we may, therefore, be forced to accept less detailed, but more
tractable, mathematical descriptions of the internal mechanisms of a biological
system.   This conflict between the microscopic and the mascroscopic is well art-
iculated in a paper by ANDREWS (1970)[1], who, for those not conversant with the
intricacies of the biochemical kinetic theory, gives an excellent introduction to
the subject.   On the other hand, ANDREWS (1975b)[3] also states admirably the
benefits of applying the techniques of systems analysis to water pollution control
problems.
Summarising our experience in this area we have found the following identification and estimation schemes to be of considerable value in the modelling of
biological process dynamics:
    (a)   for black box models:

        (i)   Maximum likelihood (ML1) (ÅSTRÖM and BOHLIN (1965)[4] - applic-
               ation: BECK (1974)[6].

        (ii)   (Recursive) Instrumental Variable-Approximate Maximum Likelihood
               (IVAML) (YOUNG (1974)[51] - application: BECK and WHITEHEAD
               (1975)[10].

    (b)   for internally descriptive models:

        (i)   (Recursive) Extended Kalman Filter (EKF) (JAZWINSKI (1970)[31]
               - application: BECK and YOUNG (1975b)[12].

        (ii)   Maximum likelihood (ML2) ÅSTRÖM and EYKHOFF (1971)[5] - applic-
               ation : BECK (1975)[7].

        (iii) (as applied to a model of the type eqn(4)) (Recursive) Multi-
               variable extension to IVAML (MIVAML) (YOUNG and WHITEHEAD (1975)
               [52]- application: WHITEHEAD and YOUNG, (1975a).

The purpose of this section is to describe the application of the methods by means
of a number of example case studies which illustrate both the ideas presented in
section 3 and some specific difficulties of modelling biological processes.

4.1.   Experimental Design (the activated-sludge process).

The activated sludge process (figure 3) is commonly used in the biological
treatment of the liquids waste stream passing from the primary sedimentation units
(see figure 1).   Various species of aerobic organisms take part in autocatalytic
reactions whereby complex waste organic materials, acting as substrates (or nutrients) for the organisms, are broken down to simple end-products such s carbon
dioxide and water.   The organisms, attached to a slurry-like medium (activated
sludge), are kept in suspension and an aerobic environment by the mixing action
of air blown into the unit from diffusers placed along the base of the channel.
The effluent from the aeration basin is passed to a secondary clarifier unit
where the solids are separated from the final effluent and returned to the aeration basin with some (controlled) wastage.
Theoretical, internally descriptive, dynamic models of the activated sludge
process have been developed by several people (BUSBY and ANDREWS (1973)[17], JONES
(1975)[33], HÄMÄLÄINEN et al (1975)[26]; inclusion of the clarifier dynamics is a

further important consideration for control applications (BRYANT and WILCOX (1972)
16, HÄMÄLÄINEN et al (1975)26).   A central feature of these models is a growth
function for the micro-organisms proposed by MONOD (1942)37:   for a given concentration S of _specific rate-limiting_ substrate i.e. organic pollutant, the growth
of a concentration M of a micro-organism species is described by the following
kinetic mechanism,

$$\dot{M} = \hat{\mu} \left[\frac{S}{S+K_s} \right] M \tag{5}$$

where $\hat{\mu}$ and K_s are constants.   The Monod function of eqn (5) is a fundamental
law of micro-organism growth; clear parallels can be drawn between its application here and its application to anaerobic digestion (section 4.2) and to river
water quality modelling (section 4.4).
      The dynamic behaviour of activated sludge is not well understood.   The exist-
ing theoretical models have only been verified in a largely qualitative manner.
However, it is neither a trivial problem to design a suitable experiment, nor a
simple matter of effecting such an experiment to obtain the requisite field data.
Figure 3(a) shows a preliminary set of desirable points for observation of the
process dynamics: we require information about the mass balances around each
division/confluence of the material fluxes and about the _spatially_-varying dynamic
behaviour of the aerator basin (and eventually the clarifier unit).   A first indication of the process characteristics would be given by _what_ the system (subsystem)* inputs are seen to do to the system (subsystem) outputs, i.e. a black box
model.   Later we would examine _how_ the outputs respond to the input disturbances,
i.e. an internally descriptive model.   Having specified the observation points,
which variables should be observed? Let us suggest the following: dissolved
oxygen (DO) concentration, micro-organism concentration (M), and substrate concentration (S), together with volumetric flow-rate.   Now, while the automated
measurement of DO is well established, only a correlative measure (suspended
solids) is presently available for the measurement of M, and for S one might have
considered using the BOD test.   If BOD measurement is circumvented by using
ammonia and organic carbon contents (BRIGGS (1975)15) as indices of the (waste)
substrate strength, we may be approaching more closely a practically feasible
experiment.   But a priori, the acquired data may only be a blurred view of the
real nature of activated sludge process dynamics.   Indeed, the act of observing
this biological system is a good illustration of the conflict between our macroscopic insight into microscopic detail ** (see also section 4.2).
      Additional problems of experimental design for activated sludge relate to
the process's characteristic modes of dynamic behaviour, which show a wide spectrum of speeds of response.   These range from the relatively fast (of the order
of seconds) response for the DO/blower speed dynamics to much slower responses
(of the order of hours and days) associated with micro-organism/substrate interaction.   Consequently, the choices of sampling rate and duration of the experiment are almost certain to be poorly matched for the observation of all the modes
of behaviour simultaneously.   It may suffice, in practice, to identify _two_ models
separately, providing it can be assumed that there is a discrete distinction between the order of magnitude of the time constants.   A long term model could
apply to the characterisation of micro-organism/substrate trajectories, while a
short-term model might describe the DO dynamics as short-term perturbations about
the long-term trajectories.   A conceptual separation of this kind seems to be

---

* See figure 3(b).

** Notice (i) that in a laboratory-scale experiment the observer has good control
over his experimental conditions with the potential for using more sophisticated
instrumentation; (ii) that a model derived from field data, however crude those
data are, is still a model worthy of application since automatic control will
ultimately be implemented through the same observation process.

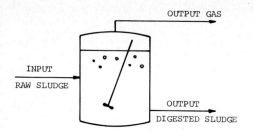

Figure 4   The anaerobic
           digestion process

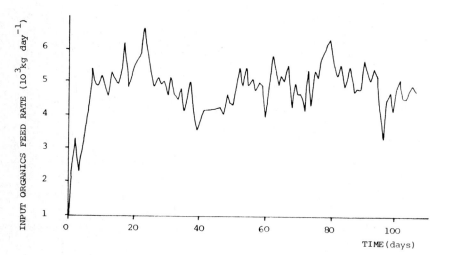

Figure 5   Observed input organics feed rate, u_1

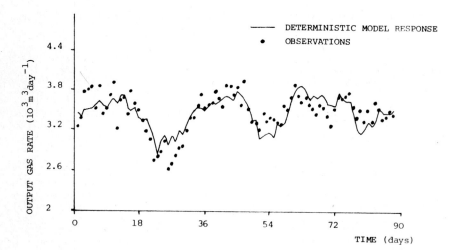

Figure 6   Observed and deterministic model outputs for the digester
           gas production rate, y

intuitively reasonable and, to some extent, it reflects the logistics of experimental design.   By manipulating the air-blower speed in an artificial manner the
DO could be perturbed about a mean level of 1.5 mg/ℓ, say, but constrained within
the limits 1.0 mg/ℓ and 2.0 mg/ℓ * for reasons of process stability (a PRBS signal
would have particularly attractive properties here).   In contrast, a first attempt
at establishing a model for micro-organism/substrate interaction could probably be
effected by observing the natural plant excitation (i.e. normal operation) over a
period of weeks.

Experimentation along these lines has been adopted in a recent study by
OLSSON (1975)40; his results should provide a firm basis in considering both the
data collection and analysis phases of activated-sludge process examination.

4.2.   Black box models (anaerobic digestion)

Anaerobic digestion (figure 4) is a biological process for the treatment of
the separated solids wastes stream.   It is carried out in a heated sealed vessel
and,as the name suggests, cultures of strictly anaerobic micro-organisms are
supported by the nutrient complex organic wastes which are decomposed in a series
of autocatalytic reactions.   The insoluble organics are first dissolved by extra-
cellular enzymes; acid-producing bacteria then decompose the soluble organics to
give volatile acids, which in turn are converted by methane-producing bacteria
into the final products, methane and carbon dioxide.   This last step is generally
believed to be rate-limiting and can, therefore, be assumed to be the only significant biochemical reaction in the overall digestion process.   An internally descriptive dynamic model based on this assumption, and incorporating a modification
of the Monod kinetics, has been presented by ANDREWS (1975)2; like the theoretical
models for activated sludge, it is a qualitative, but not completely quantitative,
representation of the real system.

Nevertheless, it is still feasible to use the model in an analysis of process
stability or in a control system synthesis context, as reported by GILLILAND (1974)
18.   But the verification of the model against field data remains an awkward
problem.   And not the least of these problems is that of defining which nutrient
S is rate-limiting (as implied by eqn (5)) to the heterogenous collection of
micro-organism species described by M.   It would seem, therefore, that a first
attempt at identifying the process dynamics might assume a black box conception
of the system.   For in view of the general lack of field data an internally descriptive model would appear to be too complicated to justify systematic identification and estimation at this stage.   A black box approach is used in this instance
to establish the time-dependency of some basic cause-effect relationships for the
process dynamics.   The construction of an internally descriptive model might then
be approached piecewise by carefully drawing inferences from the black box modelling results.

It is almost inevitable that a proper study of anaerobic digestion dynamics
is hampered by the lack of suitable field data.   Figure 5 shows a typical pattern
for the daily organics feed rate (defined as the percentage volatile matter in the
dried raw sludge) to a primary heated digester at Norwich Sewage Works for the
period December 1968 to February 1969.   Broadly speaking, this time series exhibits a fairly steady nature with a small signal/noise ratio.   In other words, it is
doubtful that such an input signal is persistently disturbing the process dynamics
and the prospects for identifying any cause-effect relationships from such noisy
data seem remote.   But with some perseverance in the liberal application of
cross-correlation analysis a preliminary structure of a model for the output gas
rate, y(k)(in m^3/day), is given by

---

* These limits are generally acknowledged to be the most suitable for normal process operation.

** Note however, that MOSEY and HUGHES (1975)38 have published a considerable
volume of data on the dynamic responses of anaerobic digestion to toxic heavy
metal ions using a laboratory-scale plant.

$$y(k) = 0.354\ y(k-1) + 99.3u_1(k) - 26.1u_1\ (k-1)$$

$$-2.79u_2\ (k) - 0.116u_2\ (k-1) - 1.23u_2\ (k-2) - 1.44u_2\ (k-3) - 1.35u_2(k-4)$$

$$-0.272u_3\ (k-2) + 0.641u_3\ (k-11) + 0.426u_3\ (k-12) \qquad\qquad (6)$$

Here u_1 is the input organics feed rate (kg/day), u_2 is the volatile acids concentration of the digesting sludge (mg/ℓ acetic acid), and u_3 is the alkalinity
of the digester contents (mg/ℓ calcium carbonate); the parameters are estimated
according to an IVAML technique. Figure 6 presents a comparison between the
deterministic model response, eqn (6), and the observed output gas rate.   At
this early stage, when the model really requires further analysis and simplification if at all feasible, it might be suggested from eqn (6) that any disturbance
in u_1 or u_2 produces an immediate response in the output gas rate y.   But such
an interpretation should be treated with caution since the relatively slow sampling frequency (once per day) is probably masking the true, albeit quite fast,
dynamic relationships between u_1, u_2, and y.   On the other hand, the input/output
relationship for u_3 and y displays a pure time delay of some two to ten days.
Again, the significance of this result is debatable, especially in view of the
relative brevity of the data record length.

Any further interpretation of the model structure is, in **short**, dangerous.
The model almost certainly suffers from the following inadequacies: (i) it is
strictly specific both to the sample data set and to the limited operational
range observed over the period of the data; (ii) it is a linear model of a
strongly non-linear process.   A next stage in the analysis might include an
examination of possible time-variations in the parameters.   The error between
the model and the observed data appears to oscillate slowly in a "deterministic"
manner which could have a correlation with variations in u_1, u_2, or u_3.   This
might lead to the introduction of either time-varying model coefficients (see
section 4.3.) or non-linearities, e.g. a term $u_2^2(k)$, into eqn (6).

4.3.   Recursive parameter estimation in black box models (DO-BOD interaction in a reach of river).

The following sections of the paper are concerned primarily with the modelling of river water quality dynamics as quantified by DO-BOD interaction.   A particular set of data from a 4.7 km reach of the river Cam has been the subject of
intensive study with a wide variety of identification and parameter estimation
techniques.   Many of the views expressed here are based upon this experience;
the individual results are reported fully elsewhere (BECK (1975a)[7], BECK and
WHITEHEAD (1975)[10], BECK and YOUNG (1975a)[11], (1975b)[12], YOUNG and WHITEHEAD (1975)
[52]) and are reviewed in BECK (1975c)[9].

It is found that two independent multiple input/single output, black box
models can be identified and estimated with an ML1 technique to give (BECK (1974)
[6]),

$$\text{DO:} \quad y_1\ (k) = -a_{11}y_1(k-1) + b_{11}u_1(k-1) + b_{30}u_3(k) + b_{31}u_3(k-1) \qquad (a) \left.\begin{array}{c}\\\\\end{array}\right\} (7)$$

$$\text{BOD:} \quad y_2(k) = -a_{21}y_2(k-1) + b_{21}u_2(k-1) + b_{32}u_3(k-2) + b_{34}u_3(k-4) \qquad (b)$$

in which y_1, y_2 are the downstream (output) DO, BOD concentrations (mg/ℓ), u_1, u_2
are the upstream (input) BO, BOD concentrations (mg/ℓ) and u_3 is the sunlight
incident on the reach of river (hrs/day).   We may mention in passing that the
implications of the dynamic structure of eqn (7) are highly significant in terms
of identifying an internally descriptive model for the interaction of the sunlight,
and hence populations of algae, with the DO and BOD (BECK (1975a)[7]).

Having estimated the model parameters with an off-line procedure, it is interesting to reassess the model for the possibility of time-variable parameters.
Thus, given an identical model structure an IVAML estimation technique indicates
that the parameters b_{30} and b_{31} are subject to a marked amount of time-variability,
figure 7 (BECK and WHITEHEAD (1975)[10]).   This time-dependency of the parameters is

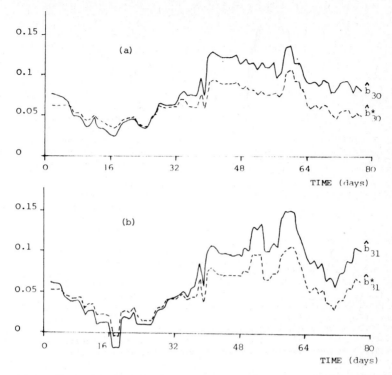

Figure 7   Recursive IVAML parameter estimates for b_{30}, b_{30}^* (a) and b_{31}, b_{31}^* (b) for the DO models of eqns (7a) and (8)

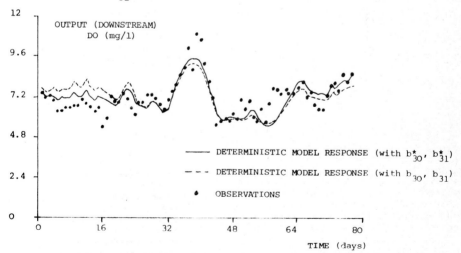

Figure 8   Observed and deterministic model responses, i.e. eqns (7a) and (8), for the downstream DO

correlated with the observed volumetric flow-rate in the river Q (m^3/day), i.e.
with the retention-time properties of the reach V/Q, where V is assumed to be the
constant volumetric hold-up in the reach (m^3). Thus, redefining eqn (7a), such
that *

$$y_1(k) = - a_{11} y_1(k-1) + b_{11} u_1(k-1) + b_{30}^* (V/Q(k))u_3(k) + b_{31}^* (V/Q(k-1))u_3(k-1)$$

$$(8)$$

provides more sensibly stationary time-invariant estimates of b_{30}^* and b_{31}^* and an
improved performance of the model, see figures 7 and 8. Moreover, the interpretation of eqn (8), as with eqn (7), gives additional insight into the physical
behaviour of the system dynamics, i.e. possible effects of turbidity conditions
on the growth of algae (BECK (1975c)9).

It is important to note that the desire to obtain a model with time-invariant
parameters is a fundamental aspect of identification and parameter estimation.
Not only does it give the model greater scope for more general application to
dynamic processes which have seasonal variations (e.g. WHITEHEAD and YOUNG (1975b)
49), but it is also a more precise and concise representation of the information
contained in the data. Indeed, time-invariance of the recursive parameter estimates provides a useful check on the sufficiency of the identified model structure.

4.4.   Identification and parameter estimation of internally descriptive models.
        (DO -BOD interaction in a reach of river).

The idea of applying "time-invariance of the parameter estimates" as a
criterion for identification has proved to be an invaluable procedure for the
analysis and synthesis of a DO-BOD-algae model. The EKF is one method which is
capable of implementing such a criterion; briefly, it is derived as follows. Let
us suppose that we have a vector of parameters $\underline{\alpha}$ which are to be estimated from
field data. In the first instance let us assume further that this vector is
composed of unknown, or poorly quantified, elements of the matrices A and B in
eqn (3a). It is now possible to augment the state vector dynamics by a set of
differential equations for the dynamic variations of the parameters so that we
have,

$$\begin{bmatrix} \dot{\underline{x}}(t) \\ \hline \dot{\underline{\alpha}}(t) \end{bmatrix} = f \left\{ \begin{bmatrix} \underline{x}(t) \\ \hline \underline{\alpha}(t) \end{bmatrix}, \underline{u}(t) \right\} + \underline{\xi}'(t) \qquad (9a)$$

with discrete-time observations, c.f. eqn (3b),

$$\underline{y}(k) = C' \begin{bmatrix} \underline{x}(k) \\ \hline \underline{\alpha}(k) \end{bmatrix} + \underline{n}(k) \qquad (9b)$$

where $\underline{f}$ is a non-linear vector function and $C' = \begin{bmatrix} C & \vdots & 0 \end{bmatrix}$ **. The EKF is a
particular linearised form of the non-linear filter which is required for the
simultaneous (recursive) estimation of the states $\underline{x}$ and parameters $\underline{\alpha}$ of the
process described by eqn (9).

The identification of a DO-BOD model in this manner is reported fully in an
earlier paper (BECK and YOUNG (1975b)12). Of particular importance to the discussion here is the innovation of a "sustained sunlight effect" (BECK and YOUNG
(1975a)11) which enables the DO-BOD model to predict the quantitative interaction
of an algal population with the DO and BOD. Subsequent analysis of the data
shows that a fourth-order internally descriptive model can be hypothesised, and
partially verified, for the combined DO-BOD-algae interaction. The concentrations

---

*For our purposes here it is not necessary to discuss the stochastic components
of the models.

** The prime notation in this and following equations indicates merely that the
order of $\underline{\xi}'$ differs from that of eqn (3a).

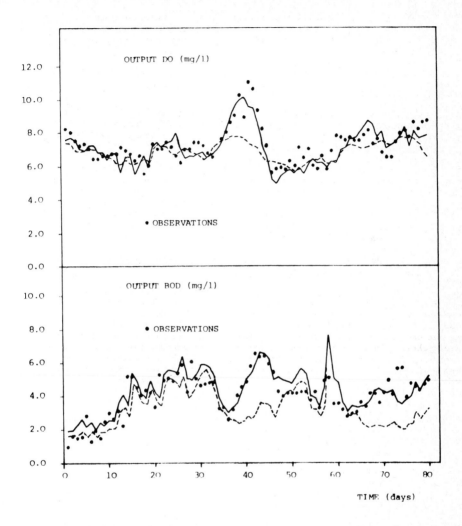

Figure 9   Deterministic DO and BOD responses for an internally
descriptive DO-BOD-algae interaction model; dashed lines
indicate responses with no algal populations assumed present

of the live and dead algal populations are the additional state variables and a
Monod function is assumed to govern the algal growth kinetics with sunlight as
the rate-limiting "nutrient" (BECK 1975a)[7].   Figure 9 shows the deterministic
DO and BOD responses of the model and also those responses which are obtained if
algal effects are disregarded.

Further identification studies are currently in progress with the EKF applied
to several reaches of the Bedford-Ouse River.   Initial results show that possible
"measurement bias" is being detected in the BOD; specifically, this relates to
the respiratory activity of algae in the five-day, dark bottle BOD test itself.
We come, then, to a slightly more complex problem of state/parameter estimation.
Let us consider a parameter vector $\underline{\alpha}'$ which comprises elements of the A, B, and
C matrices of eqn (3); for this case we have

$$\begin{bmatrix} \underline{\dot{x}}(t) \\ ---- \\ \underline{\dot{\alpha}}'(t) \end{bmatrix} = \underline{f}' \left\{ \begin{bmatrix} \underline{x}(t) \\ ---- \\ \underline{\alpha}'(t) \end{bmatrix}, \underline{u}(t) \right\} + \underline{\xi}''(t) \tag{11a}$$

$$\underline{y}(k) = \underline{g} \left\{ \begin{bmatrix} \underline{x}(k) \\ ---- \\ \underline{\hat{\alpha}}'(k) \end{bmatrix} \right\} + \underline{n}(k) \tag{11b}$$

where $\underline{g}$ is a non-linear vector function for the observations process of eqn (11b).
It seems as if the wheel has almost turned full circle for we are now back to the
original problem of section 2, namely the observation of biological processes.   A
rather strange situation exists: in order to identify the process dynamics we
must construct a dynamic model for the batch reactor behaviour of the BOD test and
simulate it in tandem with the dynamic behaviour of the river.   A strange situation indeed but perhaps not one which should surprise us if we reflect upon the
nature of the BOD test.   For, in effect, the BOD test is a (controlled) microcosm
of a multitude of dynamic phenomena which are occurring "in-situ" in the river.

4.5.   Diagnostic checking of the model validity (DO-BOD interaction in a
       reach of river.)

Assume that we have identified a black box model of the following general
form for the downstream DO in a reach of river (BECK and WHITEHEAD (1975)[10]), c.f.
eqn (7a),

$$y_m(k) = \frac{\sum_{i=1}^{2} \hat{B}_i(z^{-1})u_i(k)}{\hat{A}(z^{-1})} \tag{12}$$

in which $\hat{A}(z^{-1})$, $\hat{B}_i(z^{-1})$, i=1, 2 (two inputs: upstream DO and sunlight) are
estimates of $A(z^{-1})$ and $B_i(z^{-1})$, and $y_m(k)$ is the predicted output DO response
given the measurements $u_i(k)$.   Computation of the model errors,

$$\varepsilon(k) = y(k) - y_m(k) \tag{13}$$

shows that they have a significantly autocorrelated nature (figure 10(a)).
Further identification and estimation of a noise process model yields the estim-
ated polynomials $\hat{C}(z^{-1})$ and $\hat{D}(z^{-1})$, such that computation of $\hat{e}(k)$, where by substitution in eqn (1),

$$\hat{e}(k) = \frac{\hat{C}(z^{-1})}{\hat{D}(z^{-1})} \left(y(k) - \frac{\sum_{i=1}^{2} \hat{B}_i(z^{-1})u_i(k)}{\hat{A}(z^{-1})} \right) \tag{14}$$

gives an estimate $\hat{e}(k)$ of the stochastic sequence e(k) which is relatively uncorrelated in time (figure 10(b)).   Other statistical checks reveal that $\hat{e}(k)$ is

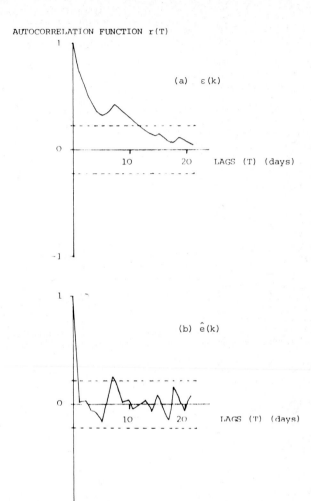

AUTOCORRELATION FUNCTION r(T)

(a) ε(k)

10   20   LAGS (T) (days)

(b) ê(k)

10   20   LAGS (T) (days)

Figure 10   Autocorrelation functions of model error series, ε(k), (a)
and residuals sequence, ê(k), (b) of a black box DO model;
dashed lines denote bounds for 95% confidence that r(T)=0
for T≠0

also independent of $u_i(k)$, i=1,2, with sufficient confidence for us to conclude
that the sample properties of $\hat{e}(k)$ approximate those assumptions made about the
nature of e(k) in the derivation of the process model, eqn (1).   The model is,
therefore, on this basis a reasonable approximation of the actual process dynamics.

4.6.   Further studies in biological process modelling.

Dynamic modelling and the identification/parameter estimation of biological
processes is a relatively young area of study.   For example, most of the references
in this paper indicate that the majority of the results have been obtained in the
past five years.   And it would appear that the derivation and verification of
these models has only very recently been approached in the manner of systems identification and parameter estimation as interpreted by the control and systems analysis discipline.   This is probably a result of the pronounced lack of field data.
Yet there has been a distinct lag between the application of such techniques to
general industrial processes and their application to the biological processes
discussed here.   Again this could be attributed to instrumentation problems but
it is equally probable that the delay is a consequence of the deeply ingrained
attitude that wastewater treatment and water quality are the "poor relations" of
the more profit-motivated industries.
In the literature there have been few straightforward applications of ident-
ification/estimation to field data.   SHASTRY et al (1973)44 have obtained maximum
likelihood estimates for the parameters of DO-BOD interaction models, but only
from "steady-state" spatially-distributed data.   The maximisation of the likelihood function can be posed as a problem of optimisation; similarly, therefore,
the work of POWERS and CANALE (1975) tends to be more concerned with the application of optimisation techniques than with the application of estimation techniques.
Univariate time-series analysis (as opposed to input/output time-series analysis)
studies, after BOX and JENKINS (1970)14, are also gaining popular acclaim in the
environmental engineering literature, e.g. HUCK and FARQUHAR (1974)27, BERTHOEUX
et al (1975)13.   Finally, with a much broader outlook, dynamic modelling of ecological systems is receiving active interest, both for small-scale sewage treatment
communities (CURDS (1973)19, JAMES (1975)30) and for large-scale marine (SJÖBERG
et al (1972)46) and terrestial environments (JEFFERS (1975)32).

5.   Conclusions.

A brief introductory survey of some of the underlying concepts and ideas of
system identification and parameter estimation has been presented.   We have
attempted wherever possible to avoid any discussion of the theoretical aspects,
and have, in preference, concentrated upon the simpler, more practical, side of
the subject.   This may tend to give the treatment of identification/estimation
a somewhat heuristic nature, but then if it can be read as a "user's guide" our
objectives have been fulfilled.
Bearing in mind the very real problems of data collection and instrumentation
in biological processes, the applications section of the paper is an illustrative
development and discussion of the preceding theory section.   Each phase in the
development of a dynamic model is enlarged upon and supported by evidence from
case studies.   It is apparent that the simple black box approach has had an
important part to play, probably because it is the first step in acquiring the
a priori knowledge which would be necessary for the identification of the inherently more complex internally descriptive models.   But no particular strategy for
the derivation of biological process models has emerged.   As with any other type
of system, the model-builder should use his a priori knowledge with prudence and
allow the data to speak for themselves.   Of course, system identification and
parameter estimation as such is a relatively new subject.   While the ensemble
of techniques summarised here is a powerful tool of analysis, there are notable
gaps in its ability to solve all the problems, especially in the area of internally
descriptive model identification.
Although there has been much debate over the relative merits and demerits of

the individual procedures (often the result of varying personal preferences),
 in practice each method can still yield its own piece of information about
the nature of the system's dynamics (see e.g. BECK (1975c)9).   Above all, the
process of modelling is a continuing evolution which depends upon the interplay
between experiment, analysis, and synthesis.   A new experiment is all the more
stimulating for the very reason that any preconceived expectations of the results
to be obtained from that experiment are (more often than not in our experience)
quite misguided.

References

1.   ANDREWS J.F. (1970), "Kinetics of biological processes used for wastewater
      treatment", Workshop on Research Problems in Air and Water Pollution, Univer-
      sity of Colorado, Boulder, Colorado, August.
2.   ANDREWS J.F. (1975a), "Dynamic models and computer simulation of wastewater
      treatment systems", in "Computer simulation of water resources systems" (Ed.
      G.C. VANSTEENKISTE), North-Holland, Amsterdam, pp 457-466.
3.   ANDREWS J.F. (1975b), "Introduction to systems engineering in water pollution
      control" in "The use of mathematical models in water pollution control" (Ed.
      A. JAMES), John Wiley & Sons, London, (in the press).
4.   ÅSTRÖM K.J. and BOHLIN T. (1975), "Numerical identification of linear dynamic
      systems from normal operating records", Proc. IFAC Symp. on the Theory of
      self-adaptive Control Systems", Teddington, England.
5.   ÅSTRÖM K.J. and EYKHOFF P. (1971), "System identification - a survey", Auto-
      matica, 7, No.2, pp.123-162.
6.   BECK M.B. (1974), "Maximum likelihood identification applied to DO-BOD-algae
      models for a freshwater stream", Report 7431(C), Lund Inst. Techn., Div. Aut.
      Contr., Sweden.
7.   BECK M.B. (1975a), "The identification of algal population dynamics in a
      freshwater stream", in "Computer simulation of water resources systems" (Ed.
      G.C. VANSTEENKISTE), North Holland, Amsterdam, pp. 483-494.
8.   BECK M.B. (1975b), "Dynamic modelling and control applications in water
      quality maintenance", Report CUED/F - Control/TR92, Engng.Dept., Cambridge.
9.   BECK M.B. (1975c), "Modelling of dissolved oxygen in a non-tidal stream", in
      "The use of mathematical models in water pollution control" (Ed. A. JAMES),
      John Wiley & Sons, London (in the press).
10.   BECK M.B. and WHITEHEAD P.G.(1975), in preparation.
11.   BECK M.B. and YOUNG P.C. (1975a), "A dynamic model for DO-BOD relationships
      in a non-tidal stream", Wat. Res., 9, No.9, pp. 769-776.
12.   BECK M.B. and YOUNG P.C. (1975b), "Identification and parameter estimation of
      DO-BOD models using the extended Kalman filter", Report CUED/F - Control/TR93,
      Engng. Dept., Cambridge.
13.   BERTHOUEX P.M., HUNTER W.G., PALLESEN L.C., and SHIH C-Y., (1975), "Modelling
      sewage treatment plant input BOD data", Proc. A.S.C.E., J. Env. Eng. Div.,
      101, No. EE1, pp. 127-138.
14.   BOX G.E.P. and JENKINS G.M. (1970), "Time-series analysis, forecasting and
      control", Holden-Day, San Francisco.
15.   BRIGGS R. (1975), "Instrumentation for monitoring water quality", Wat.Treatm.
      Exam., 24, Part 1, pp. 23-45.
16.   BRYANT J.O. and WILCOX L.C. (1972), "Real-time simulation of the conventipnal
      activated-sludge process", Paper 25-3, Proc. JACC, Stanford University, Calif-
      ornia, pp. 701-716.
17.   BUSBY J.B. and ANDREWS J.F. (1973), "Dynamic modelling and control strategies
      for the activated-sludge process", 46th Annual Conf. of the Wat. Poll. Contr.
      Fedn., Cleveland, October.
18.   COLLINS A.S. and GILLILAND B.E. (1975), "Control of anaerobic digestion pro-
      cess", Proc. A.S.C.E., J.Env.Eng. Div., 100, No. EE2, 487-506.
19.   CURDS C.R. (1973), "A theoretical study of factors influencing the microbial
      population dynamics of the activated-sludge process - I the effects of diurnal
      variations of sewage and carniverous ciliated protozoa", Wat. Res., 7, pp.

1269-1284.

20.   EYKHOFF P. (1974) "System identification – parameter and state estimation",
      John Wiley & Sons, London.

21.   GILLESPIE D.W. (1975), "The application of systems engineering techniques to
      the modelling of new town growth", P.T.R.C. summer Annual Meeting, University
      of Warwick, July.

22.   GRAEF S.P. and ANDREWS J.F. (1974), "Stability and control of anaerobic
      digestion", J.W.P.C.F., 46, No.4., pp 666-683.

23.   GUSTAVSSON I. (1972), "Comparison of different methods for identification of
      industrial processes", Automatica, 8, pp. 127-142.

24.   GUSTAVSSON I. (1975), "Survey of applications of identification in chemical
      and physical processes", Automatica, 11, pp. 3-24.

25.   GUSTAVSSON I., SELANDER S., and WIESLANDER J. (1973), "IDPAC – User's Guide",
      Report 7331, Lund Inst. Techn., Div. Aut. Contr., Sweden.

26.   HÄMÄLÄINEN R.P., HALME A., and GYLLENBERG A., (1975), "A control model for
      activated sludge wastewater treatment process", Preprints, 6th IFAC World
      Congress, Paper 61.6, Boston, Massachusetts.

27.   HUCK P.M. and FARQUHAR G.J. (1974), "Water quality models using the BOX –
      JENKINS method", Proc. A.S.C.E., J. Env. Eng. Div., 100, No. EE3, pp 733-752.

28.   ISERMANN R. (1975), "Modelling and identification of dynamic processes – an
      extract" in "Computer simulation of water resources systems" (ed. G.C. VANSTEE-
      NKISTE), North-Holland, Amsterdam, pp. 7-37.

29.   ISERMANN R., BAUR U., BAMBERGER W., KNEPPO P., and SIEBERT H. (1974), "Comp-
      arison of six on-line identification and parameter estimation methods",
      Automatica, 10, pp. 81-103.

30.   JAMES A. (1975), "An ecological model of a percolating filter", in "The use
      of mathematical models in water pollution control" (Ed. A. JAMES), John
      Wiley and Sons, London (in the press).

31.   JAZWINSKI A.H. (1970), "Stochastic processes and filtering theory", Academic
      Press, New York.

32.   JEFFERS J.N.R. (1975), "Systems analysis and modelling strategies in ecology"
      in "The use of mathematical models in water pollution control" (Ed. A. JAMES),
      John Wiley and Sons, London (in the press).

33.   JONES G.L. (1975), "A mathematical model for bacterial growth and substrate
      utilisation in the activated sludge process" in "The use of mathematical
      models in water pollution control" (Ed. A. JAMES), John Wiley and Sons, London
      (In the press).

34.   KARPLUS W.J. (1975), "The future of mathematical models of water resources
      systems", Proc. IFIP Working Conference on "Biosystems Simulation in water
      resources and waste problems", Bruges, Belgium, September.

35.   KLINCK M. (1975), "Simulation aided modelling of the dynamic behaviour for
      some elements of surface water treatment plant" in "Computer simulation of
      water resources systems" (Ed. G.C. VANSTEENKISTE), North-Holland, Amsterdam,
      pp. 467-475.

36.   KOIVO A.J. and PHILLIPS G.R. (1971), "Identification of mathematical models
      for DO and BOD concentrations in polluted streams from noise corrupted measure-
      ments", Wat. Res. Res., 7, No.4. pp. 853-862.

37.   MONOD J. (1942), "Recherches sur la croissance des cultures bacteriennes",
      Hermann et cie, Paris.

38.   MOSEY F.E. and HUGHES D.A. (1975), "The toxicity of heavy metal ions to
      anaerobic digestion", J. Inst. Wat. Poll. Contr., No.1, pp. 3-24.

39.   NEUMAN S.P. (1975) "Role of subjective value judgement in parameter identific-
      ation", in "Computer simulation of water resources systems" (Ed. G.C. VANSTEE-
      NKISTE), North-Holland, Amsterdam, pp. 59-84.

40.   OLSSON G. (1975), in preparation.

41.   OLSSON G., DAHLQVIST K-I., EKLUND K., and ULMGREN L. (1973), "Control prob-
      lems in wastewater treatment plants", Report, The Axel Johnson Institute for
      Industrial Research, Nynäshamn, Sweden.

42.   POWERS W.F. and CANALE R.P. (1975), "Some applications of optimisation tech-
      niques to water quality modelling and control", I.E.E.E. Trans., SMC-5, No.3,
      pp. 312-321.

43. SARIDIS G.N. (1974), "Comparison of six on-line identification algorithms",
     Automatica, 10, pp. 69-79.
44. SHASTRY J.S., FAN L.T., and ERICKSON L.E. (1973) "Non-linear parameter estim-
     ation in water quality modelling", Proc. A.S.C.E., J. Env.Eng.Div., 99, No.
     EE3, pp. 315-331.
45. SHELLSWELL S.H. (1972), "A Computer Aided Procedure for Time-series Analysis
     and Identification of Noisy Processes (CAPTAIN)", Report CUED/B-Control/TR25,
     Engng.Dept., Cambridge.
46. SJÖBERG S., WULFF F., and WÅHLSTRÖM P. (1972), "Computer simulations of
     hydrochemical and biological processes in the Baltic", Report No.1, Asko
     Laboratory, Sweden.
47. STEEL E.W. (1953), "Water supply and sewerage" (3rd Edition), McGraw-Hill,
     New York, p.265.
48. WHITEHEAD P.G. and YOUNG P.C. (1975a), "A dynamic stochastic model for water
     quality in part of the Bedford-Ouse River system", in "Computer simulation
     of water resources systems" (Ed. G.C. VANSTEENKISTE), North-Holland, Amster-
     dam, pp. 417-438.
49. WHITEHEAD P.G. and YOUNG P.C. (1975b), "The Bedford-Ouse Study Dynamic Model-
     fourth report to the Steering Group of the Great Ouse Associated Committee",
     Technical Note CN/75/1, Engng.Dept., Cambridge.
50. YOUNG P.C. (1969), "Applying parameter estimation to dynamic systems - part 1"
     Contr.Engng, 16, No.10, pp. 119-125.
51. YOUNG P.C. (1974), "A recursive approach to time-series analysis", Bull Inst.
     Maths. Appl. (IMA), 10, Nos.5/6, pp. 209-224.
52. YOUNG P.C. and WHITEHEAD P.G. (1975), "A recursive approach to time-series
     analysis for multivariable systems", in "Computer simulation of water res-
     ources systems" (Ed. G.C. VANSTEENKISTE), North-Holland, Amsterdam, pp. 39-52.

DISCUSSION

*I think it is quite an enterprise to look at a biological process model,
and I am speaking as a chemist also in the biochemistry region. Our experiments
are always of 2 different kinds. You can make a set up experiment, isolating the
factor of which you try to see the effect. On the other hand, you have an experiment just which you can consider as an observation experiment, something which is
going on in nature, in practice and just observe. Then you have all the parameters
of the acting factors together. When studying the gas output model in your closed
system, more or less, you mention some factors and from the biological point of
view, there are so many : for example the factor alkalinity. So I ask you : why
alkalinity ? You have spoken also about pH, and volatile acids.
I consider such a number of parameters and factors, how did you decide to choose
just these few ones ? You might get an analogous response considering other factors, for example the presence of tracers of heavy metals, which influences enor-
mously the biological activity proceeding to gas production.   (COTTENIE)*

These particular values were the only ones that we measured on this actual
plant. I do not understand the significance of the model I derived yet, but I'm
trying to use it as an illustration and perhaps as a means of projecting future
research.   (BECK)

Are you sure about the relation between cause and effect ?   (COTTENIE)

No, the trouble is that it tends to be so specific to the data. There are so many problems in that model that I cannot explain anything very much. I'm not particularly happy about that, but maybe there is something to come out of the diffusion between biologists and modellers. (BECK)

This is the meaning of my question. Shouldn't we, biologists, chemists, mathematicians and modelists, stick together and see what can be meaningful for us ? (COTTENIE)

This is where the difficulties come in. Somebody like myself is confused by looking at the absolute mass of biological detail. I think somewhere we have to leave our own respective details and come to each other. The conversation is extremely important. One who is particularly interested in this matter is professor Andrews who was here last year. On the one side he wrote a paper about the bio-chemical kinetics, on the other side he wrote about a systems analysis of waste-water treatment problems. This makes things more understandable for people on both sides. (BECK)

Isn't it possible to perform a kind of multidimensional analysis ? I'm thinking of a factorial analysis of correspondance, on the set of data that you have detected, before doing a specialized treatment to the data you feed into the problem. You could do for example a correspondance analysis and see which are the factors that may be correlated and that may influence your phenomena. Then, having this model, with this approach, the first idea is present of what is the definite model. (DE MARSILY)

This is one technique, but what may be possible in the future is the ap-plication of pattern recognition to this time series data.
I'm only saying that one can recognize a number of features in the data which will give you this kind of information about what affects what. In anaerobic digestion it may very well be that temperature affects the output gas rate, rather than that gas rate affects temperature. One does not know which way the whole relationship actually goes, and it is quite like this in economic systems as well. (BECK)

Of course this is a possibility, but I'm wondering about the fact that modeling people and mathematicians try always to have their own experiments. You suggest to take more data from an experiment which has been made for that thing. But, at present, we are looking to papers, published 10 à 20 years ago, where have been made an enormous amount of experiments, which have never been studied in de-tail from the mathematical side. Many of these people have only looked at the ef-fect, and made conclusions, about what is just misible. Looking to this, with a mathematician's eyes, you can see much more than they have seen. You can use their figures in a much better way (?) I don't think that you always need to repeat by yourself all those experiments. (COTTENIE)

I think this is true. You seem to be very conversant with anaerobic diges-tion. I came across papers from some people of the Water Resource Center at Stevenage in England. They made some experiments on this subject too, to look at toxic effects on the output gas rate. They derived lots of time-series. And I feel sure that they have not identified fully those time-series themselves. There was one drawback in that a laboratory model was used instead of the actual process. To some extent you cannot really generalize from the laboratory scale to the actual process plant itself. (BECK)

I understand one of the problems with this type of biological model, where you don't really know what effects what. If those sort of measurements are avail-able to you, and you have to work with the measurements you have, it is a very im-portant point that experiments have been done in the past, relating other factors

*to the effect that you are measuring, factors that were not actually measured in
the system you consider. Wouldn't it be feasible to use those experiments and feed
them into your model, in order to perform a sensitivity analysis which could eventually tell you whether or not these measurements actually have to be made in the
particular system you are considering. What I'm saying is : could you use the model as it is today, perhaps with some modifications, to direct future data acquisition, and since for example the effect of heavy metals, was not actually measured
in the system you consider, could you possibly use previous experiments, laboratory or otherwise to perform such an analysis. (NEUMAN)*

I think so, very definitely. One really wants to use all the information
that is available, and in trying to obtain a model of anaerobic digestion, I really wanted to see what information I can get out of it, e.g. designing another experiment. I have a feeling that, in this area, there is a lack of information on
process behaviour, and in designing experiments, one would like to disturb the
system in a more deterministic manner than what happens under normal process operation. One would like to set up at least an experiment where one can measure far
more of the variables in the system. By getting this preliminary model, one starts
with a black box representation which was made a little bit grey ; perhaps, performing another experiment can get us closer to the white box representation.
(BECK)

*Do you plan actually with the system that you are considering to make a
sensitivity analysis and to use this model to direct in the future a data acquisition in the reach of the river ?
Are you going to suggest that one has to measure for example not only sunlight,
but also the presence of heavy metals or other factors ? (NEUMAN)*

Yes, actually we did not expect the sunlight effect to be there. We just
measured the dissolved oxygen and biochemical oxygen demand and, occasionally
we also had measurements of the sunlight each day. When we came to the next time
(we did some experiments elsewhere) we measured also the amount of algae in the
river ; so now, we have a measurement on the algae in the same way as sunlight,
BOD and DO. We have done this experiment and it turns out now that one would like
to join the effect of the nitrogen cycle to the algae-BOD-DO model, getting even
more complex. And therefore we have done another experiment this year, a control
experiment with artificial aeration of the river. We measured ammonium and nitrate
as well this time. What happens is : one does an experiment and finds out what
measurements you should make next time. So one tries to make more experiments,
hopefully to obtain more information. (BECK)

System Simulation in Water Resources, ed. G.C. VANSTEENKISTE
1976, North-Holland Publishing Company

TWO TYPICAL EXAMPLES OF APPLICATION OF DISPERSION METHODOLOGY AND MODELING TO GROUNDWATER POLLUTION

Jean J. Fried
Professeur à l'Université Louis Pasteur
Strasbourg, France

INTRODUCTION

When confronted to a groundwater pollution problem, the responsible people should ask several questions :

i/ what is the nature of the pollution :

. is it miscible or not to water ?

. what are its physical and chemical properties ?

. what sort of danger does it present ?

ii/ what is the scale of the pollution :

. what is the total amount of pollution ?

. what is the strength of the pollution source ?

. what are the characteristic dimensions and geometry of the pollution source ?

. what is the invaded volume of soil ?

. what is the duration of the pollution ?

The ways and means of answering these questions are thoroughly discussed in Fried (1975), where a complete methodology of groundwater pollution studies is given. This methodology is based upon the use of the dispersion schema and a careful mixing of modeling and fizld experimental techniques. We wish to present two cases here which illustrate the application of this methodology; these examples are general enough but also typical enough to provide a good basis for discussion. These examples are derived from the personal experience of the author and the situation described encountered recently.

POLLUTION HAZARDS IN A LARGE AQUIFER, WHICH IS AN IMPORTANT WATER RESOURCE OF AN URBAN COMMUNITY

An urban community takes most of its water from wells pumping an alluvial aquifer and these wells must be protected against various possible pollutions such as accidents, sanitary landfills, fertilizers. In terms of pollutant injections these cases are represented by, respectively, injections localized in time and space, injections localized in space but lasting long, injections in large areas and lasting long.

It will be necessary then

i/ to quickly estimate the probability of a pollution flowing accidentally through a pumping well.

ii/ to define the influence of present or unavoidable pollutions in the wells, especially as a function of pumping regimes.

iii/ to define pollution sensitive zones in order to adjust the setting of new wells.

iv/ to derive a large scale model as a quantitative support of prediction and management.

v/ to inform the public by simple visualization of the pollution evolution.

The objectives being thus known, the problem must then be correctly defined : at this stage, some choice of the models has to be made and decision criteria derived from rough preliminary studies, which mainly consist in inquiries with local authorities to gather some knowledge of the type of existing and expected pollutions. The objectives show that the problem is multiscale and most probably both convective and dispersive models will be necessary; the sequence of options should be included in the study programme.

The study programme is organized in a sequence of steps which reflect the necessity of carefully separating the various scales and of proceeding from the local to the regional scale.

The domain is partitioned in zones presenting some geological homogeneity as displayed by the preliminary studies. Each zone is divided up into experimental areas, comprising one or several wells. To give an order of magnitude,experiments have been conducted on alluvial aquifers, on experimental areas of 0.002 to 3 km^2, on zones of 10 to 50 km^2 and in domaine of 50 to 300 km^2 and, on fissured aquifers in domains up to 3000 km^2.

On each experimental area, then, experiments will be performed to collect hydraulic parameters (such as porosities and permeabilities) and pollution parameters (such as dispersion coefficients). These parameters will be usad as such in predictive models answering objectives i/ and ii/

Such an experimental area is an elementary block of a larger model representing the zone : first, compatibility conditions at the boundaries of the blocks, especially flux conservations, are derived between the experimental area models, then a mean equivalent model is derived, by computing new sets of equivalent dispersion coefficients, absorbing block boundary conditions and using new zonal boundary conditions.

The zonal models will be adjusted on existing pollution and answer objective c . The zone are then used as elementary blocks of a model of the domain, first as a juxtaposition of zonal models with compatibility conditions at the zonal boundaries, then within a domain equivalent model with large scale equivalent coefficients.

At this stage, dispersion may sometimes be neglected and the domain model will consist of a convective model, i.e. a balance of matter.
Objectives iii/ and iv/ are then answered
This programme has been summarized on the flow chart 1

The models are bidimensional, for general domains. The complete dispersion matrix will be used (and not only a diagonal form) in canonical rectangular axes, with classical change of coordinates formulas to switch from the general form to the diagonal form and conversely.

The results will be forecasting models, the maps of pollution sensitive zones (velocity and dispersion coefficient maps) and type-curves of concentrations.

THE SETTING OF SANITARY LANDFILLS NEAR AN URBAN COMMUNITY

A town is quickly developing and increases its reliance on an underlying unconfined aquifer by setting new grids of pumping wells ; at the same time it has to built two new sanitary landfills near an existing one, not too far from the wells. The local authorities wish to forecast the pollution coming from the existing and future landfills and the influence of the various pumping programmes, and the seasonal nature of the surface recharge on its evolution. It is a highly transient, non-steady problem that can be most accurately handled by a mathematical model of the pollution.

Even if no accurate information has been provided concerning the composition of the wastes, it can be assumed (unless stated otherwise by the authorities) that they consist chiefly of wastes from urban areas which generate compounds such as sulfates, sulfites,... miscible with the water of the aquifer and a dispersion model will be fit to determine the pollution concentration levels compared to an admissible pollution threshold in the water of the aquifer.

The study programme is divided up into three stages, each stage providing a set of usable results allowing evaluations of the pollution with increasing accuracy, which allows to consider one stage after the other in the financial planning of the operation : this procedure is interesting for urban communities which do not have to plan large expenses at once.

. Stage 1 is an initial field study, corresponding to the preliminary studies of the general methodology (Fried, 1975). It consists in studying the available data in order to determine the various pollution thresholds, the geological features (especially the zones where significant vertical permeabilities contrasts may be expected), the piezometry and the expected flow lines.

Also, and this is most important, the existing landfill may be considered as a source of environmental tracers and should be monitored by using already existing wells and sampling their water for chemical analysis, and by drilling new multiple level wells at positions given by the piezometric map.

. Stage 2 corresponding to the determination of the pollution modelling parameters (velocities, dispersion coefficients) in the field, consists in monitoring the existing pollution (by measuring water resistivities with electrical borings, for instance, if stage 1 shows that pollution changes the water resistivity), refining the geological knowledge in the proposed sites (by drilling new wells or by geophysical methods), collecting the necessary data for the determination of dispersion parameters (by injecting an artificial miscible pollutant, such as salt water, and recording its spreading, by surface resistivity measurements for instance, trying to separate the influence of the lower and the upper aquifer strata), determining the dispersion coefficients (by interpreting the field experiments with a numerical model).

. Stage 3 corresponding to the derivation and use of a forecasting and mathematical model, consists in integrating the various results of stages 1 and 2 into hydrologic and dispersion models representing the whole domain influenced by the landfills.

The expected results are then as follows :

. Stage 1 will yield a general knowledge of the behaviour of pollution on the proposed landfills (such as the nature of potential pollutions, the possible average horizontal extension of pollution clouds with time, the possible average vertical extension of pollution clouds and the determination of the layers most sensitive and most affected by pollution) and guidelines to the choice of the forecasting model and its scale (such as the determination of the behaviour of the pollution in a vertical section, a choice of the field experiments with tracers to collect dispersion parameters and the determination of the position and of the number of necessary wells for further exoeriments to collect dispersion parameters).

. Stage 2 will yield numerical values of the dispersion coefficients at the various sites, numerical values of water velocities in the aquifer and a refined map of flowlines, a detailed knowledge of the geological features near the sites, a thorough knowledge of the pollution paths vertically and horizontally and a set of rules of thumb allowing the forecasting of the pollution for steady state conditions and various well distributions.

. Stage 3 will yield a mathematical model, composed of a hydrological model and of a dispersion model, to manage water quality in the landfill zone and the determination of a belt of warning stations to continuously adjust and correct the forecasting tools in case of local variations.

CONCLUSION

        Both examples are taken from studies effectively performed by the author, where the methodology, the analysis of the system and the mathematical models have proved very efficient tools in setting, ordering and solving such pollution problems.

REFERENCE

Fried, J.J. (1975). Groundwater Pollution : Theory, Methodology, Modelling and
                     Practical Rules - Elsevier Pub. Co (330 pp)
                     (to be published in 1975)

DISCUSSION

We see that more or less there is a conflict between the last 2 papers. We heard from dr. Simundich how he has attempted to do the modeling of a particular basin, and he had lots of problems.
Here we heard a more hopeful story. I guess, the basis of it is that what you are proposing, the essence of your methods is that you go out and collect data from the particular areas you are working in, whereas Tom had to put up with the data that were given. (PECK)

You are right. Our method is to collect new data also. Otherwise we do not start any model.
As dr. Vachaud said this morning, we have to adapt our data collecting to the type of model we are using. This has been our philosophy for a couple of years. (FRIED)

That is the attitude most people had, also in our case.
But then comes the question of the management : how much data, how often should we sample, what spacing should we have in this basin ? Should we have wells every 50 feet ? Do we have to take continuous readings or what ? (SIMUNDICH)

There are theoretical and practical answers to that problem. It has been treated for example in de Marsily's laboratory, at the school of mines, by using kriging methods to optimize the well distribution, to optimize the implementation of testing.
I don't know whether de Marsily is still working on these methods ? (FRIED)

We are using them. (DE MARSILY)

Using also the specialized method of Matheron at the school of mines, introducing an optimal linear predictor, we try to put into our methodology also these techniques in order to answer the management question. (FRIED)

This does not suffer from scaling problems ? Do you run your experiments on small scale or is this a large scale ? (SIMUNDICH)

The principle of proceeding in that case is rather simple. You can start with a very loose spread and make an estimation variance test. If your estimation variance is higher than you assume the error, then you put new wells, but only in those areas where the variance of estimation is higher than the admissible error. Those techniques are used especially by the people at the school of mines. You know that, more inherently my 2nd example was divided into 3 stages. At each stage the management could say : now that's far enough for us, we spent enough money and we are satisfied with the data. (FRIED)

You seem to be trying to answer 2 questions that I would call technical questions. There is another one partly technical, partly legal, when you face the problem of groundwater pollution. That is : who did it ? Sometimes it is very clear, when water is leaking from a specific place, but sometimes it is not clear at all. How would you go about to solve this problem ? (WAJC)

For groundwater, I don't know whether anything has been done. But there is a very good example taken from the experiments made by Emsellem in France, where he tried by a deconvolution method to find the origin of pollution in a stream by computing the transfer function of the stream from the results of given experiments.

In other words, once he has the transfer function, he hoped to find the origin, just looking at the input response.
As there were only a few industries, he could select the one just looking at the distance given by his transfer function. That has been tried in France, but only for surface water. Perhaps this matter can be extended to groundwater. This is dependent on the validity of the deconvolution method, which would be rather controversial. (FRIED)

   In Israël some lake was polluted systematically primarily by nitrates and phosphates. The big question was not who is the big industrialist, who is polluting, but who is the big farmer who is doing that ?
Was it the Hule valley upstream where pig deposits have been drained, and as a result of their contact with the atmosphere, started oxidising, creating nitrates ? Or perhaps some other source ? Is there a way of identifying other potential sources of pollution ?
In this particular study, most of the hydrological system through which the nitrates could possibly flow were near the surface water phase, either in the Jordan river itself, or in shallow affluents in soils. In this case it was too difficult to know the polluter just by measuring concentrations at various points. (NEUMAN)

PART TWO

WATER RESOURCES SIMULATION AS A SYNTHESIS PROBLEM

System Simulation in Water Resources, ed. G.C. VANSTEENKISTE
1976, North-Holland Publishing Company

IDENTIFICATION OF LINEAR HYDROLOGIC SYSTEMS'
RESPONSE FROM SHORT RECORDS IN THE
PRESENCE OF NOISE

Shlomo P. Neuman[1] and Ghislain de Marsily[2]

ABSTRACT

In identifying the impulse response function of a linear hydrologic
system on the basis of a short input-output record one often finds that
the results are very sensitive to minor errors in the data. In particular, low-amplitude random errors in the input-output record tend to
cause severe oscillations in the response function, thereby making it
difficult to obtain a physically realizable solution by conventional
methods. One way to obtain a physically meaningful impulse response
function from a relatively short hydrologic record (e.g., the record of
a single storm) is to use parametric programming. This makes it possible
to generate a continuous set of eventual alternative solutions to the
deconvolution problem, together with a bicriterion function representing
these alternatives. The shape of the bicriterion curve is then used by
the hydrologist as a guide in selecting a narrow range of acceptable
solutions which satisfy his concept about the physical nature of the
system under investigation.

INTRODUCTION

The concept of a lumped, stationary, deterministic linear system leads to
a useful operational tool in surface as well as subsurface hydrology. Mathematically, the relation between input and output in such a system is expressed
by the convolution integral

$$y = \int_{-\infty}^{t} u(t-\tau) \, x(\tau) \, d\tau \qquad (1)$$

where t is time, x is input, y is output, and u is the impulse response function
of the system.

In practice the response function is often unknown and must be determined
from an observed set of input and output data. This process of identifying the
impulse response function is known as deconvolution.

Numerous methods of performing deconvolution on discrete data have been
reported in the literature (Graupe, 1972). However, a difficulty is often encountered in applying existing methods to real world data due to the inherent
instability of the deconvolution process. Blank et al. (1971) and Delleur and
Rao (1971) have shown that the impulse response function is extremely sensitive
to minor errors in the input-output record when the latter represents a single
hydrologic event (such as an isolated storm). In particular, low-amplitude
random errors in the input-output data tend to cause severe oscillations in the
response function, thereby making it often impossible to obtain a physically
realizable solution by conventional methods.

[1] Department of Hydrology and Water Resources, The University of Arizona, Tucson,
Arizona 85721. On leave from the Institute of Soil and Water, Agricultural
Research Organization, P.O. Box 6, Bet Dagan, Israel.

[2] Centre d'Informatique Géologique, École Nationale Supérieure des Mines, 35 rue
Saint-Honoré, 77305 - Fontainebleau, France.

This finding is further supported by the more recent work of Natale and Todini (1974) and Todini (1975) in connection with the Arno river basin in Italy. They developed a quadratic programming approach to deconvolution which leads to a stable and consistent solution when one considers the average of response functions obtained from several hydrologic events. However, the response functions obtained from individual events tend to be vastly different from each other, indicating that these functions are highly sensitive to noise. Thus, the method may not be suitable for the analysis of short records representing only one or two distinct events.

One way to remedy this situation is by artificially filtering the input-output record to eliminate high-frequency oscillations. However, since the nature and extent of noise is seldom known a priori, one cannot be sure as to the proper choice of a cut-off frequency. Such filtering also causes a loss of data at the endpoints of the record and should therefore be avoided when the number of data points is small. Delleur and Rao (1971) found that filtering the impulse response function itself may help to eliminate high-frequency oscillations, but is less effective when the frequency is relatively low. Such low-frequency oscillations may be expected to occur in hdyrologic systems due to nonlinearities and various systematic errors.

An efficient method for controlling the instability of the deconvolution process has been developed by Emsellem and de Marsily (1969, 1971, 1973). According to their approach, the response function is initially embedded in a vector space of low dimension (limited number of Walsh functions) and the coordinates of the response function in this space are determined by least squares. The dimension of the vector space is then gradually increased until it is established that a further refinement of the solution will lead to oscillatory results. An important feature of this method is that it enables one to impose arbitrary lower and upper bounds on the individual values of the discrete response function and to continually smooth the result during the computation. The method has also been extended to nonstationary linear systems (Poitrinal and de Marsily, 1973) similar to those considered more recently by Diskin and Boneh (1974).

The purpose of this paper is to propose an alternative method for obtaining a stable and physically meaningful impulse response function from a relatively short hydrologic record (such as a single storm) by using parametric linear programming. The formal programming approach is used merely as a means of generating a continuous set of possible alternative solutions to the deconvolution problem together with a bicriterion function representing these alternatives. Since the computer has used all the available quantitative information without being able to identify a single solution which is "best" from the standpoint of both residual error and physical plausibility, the selection process must be supplemented by qualitative information based on the hydrologist's professional experience. Thus, the hydrologist can use the bicriterion curve as a guide in selecting a narrow range of acceptable solutions which satisfy his concept about what the shape of the response function should be in terms of degree of smoothness, positioning of peaks and valleys, and the area under the response curve. The method has been applied to actual field data and is illustrated in this paper by a theoretical example. The results are compared with those obtained by a modification of the method of Poitrinal and de Marsily (1973). A possibility of extending the parametric programming approach to nonstationary linear systems is indicated.

SINGLE-CRITERION LINEAR PROGRAMMING APPROACH

Consider a discrete input-output record of length T in which the data are prescribed at equal time intervals $\Delta t = T/N$, where N is an integer. Suppose that the record consists of $N+1$ instantaneous output values, y_n, measured at $t_n = t_0 + n\Delta t$, where $n = 0, 1, 2, \ldots, N$, and of N continuous input values, x_n, measured during the intervals $\Delta t = t_n - t_{n-1}$, where $n = 1, 2, \ldots, N$. If the memory of the system is assumed to be not more than $M\Delta t$, then (1) can be rewritten in the form:

$$y_n = \Delta t \sum_{i=n+1-M}^{n} u_{n+1-i} x_i + \varepsilon_n \qquad (2)$$

$$n = 1, 2, \ldots, N$$

where $u_1, u_2, \ldots, u_M$ is a sequence of average values of the response function over the time intervals Δt, and ε_n are residual errors. Implicit in equation 2 is the assumption that $y_0 = 0$ and all earlier effects of x_n (for $n<1$) have completely dissipated. The deconvolution problem consists of determining the unknown values of u_m in some optimal fashion without necessarily having any prior information about the nature of the residual errors, ε_n. If the true memory of the system is greater than $M\Delta t$, the response function will be truncated.

A straight forward linear programming approach to this problem might call for the minimization of the following error functional

$$J_c = \sum_{n=1}^{N} (p_n + q_n) \qquad (3)$$

subject to the constraints

$$\Delta t \sum_{i=n+1-M}^{n} u_{n+1-i} x_i - y_n + p_n - q_n = 0 \qquad (4)$$

$$p_n, q_n \geq 0; \quad n = 1, 2, \ldots, N \qquad (5)$$

$$\sum_{m=1}^{M} u_m \leq C \qquad (6)$$

$$u_m \geq u_m^L; \quad m = 1, \ldots, M \qquad (7)$$

where p_n and q_n are slack variables, C is a constant depending on the units, and u_m^L are prescribed lower limits for the values of u_m (zero if u is expected to be non-negative). If x and y are expressed in the same units then $C = 1$ and (6) indicates that the area under the response function should not be more than unity. However, this area may be less than unity when the true memory of the system exceeds either $M\Delta t$ or $N\Delta t$ (i.e., the response function is truncated), or when only a part of the measured input actually participates in generating the output (i.e., a portion of the input effect is consistently lost during the operation of the system). The calibration criterion, J_c, represents the sum of the absolute residual errors, $|\varepsilon_n|$ (note that either p_n or q_n must always lie outside the basis and must therefore be zero. For a definition of the term basis vector in linear programming refer to Hadley (1962, p. 43)). Another possibility would be to use a minimax criterion, but our experience with deconvolution indicates that the criterion defined in (3) leads to far better results.

The single-criterion deconvolution problem defined by (3) - (7) does not impose any restriction on the shape of the resulting impulse response function. It is easy to demonstrate that such an approach may lead to unstable results which are physically unacceptable. To do so, let us consider a hypothetical linear system similar to that considered previously by Delleur and Rao (1971). In this example the response function is given exactly by

$$u(t) = t(e^{8-t}-1) / (e^8-41); \quad 0 \leq t \leq 8$$

When the input is defined as

$$x(t) = t(1-t)e^{1-t} (e^8-41); \quad 0 \le t \le 1$$

then the output can be evaluated exactly to be

$$y(t) = e^{9-t} t^3(2-t) / 12 + e^{1-t} (\ ^2+3t+4) - e(4-t); \quad 0 \le t < 1$$

$$y(t) = e^{9-t} (2t-1) / 12 + (11-3t) - e(4-t); \quad\quad\quad 1 \le t < 8$$

$$y(t) = (e^{9-t}/12) [12t^2-130t+335-(t-8)^2(152-14t-t^2)]$$
$$+ (11-3t); \quad\quad\quad\quad\quad\quad 8 \le t \le 9$$

For the purpose of deconvolution we have divided the time interval T = 9 into 90 equal increments of size Δt = 0.1. Figure 1 shows average values of the

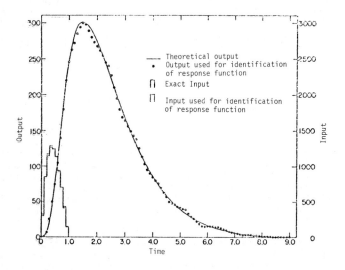

Figure 1. Input-output record for example problem.

exact input over each time increment, as well as the exact theoretical output. This figure also shows the actual discrete input-output records used for the analysis and it is seen that both records have been artificially corrupted by a slight but discernible noise. The noise imposed upon the output record includes a systematic low frequency ondulation about the decending limb of the theoretical curve. When these data are used to identify u by a linear programming approach based on (3) - (7) with C in (6) set equal to unity, the result is highly oscil-latory as indicated by the broken line in Figure 2. Note that the frequency of these oscillations is higher than the frequency of the systematic ondulations shown in Figure 1, indicating that at least part of the instability may stem from high frequency random errors in the input-output data.

The oscillatory result in Figure 2 is by no means an artifact of the linear programming approach. A similar phenomenon has been observed by using other methods, for example, Fourier and Z transforms (Delleur and Rao, 1971), least squares (Cole et al., 1972), etc.

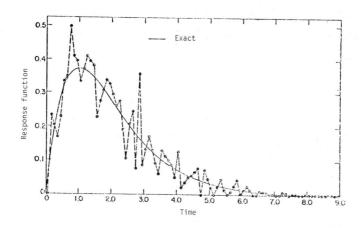

Figure 2.   Response function obtained when solution is
kept non-negative.

BICRITERION APPROACH

From the above example it is obvious that the deconvolution problem defined by (3) - (7) does not contain sufficient information to guarantee a physically realizable response function. Moreover, different input-output records
from a given system may be expected to result in vastly different response
functions because the shape of these functions is highly sensitive to minor
variations in the level of noise. Thus, we must ask ourselves the question what
other information could we feed into the problem that would help us to minimize
the effect of noise on the solution? Since all the available quantitative information has already been considered in equations 3-7, any additional information
must necessarily be of a purely qualitative nature. This is especially true in
environmental systems because here the statistical nature of the errors is
usually unknown.

Considering the fact that most hydrologic systems are characterized by a
highly pronounced damping quality, we may expect the response function of such
systems to be reasonably smooth. However, some hydrologic systems such as
karstic aquifers may give rise to polymodal response functions containing more
than just a single peak (Bouillon et al., 1973). These functions exhibit low
frequency oscillations which can be justified on physical grounds, and we are
thus faced with the question what degree of smoothness should we try to impose on
the solution without impairing the true physical nature of the response function?
As we shall see below, there is an infinite number of near optimal alternative
solutions to the deconvolution problem (in terms of the magnitude of the fit
criterion J_c) that may have varying degrees of smoothness. To choose between
these alternatives, it is helpful to establish an additional criterion of optimality providing a measure for the physical plausibility of any set of u_m values.
This will enable us to compare various alternative solutions from the standpoint
of a) closeness to a physically acceptable solution, and b) degree of consistency (or fit) with the convolution integral as expressed by the magnitude of
the error functional, J_c.

Let a_m be the difference between any two successive values of u_m so that

$$u_{m-1} - u_m + a_m = 0; \quad m = 1, 2, \ldots, M \qquad (8)$$

where it is understood that $u_0 = 0$. In order to control the degree of smoothness of u, we need to control the rate at which the slope of u varies with time at each point. In other words, we want to control the third derivative of the response function with respect to time. Thus, we are led to the following definition of a linear plausibility (smoothness) criterion,

$$J_p = \sum_{m=1}^{M-2} (r_m + s_m) \qquad (9)$$

subject to the constraints

$$(a_m - a_{m+1}) - (a_{m+1} - a_{m+2}) + r_m - s_m = 0 \qquad (10)$$

$$m = 1, 2, \ldots, M-2$$

$$r_m, s_m \geq 0; \qquad m = 1, 2, \ldots, M \qquad (11)$$

where r_m and s_m are slack variables. When $J_p = 0$, the rate at which the slope of u changes is fixed, meaning that u is a smooth curve with a gradually varying slope. Thus, $J_p = 0$ corresponds to maximum smoothness, and our objective then should be to minimize the value of J_p. Another possibility would be to use a minimax criterion, but our experience indicates that the criterion defined in (9) always leads to far better results.

GENERATION OF BICRITERION CURVE AND ALTERNATIVE SOLUTIONS

The relationship between the calibration criterion, J_c, and the plausibility criterion, J_p, can be conveniently obtained with the aid of parametric linear programming. The approach is to minimize J_c in (3) subject to the constraints (4) - (11) as well as the parametric constraint

$$J_p \leq \theta; \quad \theta \geq 0 \qquad (12)$$

where θ is a parameter that varies continuously between any two specified limits. By use of standard linear programming routines such as IBM's MPS/360 and MPSX or CDC's Optima, one can in this way obtain values of J_c corresponding to each value of θ within the interval $[0, \infty)$. For a given linear system and a given set of data, the result is a unique relationship such as that shown in Figures 3 and 5. The resulting bicriterion curve is piecewise linear, consisting of straight line segments intersecting at points where changing the value of θ requires changing the components of the basis vector. Eventually, a point is reached where θ can be increased indefinitely while the same basis and the minimum value of J_c are maintained. At this point, execution of the parametric programming routine is automatically halted and the bicriterion function is complete. Each point on the bicriterion curve represents a different set of u_m values, so that one has an infinite number of alternative solutions, each of which is characterized by different values of the ordered pair of numbers $\{J_c, J_p\}$.

Since there is always uncertainty regarding the proper choice of optimality criteria and the adequacy of data, the bicriterion function does not represent all the possible solutions to the deconvolution problem. Instead, the best possible solution (i.e., the one optimizing the predictive capabilities of the linear model) lies somewhere in the neighborhood of this function within a range of uncertainty the limits of which are generally unknown. To consider all the possibilities within this range, more must be known about the statistical nature of the various errors that enter into the deconvolution problem. In the absence of such knowledge, the bicriterion method can be viewed as a means for approaching the issue of uncertainty with the aid of deterministic mathematical programming techniques.

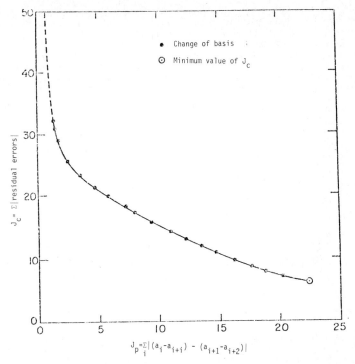

Figure 3. Bicriterion function without modality constraints.

        Figure 3 shows a bicriterion function as obtained by parametric program-
ming with the aid of MPSX for the sample problem described earlier. The result
is based on equations 3-12 with all the values of u_m^i in (7) set equal to zero.
It is seen that the curve consists of two distinct segments, one steep and the
other relatively flat. Since the maximum value of J_c (at $J_p = 0$) is very large,
the plausibility criterion can be reduced from $J_p \approx 22.4$ down to about $J_p \approx 2.0$
without significantly affecting the relative magnitude of the fit criterion, J_c.
In other words, the response function can be smoothed considerably without any
significant effect on its ability to reproduce the observed output. The shape
of the bicriterion function provides us with an indication as to how much we are
allowed to smooth the response function without at the same time introducing
significant errors into the final solution. We feel that this is much preferred
over artificial filtering of the response function which disregards the goodness
of fit question.

        The bicriterion function does not indicate which particular solution out
of all the possible alternatives actually optimizes the predictive capabilities
of the linear model. It nevertheless indicates to us a narrow range of dominant
solutions which appear to possess better qualities than solutions lying outside
this range. The width of this range reflects our uncertainty regarding the
effects of fit (as expressed by J_c) and shape (as expressed by J_p) on the quality
of the impulse response function. Inside this range, the final choice depends
on personal judgement and is therefore rather arbitrary.

        In our example, the solution corresponding to the minimum value of J_c
(≈ 6.1) and maximum value of J_p (≈ 22.4) is represented by the highly oscillatory

broken curve in Figure 2. The solution at J_p = 2.0 and $J_c \simeq$ 27.4 is shown by the broken curve in Figure 4. Although this latter solution is much smoother than the one in Figure 2, it is still oscillatory. This does not usually happen with real data and, in our case, seems to be caused by the oscillatory systematic noise that we have superimposed on the output data in Figure 1. We will now show that this solution can be further modified (or perhaps improved) by introducing additional prior assumptions about the desired shape of the response function.

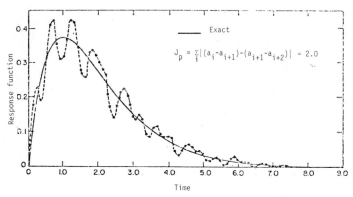

Figure 4. Solution without modality constraints.

ADDITIONAL MODALITY CONSTRAINTS

The response function in Figure 4 can be smoothed simply by modifying the signs in (8). In smoothing this function we are in effect hypothesizing that the oscillations are not necessarily a characteristic of the system, but that they may be an artifact of the errors. To test this hypothesis, we recognize from the overall shape of the curve in Figure 4 that the true response function may have a single peak in the neighborhood of u_{10} (other hypotheses based on prior familiarity of the system may also be tested). We can make u into a unimodal function with the peak located at u_{10} merely by modifying (8) according to

$$\left. \begin{array}{l} u_{m-1} - u_m + a_m = 0; \ m \le 10 \\ u_{m-1} - u_m - a_m = 0; \ m > 10 \end{array} \right\} \ a_m \ge 0 \qquad (13)$$

When the parametric programming procedure is repeated using these new modality constraints, the result is the bicriterion function in Figure 5. It is immediately evident that J_c is now much greater than in Figure 3; the minimum value is 73 instead of 6.1. If we would rely solely on the minimization of J_c without using a plausibility criterion, we would obtain the solution shown in Figure 6 (corresponding to $J_p \simeq 2.4$ and $J_c \simeq 73$). However, this result can be considerably improved by choosing a solution at a lower value of J_p. For example, Figure 7 shows what happens when we choose a solution at J_p = 0.1 and J_c 95. The result is obviously excellent in spite of the slight residual ondulation of the descending limb. These slight oscillations are in phase with those which we have previously imposed on the output (compare Figures 1 and 7) and they have exactly the same frequency. This strongly suggests that our hypothesis was correct and what we see in Figure 7 is indeed only due to the systematic noise in the output record, whereas the effect of random noise has been completely eliminated by our method.

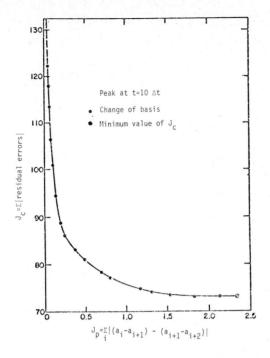

Figure 5. Bicriterion function when peak is imposed at u_{10}.

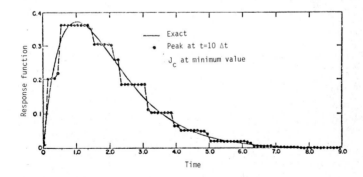

Figure 6. Solution when peak is imposed at u_{10} and J_c is minimum.

An interesting question is what would happen if, in examining Figure 4, we would decide by mistake that the peak is located not at u_{10} but, for example, at u_7. We examined this question and found that in the particular example

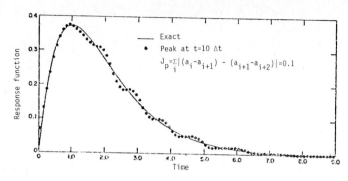

Figure 7.   Solution when peak is imposed at u_{10} and J_p = 0.1.

considered here, the solution is not very sensitive to minor errors in the positioning of the peak. Note that it is possible to impose not only one peak, but several peaks and valleys, provided that their position can be determined from the overall shape of a solution initially obtained without modality constraints.

COMPARISON WITH THE METHOD OF EMSELLEM, DE MARSILY, AND POITRINAL

Our multi-criterion approach to the deconvolution problem has many conceptual similarities with the method of Emsellem and de Marsily (1969) and Poitrinal and de Marsily (1973) described briefly in the introduction. A plausibility criterion measuring the smoothness of the response function is implicitly included in their procedure but the method does not generate a complete range of alternative solutions. It is therefore interesting to compare the performance of both.

When the data in Figure 1 are treated by the computer program DUAMEL of Poitrinal and de Marsily (1973), the resulting shape of the response function is almost identical to our result in Figure 4, indicating that the original version of their method was unable to eliminate low frequency oscillations caused by systematic noise.

Our next step was to modify their computer program in a manner that would enable us to control the modality (i.e., relative positions of peaks and valleys along the time axis) of the response function. The solution is shown in Figure 8 and from a comparison with the result of our parametric programming approach (Figure 7) it is evident that in principle, both methods are capable of producing nearly identical results.

When computer times are compared, the parametric programming approach has a disadvantage in that it utilizes commercially available linear programming routines such as MPSX which, at the present time, are relatively slow. The least square procedure performed by DUAMEL is therefore relatively fast, especially when large sets of data are to be processed. It is hoped that this will be remedied in the future with the development of faster linear programming codes.

On the other hand, parametric programming has at least two advantages: a) It enables one to obtain a continuous relationship between J_c and J_p, thereby providing the analyst with more control over his choice of the "best" response function, and b) it enables one to impose a wider range of constraints on the desired shape of the solution, thereby providing the analyst with more flexibility in dealing with the deconvolution problem. The method can also be extended to non-stationary linear systems of the type considered originally by Poitrinal

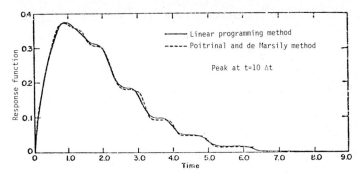

Figure 8. Solution using modified version of program DUAMEL
when peak is imposed at u_{10} compared with equivalent solution using parametric programming.

and de Marsily (1973) and more recently by Diskin and Boneh (1974). We hope to
accomplish this task in the future.

ACKNOWLEDGEMENT

Part of this work was made possible through a scientific exchange program
organized by the Israeli National Council for Research and Development and the
French Ministère des Affaires Etrangères, Direction Générale des Relations
Culturelles Scientifiques et Techniques, in July 1974.

REFERENCES

Blank, D., J. W. Delleur and A. Giorgini (1971). Oscillatory kernel functions in
linear hydrologic models. Water Resour. Res., 7(5), p. 1102.

Bouillin, O., J. Flandrin, J. Forkasiewicz, H. Paloc and D. Poitrinal (1973).
Contribution à la connaissance hydrodynamique d'un réservoir calcaire
d'après l'exemple fourni par la Fontaine de Vaucluse. 2° Convegno
Internazionale sulle Acque Sotterrane, Palermo.

Cole, J. A., H. Hirsch and B. M. Thorn (1972). Finding natural recharge patterns
and abstraction phases to maximize yield of aquifers. Proceedings,
International Symposium on Mathematical Modelling Techniques in Water
Resources Systems, Ottawa, Canada, V. 2, p. 241.

Delleur, J. W. and R. A. Rao (1971). Linear systems analysis in hydrology - The
transform approach, the kernel oscillations and the effect of noise, in
Systems Approach to Hydrology, pp. 116-139, Water Resources Publications,
Fort Collins, Colorado.

Diskin, M. H. and A. Boneh (1974). The kernel function of linear non-stationary
surface runoff systems, Water Resour. Res., 10(4), p. 753.

Emsellem, Y. and G. de Marsily (1969). Le problème inverse et la déconvolution,
La Houille Blanche, No. 8, p. 861.

Emsellem, Y., G. de Marsily, D. Poitrinal and M. Ratsimiebo (1971). Déconvolution et identification automatique de paramètres en hydrologie,
International Symposium on Mathematical Models in Hydrology, IASH, Warsaw.

Emsellem, Y. and G. de Marsily (1971). An automatic solution for the inverse
problem, Water Resour. Res., 7(5), p. 1264.

Graupe, D. (1972). Identification of Systems, Van Nostrand Reinhold Co., New
      York.

Hadley, G. (1962). Linear Programming, Addison-Wesley, Reading, Mass.

Natale, L. and E. Todini (1974). A stable physically constrained parameter esti-
      mation technique for linear models using quadratic programming. Hydraulic
      Institute of the University of Pavia, Italy.

Poitrinal, D. and G. de Marsily (1973). Relation du type entrée-sortie en
      hydrogéologie: procédé d'identification de l'opérateur, Bull. B.R.G.M.,
      2ème série, section 3, No. 2, p. 119.

Todini, E. (1975). The Arno river model: Problems, methodologies and techniques,
      in Computer Simulation of Water Resources Systems, G. C. Vansteenkiste,
      ed., North-Holland Publishing Co., Amsterdam, and American Elsevier
      Publishing Co., New York, p. 199.

DISCUSSION

*Do you try to balance the number of parameters you are using to characte-
rize your system ?
The more number of parameters you use, the more the model is specific to the experimental system.
It seems to me that intuitively, in this bicriterion function, you make a playoff
between the number of parameters you put into the model, so that in some sense it
has a more general application to other experimental systems other than the one
of which you derived the model. And that stimulates your reason of fit in a specific case. So is it a kind of balance between the specific and the general ? (BECK)*

Perhaps before talking about parametric programming I should go back to
the method used by Emsellem, de Marsily and Poitrinal. They first represent the
system by a single parameter, then increase the number to 2, 4, 8, etc. The idea
is to increase the number of parameters successively until, by observing the shape
of the bicriterion function. You decide that this is the maximum number of parameters to be considered given your input-output record. What the linear programming does is essentially the same in a different way. It is true that you start
with a fixed number of parameters based on a prior assumption about the memory
of your system.
When you set the J_p-criterion to zero, the effect is to impose just a single parameter on your system. The next step is to continuously increase the range within
which the parameters are allowed to vary, until the results will start oscillating,
and then stop. Thus, instead of controlling the frequency of our resolution, we
control its amplitude. (NEUMAN)

*If you derive a model with a given set of data and with many parameters in
it, it is more than likely that, because of the large number of parameters, the
model will tend to be very specific, just to the set of data for which you derived
your model. I agree with you in a sense that the understanding of the physical behaviour of the system is incredibily important in deriving the model and there are
some questions we can't get around mathematically in abstraction of the physical
process. (BECK)*

I would like to be able to quantify some of this qualitative information which I'm putting into the model, and I'm raising the question : Does anybody have a particular suggestion ? One way for example to impose smoothness is to use spline functions. In this particular case, we did not want to do this because our problem would become nonlinear. However, perhaps there would be another way of somehow quantifying our prior information. This untreated information I'm trying to feed into my identification process makes me unhappy.
It seems to be the best we can do today but perhaps there are some techniques I'm not aware of. (NEUMAN)

You could try to reduce the number of parameters. But in this peculiar case you have to ask all the ordinates of output response function. If you simulate that response function, with an autoregressive moving average process, I mean the input-output autoregressive on the output and moving average on them, you may have the same number of the input response function on the raising part, but for the tail, you may have a very small number of parameters, say 2 or 3. In which case you eliminate a very big amount of parameters you have to estimate. (TODINI)

Suppose that I adopt such a model, and I use a smaller number of parameters. How do I go about the second step of actually looking at the effect of the oscilation versus the fit function ? That is very important. I don't just want to smooth I want to get an idea of how the smoothing affects the fit. (NEUMAN)

You may have a dead point if you statistically test your residuals, to see how your model was built.
This is the only thing I can find about it. (TODINI)

Perhaps this is something to look at. (NEUMAN)

You have to put in the shape of your curve. You guess the peak in your program now ? (LOMEN)

You don't have to. This was the 2nd step. We did it in 2 stages. Stage one : I don't assume anything about the position of my peak. I only smooth. The effect of that is to eliminate high frequencies. In natural systems, very often you only have these frequencies. You may not have any low frequencies, in which case that would be enough. If you do have systematic errors like I showed before, their effect cannot be eliminated simply by eliminating the Nyquist frequencies. The next step then would be to hypothesize that these oscilations are not an inherent part of the system, but an artifact of your noise. How do we test this ? Let us impose a peak at a point indicated by the early results and see whether or not that changes drastically the fit, J_c. If it does not, you may say : yes, I'm going to accept this hypothesis. Eventually, when your data base increases, you go back and improve the result. The position of the peak is an additional constraint on our system, which may or may not be necessary. (NEUMAN)

Here you have a problem which is more complicated than the estimating of parameters. In fact you have to estimate the structure of your model and then you have to estimate parameters. Saying that your peak is in a determined position, that means that you have estimated or given a certain assumption of the structure of your model. (TODINI)

Not really, because by going through the first stage of smoothing, the overall shape of the result suggests a position for the peak. The data themselves suggest it. (NEUMAN)

It is not the structure of your model you usually identify from your data. You try to identify first the structure, and then you identify the parameters relevant to that structure. The structure is the thing that will remain on another set of data, while the parameters will change. (TODINI)

That's really what we are doing. We are estimating the structure (position of the peak) from the partial result we obtain from the 1st step. The other part of our information comes from a knowledge of the system, if it exists, or you may rely only on the data themselves. You can use both or just one of them. (NEUMAN)

There is a problem of control theory. If you consider your J_c and the ordinate J_p as equally weighted, as far as cost is concerned, what I'd want to do is minimize the distance to the origin. If both of these are equally important, the place of best fit along the curve is the one which has minimum distance to the origin. (LOMEN)

This is a good point, also discussed in my paper last year. The two error criteria do not have a common base, they are measured in different units, they tell us something completely different about the nature of the system. I have thought at the beginning to weight them somehow, but could not find a proper way to do this. This is an interaction game ; the only thing the computer does is develop the bicriterion function for you. Then you intervene and say : the computer has done his best, and you have to use your intuition to determine what to do next. I would like to have an algorithm instead, and what you are suggesting might be one way to go about it. How do we assign weights to J_c and J_p ? I don't know. (NEUMAN)

If you want to make a choice of the point on this curve which you will choose as the best solution mathematically, then you use all the interest of mathematics, that you have come to a point where the hydrologist makes the decision. And he wants to make it himself rather than others. (DE MARSILY)

In decision theory, there are ways to develop utility functions, which help to quantify your decision process. I wonder if anybody in the audience would suggest any kind of utility function ? (NEUMAN)

This is something very subjective. (BECK)

The question is : is there a higher degree of quantification I could achieve than what I described here ? Did I use all the information that I could ? Did I quantify all the information I could, or did I leave some of it unquantified ? I think there is something left behind which should be quantified. That's the question.

There are other fields in hydrology where your method could be used and where the signals are quite different. For instance in biomechanics we have highly periodical signals. Do you think that your method could be used in such cases ? I don't think that your smoothness criteria would fit this time ! (FRIED)

I don't think it is a matter of the input. It is a matter of what is the true nature of the transfer function. If you got an oscilating transfer function, for example in earthquake engineering, they are not smooth and there is no damping. There is no way to use this approach, because the assumption is that you know something about the shape of the function. Whereas in earthquakes there is nothing you know about the shape of your function. It may be wiggling. This wiggling function I showed might be the true physical transfer function. (NEUMAN)

We have highly periodical functions and the transfer function may be perio-dical too. (FRIED)

You certainly could not use it. This is restricted to highly damped systems.
(NEUMAN)

You have a highly damped system, and you use this as a criterion. Couldn't one use periodicity as a criterion in a study where periodicity exists ? (LOMEN)

You would have to use different physical criteria. In our case J_p is the sum of the 3rd derivatives. If you know something else about the desired shape of the transfer function, I don't see why you should not be able to use it. (NEUMAN)

This is what we are looking for. Our transfer functions are sometimes not highly periodical, sometimes not periodical, but wiggling.
FFT-methods make it seem to be rather evident, I must say. (FRIED)

FFT is good, but it does not solve this particular problem.
FFT does not treat the errors. It takes the I/O record as it is and transforms it, but the error remains and affects your results. (NEUMAN)

Your aim is to get back to distributed parameter systems. Are you going to limitate to single point source inputs ? (SIMUNDICH)

Not necessarily. (NEUMAN)

Do you have any problems when you go to a distributed input ? (SIMUNDICH)

Some particular problems I'm actually looking at are aquifer models des-cribed by partial differential equations that are solved by finite difference or finite element techniques.
One of the greatest difficulties there is identifying the input functions. These are often not known. They may vary with time.
If we can find models that describe for example flow in the unsaturated zone from the soil surface down to the water table using a small number of parameters, then perhaps we will be more successful. If on the other hand we treat input as unknown parameters, then every time step will introduce new parameters, and I don't see how to solve this problem. (NEUMAN)

I'm thinking about the computation of our first model. We had the following problem : you have more than 1 input. It is very difficult to use superposition. You cannot let this away putting it to zero and look at the other, trying to iden-tify the function at the other input. (SIMUNDICH)

These inputs are distributed in space and time. Suppose they were only distributed in space, like in a steady-state problem. In this case we have a fixed number of parameters to identify. There is a fixed number of inputs you have to identify in the steady-state problem, and there is a fixed number of parameters such as transmissivity. Let's say you have 20 of those. Maybe you look at a single record, a single set of measurements by piezometers, giving a piezometric map from which you try to pick out the parameters.
Maybe your sample is too small to get anything meaningful. Sometimes even 6 samples will not improve the results because they are interrelated. The shape of your piezometric surface is very similar to the shape of the surface 3 or 2 months later, and you are not looking at statistically independant data.
However, if you are able to manipulate your system by changing for example the

directions of flow, you may get different maps, corresponding to different boundary conditions. You are then really increasing the size of your effective record. And perhaps this would be 1 way to look at this kind of systems. In transient (non steady-state) conditions, the input varies in time. You should try to express the input function in terms of as few parameters as possible.   (NEUMAN)

The essence of my question is : going from the lumped into the distributed system, you get an infinite dimensional state-space, and your data are not increasing as much as the complexity of the problem is. When you use finite difference, you reduce the dimensions to let us say 1 000 or 10 000.   (SIMUNDICH)

It depends on the kind of system you are dealing with. In a former study, I had to determine 1 parameter from 12 measurements on a cross section of the water table. I was not succesful in that particular case. It turned out that the system was still highly underdetermined. There was no way to determine the parameter. (NEUMAN)

*System Simulation in Water Resources, ed. G.C. VANSTEENKISTE
1976, North-Holland Publishing Company*

A RAINFALL RUNOFF KALMAN FILTER MODEL

E. Todini
IBM Scientific Centre, Pisa

and

D. Bouillot
Etudiant E. N. S. I. M. A. G. Grenoble

ABSTRACT

In most recent years on-line rainfall-runoff models, which may
provide real time forecasts of discharges in a river, have become
of great interest.

Kalman filtering techniques with their recursive algorithms seem
to be particularly suited to this purpose, both for the possibility
of reestimating the parameters of the model, and for the limited
computer dimensions required.

In this paper an on-line rainfall-runoff model of the river Sieve
(a tributary of the Arno river in Italy) is presented which is based
on Kalman filters and which uses the Instrumental Variables -
Approximate Maximum Likelihood (IV-AML) approach to perform
a recursive estimate both of the parameters of the model and of
the parameters relevant to a possible structure of the residuals.

INTRODUCTION

The Sieve river, with its 840 km^2 of catchment area, is one of the most
important tributaries of the Arno river.

During flood events its contribution becomes of great interest, since it
joins the main channel some 20 km upstream of the city of Florence.

Therefore an on-line model of the Sieve river could highly improve the
efficiency of a flood warning system.

In this paper an on-line model of the Sieve river which has been set up
using an algorithm based on Kalman filters is presented. Kalman filters
theory is beyond the scope of the present paper; the interested reader may
consult [2], [3], [4], [8], [11] for a deeper discussion.

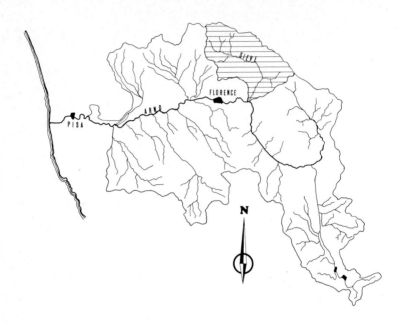

Fig. 1 - The Arno river catchment area

PRELIMINARY ANALYSIS OF DATA

     The input-output data of a three month flood period available on continuous records were sampled at discrete time intervals Δt of two hours.

     The discharge data q_t were obtained from the water levels measured at the gauging station of Fornacina by using the rating curve relevant to the same station.

     Moreover the lumped input rainfall data p_t were obtained as a weighted average of eight recording rain-gauges (fig. 2), by means of Thiessen polygons.

     A preliminary analysis of the input-output data was performed in order to check for stationarity by plotting and analizing both the autocorrelation function and the partial autocorrelation function of the raw data p_t and q_t, of their first differences ∇p_t and ∇q_t, and of their second differences $\nabla^2 p_t$ and $\nabla^2 q_t$ [1].

     Since both the time series did not show marked nonstationarities it was decided to use the raw data p_t and q_t without differentiation to set up the input-output model.

Fig. 2 - The Sieve river catchment area

MODEL IDENTIFICATION

Although examples of Kalman filter models which use a moving average representation of the impulse response of the system, namely the Instant Unit Hydrograph (IUH), can be found in the literature [5] , a more appropriate representation can be adopted in order to reduce to a minimum value the model order and hence the number of significant parameters to be estimated.

Thus parsimony being one of the main objectives of this modeling effort, an autoregressive moving average (ARMA) representation of the impulse response of the system was adopted [1] , the autoregressive term taking into account all the decaying portion of the IUH

$$(1+\delta_1 B+\delta_2 B^2+\cdots+\delta_i B^i+\cdots+\delta_r B^r)q_t=(\omega_0+\omega_1 B^1+\omega_2 B^2+\cdots+\omega_j B^j+\cdots+\omega_s B^s)p_{t-b}+\varepsilon_t \quad (1)$$

where B is the backward shift operator (namely $q_{t-\tau} = B^\tau q_t$, $\forall \tau \geqslant 0$); r is the order of the autoregressive term, s is the order of the moving average term, b is the time lag between the first significant response of the system to a given impulse, and the impulse itself; ε_t is a zero mean normally distributed random disturbance to the system, while δ_i , i = 1,..., r and ω_j , j = 0,..., s represent the model parameters to be estimated.

The problem of model identification consists in the determination of the most appropriate r, s and b values.

This can be done by analizing a rough approximation of the impulse response of the system : thus Box and Jenkins (1970) suggest to avoid a direct matrix inversion by prewhitening the input function and by applying the same transformation to the output function.

In fact it can be easily shown that if the input function is a white noise then

$$\hat{u}_k = \frac{\sigma_\beta}{\sigma_\alpha} \, \rho_{\alpha\beta}(k)$$

(2)

represents the impulse response function at lag k where $\rho_{\alpha\beta}(k)$ is the crosscorrelation function at lag k between the input α_t and the output β_t while σ_α and σ_β are the standard deviations of α_t and β_t .

Hence $\hat{\alpha}_t$ being the prewhitened input function and $\hat{\beta}_t$ the modified output function, the crosscorrelation function between $\hat{\alpha}_t$ and $\hat{\beta}_t$ was estimated together with a first approximation of the impulse response and of the step response of the system.

Using the estimated crosscorrelation function, shown in fig. 3 together with the two standard deviations limits estimated by means of a formula by Bartlett, and comparing the shapes of the impulse response and of the step response (fig. 4, 5) with the ones shown in [1] , an appropriate structure can be found for the Sieve model.

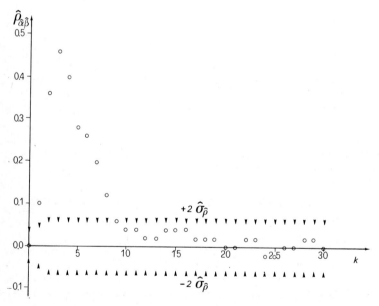

Fig. 3 - Crosscorrelation function $\hat{\rho}_{\hat{\alpha}\hat{\beta}}$ between prewhitened input
and consequently modified output $\pm 2\,\hat{\sigma}_{\hat{\rho}}$ limits

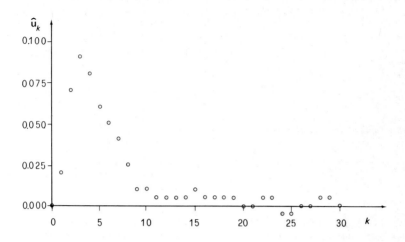

Fig. 4 - Impulse response function $\hat{u}_k$

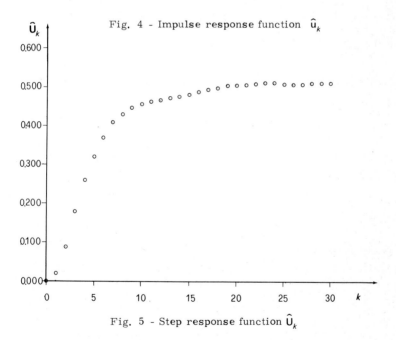

Fig. 5 - Step response function $\hat{U}_k$

As a result of this analysis the proposed input-output model for the Sieve has r=1, s=2, b=1

$$(1 + \delta B)\, q_t = (\, \omega_0 + \omega_1 B + \omega_2 B^2)\, p_{t-1} + \varepsilon_t \qquad (3)$$

Moreover a first guess estimate of the four parameters can be derived from the rough estimate of the impulse response, since

$$\hat{u}_0 = 0, \quad \hat{u}_1 = \hat{\omega}_0, \quad \hat{u}_2 = \hat{\omega}_1 + \hat{\delta} u_1, \quad \hat{u}_3 = \hat{\omega}_2 + \hat{\delta}\,\hat{u}_2, \quad \hat{u}_4 = \hat{\delta}\,\hat{u}_3,$$

thus $\hat{\delta} = -0.87, \quad \hat{\omega}_0 = 0.01909, \quad \hat{\omega}_1 = 0.05423, \quad \hat{\omega}_2 = 0.02902$

PARAMETER ESTIMATION

Once the structure of the model was identified, a state-space notation was adopted to allow for a recursive estimation algorithm.

System model

$$\mathbf{x}_t = \boldsymbol{\Phi}_{t-1}\mathbf{x}_{t-1} + \boldsymbol{\Lambda}_{t-1}\mathbf{p}_{t-b} + \mathbf{w}_{t-1} \tag{4 a}$$

Measurement model

$$\mathbf{q}_t = \mathbf{H}_t\,\mathbf{x}_t + \mathbf{v}_t \tag{4 b}$$

where

$\mathbf{x}_t = |x_t \quad x_{t-1} \quad \cdots\cdots \quad x_{t-(r-1)}|^T$ 　(r)　　state vector

$\mathbf{q}_t = |q_t \quad q_{t-1} \quad \cdots\cdots \quad q_{t-(r-1)}|^T$ 　(r)　　measured output vector

$\mathbf{p}_{t-b} = |p_{t-b} \quad p_{t-b-1} \quad \cdots\cdots \quad p_{t-b-s}|^T$ 　(s+1)　measured input vector

$\mathbf{w}_t = |w_t \quad 0 \quad \cdots\cdots\cdots \quad 0|^T$ 　(r)　　model perturbation vector
　　　　　　　　　　　　　　　　　　　　$\mathbf{w}_t \sim \mathbf{N}(0, \mathbf{Q}_t)$

$\mathbf{v}_t = |v_t \quad v_{t-1} \quad \cdots\cdots \quad v_{t-(r-1)}|^T$ 　(r)　　output measurement noise vector
　　　　　　　　　　　　　　　　　　　　$\mathbf{v}_t \sim \mathbf{N}(0, \mathbf{R}_t)$

$$\boldsymbol{\Phi}_{t-1} = \begin{vmatrix} -\delta_1 & -\delta_2 & \cdots\cdots & -\delta_r \\ 1 & 0 & \cdots\cdots & 0 \\ 0 & 1 & \cdots\cdots & 0 \\ \multicolumn{4}{c}{\cdots\cdots\cdots\cdots\cdots\cdots} \\ 0 & 0 & \cdots\cdots & 1 \end{vmatrix}$$
　(r, r)　　state transition matrix

$$\boldsymbol{\Lambda}_{t-1} = \begin{vmatrix} \omega_0 & \omega_1 & \cdots\cdots & \omega_s \\ 0 & 0 & \cdots\cdots & 0 \\ 0 & 0 & \cdots\cdots & 0 \\ \multicolumn{4}{c}{\cdots\cdots\cdots\cdots\cdots\cdots} \\ 0 & 0 & \cdots\cdots & 0 \end{vmatrix}$$
　(r, s+1)　input weighting matrix

$$\mathbf{H}_t = \mathbf{I}$$
　(r, r)　　measurement scaling matrix
　　　　　　$\mathbf{I}$ = identity matrix

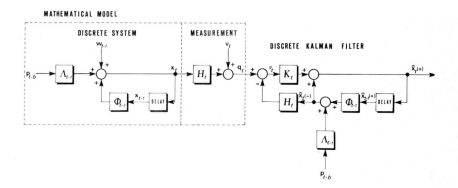

Fig. 6 - System model and Discrete Kalman filter

In fig. 6 a sketch of the mathematical model and of the Kalman filter used is presented where K_t is the (r, r) Kalman gain matrix, v_t is the residual of the filter (namely $v_t = q_t - H_t \hat{x}_t(-)$), $\hat{x}_t(-)$ is the estimate of the state vector at time t prior to the measurement q_t and $\hat{x}_t(+)$ is the estimate after the measurement q_t .

Rao and Delleur (1971) showed that in this hydrological problem the output is relatively noise free compared to the noise inbedded in the input data. It is therefore convenient to assume the measurement model (4 b) to be noise free and to concentrate all the noise effect in the model perturbation w_t .

The validity of this assumption was also proved by preliminary runs of the model where an estimate of the variance matrix R_t was computed recursively from an estimate of v_t (that is $\hat{v}_t = q_t - H_t \hat{x}_t(+)$), in that $\hat{R}_t$. tended rapidly to zero, while K_t tended to I , the identity matrix.

Thus in the final Sieve model the variance matrix R_t was assumed to be a zero matrix (which implies $K_t = I$), while the variance matrix Q_t was assumed to equal the $(r, r) \hat{Q}_{t-1}$ matrix computed recursively from an estimate of w_{t-1}, that is $\hat{w}_{t-1} = K_t [q_t - H_t \hat{x}_t(-)]$.

The program used in the modeling effort has been implemented in APL. a conversational programming language which is particularly suited for matrix operations.

At the moment it has been written for the single input case, but it can be easily modified to allow for multiple inputs by modifying the definitions of vector $\mathbf{p}_{t-b}$ and of matrix Λ_{t-1} as follows :

$$\mathbf{p}_{t-b} = |\, p^{T(1)}_{t-b} \vdots p^{T(2)}_{t-b} \vdots \cdots \vdots p^{T(i)}_{t-b} \vdots \cdots \vdots p^{T(n)}_{t-b}|^T$$

(n(s+1)) measured inputs partitioned vector

$$\Lambda_{t-1} = |\, \Lambda^{(1)}_{t-1} \vdots \Lambda^{(2)}_{t-1} \cdots \vdots \Lambda^{(i)}_{t-1} \cdots \vdots \Lambda^{(n)}_{t-1}|$$

(r, n(s+1)) inputs weighting partitioned matrix

$i = 1, \ldots$, n with n the number of controlled inputs and where $p_{t-b}^{(i)}$ and $\Lambda^{(i)}_{t-1}$ represent the input vector and the weighting matrix relevant to the ith input.

This modification becomes important when a non-linear model of the CLS (Constrained Linear Systems) type has to be implemented by using multiple inputs and a threshold to simulate the non linear behaviour of the system [9].

A recursive algorithm, based on the Instrumental Variables approach, which has been proved to be very efficient in the presence of a high level of noise [6], is used to provide an estimate of the r+s parameters of the model, namely the first row of matrix Φ_{t-1} and the first row of matrix Λ_{t-1}. The interested reader may find a clear description of this algorithm in [10] [11] [12].

In addition and Approximate Maximum Likelihood algorithm which is also described in [11] and [12] allows for the estimation of the parameters relevant to the model of the residuals ν_t .

RESULTS

To calibrate the model of the Sieve river only four parameters needed to be estimated. This was done by iterating on the available data set several times until the value of the parameters became stable.

In fig. 7, 8, 9, 10 the values of the four parameters are plotted versus t during the first run through the data.

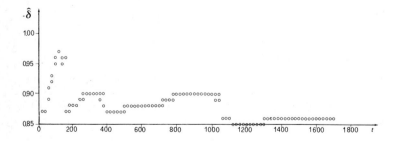

Fig. 7 - Parameter - $\hat{\delta}$ versus t

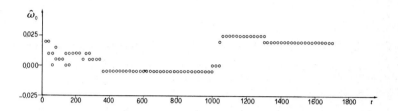

Fig. 8 - Parameter $\hat{\omega}_0$ versus t

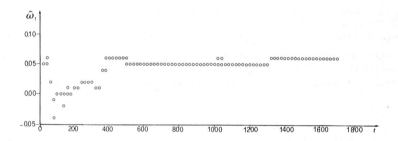

Fig. 9 - Parameter $\hat{\omega}_1$ versus t

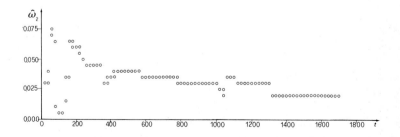

Fig. 10 - Parameter $\hat{\omega}_2$ versus t

The final values of the parameters where found to be very close to the initial guess values

$$\hat{\delta} = -0.86455$$
$$\hat{\omega}_0 = 0.0194$$
$$\hat{\omega}_1 = 0.0552$$
$$\hat{\omega}_2 = 0.0204$$

In fig. 11 the plot of the $1\,\Delta t$ in advance prediction $\hat{x}_t(-)$ is shown versus 1962 values of the measured discharge q_t , while in fig. 12 a shorter period about the peak is shown more in detail.

CONCLUSIONS

The ability of the model of predicting $1\,\Delta t$ in advance is better shown by the value of the standard deviation of the residuals $\hat{\sigma}_v = 10.31 \, m^3/sec$, which is about $1/3$ of the standard deviation of the residuals obtained without updating the prediction $\hat{x}_t$ by means of the measurement q_t . This can be regarded as a very good performance though it should be noted that if this model is no more feeded by new measurements of the output discharges it will resort to the usual linear IUH type models with a noticeable increase in the variance of prediction.

Apart from the performance of the model the authors would like to stress its ability of estimating at each time step not only the state vector, but also the parameters relevant to its own structure. This is a very useful way of taking into account some time dependent modifications in the input-output behaviour while a CLS type structure should be given to the model to account for the non-linear behaviour of the rainfall-runoff process.

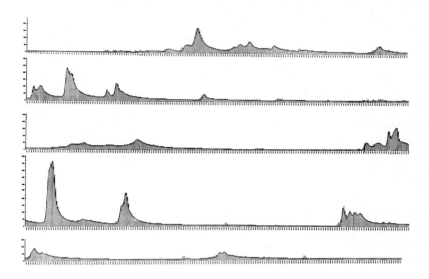

Fig. 11 - One Δt in advance prediction versus measured discharges
Flood event started on November 23, 1959

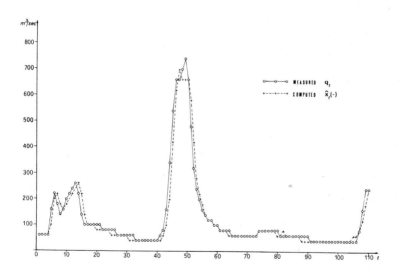

Fig. 12 - One Δt in advance prediction versus measured discharges
about the peak   measured discharge

REFERENCES

[1]   Box, G.E.P. and Jenkins, G.M. (1970). Time Series Analysis
        Forecasting and Control, Holden Day, S. Francisco.

[2]   Gelb, A. and al. (1974). Applied Optimal Estimation, The MIT Press.

[3]   Kalman, R.E. (1960). A New Approach to Linear Filtering and
        Prediction Problems. Trans. ASME J. Basic Eng., 82-D, 35.

[4]   Kalman, R.E. and Bucy, R.S. (1961). New Results in Linear Filtering
        and Prediction Theory. Trans. ASME J. Basic Eng., 83-D, 95.

[5]   Hino, M. (1973). On-Line Prediction of Hydrologic System. XVth
        Congress of IAHR, Istanbul.

[6]   Iserman, R. (1975). Modeling and Identification of Dynamic Processes;
        an extract, Proc. IFIP Working Conference on Modeling and
        Simulation of Water Resources Systems, North Holland.

[7]   Rao, R.A. and Delleur, J.W. (1971). The Instantaneous Unit
        Hydrograph: its calculation by the transform method and noise
        control by digital filtering. Purdue University Water Resources
        Center, Tech. Rep. 20.

[8]   Sage, A.P. and Melsa, J.L. (1971). Estimation Theory with
        applications to communications and control. Mc Graw Hill Book
        Company.

[9]   Todini, E. and Wallis, J.R. (1974). Using CLS for Continuous Daily or
        Longer Period Rainfall-Runoff Modeling. Workshop on
        Mathematical Models in Hydrology, Pisa.

[10]   Whitehead, P. and Young, P.C. (1975). A dynamic stochastic model
        for water quality in part of the Bedford-Ouse river system.
        Proc. IFIP Working Conference on Modeling and Simulation of
        Water Resources Systems, North Holland.

[11]   Young, P.C. (1974). A recursive approach to time series analysis.
        Bull. Inst. of Math. and its App. (IMA), vol. 10, nos. 5/6,
        pp. 209-224.

[12]   Young, P.C. and Whitehead, P. (1975). A recursive approach to time-
        series analysis for multivariate systems. Proc. IFIP Working
        Conference on Modeling and Simulation of Water Resources
        Systems, North Holland.

DISCUSSION

Is that matrix there a certain error criterion ?   (LOMEN)

Yes, that matrix represents the variance of the error of estimate of the
state variable prior to the measurement, and in this case its trace can be regarded
as the sum of squares of the residuals which has to be minimized to estimate the
parameters.   (TODINI)

Can you use the Kalman filter backwards on your data set ?   (PECK)

Sometimes when you use the Kalman filtering, you can in fact at a time t have estimates of your parameters, and then look back to the data and do a smoothing operation, and try to update all the estimates on the basis of all this past information you have. But the advantage of the Kalman filter is supposed to be the fact that it is a recursive estimation scheme. You don't have to retain all the data in the huge matrix. (BECK)

You just retain in the computer memory a very small amount of numerical quantities that carry sufficient information you need to update your estimates by using a recursive least squares algorithm. (TODINI)

Those recursive formulas are effectively taking your loss function as a square error criterion, and then you put it in a recursive form. In other words, you minimize that loss function. You can, in fact, write it in a recursive formula. What you have today, is what we had yesterday plus some corrections. (BECK)

Instead of using a least squares algorithm on the whole data set, you start minimizing the sum of squares of errors on a few data, say n, then you have a recursive formula that allows you to introduce a new measurement and have the estimate of your parameters that minimizes the sum of squares of errors on n+1 data. (TODINI)

Is the Kalman filtering a short term prediction method of one dt ahead ? So, as the number of dt's becomes larger, in other words as you try to predict further ahead, I guess you run into problems that are getting worse and worse. (PECK)

Yes, you have in fact, but you also have a matrix which expresses the confidence that you have in your prediction. (BECK)

You plotted parameters versus time. I found it very intrigant that for small values of time, at the beginning, you reach a sort of minimum level of time untill it leveled off. What is this level in terms of number of data considered ? (NEUMAN)

More than on the number of data, in this case it depends on how good the starting estimates of the parameters and the starting assumptions on the statistical characteristics of the noise terms were. In this case the estimates of the values of the parameters were not that for from the ones found at the end, conversely the first estimates of the variance matrices used were really wrong. For instance we started the process putting the variance matrix of the residual equal I, the identity matrix, while at the end its trace (the sum of squares of the residuals) is approximately 100. Therefore, bearing also in mind that there was almost no rainfall signal in the first hundredth of data, it took approximately four hundred time steps before getting a stable solution of the parameters. (TODINI)

System Simulation in Water Resources, ed. G.C. VANSTEENKISTE
1976, North-Holland Publishing Company

DYNAMIC MODELS IN THE PLANNING ROLE

P. Whitehead[*]

Control and Systems Division
Dept. of Engineering University of Cambridge
Cambridge, England

Abstract

The paper discusses the application of Monte Carlo simulation techniques to dynamic water quality models developed for a 55 kilometre stretch of the Bedford Ouse in Central Eastern England. The stochastic simulation provides forecasts of water quality at a downstream abstraction point in terms of probability distributions which are compared with water quality standards also defined in probabalistic terms. Effluent from the new city of Milton Keynes enters the river at an upstream point and the impact of the effluent on the aquatic environment is assessed together with the sensitivity of the water quality model to parametric uncertainty.

1.   Introduction

It is now genally admitted that day to day river water quality management must involve some appreciation of the dynamic aspects of river pollution since it is the *transient* violations of water quality standards that cause most problems in the short term. In line with these requirements a study of the Bedford Ouse River System in Central Eastern England was initiated in 1972 by the Great Ouse River Division of the Anglian Water Authority and the Department of the Environment, in association with the Control Division of the Engineering Department, University of Cambridge. The objectives of the study are to assess the short term control of future water re-use problems and the future resource allocation required to meet the increasing domestic and industrial demand in the South East of England.

In particular, the control division is concerned with the day to day aspects of the river behaviour involving the development of dynamic stochastic models of water quality and the application of these models to operational water resource problems. One typical application is the maintenance of DO (Dissolved Oxygen) levels immediately downstream of large effluent discharges using the techniques of feedback control (Whitehead 1975). Whilst the models developed in the Bedford Ouse Study provide a useful tool for the design and analysis of such control systems, the models describe in addition to the dynamic behaviour, the stochastic aspects of the system. This emphasis on the need for stochastic rather than purely deterministic models arises because it is rarely, if ever, possible to explain all the phenomena in river systems by exact (i.e. deterministic) physico-chemical relationships and some random effects and uncertainties are inevitable. The effect of the random component in the models may be measured in terms of statistics, such as the mean and variance of the unexplained error; statistics which provide an estimate of the inherent uncertainty of the system.

In management and planning studies one of the major needs is for adequate forecasting of possible future conditions. Since the information required for forecasting includes quantitative evaluation of the stochastic aspects of the system, it is clear that models such as those discussed in previous reports (Whitehead and Young, 1974) are particularly important to any systematic approach to management and planning decision making. The stochastic model enables the system analyst to make forecasts not only of the mean value but also, for example, of the probability distribution about this mean. In this way the analyst or

---

[*] Paul Whitehead is a Member of Wolfson College.

model user obtains some idea of the basic uncertainty in his forecasts and can make decisions with this uncertainty in mind.   This is in contrast to the usual approach in many planning exercises where there is a tendency to either ignore the inherent uncertainty, or at least consider it as a very secondary aspect of the problem.

In this paper we consider the application of Monte Carlo simulation techniques to the stochastic water quality model of the Bedford Ouse.   The model validity is tested in a sensitivity analysis and then the impact of effluent from the developing new City of Milton Keynes is assessed in a probabalistic manner.

2.   River System Description

The stretch of the Bedford Ouse of interest in the study is between the discharge point of Milton Keynes effluent at Tickford Abbey and the Bedford Waterboard abstraction plant 55kms downstream at Clapham.   The principal features are shown in Figure 1 together with the flow gauging stations at Newport Pagnell and Bedford which define the upstream and downstream boundaries of the system.

3.   The Combined Flow and Quality Model

A detailed description of the Bedford Ouse flow and BOD-DO (Biochemical Oxygen Demand - Dissolved Oxygen) water quality model is presented by Whitehead and Young (1974) but the combined system models are represented schematically in Figure 2.   A deterministic multi-reach flow model is enhanced using stochastic time-series models to describe the rainfall-runoff effects.   Flow information at each reach is transferred to the water quality models which themselves contain both deterministic and stochastic aspects;   the former representing the estimated dynamic behaviour of the physico-chemical phenomena and the latter representing the residual noise and distributed effects on the river reach.   The BOD-DO water quality models are estimated against field data using a multivariable extension of the instrumental variable approximate maximum likelihood (IVAML) technique of time-series analysis (Young and Whitehead 1974) and the BOD-DO models are of the following discrete time form.

$$\text{BOD:} \quad x_{1k} = k_1 \frac{V_m}{Q_{k-1}} x_{1,k-1} + k_2 u_{1,k-1} + k_3 S_{k-1} \tag{1}$$

$$\text{DO:} \quad x_{2k} = k_4 x_{1,k-1} + k_5 \frac{V_m}{Q_{k-1}} x_{2,k-1} + k_6 u_{2,k-1} + k_7 S_{k-1} + k_8 c_{s,k-1} \tag{2}$$

where x_1 is the BOD at the output of the reach, which can be considered as an aggregate or macro measure of the oxygen absorbing potential of substances in the stream (such as decaying organic material from effluent discharges), and is defined as the oxygen absorbed in mg ℓ^{-1} over a five day period by a sample of river water in the absence of light at a constant temperature of 20°C;

x_2 is the DO at the output of the reach (mg ℓ^{-1});

Q is the volumetric flow rate in the stream (m^3 day^{-1});

V_m is the mean volumetric hold-up in the reach (m^3);

u_1 is the input BOD from the previous upstream reach in the river system (mg ℓ^{-1});

u_2 is the input DO from the previous upstream reach (mg ℓ^{-1});

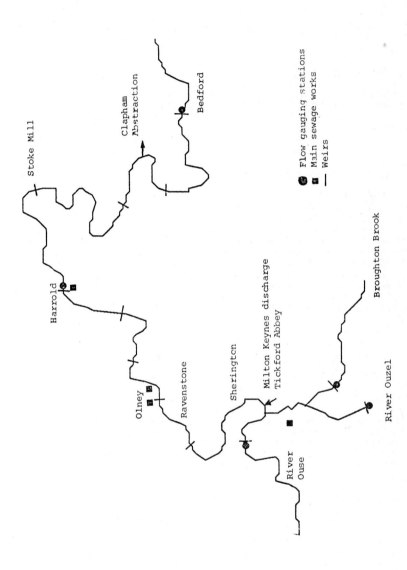

Figure 1   Map of the Bedford Ouse System.

S   is a term dependent upon sunlight hours and chlorophyl A level to
account for photosynthetic effects such as algal growth and decay
(see Whitehead 1975) (mg ℓ^{-1});

C_s is the saturation concentration of DO (mg ℓ^{-1});

and $k_1, k_2, \ldots, k_8$ are coefficients or parameters which will be either constant
or slowly time-variable depending on the period of
observation.

This second order coupled system describe the downstream BOD and DO as a
function of the upstream water quality, previous downstream BOD and DO levels and
other system inputs such as sunlight and the oxygen saturation concentration.
The model has the practical advantage of being able to forecast downstream water
quality based on upstream observations and this aspect is of particular utility in
the Bedford Ouse study where a knowledge of the effects of Milton Keynes effluent
on the water quality at Clapham is required.

It has already been mentioned that the models have been estimated against
field data but that the measurement of non-conservative states such as BOD and DO is
difficult because of the need to "freeze" the decay and chemical processes during
transit from the river to the laboratory.   A wide range of chemical techniques
are available to obviate this problem but measurement errors are still significant.
Additional human errors, problems of chemical purity and accuracy of analytical
procedure all contribute to these errors and a number of experiments conducted by
the Great Ouse River Division of the Anglian Water Authority (1974) indicate noise
levels of the order of 2% on DO and 9% on BOD.   From these results the BOD is
shown to be less accurate than the DO measurement and this has an important
bearing on the modelling of water quality since it reflects the need for a
statical assessment of water quality to account for measurement "noise".   In
addition, minor tributaries and influents along the reach affect the quality and
these noise effects together with the measurement errors may be described by an
additional term ξ in the observation equation

$$y_k = x_k + \xi_k$$

Here, the observation y of a variable x is corrupted by a stochastic noise
term ξ on day k.   The modelling of the stochastic terms is described fully by
Young and Whitehead (1974) and it will suffice here to state that, as shown in
Figure 1, the noise terms are added to the outputs of the physico-chemical models.

The coefficients of the water quality models (1) and (2) have been
estimated using field data collected by the Great Ouse River Division of the
Anglian Water Authority and typical forecasts of the model over summer and winter
data are shown by Whitehead (1975) to be adequately forecast using the discrete
time-series models.*

4.   The Monte Carlo Simulation Technique

In order to obtain water quality forecasts in terms of probability
distributions the Monte Carlo simulation technique Berthouex and Brow,(1969) is
utilised;   an approach which is extremely useful in those situations where
analytical solutions are difficult or even impossible to obtain because of the
non-linear nature of the system.   In the case of the Bedford Ouse system the
problem is too complex for a precise analytical solution and Monte Carlo

----

*A similar differential equation model for BOD and DO developed by Beck (1975) has
been verified using data collected on the River Cam;   the reach of the Cam lies
downstream of Cambridge sewage works and the higher levels of BOD are adequately
forecast using the model.

simulation is therefore required. The system calculations (dynamic simulations in the present context) are performed a large number of times, each time with the values for the stochastic inputs or uncertain parameters selected at random from their assumed (i.e. estimated) parent probability distributions. Each such random experiment or simulation yields a different result for any variable of interest and when all these results are taken together the required probability distributions can be ascertained to any required degree of accuracy from the sample statistics.

The degree of accuracy of the probability distribution function estimated from Monte Carlo simulation is a function of the number of random simulations used to calculate the sample statistics, but it is possible to quantify the degree of uncertainty on the distribution using non-parametric statistical tests such as the Kolmogorov and the Kolmogorov - Rényi statistics (see B. Spear 1968).

Monte-Carlo simulation is a flexible, albeit computationally expensive, tool with which to investigate certain design problems. For example, the water quality standards discussed by Taylor (1975) are presented in terms of distribution functions and, therefore, provide a reference against which the water quality at Clapham can be tested. It would be possible, therefore, to perform Monte-Carlo simulation analysis using the water quality models developed for the study section of the Bedford Ouse and making various assumptions about future levels of effluent input from Milton Keynes sewage works. The outcome of such an analysis would be probability density functions for the water quality states which could be compared directly with the designed water quality standards. Such information would be extremely useful in assessing the impact of influent on the system and determining the degree of treatment necessary at Milton Keynes in order to ensure a satisfactory water quality at the abstraction point.

A second objective of Monte-Carlo simulation studies is for assessing the sensitivity of water quality models to the inherent uncertainty on the estimated parameters. The parameter estimates are obtained together with a covariance matrix which indicates the degree of uncertainty or variance of the estimate from its true (but unknown) value. The variation of each parameter within the probability distribution function defined by these statistics may be of significance in terms of its effect on the model output variables: Monte-Carlo simulation, in effect, provides a systematic method for randomly varying the model parameters in order to observe their effect on the output variations.

5.   Simulation System Description

It has already been mentioned that in order to apply Monte Carlo simulation analysis to a particular problem certain apriori information is required on the stochastic aspects of the system description. Many researchers have described hydrological systems by statistical components and the application of stochastic simulation to rainfall - runoff - reservoir problems and other similar systems as well established   (Jamieson et al - 1974).   Equivalent water quality problems have not been considered in the context of uncertainty and, as such, there are few applications of simulation in this area. Page and Warn (1974), however, have assessed the long term quality problems associated with Empington Reservoir via simulation where different pumping strategies produce different water quality situations and an optimum exists in terms of the total cost of pumping and water treatment.

The water quality model of the Bedford Ouse describes the day to day variations in water quality and accounts for the stochastic aspects in various ways.   The model may, therefore, be used in a stochastic simulation study to provide information on the distributions of water quality at the Clapham abstraction point.   Figure 2 shows the structure and interconnections of the flow and quality models and a full simulation analysis of the system would involve the generation of synthetic rainfall data, upstream flow data, upstream BOD and DO

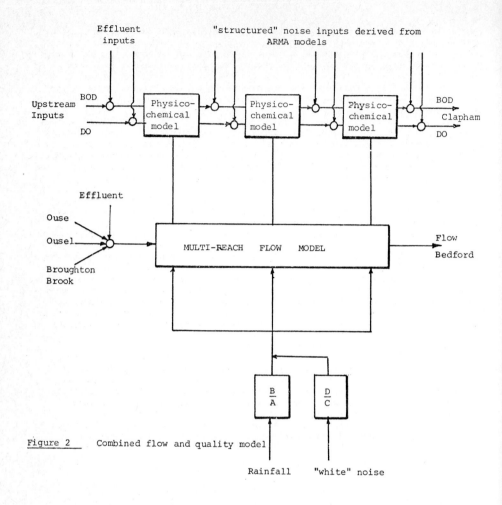

Figure 2   Combined flow and quality model

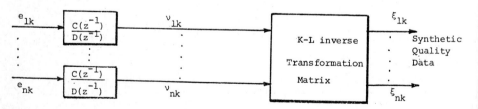

Figure 3   Block diagram of synthetic quality data
            generation.

data, temperature data, sunlight data and chlorophyll A data. In other words all the system inputs. Such a simulation would be extremely complex in terms of data generation and computationally prohibitive. It is therefore desirable to reduce the computational load without destroying the flexibility of the technique.

One method of simplifying this problem is to consider the flow and rainfall data known for a specific year. Flow and rainfall records are readily available and the complete simulation analysis may be repeated using different types of rainfall and flow behaviour. In this manner the effect of "wet", "dry" or "average" years may be considered. In this way, the simulation problem reduces to the generation of quality data at the upstream boundary and the generation of suitable noise components at the reach boundaries. Even this presents some statistical problems since the upstream quality states BOD and DO are correlated with sunlight, chlorophyll A, and temperature in addition to being correlated in time.

One solution to the problem lies in the correlated noise identification problems discussed by Young and Whitehead (1974). The Karhunen-Loeve transformation is used to decorrelate approximately the input variables and the resultant "instantaneously" uncorrelated noise series are modelled using the time series techniques of approximate maximum likelihood. Table 1 contains the ARMA* models evaluated for the input data (BOD, DO, temperature, sunlight hours and chlorophyll A), and the K-L transformation matrix. In a typical simulation run the models are activated according to Figures 2 and 3. Initially the flow model produces streamflow data at each quality reach based on actual rainfall and flow data for a specific year. Synthetic quality data and other input variables are generated as shown from white noise. The process involves generating the serially correlated noise data via the ARMA* models and then cross-correlating by use of the inverse of the K-L transformation matrix.

At the reach boundaries additional "coloured" noise signals are generated and these reflect the stochastic disturbances down the river system. Also the growth of algae along the river and the additional photosynthetic effects at the lower reaches of the river due to the enlarged algal population are included in the simulation. The input-output relationship between the upstream and downstream chlorophyll A measurements indicate a first order discrete time model, and from an instrumental variable estimation procedure the following model was obtained.

$$Cd_k = 0.29\ Cd_{k-1} + 0.97\ Cu_k + e_k$$

where Cd_k is the downstream chlorophyll A mg/m^3 (mean 35.5) Cu_k is the upstream chlorophyll A (mean 15.1) and e_k is a serially uncorrelated zero mean series at time k.

The downstream boundary of the third quality reach represents the Clapham abstration point and the distribution of water quality at this location is of particular interest. The simulation of the model for the given stochastic variables chosen at random from their parent distributions provide a single point on the distribution curves of BOD and DO at Clapham. From a number of such realizations, an ensemble average forecast distribution may be computed, and it can be shown that the deviation D_n of the forecast distribution $S_n(x)$ obtained in this manner, from the true but unknown distribution $F(x)$ is related to the number of realizations, n.

---

*Autoregressive Moving Average Models in the statistical literature (Box and Jenkins 1969)

TABLE 1

	BOD mg/l	DO mg/l	Temperature °C	Sunlight Hrs	Chlorophyll A mg/m
Variance δ^2 of e_k series	0.6646	0.8137	1.2230	1.1445	1.0440
$v_{ik} = \dfrac{C(Z^{-1})e_i}{D(Z^{-1})}{}_{ik}$	$\dfrac{C}{D}$	$\dfrac{C}{D}$	$\dfrac{C}{D}$	$\dfrac{C}{D}$	$\dfrac{C}{D}$
ARMA TIME SERIES MODELS	$\dfrac{(1-0.0205\,Z^{-1})}{(1-0.157Z^{-1})}$	$\dfrac{1}{(1-0.2Z^{-1})}$	$\dfrac{1}{(1-0.836Z^{-1}+0.09Z^{-2}+0.12Z^{-3})}$	$\dfrac{1}{(1-0.432Z^{-1}-0.134Z^{-2})}$	$\dfrac{1}{(1-0.364Z^{-1}-0.179Z^{-2})}$
Mean ξ_k series	2.28	8.12	18.35	5.08	15.15
St.Deviation of ξ_k series	0.6727	0.8473	1.4123	3.7253	8.4796
INVERSE K-L TRANSFORM-ATION MATRIX		0.152 -0.6732 -0.1470 0.7070 -0.0428	0.4757 0.4972 -0.6019 0.2645 0.3070	0.6428 -0.0397 0.6631 -0.0151 0.3813	-0.3339 -0.4754 -0.3122 0.4479 -0.1849 0.3772 -0.2127 0.6199 0.8436 0.2166

where z is the z transform operation i.e. $z^{-1}\,v_k = v_{k-1}$

This latter result is extremely useful and has been used, for example, by Spear (1968) to assess the confidence limits associated with a distribution. Whatever random variable is chosen as a measure of the system characteristics, it is possible to state a priori the number of sample realizations required to estimate the true distribution function to a given accuracy. Moreover, the number of samples is not dependent on the number of system parameters but only on the required accuracy.

A proof of the properties of this statistical test is given by Kendal and Stuart (1961) and the test may be best illustrated by application to the water quality problem; for instance suppose we wish to obtain a distribution of DO and BOD at Clapham and we require the true distribution F(x) to lie within ± 10% of our forecast distribution with a 95% confidence level. In this situation $D_n = 0.1$ (Kendal and Stuart 1961) and at the 95 confidence level

$$D_n = 0.1 = \frac{1.36}{\sqrt{n}}$$

i.e. n = 186

It is required, therefore, that 186 realizations are necessary to satisfy the confidence criteria.

With this information a simulation run over 186 equivalent summer periods should provide a distribution for BOD and DO at Clapham which closely corresponds with the actual distribution obtained from the summer river data. The discrete

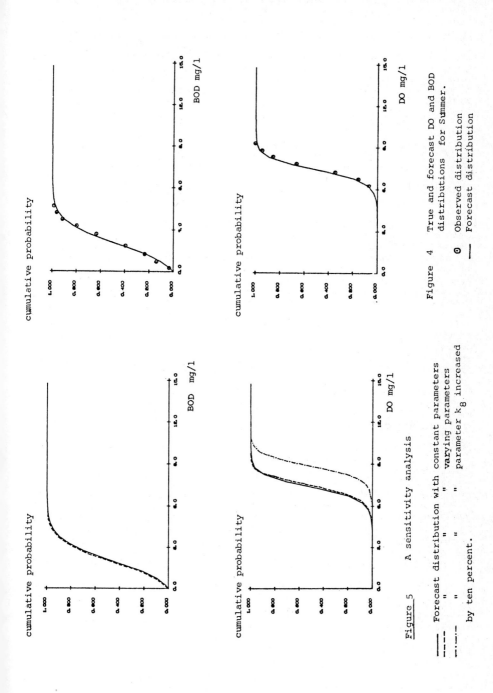

Figure 4   True and forecast DO and BOD
            distributions for Summer.
            ⊙   Observed distribution
            ── Forecast distribution

Figure 5   A sensitivity analysis

──── Forecast distribution with constant parameters
──── "   "   "   varying parameters
──·── "   "   "   parameter k_8 increased
      by ten percent.

time nature of the models help to reduce computation time to 35 minutes on the
4130 Elliot Computer for the full stochastic simulation.   The Monte Carlo
simulation is defined here as the complete stochastic simulation of 186 summer
periods and not just one realization.   The distribution from the observed summer
data is shown in Figure 4 and this can be considered as the "true" distribution.
It is clear that it lies well within the 95% confidence limits set as being ± 10%
of the forecast distribution obtained from the simulation.   The close
correspondence of the true and forecast distribution for both BOD and DO provides
a useful check on the efficacy of the statistical assessment of the dynamic
behaviour of the river.

6.   A Sensitivity Analysis

      During the modelling exercise (Whitehead 1975), the parameters were
estimated using the recursive multivariable IVAML time series algorithms.   These
"best" parameter estimates in fact lie at the centre of a range of parameter
values which can be assumed to form a Gaussian distribution provided the basic
stochastic disturbances are assumed Gaussian.   The variance associated with each
parameter defines the spread of the distribution and again an approximate
estimate of this error variance can be obtained from the estimation analysis.
The sensitivity of the model to changes in the parameter may be considered,
therefore, by performing a Monte Carlo analysis with the parameters selected at
random from the Gaussian distribution defined by the covariance matrix of the
estimation errors.   In other words, during an identical simulation run to that
described above the parameters were assumed to be stochastic variables with a
statistical distribution defined by the estimation results.   In this manner,
over many realizations, a sensitivity analysis on the parameter uncertainty can
be obtained.

      Figure 5 contains the original forecast distribution assuming constant
parameter estimates and the distribution from the sensitivity analysis with the
parametric uncertainty introduced.   The minimal difference between these
distributions tends to suggest that the model output is relatively insensitive to
parameter variations provided the variations are small and within the error
bounds defined by the estimation algorithms.   The standard errors associated with
each parameter tend to be small on those parameters which significantly affect the
model output such as the "reaeration" parameter k_8.   A simulation run with this
parameter increased by 10%, for instance, gave a shifted distribution, shown in
Figure 5, approximately 1.5 mg/l of DO higher than the original forecast
distribution.   This has important implications for the generality of the model
since, whilst the model structure is adequate for both the River Cam and the
River Ouse the model parameters differ considerably.   The distribution results
suggest that parameters should be estimated using the statistical algorithms
before the models are used in any design or planning role.   Guessed parameter
values are invariably inaccurate to the extent of 10% and conclusions drawn from
studies using guessed parameter values are likely to be misleading.   A
conclusion which is particularly interesting when it is realized that most water
quality models being used for planning at the present time tend to be much less
rigourously estimated than those discussed in this dissertation.

7.   A Statistical Assessment of the Effluent Impact on the Aquatic Environment

      The planning of water resource systems is fraught with many intangibles
and uncertainties: population trends are likely to change in the future; Milton
Keynes New City will almost certainly develop beyond the planned size, as has
happened in many new town developments (Schaffer 1970); flood or drought years
will affect the extremes of behaviour.   All these effects introduce a degree of
uncertainty that can make realistic forecasting into the *distant* future a
dangerous and misleading exercise.

Perhaps a more realistic approach to forecasting would be with a time horizon of 5 years but using an updated "intermediate" forecast based on the latest information every two years.   Forecast population and effluent discharge rates are defined to some extent by planning consents for industrial and domestic building programs and a short term forecast would be reasonably accurate.   Also it may be argued that whilst major sewage works need to be planned ten or twenty years ahead, there is some flexibility in the short term because the possibility of improving existing treatment plants via the addition, for example, of tertiary treatment or, alternatively, by the further extension of primary and secondary treatment.   The "rolling" plan, as it might be called, would therefore, be based on the latest information on river dynamics and other important variables.

With this approach in mind an initial assessment of the impact of Milton Keynes effluent on the aquatic environment in the Bedford Ouse was obtained using the Monte Carlo simulation.   The stochastic simulation of the river described in section 5 was repeated but with an additional effluent input at the upstream boundary to represent the Milton Keynes effluent discharge.

Altogether three effluent conditions were considered with discharge rates of 4, 8 and 20 mgd (million gallons per day) and with BOD levels of 5, 10 and 10 mg/l respectively.   It was assumed that the effluent had no dissolved oxygen present; a condition that represents the worst situation but which is not unrealistic as the effluent is to be pumped direct from the treatment works via a three mile pipe into the river.   Finally the BOD levels in the effluent fluctuate in practice and so a stochastic component defined by a noise signal of variance 1, 4 and 4 mg/l respectively as added to the three BOD levels.

The distribution for BOD and DO at Clapham given these three effluent conditions are compared with the present situation in Figure 6.   At the low discharge rate conditions there is comparatively little effect on the aquatic environment.   However, at the 20 mgd condition the mean BOD level has risen to 4.5 mg/l and the mean DO level has fallen to 6.5 mg/l.   These conditions contravene the criteria for BOD and DO discussed by Taylor (1974), where the mean BOD value should be less than 3 mg/l and the mean DO greater than 7.5 mg/l.   This situation is accentuated at the minimum point of the oxygen sag curve which occurs approximately at Olney, the downstream boundary of the first reach.   The DO distributions at the 20 mgd discharge computed from the quality data at the first reach, shown in Figure 7, indicates an even lower DO mean level of 5.5 mg/l.

The two other conditions in the quality criteria are,

1)   for 99% of the time the dissolved oxygen should be greater than or equal to 3 mg/l and

11)   for 95% of the time the dissolved oxygen should be greater than or equal to 5 mg/l.

The distribution of DO at Olney satisfies the first condition but just contravenes the second condition as the distribution is above the 5 mg/l level for 94.7% of the time.   Since the true distribution lies within ± 10% of this value, the worst condition could produce a confidence level of 84.7%.   However, this assumes that the confidence band is of constant width about the sample distribution function and a better assessment of the worst condition may be ascertained using a statistical test developed by Renyi (1953).   The primary advantage of Renyi's statistic is that a smaller confidence band will be obtained for small values of $Sn(x)$, the forecast distribution, than the Kolmogorov statistic.   Instead of a confidence band of constant width about the sample distribution function the Renyi statistic provides a confidence band around $Sn(x)$ that is proportional to $F(x)$, defined as

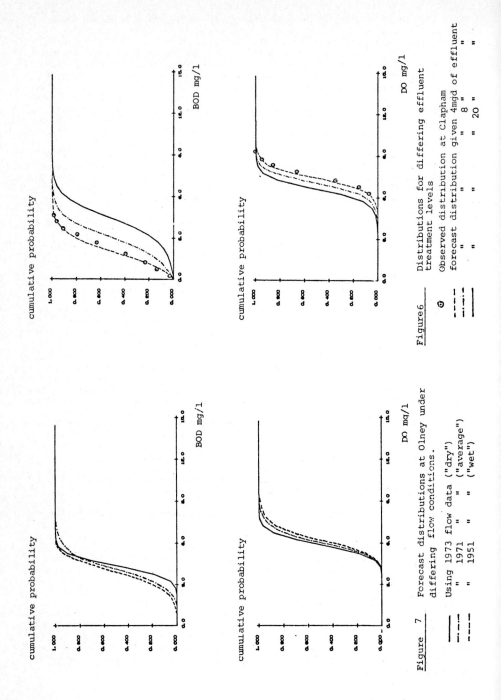

Figure 6   Distributions for differing effluent treatment levels

⊖   Observed distribution at Clapham
‒ ‒ ‒   forecast distribution given 4mgd of effluent
‒ · ‒ · ‒   "   "   "   8   "   "
————   "   "   "   20   "   "

Figure 7   Forecast distributions at Olney under differing flow conditions.

————   Using 1973 flow data ("dry")
‒ · ‒ · ‒   "   1971   "   "   ("average")
‒ ‒ ‒   "   1951   "   "   ("wet")

$$\frac{Sn(x)}{1 + \dfrac{y}{\sqrt{n}}} < F(x) < \frac{Sn(x)}{1 - \dfrac{y}{\sqrt{n}}}$$

where y is obtained from a table of the asymptotic distribution of the Reny's statistic.   The value of a in the table is chosen to be a≤ Sn(x);   a condition of the Renyi theorem.   In the water quality example Sn(x) is 0.053 and therefore a = 0.05 represents a suitable value.   The Renyi's statistic yields a distribution range of 0.032 < F(x) < 0.141 with probability 0.898.   Under the worst conditions, therefore, there is a 90% probability that the dissolved oxygen level will be below 5 mg/l for 15% of the time.   In other words there is a 90% chance that the standard will be contravened one day in every seven.

This result is, however, only an initial assessment of the impact of Milton Keynes effluent on the aquatic environment and an updated forecast based on a reestimated model in two years time may indicate an improved situation.   On the other hand, the DO levels may be adversely affected by the changing biological nature of the river and some form of control action may be necessary to improve the DO distribution.   For instance, a large lagoon close to the discharge point at Tickford Abbey could be used as a retention lagoon and a relatively simple control scheme such as that discussed by Young and Beck (1974) for flow augmentation could provide sufficient control to avoid low DO levels in the Bedford Ouse.

The effect of varying flow conditions from year to year may be illustrated using rainfall and flow data for the years 1971 and 1951.   In comparison to the dry 1973 flow conditions already considered these represent "average" and "high" precipitation and flow years respectively.   The introduction of these now flow conditions into the Monte Carlo analysis effectively alters the shape of the DO distribution, as shown in Figure 7.   The DO mean increases by 0.2 and 0.5 mg/l respectively;   an increase due primarily to the additional aeration at higher flow rate.   As might be expected the higher flow rates effectively dilute the BOD inputs from the effluent and, therefore, reduce the BOD levels in the river.

8.   Conclusions

One of the objectives of the model building phase was to construct a relatively low order model capable of describing transient behaviour in addition to the stochastic aspects of the aquatic environment.   The stochastic aspects have provided forecasts in terms of probability distributions and the distributions themselves reflect the day to day or dynamic behaviour of the river, providing, as they do, information on the water quality extremes.   Such information is considered invaluable if realistic planning strategies are to be developed since it is the extremes of behaviour or the transient violations in water quality standards that cause problems in the short term.

The sensitivity of the model to parameter variations has been found to be significant and forecasts made using guessed parameter values are likely to be highly misleading.   It is suggested therefore that water quality models should always be estimated and validated against field data prior to their application to planning problems.

Finally the impact of Milton Keynes effluent on the aquatic environment has been assessed using the dynamic stochastic models in a stochastic simulation. The need for some additional treatment or for a form of control on the effluent discharge has been initially demonstrated and the Monte Carlo technique could now be applied in a design role to establish the degree treatment or control necessary to meet the required water quality specifications.

References

Beck, M. B., and Young, P. C., (1975), A Dynamic Model for BOD-DO Relationships
in a Non-Tidal River, Water Research, to be published 1975.

Berthouex, P. M. and Brow, L. C., (1969), Monte Carlo Simulation of Industrial
Waste Discharges, A.S.C.E., J.S.E.D., October.

Box, G, and Jenkins, G. M. (1970), Time Series Analysis Forecasting and Control,
Holden Day.

Kendall, M. G., and Stuart, A., (1961),Advanced Theory of Statistics, Griffin.

Page, C and Warn, A. E., (1974), Water Quality Considerations in the Design of
Water Resource Systems, Water Research, Vol.8., pp 969 to 975.

Rényi, A., (1953), On the Theory of Order Statistics, Acta. Math., Acad. Science,
Hungary pp 191-231.

Spear, B., (1968), Low Frequency Instabilities in Liquid Propelant Rocket Engines,
Ph.D. Dissertation, University of Cambridge Engineering Department.

Schaffer, F. (1970), The New Town Story, Paladin.

Taylor, N. (Editor) (1974), The Second Annual Report to the Steering Group, The
Bedford Ouse Study, Great Ouse River Division, Anglian Water Authority.

Whitehead, P. G. (1975), A Control and Systems Analysis of Artificial Instream
Aeration, 7th IFIP Conference on Optimization Techniques, Nice.

Whitehead, P. G. (1975), A Dynamic Stochastic Model for a Non-Tidal River,
Symposium on Water Quality Modelling of the Bedford Ouse, Churchill College,
Cambridge, Organised by the Anglian Water Authority.

Whitehead, P. G., and Young, P. C. (1974), A Dynamic Stochastic Model for Water
Quality in part of the Bedford Ouse River System, Proc. IFIP Working Conf. on
Modelling and Simulation of Water Resources Systems.   Ghent. Belgium (July/
August) North-Holland. Amsterdam.

Young, P. C., and Beck, M. G. (1974), The Modelling and Control of Water Quality
in a River System, Automatica 10.5. 455-468.

Young, P. C., and Whitehead, P. G. (1974), A Recursive Approach to Time-Series
Analysis for Multivariable Systems.   Proc. IFIP Working Conf. on Modelling and
Simulation of Water Resource Systems. Ghent. Belgium (July/August) North Holland,
Amsterdam.

DISCUSSION

*What kind of probability distribution function your disturbances do they
have ? Could your trying, as I understood, to preserve the mean and the standard
deviations, influence the cross-correlation matrix ?
This was on the assumption that they are distributed as a normal- are they ?
(TODINI)*

In order to generate synthetic water quality data, you have to initially
determine the models and the transformation matrix. Water quality data is decorre-
lated using the transformation matrix, and then each of the independent series is
analysed in a time series manner. The inherent assumption in estimating these
models is that the final noise series is white i.e. zero mean serrially uncorrelated and Gaussian in distribution. (WHITEHEAD)

*Here you have a noise which is white. You correlated it with the input
responses you have and you obtain that your results are independent.
Then you give the structure of your cross-correlation matrix. What you are trying
to preserve is something you observed. (TODINI)*

Yes, I want the synthetic quality data to have the same statistical properties as the actual data. (WHITEHEAD)

*I had experiences in generating synthetic tables. If they are distributed
like this chart for instance (log - normal) you can get into big trouble, concerning the standard deviation of the generated sequences. (TODINI)*

*I had similar problems with some work I have done in the Illinois and
Texas river basins. A wrong assumption about the distribution creates huge errors
in the generated flows of so much that hydrologists would never accept them.
The distribution of your naturally occuring data is as important as your analysis.
A lot of it comes back to some work done by (Nicolas Potalis) of the US. geological
Survey, and Fiering in Harvard University. He came up with another approach. Another
person found an error in his algorithm and the method was corrected for this pro-
blem.*

He used regression analysis to estimate the parameters in his model, which
gave him biased estimates. If there is noise on the data and the model is structured
then biased estimates will always be obtained with regression analysis.
(WHITEHEAD)

*I think that your approach is more general than the (Potalis) algorithm and
the Fiering algorithm, because they suppose that the processes were only autoregressive of the first order. What they want to preserve is only the first order
cross-covariance matrix of an autoregressive process. Here you have some ARIMA
process. (TODINI)*

*Are you also interested in the autocorrelation functions of the output in
time, because, I suppose you are not only interested in what percentage of time the
consequences exceed limits, but also how long they exceed. (DE BOER)*

This is a first order autoregressive model. In this matrix you have the
autoregressive parameters, and if you wanted to do it, you could simulate on it.
(WHITEHEAD)

Do you know the size of the autoregressive parameters ?   (DE BOER)

They are the order of 0.4 which is a significant degree of autocorrelation.
                                                              (WHITEHEAD)

System Simulation in Water Resources, ed. G.C. VANSTEENKISTE
1976, North-Holland Publishing Company

MODELING OF THE BIODEGRADATION OF GLUCOSE IN SOIL

by

R. Vanloocke and W. Verstraete
Laboratorium for general and industrial microbiology
Dir. Prof. Dr. Ir. J.P. Voets
State University Ghent
Ghent, Belgium

J. Spriet and J. Mercy
Siminar for applied mathematics and biometrics
Dir. Prof. Ir. G. Van Steenkiste
State University Ghent
Ghent, Belgium

ABSTRACT

When a soil is polluted with an organic water-soluble
compound both physico-chemical and biological phenomena have to be taken into account. Indeed, part of
the compound absorbs to the solid soil matrix and is
therefore subject to sorption - desorption processes.
This part is subsequently biodegraded by the soil
biomass which is a biological phenomenon. The part of
the pollutant remaining as solute in the soil water-
phase is subsequently leached to the subsoil and to
the groundwater.

This paper deals with the breakdown of glucose in soil.
The principal aim is to develop a model which describes
the concentration of the organic compound dissolved in
the soil water-phase as a function of time. Indeed it
is the amount of pollutant present in the mobile aqueous
phase which constitutes a threat to the groundwater.
The structure of the model is determined and the unknown
parameters estimated using an optimization technique. In
addition an attempt is made to quantitatively evaluate
the initial substrate-specific biomass as well as the
evolution of carbon dioxide as a consequence of the
biodegradation of the substrate.

INTRODUCTION

The microbial breakdown of organic compounds in natural environments has received ample attention during the last decades. Research has particularly been focused on questions regarding molecular recalcitrance, biodegradation pathways, residual metabolites and
influence of environmental parameters. In contrast herewith, the
kinetics and the overall quantitative aspects of these biodegradation phenomena have hardly been studied. This is rather unfortunate
since for environmental engineering purposes, particularly the
quantitative aspects of microbial transformations must be known.
Some of the more important models currently used to simulate

biodegradation phenomena have been reviewed by Verstraete and
Vanloocke (1975).

When a biodegradable carbon source is added to the soil,
both physico-chemical and biological phenomena have to be taken into
account. Indeed, the carbon source is at the same time subject to
sorption-desorption processes from the soil complex and to biodegradation processes from the soil microbiota. The latter is considered
to be adsorbed to the soil matrix. Hence, a model which represents
the disappearance of the C-source has to comprise physico-chemical
as well as biological parameters.

This paper deals with the breakdown of glucose in soil. Glucose
was selected as a model compound for water-soluble biodegradable organic pollutants. The principal aim of this study is to develop a
model which describes the concentration of the organic compound dissolved in the soilwater phase as a function of time. Indeed, it is
the amount of pollutant in the mobile aqueous phase, which constitutes a threat to groundwater quality. For this purpose, a substrate
model was developed. In addition to this model, the evolution of the
microbial metabolites in the soil as a consequence of the biodegradation processes was studied by means of a so-called metabolite
model.

MODELING

The modeling has been performed in two steps. On the basis
of known physico-chemical and biological unit processes, some model
structures were proposed. After selection of the most promising
structure, parameter adjustement has been performed according to the
procedure outlined in Fig. 1.
The different block units of the scheme on Fig. 1 are now discussed.

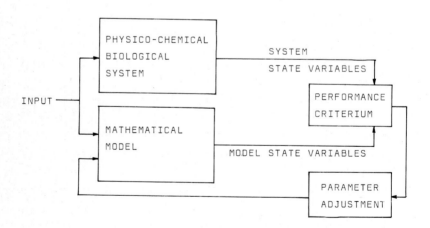

Fig. 1. Procedure used for parameter adjustment

Physico-chemical biological system

The physico-chemical and biological phenomena as described in the introduction are too complex to handle. Therefore controlled experiments have been set up to delineate the biodegradation phenomenon.

Batches of an acidic podzol (pH 4.5) were amended with various amounts of glucose. The soils were kept at about 75 % of their field capacity and incubated at 20° C, unless otherwise indicated. From these batches, samples were incubated in the Sapromat electrolytic respirometer and their O_2-uptake was monitored continuously (Verstraete et al. 1974; Voets et al. 1974). From these oxygen-uptake curves, the CO_2-production was calculated by assuming that every mole of oxygen consumed for the aerobic metabolism of glucose resulted in the production of one mole of CO_2 (RQ = 1 for glucose). To check the latter assumption, the total amount of CO_2 entrapped into the KOH-solution present in the Sapromat cell was determined titrimetrically at the end of the incubation period. To determine the amount of glucose remaining in the soil, 100 grams of soil were suspended in 50 ml of aqua dest, centrifuged at 10.000 xg during 20 min and subsequently separated in a cake and a supernatant phase. The supernatant was furthermore filtered over a Millipore 0.45 μ filter. Finally, the filtrate was analysed for its content of free glucose by the specific Merck-o-test Blutzucker (art. 3322, GOD-method) enzymatic method.

The system state variables that could be measured are thus the CO_2-production and the unadsorbed glucose in the soil. The latter variable is only available in discrete form due to the measurement technique.

To test the models the following experiments were set up :

A. Podzol, pH 4.5, 20° C.
  A.1. glucose addition 80 mg C kg^{-1}
  A.2. glucose addition 120 mg C kg^{-1}
  A.3. glucose addition 160 mg C kg^{-1}
  A.4. glucose addition 200 mg C kg^{-1}
  A.5. glucose addition 240 mg C kg^{-1}

B. Podzol consisting out of one part normal soil and one part soil sterilized by fumigation with CH_3Br; pH 4.5; 20° C.
  B.1. glucose addition 80 mg C kg^{-1}
  B.2. glucose addition 120 mg C kg^{-1}
  B.3. glucose addition 160 mg C kg^{-1}
  B.4. glucose addition 200 mg C kg^{-1}
  B.5. glucose addition 240 mg C kg^{-1}

The measurements for glucose - breakdown and CO_2-production are given in Table 1.

Mathematical model

The model has been developed in two parts, a substrate model using the glucose uptake as system variable and a metabolite model using the CO_2 production as system variable. Both models form together a suitable methematical description for the phenomena occuring in the experiments.

- ## Substrate model

Paul and Domsch (1972) proposed a model for the nitrification process in the soil. This model was adapted to the problem of biodegradation of glucose in soil :

$$\frac{dS_f}{dt} = - k_1 S_f (S_1^o - S_1)$$

$$\frac{dS_1}{dt} = k_1 S_f (S_1^o - S_1) - B$$

S_f : concentration of glucose not absorbed to the soil matrix (mg C/kg soil)

S_1 : concentration of glucose absorbed to the soil matrix (mg C/kg soil)

S_1^o : initial amount of glucose absorbed to the soil matrix (mg C/kg soil)

k_1 : sorption rate constant (kg/mg C -day)

B : amount of glucose degraded in the soil per unit time (mg C/kg soil-day)

The model structures have been retained for the breakdown of the organic pollutant by the soil biomass :

- In the first one the biodegradation is proportional to the biomass, which is assumed to increase linearly and dependent on the available substrate according to a Monod law

$$B = \frac{q_m (S_1 - S_1^{ir}) \quad Xo - Y (S_1^o - S_1)}{1 + (S_1 - S_1^{ir})} \tag{1}$$

TABLE 1. : Experimental values for the physico-chemical biological
systems.

a. Normal soil amended with glucose

Days	A1 S_f $S_o = 80$	A2 $S_o = 120$	A3 $S_o = 160$
0.0	66	116	153
0.5	36	80	140
1.0	13	45	104
1.5	9	18	53
2.0	1	6	16
2.5	0	3	1
3.0	0	0	0

S_f : glucose not absorbed to soil matrix

S_o : total initial amount of glucose added to podzol

Days	Y A1 $S_o = 80$	A2 $S_o = 120$	A3 $S_o = 160$	A4 $S_o = 200$	A5 $S_o = 240$
0.0	0	0	0	0	0
0.5	2	8	2	8	11
1.0	5	18	7	19	23
1.5	8	25	10	35	40
2.0	12	30	17	44	56
2.5	15	32	32	50	66
3.0	18	33	42	54	71
3.5	22	33	46	56	74
4.0	24	33	48	57	76
4.5	26	33	49	59	78
5.0	27	34	50	61	81
5.5	27	34	50	62	83
6.0	28	35	51	63	86
6.5	29	36	52	65	87

TABLE I. : Experimental values for the physico-chemical biological
systems.

b. Fumigated soil amended with glucose.

Days	S_f		
	B1 $S_o = 80$	B2 $S_o = 120$	B3 $S_o = 160$
0.0	78	95	152
0.5	76	87	151
1.0	75	70	146
1.5	70	42	136
2.0	55	15	113
2.5	28	5	81
3.0	14	1	40
3.5	8	0	15
4.0	6		7
4.5	4		3

Days	Y			
	B1 $S_o = 80$	B3 $S_o = 160$	B4 $S_o = 200$	B5 $S_o = 240$
0.0	0	0	0	0
0.5	3	2	6	4
1.0	4	3	12	8
1.5	5	3	20	13
2.0	6	3	34	20
2.5	14	19	49	30
3.0	21	41	58	42
3.5	24	48	62	53
4.0	26	54	65	64
4.5	27	57	69	76
5.0	28	58	75	91
5.5	28	60	78	106
6.0	28	62	83	112
6.5	-	-	85	113

q_m : maximum rate of substrate conversion per unit biomass
and per day (mg C/day-mg biomass-C)
l : half saturation constant for microbial growth
(mg C/kg soil)
Xo : initial biomass (mg biomass-C/kg soil)
Y : biomass yield per mg substrate (mg biomass-C/mg substrate-C)
S_1^{ir} : amount of glucose irreversibly absorbed and no more
available for biodegradation (mg C/kg soil)

- In the second model structure, the biodegradation is proportional
to the substrate available for biodegradation, multiplied by a
bioactivity factor which varies according to an extended Michaelis-
Menten equation

$$B = k_2 E (S_1 - S_1^{ir}) \qquad (2a)$$

$$\frac{dE}{dt} = E \frac{\mu_m (S_1 - S_1^{ir})}{1 + (S_1 - S_1^{ir})} - d \qquad (2b)$$

μ_m : maximum specific growth rate of the soil microorganisms
(1/day)
l : half saturation constant for microbial growth
(mg C/kg soil)
d : the die-off rate of the microbiota (1/day)
k_2 : proportionality constant
(kg soil/mg C)
E : bioactivity representing an enzymatic potential
(mg C convertable/day.kg soil)
E = q x b

$$\frac{\text{mg substrate-C potentially convertable/kg soil.day}}{\text{mg active biomass-C/kg soil}} \text{x}$$

$$\frac{\text{mg active biomass-C}}{\text{kg soil}}$$

To decide which model was most suitable to fit the data,
both models were implemented on an analogue computer and a wide
variety of values for the parameters were tested. It was found that
the general shape of the curve representing S_f as a function of time
was linear for structure 1 and sigmoidal for structure 2. Comparison
between the mathematical results thus obtained and the experimental
values indicated that model structure 1 was not at all suited to represent the soil biochemical system. Model structure 2 however appeared to warrant further research.

- Metabolite model

The respiration curve permits to evaluate the kinetics of
the breakdown of the carbonaceous substrate in the soil ecosystem.
This curve has a typical sigmoidal shape. Such curves can be represented by the equation proposed by De Revelle et al. (1965) :

$$\frac{dy}{dt} = k (y + b) (c_o - y) \qquad (3)$$

y : amount of CO_2-C produced (mg CO_2-C/kg soil)
t : time (day)
c_o : ultimate CO_2-C production (mg CO_2-C/kg soil)
b : initial substrate-specific biomass (mg C-biomass/kg soil)
k : rate constant (1/day)

Since the respiration curves mostly turn out to be asymmetric, the following modification of the De Revelle equation was used :

$$\frac{dy^{1/a}}{dt} = k \ (y^{1/a} + b) \ (c_o - y^{1/a}) \qquad (4)$$

$$y = \left[c_o - \frac{b + c_o}{\frac{b}{c_o}e^{k(c_o + b)t} + 1} \right]^a \qquad (5)$$

a_a : coefficient of asymmetry
c_o^a : ultimate CO_2-C production (mg C/kg soil)
b^a : initial substrate-specific biomass (mg biomass-C/kg soil)

Simulation method

The differential equation of the metabolite model can be solved analytically. However for the substrate model, which is a set of non-linear differential equations a numerical integration scheme has to be selected.

To limit the overal computation time and to have a measure of the truncation error, a predictor - modifier - corrector method was used. As a relatively large number of steps in the time domain has to be taken, a scheme with sufficient computational stability was chosen :

Predictor　　$P_{i+1} = Y_{i-3} + \frac{4}{3} h \ (2Y'_i - Y'_{i-1} - 2Y'_{i-2})$

Modifier　　$m_{i+1} = P_{i+1} - \frac{112}{121} (P_i - C_i)$

$m'_{i+1} = f \ (x_{i+1}, m_{i+1})$

Corrector　　$C_{i+1} = \frac{9}{8} Y_{i-2} + \frac{3}{8} h \ (m'_{i+1} + 2Y'_i - Y'_{i-1}) - \frac{1}{8}Y_{i-2}$

Final value　$Y_{i+1} = C_{i+1} + \frac{9}{121} (P_{i+1} - C_{i+1})$

As the method is not self-starting, a fourth-order Runge Kutta program was added to start the integration.

The integration was performed and checked with different sets of parameter values to be sure that errors due to the numerical integration should not influence the optimisation used for determining the parameters.

- Criterium function

        The criterium function chosen was the sum of the squares of
the differences between calculated and measured values.

$$I = \Sigma_{i=1}^{n} (S_{fi} - S_{fi\ measured})^2 \quad ; \text{ substrate model}$$

$$I = \Sigma_{i=1}^{n} (y_i - y_{i\ measured})^2 \quad ; \text{ metabolite model}$$

S_{fi} :concentration of not-absorbed glucose, model state
        variable

$S_{fi\ measured}$:concentration of not-absorbed glucose,
                system state variable

y_i:concentration of CO_2, model state variable

$y_{i\ measured}$: concentration of CO_2, system state variable

- Optimization procedure (parameter adjustment)

        The model can be viewed as a specific mathematical problem
of the following form :

$$\overset{o}{x} : \underline{f} (\underline{x}, \underline{p}) \quad \underline{x} (t = o) = \underline{x}_o$$

$\underline{x}$: model state variable
$\underline{f}$: non-linear real-valued vector function
$\underline{p}$: parameter vector
$\underline{x}_o$: initial values

        The solutions $\underline{x}$ (t, $\underline{p}$, $\underline{x}_o$) are functions of time, the para-
meters and the initial conditions.

$$I (\underline{p}, \underline{x}_o) = \Sigma^n (\underline{x}_i - x_{i\ meas.})^T Q (\underline{x}_i - x_{i\ measured})$$

I : is an objective function
$\underline{x}_{i\ measured}$: measured values of the state variables
$\underline{x}_i$: calculated values
Q : positive semi-definite matrix

It is known that if $\underline{f}$ is continuous in its variables and has continuous partial derivatives on a given closed domain, the solutions
are unique and differentiable in t, $\underline{p}$ and $\underline{x}_o$. It follows that I
will be differentiable in t, in $\underline{p}$ and $\underline{x}_o$ on that domain.

The given model satisfies the conditions for a domain

$$e_j < p_j < \infty$$

$$e_k < x_k < \max_i (x_{ki})$$

e_j, e_k are small positive quantities. Hence, the objective function
is sufficiently smooth so that the used optimization techniques are
globally convergent and the solutions will be strictly local minima.

        The set of parameter values of the mathematical model are
these values which minimize the criterium function.

After some preliminary work on the analogue computer it was found that the criterium function showed many curved valleys and many local minima. As analytical expressions for the derivatives are not available, and the shape of the objective function is complicated, direct search techniques were applied. A random search method which is well known and a method of rotating coordinates was chosen. The latter algoritm works as follows :

Given x_0 (x vector of parameters to be optimized) and a set of ortho-normal directions in parameter space $D = (d_0, d_1, ... d_{n-1})$, initially these are the coordinate axes. A set of steplengths $(a_0, a_1 ... a_{n-1})$ along the directions is searched for :

$$a_j = \min_a f(x_j + a d_j)$$

$$x_{j+1} = x_j + a_j d_j$$

Doubling and halving an initial step is used to find the steplength a_j. Then the coordinate system is rotated in such a way that one axis is oriented towards the locally estimated direction of the valley, $x_{n-1} - x_0$.
An orthogonalization procedure is used to produce a new set of orthonormal directions $D^1 = (d_0^1, d_1^1, ... d_{n-1}^1)$. The procedure is repeated with starting point x_n and orthogonal directions D^1. A suitable criterium for termination is :

$$\sum_{j=0}^{n=1} |a_j| < e \qquad e : \text{small positive quantity.}$$

Powell's orthonormalization scheme was used because it has been showed that his procedure is more efficient than the one of Gramm-Schmidt and no dangerous accumulation of round-off errors occurs. Assume the last orthonormal basis to be $(d_0, d_1 ... d_{n-1})$ with step-lengts $(a_0, a_1 ... a_{n-1})$. The directions are rearranged in such a manner that directions with zero steplength are the directions with highest index $(d'_0, d'_1, ... d'_{n-1})$ with $(a'_0, a'_1 ... a'_k, o, o, ... o)$. Then a new set $(d_0^1, d_1^1, ... d_{n-1}^1)$ is obtained as follows :

1   Set $j = k$

$$T = (a_k)^2$$

$$S = a_k d_k^1$$

2   if $j = o$, terminate
                   otherwise $$d_j^1 = \frac{(T d_{j-1}^1 - a_{j-1} S)}{\left[T (T + d_{j-1}^2) \right]^{1/2}}$$

3   Set $j = j-1$

$$T = T + (a_j)^2$$

$$S = S + a_j d_j$$

and return to step 2

The remaining vectors are

$$d_0^1 = \frac{S}{\sqrt{T}} \qquad S = \sum_{j=o}^{k} a_j d'_j$$

$$T = \sum_{j=0}^{k} a_j \underline{S_j}$$

$$\underline{d}_j^1 = \underline{d}_j' \qquad\qquad j = k + 1, k + 2, \ldots, n - 1$$

RESULTS AND DISCUSSION

Metabolite model

This model permits to estimate mathematically the initial substrate-specific active biomass as well as the amount of carbon which ultimately is respired. The results of the simulations are re-presented in Table 2 and Fig. 2. The b^a-values for the normal soil are quite variable and average 11 µg biomass/g soil. This is rather low in view of the finding that the active biomass is normally esti-mated to range from 500-1000 µg C/g soil (Shields et al. 1973). How-ever, the b^a-values represent that part of the biomass which active-ly metabolises the substrate. It is quite conceivable that this part increases with increasing substrate levels. Indeed, as S_f increases, more and more organisms get a chance to metabolise the substrate. The fact that the b^a-values are lower in the fumigated soils is in agreement with the treatment imposed upon those soils. Furthermore, the ratio's of the biomass values in the normal and the fumigated soils aproach the theoretical value of two.

With regard to the c_o^a-values, one observes that these figures average 32 % and 41 % of the glucose-C added for the normal and the fumigated soils, respectively. The remainer 60-70 % of the carbon is either incorperated into biomass or converted to metabolites. A va-lue of 70 % for the CO_2-evolution has been reported before by Jenkinson (1966).

The maximum rate of the CO_2-production is given by k', that is the slope at the point of inflection. It can be seen that with increasing amounts of available substrate not only the amount of sub-strate-active initial biomass tends to increase, but the rate of metabolism too. These findings are in agreement with overall biologi-cal expectations to that extent.

Substrate model

This model has the following unknown parameters : S_1^o, E_o, k_1, k_2, μ_m, 1, d and S_1^{ir}. Since just an estimation of the glucose disappearance curve is available, only the product $E_o k_2$ can be ob-tained as can be seen by solving the third equation of the model and inserting the result in the second equation :

$$E(t) = E_o \exp \left[\int_o^t (\frac{\mu_m S_1 (t)}{1 + S_1(t)} - d) \, dt \right] = E_o f(t)$$

$$\frac{dS_1}{dt} = k_1 S_f (S_1^o - S_1) - k_2 E_o (S_1 - S_1^{ir}) f(t)$$

Therefore a number of parameters were approximated by means of ad-ditional experiments.

TABLE 2. : Simulation of the CO_2-production by the metabolite model.

Normal soil	a	b^a	$c_o{}^a$	k	k'[*]	ID[**]
80 mg glucose-C	0.69	3.81	28.44	0.0078	7.13	0.9987
160 mg	0.77	1.56	51.23	0.0108	21.56	0.9943
200 mg	1.22	19.84	63.18	0.0279	25.13	0.9962
240 mg	1.07	20.44	84.51	0.0144	30.39	0.9968

Fumigated soil	a	b^a	$c_o{}^a$	k	k'	ID
80 mg glucose-C	0.65	0.94	28.13	0.0107	11.25	0.9873
160 mg	0.79	0.67	59.58	0.0107	26.09	0.9770
200 mg	1.06	10.09	83.32	0.0131	23.21	0.9920
240 mg	1.05	9.32	122.55	0.0071	25.69	0.9917

[*]   Slope at the point of inflection

[**]   Index of determination =

$$1 - \frac{\Sigma \ (Y_i - \bar{Y}_i)^2}{\Sigma \ (Y_i - \bar{Y})^2}$$

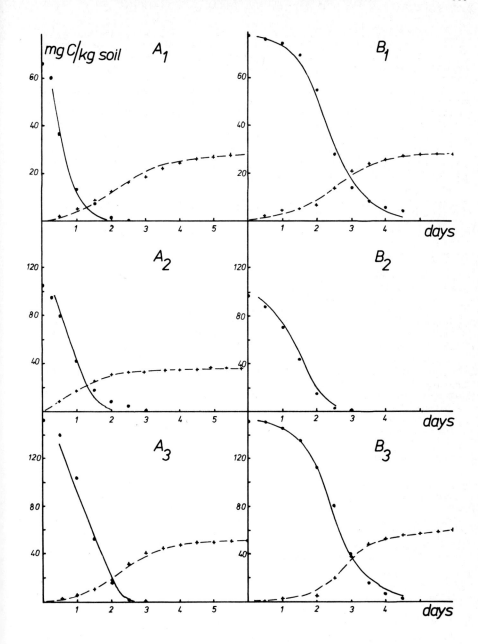

Fig. 2. Time-course of glucose disappearance in soil.
  A : normal soil
  B : soil in part treated with $CHCl_3$

  ———— : glucose disappearance
  - - - - : CO_2 formed

From a sensivity study, it could be deduced that the value
of S_1^o is very critical. Therefore in a first attempt to obtain some
information about the completely unknown parameters, S_1^o was considered to be constant and equal to 5. This value was based on an experiment in which increasing amounts of a glucose solution were added
to 25 g samples of air-dried soil. After equilibration during 15
minutes at 20° C, the amount of non-adsorbed glucose was determined
by the procedure described before. Since biodegradation during the
short incubation is negligible, the amount of non-recovered glu-
cose-carbon was considered to represent S_1^o.

For S_1^{ir} , physico-chemical considerations as well as measurements after prolonged incubation of the glucose-amended soil indicated that this value was negligible.

From the literature on microbial die-off in soil it could be
deduced that d can be assumed to approach 0.05 in the context of
these experiments (Shields et al. 1973).

Finally to estimate a value for E_o the following facts were
taken into consideration :
- in a normal soil, the maintenance metabolism averages around

$$0.05 \quad \frac{mg \ C\text{-}substrate}{mg \ C\text{-}biomass} \times \frac{1}{day}$$

- in a normal non-enriched soil a viable biomass of about 500 mg
  C/kg can be expected (Shields et al. 1973). However, the results
  of the metabolite model indicate an average of about 10 mg substrate specific active biomass/kg soil. Hence E_o must have an order of
  magnitude of about 0.5. Since this value is a rough estimate at
  the best, the calculations were started with E_o = 1.0.

The parameters k_1, k_2, μ_m and 1 have been estimated from the
substrate disappearance curves obtained with normal soil. Experiments A2, A3 were combined to increase the number of measurement
points. The following values were thus obtained for the floating
parameters :

k_1 = 1.931

k_2 = 0.00623

μ_m = 0.601

1 = 1.1

Subsequently with the latter values for k_1, k_2, μ_m and 1, the predicted disappearance curve was compared with the experimental values for the experiment A_1 and it was found that the agreement was
remarkably good (Fig. 2). Finally the S_1^o values were recalculated
for the normal soils and the following results were obtained :

Experiment	E_o	S_1^o	SSS
A1	1.	5,46	89,3
A2	1.	6,02	30,
A3	1.	4,89	279,

The validity of the model was further tested by investiga-
ting whether the results for fumigated soils could be obtained by
just varying E_o and S_1^o, where S_1^o should only show minor variations.

The following results were obtained :

Experiment	E_o	S_1^o	SSS
B1	0.299	4.25	65.2
B2	0.443	6.25	7.54
B3	0.322	4.48	64.86

From the simulated substrate curves represented in Fig. 2, it is clear that the model appropriately fits the natural phenomena. Note that the E_o values in fumigated soil are less then 0.5. This might be due to a residual toxicity in the fumigated soil. The calculted values for S_1^o approximated fairly well the measured S_1^o-values.

These results indicate that the model proposed can be adapted to the substrate disappearance curves in both the normal and the in part sterilised soil. All parameters which conceptually should not be affected by the fumigation, i.e. k_1, k_2, μ_m, l and S_1^o did not turn to be affected. The two soils only differed in terms of E_o.

It should be noted that the order of magnitude of the parameters k_1, μ_m and l, as deduced from the model, seems logic. Paul and Domsch (1972) found for NH_4^+ in soils a k_1-value of $0.05 \dfrac{1}{mmolxhr}$.

The value for glucose adsorption, expressed in the same units amounts to 0.005. This lower value is acceptable in view of the fact that, in comparison with glucose, positively charged NH_4^+-ions will react at a faster rate with the negatively charged soil complex. From the data of Behera and Wagner (1974), one can deduce for the biomass in a neutral loam soil amended with glucose a μ_m-value of $\pm$ 3.4 day^{-1}. In view of this, the value of 0.6 for the μ_m in the acidic podzol seems acceptable. No reference data on l-values in soils are known to us. The value obtained surpasses largely the l-value cited by Wright and Hobbie (1966) for the disappearance of glucose in lake water (l $\simeq$ 0.001 mg C/l) but it seems logic that in a soil system rich in organic matter, the half saturation constant for microbial growth is considerably higher than in an oligotrophic aquatic environment.

CONCLUSION

The goal of this modeling work is to develop mathematical formulas which describe the kinetic and quantitative aspects of the breakdown of organic matter in the soil. The models proposed are conceptually acceptable from the point of view of the soil chemist and the soil biochemist. The metabolite model reflects the conversion of substrate to CO_2 and it permits indirectly to obtain an estimate of the initial substrate-specific biomass. The substrate model on the other hand predicts the disappearance of the organic substrate in the soil, taking physico-chemical as well as biological phenomena into account.

These investigations are to be considered as an initial attempt to evaluate the validity and the applicability of the models to the soil system. The results obtained indicate that the models, as well as the parameters out of which they are composed, are conceptually sound. However, much more data and independent approaches are in the near future urgently needed to verify these concepts in general and these parameters in particular.

ACKNOWLEDGEMENTS

Part of this work was supported by the Belgian National
R & D Program on the Environment, Project "Groundwater", Ministry
of Science Policy Programming.

REFERENCES

Behera, B., and Wagner, G.H. (1974). Microbial growth rate in glu-
cose-amended soil. Soil. Soc. Am. Proc. 38 (4), 591-597.
Bekey, G.A. and Karplus, W.J. (1968). Hybrid Computation
(John Wiley & Sons, New York).
De Revelle, C.S., Lynn, W.R. and Riverra, M.A. (1965). Bio-oxidation
kinetics and a second order equation describing the BOD-
reaction. J. Water Pollut. Contr. Fed. 37, 1679-1692.
Dragoslav Siljaks (1969). Nonlinear systems. The parameters analysis
and Design. (John Wiley & Sons, New York).
Jacoby, S.L.S., Kowalik, J.S. and Pizzo, J.J. (1972). Iterative met-
hods for nonlinear optimization problems. (Prentice-Hall
Inc., New York).
Jenkinson, D.S. (1966). Studies on the decomposition of plant material in soil. J. Soil. Sci. 17 : 280-282.
Paul, W., und Domsch, K.H. (1972). Ein mathematisches Modell für den
Nitrifikationsprozess im Bodem. Arch. Mikrobiol. 87, 77-92.
Shields, J.A., Paul, E.A. and Lowe, W.E. (1973). Turnover of microbial tissue in soil under field conditions. Soil Biol. Biochem. 5, 753-764.
Verstraete, W., Voets, J.P. and Vanloocke, R. (1974). Three-step
measurement by the Sapromat to evaluate the BOD_5, the mineral imbalance and the toxicity of water samples. Water Res.
8, 1077-1088.
Verstraete, W., and Vanloocke, R. (1975). Mathematical modeling of
biodegradation processes. Proceeding of the Belgo-Israeli
Symposium on "Groundwater Quality and Control". Brussels,
nov. 1974. Ministry of Science Policy Programming. In press.
Voets, J.P., Vanloocke, R., and Verstraete, W. (1974). Measurement
of the biodegradation of hydrocarbons in soil samples by
combined measurement of the O_2-consumption and the CO_2-evo-
lution. Mémoires du Congrès Internationale des Hydrogéolo-
gues. Tome X, 159-166.
Wright, R.T. and Hobbie, J.E. (1966). The use of glucose and acetate
by bacteria and algae in aquatic ecosystems. Ecology 47,
447-464.

DISCUSSION

Looking at the calculations for biodecay with the normal and with the fumi-gated soils, b^a increases with increasing glucose concentration. However, there is a jump going from 160 to 200 mg glucose-C/kg soil. I am wondering what might cause these changes. (LOMEN)

Actually we don't know the reason for this jump. It is possible that at a certain substrate level important microbial groups are induced to activity. Further research is required to verify whether this is the case for 160-200 mg C/kg soil. (VANLOOCKE)

You fitted 9 parameters. How many measurements did you have for that ?
(WAJC)

Although there where 9 parameters in the initial model, we were able to give a good estimation for 5 of them so that we had to calculate only four of them namely k_1, k_2, μ_m and 1. For the calculations we have combined two experiments to increase the number of measurement points. (VANLOOCKE)

How many times did you sample during the experiments ? (BECK)

For the metabolite model, the measurement is a continuous one. For the sub-strate model, samples are taken at 12 hour intervals. All experiments are the ave-rage of two repetitions. For the estimation of the free parameters, experiments A_2 and A_3 were combined to increase the number of measurement points. (VANLOOCKE)

I suppose you are not very confident on the values of your parameters.
(WAJC)

Conceptually the parameters seem alright. Those for which some experimental values are available furthermore agree fairly well with the experimental values. However, we firmly agree that this is just a start. (VANLOOCKE)

System Simulation in Water Resources, ed. G.C. VANSTEENKISTE
1976, North-Holland Publishing Company

APPLICATION OF THE LGR SYSTEM OF TELEMEASUREMENT
ON FLOW PREDICTING

G. BAZIER and E. PERSOONS
Université Catholique de Louvain
Département de Génie Rural
Place Croix du Sud, 3
B 1348 Louvain-la-Neuve.

ABSTRACT

The aim of this paper is to describe the application to the forecasting
of river flow discharge of the LGR Telemeasurement system through public
telephone network.

A general description of the system of telemeasurement, in the case of
its use with a mini-computer, shows the advantages of the system, for
the collection of data as well as for the building and the use of a prediction model.

Such a tool will permit us to collect easily field measurements necessary for our problem of forecasting the river flow discharges of a river
basin of 752 km^2 (the Dyle upstream of Louvain).

With these data, an hydrological model of the basin is built. It proceeds in fact of three models. The first one describes the transfer relating the flow discharge at the outlet of the basin to the outflows of
the subbasins. The two other models refer to the subbasins and relate
the outflow to the rainfall.

These models will be used to forecast the flow at the outlet of the
basin.

INTRODUCTION

The elaboration of models predicting the flow discharge of a river requires, on the one hand, an history of the measurements of a great number of physical values. In order to do that, it is necessary to dispose of reliable systems of measuring sensors, of information transmission and recording as well as
of data treatment. On the other hand, the real time processing models require an
automatic system working on line.

As we shall see, the LGR telemeasurement system offers all flexibility
of satisfying those requirements.

1. DESCRIPTION OF THE LGR TELEMEASUREMENT SYSTEM

1.1. PRINCIPLE OF OPERATION

As initially developped, the LGR automatic teletransmission system is
using the public telephone network as a link between the measurement points and
a data recording center (figure 1).
Further developments have brought us to add to the recording center a mini-computer in order to enhance the flexibility and the treatment capacity of the system
which is actually composed of :
 - sensors of measured parameters
 - an Automatic Answering Equipment (AAE)

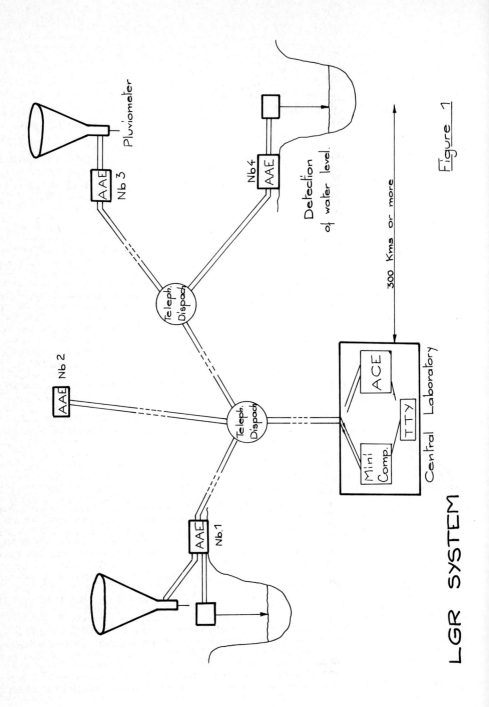

Figure 1

LGR SYSTEM

- a mini-computer which replaces the former Automatic Calling (ACE) and
  recording equipments.
The principle of operation of the actual system is the following.

The AAE is the field interface between the parameter sensor and the public telephone network. When activated by a telephone call, it sends through the
line a wave which has a frequency corresponding to the value of the measured parameter.

The mini-computer of the laboratory equiped with 64 digital inputs and
outputs is also connected to the public telephone network through a small elec-
tronic interface. The possibilities of direct access to the mass memories and
of the use of tasks (1) allow for the calling of each sensor at any moment, for
the immediate treatment of the frequency measurements, and for the storage of the
treated data on a magnetic disc and afterwards on a magnetic tape in the computer.

1.2. MEASURED PARAMETERS

Actually, 7 types of sensors can be called automatically :
- limnimeters and piezometers which give instanteneous water level;
- rain gauges which send the mean of precipitation of the preceding hour;
- temperature sensor;
- resistance blocks which indicate the soil water suction in the top two meters
  of the soil;
- anemometer and vane for the wind velocity and direction both averaged over ten
  minutes.

2. THE FLOW DISCHARGE MODELS

Our purpose is to build one or several models as simple as possible i.e.
making the best use of the measured physical values.

Thus one is lead to consider two models.

2.1. TRANSFER MODEL OF THE BASIN.

Limniphones have been installed at the outlet of several subbasins of
the Dyle basin (see figure 2).
The Dyle river mean velocity is practically constant. It is therefore possible
to determine an optimal transfer time for each subbasin, knowing a short history
of the flow discharges at the outlets of the subbasins and of the basin. A
methodology is presented by Roche (1963). By correlation, the contribution of
the unequipped subbasins can be estimated. The transfer model is of the following type :

$$Q_{t,\text{outlet}} = \sum_{j=1}^{n} Q_{t-T_j,j} \qquad\qquad 1$$

where $Q_{t-T_j,j}$ = flow discharge at time $(t - T_j)$ at the outlet of the subbasin j.

n = number of subbasins.

T_j = transfer time from the subbasin j to the outlet.

---

(1) tasks : programs ready to be activated in central memory at any moment on
the command of the operator, of a timer or of another task.

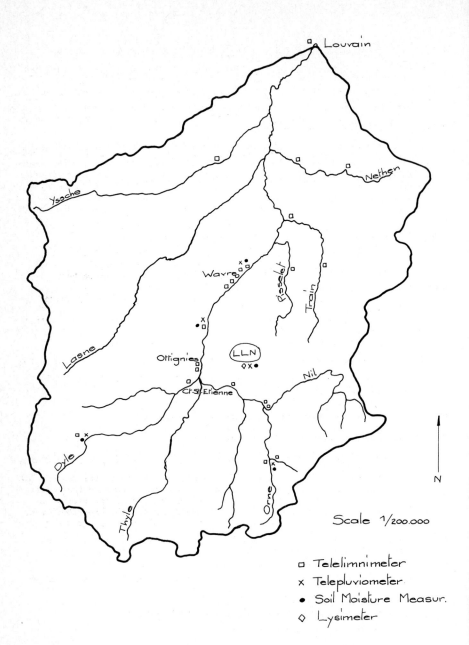

Scale 1/200.000

□ Telelimnimeter
x Telepluviometer
● Soil Moisture Measur.
◊ Lysimeter

The Dyle Basin

Figure 2

This first model is interesting for two reasons :
1) it involves only flow discharge measurements;
2) the problem of representativity of these measurements is greatly reduced due
   to the fact that the hydrological study of the Dyle basin of an area of 752
   square kilometers is divided into that of several subbasins of less than 180
   km^2.

2.2. HYDROLOGICAL MODEL OF A SUBBASIN

It is possible to increase the prediction interval of the first model by
using rainfall-flow discharge models at the scale of the subbasins.

Considering the water balance as given by the following equation :

$$P = E + C + I_e \qquad\qquad 2$$

where P is the total precipitation on the basin during a rainfall.
      C is the sum of the surface and the subsurface run-offs.
      E is the evapotranspiration measured with the help of a lysimeter and
        air temperature.
      I_e is the infiltration including the storage in the ground.

The flow discharge Q at the outlet of the subbasin can be written as :

$$Q = K (C) + B \qquad\qquad 3$$

with K (C) being a function of the run-off during the preceding times and
     B the base flow which can be estimated by piezometer measurements.

In order to forecast Q, we have to identify the relationship between P and C as
well as K (C).

2.2.1. MODEL FOR THE COMPUTATION OF C

Let us call : - Δt, the time interval between measurements
              - P_i, the precipitation between instants i and i + 1
              - C_i, the run-off during the same interval
              - θ_i, the soil moisture at time i
              - E_i, an estimation of the evapotranspiration between the instants
                i and (i + 1).

Then we write that :

$$C_i = P_i - E_i - F (\theta_i, P_i) \qquad\qquad 4$$

where F is an infiltration function which can be identified according to the
methodology developped by Cogels (1975).
The following model can thus be build :

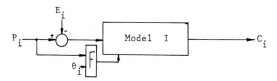

It is important to outline that the soil water status is measured at each time
step. This should allow for a good estimate of the infiltration and therefore
of C_i.

2.2.2. MODEL FOR THE COMPUTATION OF Q

By doing a few simplifications in the study of the physical relation (C, Q) it can be easily shown (Lorent, 1974) that there exists a linear relation between the outflow Q and the net rain C of the form :

$$Q_i = \sum_{k=0}^{\infty} \alpha_k \, C_{i-k} \qquad\qquad 5$$

For the case of the treatment, we shall use an equivalent form of the linear relation such as :

$$Q_i = \sum_{k=1}^{m} a_k \, Q_{i-k} + \sum_{k=0}^{m} b_k \, C_{i-k} \qquad\qquad 6$$

where the a_k and b_k are the parameters of the model that we have to identify by using a serie of measurements of Q_i and a serie of computed values of C_i.

After identification, we can use the following model :

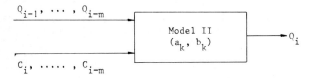

where the Q_j are measured for $j < i$
the C_j are the outputs of the model I for $j \leqslant i$

3. USE OF THE MODELS IN PREDICTING THE FLOW DISCHARGE

3.1. PRINCIPLE

Given Δt_p the prediction interval, the predicted flow discharge at the outlet at time $(t^p + \Delta t_p)$ is expressed by :

$$\hat{Q}_{outlet, t+\Delta t_p} = \sum_{j=1}^{n} \hat{Q}_{t+\Delta t_p - T_j, j} \qquad\qquad 7$$

where the $\hat{Q}_{t+\Delta t_p - T_j, j}$ are the flow discharges

either predicted at the outlet of the subbasins when $t_p > T_j$

or measured at the outlet of the subbasins when $t_p < T_j$.

At the level of the subbasins, the flow discharge prediction is made with the help of the models I and II.

It can be shown (Box-Jenkins, 1970) that the optimal prediction of Q_{i+1} from the instant i is given by model II using $\hat{C}_{i+1}$ as an estimate of C_{i+1}.

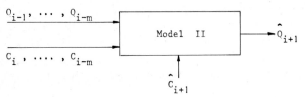

where $\hat{C}_{i+1}$ is the forecast rain and

$\hat{O}_{i+1}$ is the forecast flow discharge.

3.2. PRECISION OF THE PREDICTION

Through a statistical analysis of the built models, the prediction precision can be obtained for each prediction interval Δt_p.

Indeed, one wants, on the one hand, to predict the evolution of the flow discharge within the several hours or days after the last measurement and on the other hand, to reconstitute by interpolation the evolution of the flow discharge between two measurements. However, each measurement is costly and therefore one wants also to minimize the number of measurements to be done. According to the cost of the measurement and the precision desired with respect to the prediction and the interpolation, there must exist an optimal time interval to be defined between two measurements. This time interval will vary with time as a function of the rainfall and the statistics of the flow discharge.

3.3. USE IN REAL TIME

At an instant selected as mentionned above (3.2), the programs are activated in the central memory of the computer. The measurement points are successively called and the treated measurements become the inputs of the following model :

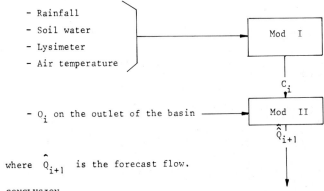

- Rainfall
- Soil water
- Lysimeter
- Air temperature

    Mod   I

- O_i on the outlet of the basin C_i Mod   II

$\hat{Q}_{i+1}$

where $\hat{Q}_{i+1}$ is the forecast flow.

CONCLUSION

The modelling of an hydrological basin, particulary when elaborated on a real time basis, involves technical problems as important as those encountered with the mathematical formulation.

With the help of the LGR telemeasurement system, such problems as remote measurement, data storage, measurement costs as well as response rapidity are easily solved.

As far as the mathematical treatment is concerned, the mini-computer offers a great flexibility of utilization which will allow for fast treatment and reduction of the data actually piling up.

REFERENCES

BOX-JENKINS, 1970 : Time series analysis forecasting and control.
                        Holden Day.
COGELS-DE BACKER, 1975 : Soil water content and potential profiles in relation
                        with the parameters of the water budget.
                        2nd IFIP Working Conference.
LORENT B., 1974 : Test of different river flow predictors.
                        Conference on computer Simulation of water resources system.
                        Ghent. IFIP.
ROCHE, 1963 : Hydrologie de Surface.
                        Ed. Gauthier-Villars.

DISCUSSION

The soil moisture measurements, you made them in a single lysimeter ?

(NEUMAN)

Yes, we will obtain them from a lysimeter, meanwhile we are using resistance blocks. (BAZIER)

At one location or many locations ? (NEUMAN)

The answer to this question is given in the paper that will be presented tomorrow by Cogels. (BAZIER)

Could you describe your function F ? (NEUMAN)

This function is for the time being non well defined, therefore we are now collecting the data and we intend to adapt this function to the data. (BAZIER)

So, this is not a working model. Just on the planning stage. (NEUMAN)

Yes, elaborating. (BAZIER)

Have you considered or have you any idea of the reliability of the telemetry system in terms of, how many times is it wrong or how often does the system break down ? (WHITEHEAD)

The reliability is function of the measurement instruments in the field, of the transmission and the recording systems.
The performance of the system can be estimated at 80 %. That means 5 % of losses due to the instrumentation on the field and 15 % due to the transmission through the telephone network (mainly busy lines). As the quality of the signal is, most of times, very good, the recording computer can work with great reliability.
(BAZIER)

What about the precision of the instruments ?   (WHITEHEAD)

The error introduced by the transmission (0,1 %) is far smaller than the error of the measurement itself (1 %) which is a function of the measured parameter. (BAZIER)

PART THREE

ON THE USE OF DEDUCTIVE INFORMATION
IN QUANTITY MODELS
OF WATER RESOURCES SYSTEMS

System Simulation in Water Resources, ed. G.C. VANSTEENKISTE
1976, North-Holland Publishing Company

SIMULATION OF MISCIBLE DISPLACEMENT IN
UNSATURATED POROUS MEDIA

G. VACHAUD, P.J. WIERENGA, J.P. GAUDET and H. JEGAT
Institut de Mécanique de Grenoble
B.P. 53 - Centre de Tri
38041 - GRENOBLE.CEDEX (FRANCE)

ABSTRACT

A number of physical approaches toward solving dispersion problems in
saturated and unsaturated porous media are reviewed. The importance of
adsorption and lateral diffusion on solute flow through soils is discussed.
It is shown that the analysis of miscible displacement experiments
on the basis of the convective-dispersion equation can lead to erroneous
conclusions concerning the rate of water movement, and the values of
the dispersion coefficient. It is concluded that in order to describe
solute movement through soil profiles of varying physical-chemical
properties and with zones of transient, steady, unsaturated and saturated water flow, a variety of models may be necessary, whose complexity
depends upon the purpose of the model.

1. INTRODUCTION

Miscible displacement occurs each time one fluid displaces another,
miscible with the first one. This phenomenon is of great importance for agronomy,
soil science, sanitary engineering or hydraulic engineering. When aqueous solution of various chemicals such as herbicides, pesticides, fertilizers, radioactive materials, salts etc.., are spread over the soil surface or are placed in
the soil, they can move downward with the water in the soil and eventually reach
the groundwater table. On the other hand sorption, precipitation and degradation
may delay downward movement. In either case it is of great importance to be able
to predict the time of transfer of surface applied chemicals to the aquifer, as
well as the amount of chemical which will reach and possibly contaminate the
aquifer and the amount which will remain in the soil. For degradable chemicals
one also needs to know the length of time the chemicals will remain in the soil,
and in which amounts.

The problems of miscible displacement have been studied extensively by
engineers interested in hydrodynamic dispersion of tracers, saline water etc..
through saturated media, particularly in connection with groundwater flow
(Bear (1972), Scheidegger (1954), Fried and Combarnous (1971)). These studies were
usually limited to the saturated domain and were mainly concerned with non-
interacting chemicals. Soil scientists on the other hand were concerned with the
transfer of chemical from the soil surface to the water table, and thus had to
deal with non-saturated flow(Nielsen and Biggar (1967), Bresler (1967)) and
adsorbing chemicals (Davidson and Mc. Dougal (1973), Van Genuchten et al (1976)).
The fields of petroleum engineering (Coats and Smith (1964)) and chemical engineering (Lapidus and Amundson (1952), Villermaux et al. (1969))have also extensively contributed to a better understanding of convective-dispersion problems.

It is the purpose of our paper to present a summary of the different
physical approaches toward solving dispersion problems, and to discuss the
merits of these approaches with respect to solute movement in saturated and unsaturated soils.

2. CONVECTIVE DISPERSION WITHOUT INTERACTION

Table 1 presents the mechanisms of movement and the equations of flow that are used to describe displacement in a porous medium of one fluid by a second fluid, miscible with the first. The flow equations are written for a saturated or an unsaturated medium, but assuming the flow to be steady.

The equations show that solute movement in porous media involves molecular diffusion, hydrodynamic dispersion and convection. The coefficients of molecular diffusion and hydrodynamic dispersion are generally combined in the apparent diffusion or apparent dispersion coefficient D_{ap}. Combination of the mass conservation equation with the equation of movement, yields an equation frequently referred to as the "convective-dispersion" equation (equation 4, table 2). Solutions of equation 4, for various sets of boundary and initial conditions have been used extensively to describe solute movement in porous material (Lapidus and Amundson (1952), De Josselin de Jong (1958), Fried and Combarnous (1971), Bear (1974)). An example of such a solution (Nielsen and Biggar (1962)) is given in Table 2, for a saturated column of soil and a step change of concentration at the entry of the column at time t = 0. Equation 5 presents the relative solute concentration at time t and depth x in the column, assuming the column is semi-infinite. The solution indicates that for a step change of concentration at the upper end of a column one should obtain an effluent concentration distribution (or break through curve, BTC) at the lower end of the column which approximately is symmetric and goes through the point C/C_0 = 0.5 and V/V_0 = 1, where V is the volume of effluent, and V_0 the volume of water in the column during displacement. However, it has frequently been shown that experimental BTC curves do not always satisfy this requirement. A displacement to the left of the point C/Co = 0.5 and V/Vo = 1 may indicate exclusion of ions by negative adsorption or by stagnant water, while displacement to the right hand side of this point indicates sorption or precipitation of ions. It appears that for unsaturated soils this displacement to the left or the right, depending on the chemical being studied, is rather the rule than the exception. It has further been observed that break through curves from experiments with unsaturated soil are seldom symmetric. Since neither the displacement nor the asymmetry in break through curves can be describes at large Peclet number with solutions of equation (4), it is obvious that equation (4) needs to be modified for conditions where these phenomena take place.

3. FLUID VERSUS SOLUTE FLOW

During fluid flow in porous media it is possible to define the local velocity as $\vec{v}(x, y, z, t)$. This is a vector whose magnitude and direction change from one point to another. The mean velocity through a given surface of voids may then be defined as v_* being the mean of $\vec{v}(x, t)$. On the other hand, the flow of water is generally defined by the Darcyan velocity, or flux density q, which is equal to the discharge at the surface per unit surface area. Since water only flows through the voids, the interstitial water velocity or pore water velocity is defined as $v' = q/\theta$, where θ is the volumetric water content. For steady, unidirectional flow of water in an incompressible porous domain, one may therefore write the identity :

$$v' = v_*$$

The parameter v' is the one which is considered in the convective term of equation 4.

Since the identity $v' = v_*$ is only valid for steady flow, one should be very careful in using solutions of equation (4) to determine rates of water movement from the rate of movement of the salt front in unsaturated soils. The advance velocity of the salt in non-interacting porous media is close to the advance velocity of the water in any of the following conditions : flow in saturated soil, flow in air dry soil, and flow in unsaturated soil which is

TABLE I

THE CLASSICAL "CONVECTIVE-DISPERSION" APPROACH

BASIC ASSUMPTIONS :

. THE SOLID MATRIX HAS NO PHYSICAL NOR CHEMICAL EFFECT AND IS ONLY A GEOMETRICAL
  BOUNDARY
. THE FLOW AFFECTS THE ENTIRE FLUID PHASE

MECHANISMS OF MOVEMENT

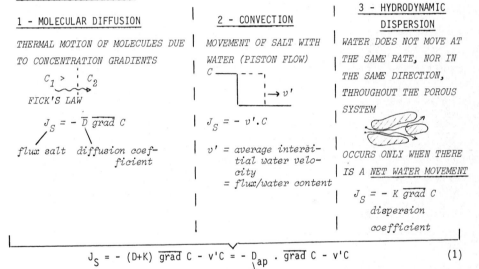

1 - MOLECULAR DIFFUSION	2 - CONVECTION	3 - HYDRODYNAMIC DISPERSION
THERMAL MOTION OF MOLECULES DUE TO CONCENTRATION GRADIENTS	*MOVEMENT OF SALT WITH WATER (PISTON FLOW)*	*WATER DOES NOT MOVE AT THE SAME RATE, NOR IN THE SAME DIRECTION, THROUGHOUT THE POROUS SYSTEM*
$c_1 > c_2$ *FICK'S LAW*	c $\quad \rightarrow v'$	
$J_S = - \overline{D} \; \overline{grad} \; C$ *flux salt diffusion coefficient*	$J_S = - v' . C$	*OCCURS ONLY WHEN THERE IS A NET WATER MOVEMENT*
	$v' =$ *average interstitial water velocity* $=$ *flux/water content*	$J_S = - K \; \overline{grad} \; C$ *dispersion coefficient*

$$J_S = - (D+K) \; \overline{grad} \; C - v'C = - D_{ap} . \overline{grad} \; C - v'C \qquad (1)$$

apparent dispersion coefficient

EQUATION OF FLOW

FOR SALT : MASS CONSERVATION : $\frac{\partial(\theta C)}{\partial t} = - \text{div} \; J_S$)
)   (2)
           EQUATION OF MOVEMENT : $J_S = - D_{ap} . \overline{grad} \; C - v'C$)

FOR WATER : MASS CONSERVATION : $\frac{\partial \theta}{\partial t} = - \text{div} \; q$)
)   (3)
            EQUATION OF MOVEMENT : $q = - K(\theta) \; \overline{grad} \; H$)

WHERE : θ = WATER CONTENT
           H = WATER POTENTIAL HEAD $V' = \frac{q}{\theta}$
           K = HYDRAULIC CONDUCTIVITY

TABLE 2

EXAMPLE OF SOLUTION OF THE "DISPERSIVE-CONVECTION" APPROACH

ASSUME THE WATER FLOW TO BE STEADY, SATURATED AND MONODIMENSIONAL (HORIZONTAL)

$$\frac{\partial C}{\partial t} = D_{ap}\frac{\partial^2 C}{\partial x^2} - v'\frac{\partial C}{\partial x} \tag{4}$$

IF $C = C_i$ $X > 0$ $t = 0$

     $C = C_0$ $X = 0$ $t > 0$

FOR A SEMI INFINITE COLUMN

$$\frac{C - C_i}{C_0 - C_i} = \frac{1}{2}\left\{erfc\left(\frac{x - v't}{\sqrt{4Dt}}\right) + exp\left(\frac{v'x}{D}\right) \cdot erfc\left(\frac{x + v't}{\sqrt{4Dt}}\right)\right\} \tag{5}$$

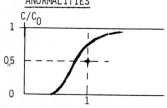

ANORMALITIES

EXCLUSION OF IONS

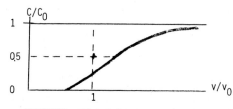

SORPTION, OR ADSORPTION OR PRECIPITATION

$$\frac{\partial C}{\partial t} + \frac{\partial S}{\partial t} = D.\frac{\partial^2 C}{\partial x^2} - \frac{\partial(v'C)}{\partial x} + \phi \tag{6}$$

amount of chemical   rate of supply
adsorbed or excluded   or loss of chemical
+ adsorption or exchange relation

kept at a constant water content (steady flow). When the water content is not
constant with time as during infiltration in soil at intermediate water contents,
the rate of water movement is related to salt movement in a more complicated
fashion. Thus Ghuman et al (1974), who studied the simultaneous movement of water
and salt in soil columns, found that the salt front coincided with the water
front in initially dry soil, but lagged behind it in the initially moist unsaturated soil. Similarly Anderson and Sorel (1974) and Kelstrup (1974) who determined the movement of natural tritium by sampling soil water, and the downward
movement of rainwater from precipitation and neutron meter data, found that the
infiltration front advanced at a rate of 3-3.5 m per month, whereas the movement of the tritium was only 4 to 4.5 m per year. Thus the advance of the
tritium front did give no indication of the rate of recharge to the groundwater
aquifer. Fig.1 presents some results on the movement of water and salt in a field
soil (Gaudet et al. (1975)). The advance of the water front was obtained from
neutron meter data and tensiometer measurements. The advance of the salt front
from sampling the soil solution in situ with suction cups. The initial water
content of the soil profile varied between $0.25 \, cm^3/cm^3$ near the surface to
$0.08 \, cm^3/cm^3$ at 150 cm. The data in Fig.2 show the downward movement of a salt
plug applied on the surface of a 94 cm long laboratory column during constant
flux infiltration with non-saline water following infiltration with saline
water. In both the field and the laboratory profiles the water front moves ahead
of the salt front due to the initial water content and the changes in water
content with time (transient water flow), and again the rate of salt displacement
does not approximate the rate of water movement.

4. CONVECTIVE-DISPERSION WITH ADSORPTION

For chemicals which adsorb or otherwise interact with the porous medium,
equation (4) needs to be modified to include a sorption term (see equation (6)).
Frequently the adsorption process can be described with a Freundlich adsorption
isotherm: $S = KC^N$, where S is the amount of solute adsorbed and C the amount
in solution, with K and N being coefficients (Van Genuchten, Davidson, Wierenga,
1974). Differentiation of this equation yields :

$$\frac{\partial S}{\partial t} = KNC^{N-1} \frac{\partial C}{\partial t} \tag{7}$$

with N = 1 and (7) in (6), excluding $\emptyset$, one obtains :

$$\frac{\partial C}{\partial t} = \frac{D \frac{\partial^2 C}{\partial x^2} - v' \frac{\partial C}{\partial x}}{1 + \rho K/\theta} = D_1 \frac{\partial^2 C}{\partial x^2} - v'_1 \frac{\partial C}{\partial x} \tag{8}$$

The term $1 + \rho K/\theta$ is often called retardation factor R_f.

It is clear from equation (8) that the retardation factor may have a large effect
on the rate of salt movement through soil, mainly due to its effect on the convective term. For saturated or steady state flow conditions the advance of the salt
front is now equal to $v'/(1 + \rho K/\theta)$, instead of v'. For example in a saturated
sand ($\theta = 0.3$, $\rho = 1.7$), a small value of K of 0.05 will give a significant
retardation of the salt front, since $v' = 1.28 v'_1$. Thus the water front would
move 28 % faster than the salt front. When the sand is unsaturated (e.g. $\theta = 0.10$)
the same small value of the adsorption coefficient causes the salt front to go
only about half as fast as the water front ($v' = 1.85 \, v'_1$). Wierenga ,
van Genuchten and Boyle (1975) found such a delay during steady flow of tritium
labeled water through unsaturated sandstone. Adsorption or isotopic exchange
resulted in value for K of 0.042 which caused the tritium to be delayed by about
0.5 pore volumes, making it a poor tracer for water movement. Note also that if
dispersion coefficients are evaluated using equation (5), the value of the dispersion coefficient obtained may include effects of adsorption, if present.

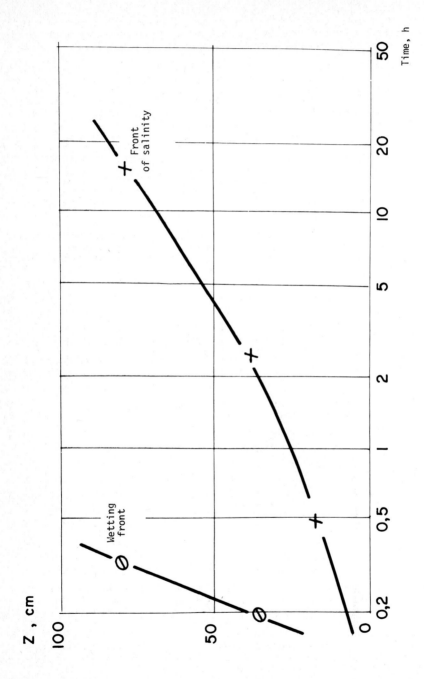

Fig. 1. Comparison between the rate of advancement of the wetting front and of the salt front during a field infiltration test with salt water

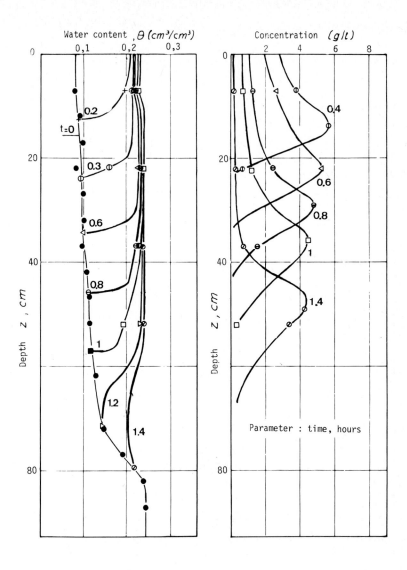

Fig. 2. Water content profiles and salt concentration profiles during a constant
flux infiltration experiment on a soil column in the Laboratory. During
this test a pulse of salt water was followed by fresh water at the same
Darcian velocity

5. CONVECTIVE DISPERSION WITH LATERAL DIFFUSION

Many experiments on solute movement through porous media, particularly those dealing with unsaturated flow, have shown asymmetrical effluent distributions (Gardner and Brooks, 1957 ; Biggar and Nielsen, 1967, Deans, 1964). To explain such tailing phenomena the concept of dead, immobile or stagnant water was introduced. One assumes that the domain is formed by the association of a solid phase, a mobile liquid phase, a stagnant liquid phase and possibly an air phase. The stagnant phase is a result of stagnant water being trapped in dead end pores and between particles. During solute displacement this water will not move, but lateral diffusion of chemicals in or out of this stagnant water is possible. Modification of equation (4) to include lateral diffusion results in the following set of differential equations :

$$\frac{\partial c_m}{\partial t} + \frac{\theta_{im}}{\theta_m} \frac{\partial c_{im}}{\partial t} = D_{ap} \frac{\partial^2 c_m}{\partial x^2} - v'_m \frac{\partial c_m}{\partial x} \qquad (9)$$

with the exchange between mobile and immobile phases given by :

$$\theta_{im} \frac{\partial c_{im}}{\partial t} = \alpha (c_m - c_{im}) \qquad (10)$$

where the subscripts m and im refer to mobile and immobile phases respectively and α is the diffusional mass transfer coefficient. Solutions of equations (9) and (10) for a semi-infinite column were obtained by Coats and Smith (1964) and by Villermaux and van Swaay (1969). Recently van Genuchten and Wierenga (1976) modified equations (9) and (10) to include adsorption on the porous medium in both the mobile and stagnant regions. Their solution is also a solution of equations (9) and (10), if their adsorption coefficient is taken equal to zero. A numerical solution of their equations with non-linear adsorption in the mobile and immobile regions is presented in another paper during this symposium (van Genuchten and Wierenga, 1976).

An application of the system described, by equations (9) and (10) is presented in fig.3 (Gaudet, Jegat, Vachaud, Wierenga, 1976). In this figure the relative salt concentration is presented versus time, as measured at 5 depths and at the exit of a 94 cm column filled with sand. The column was leached at a constant rate of 10.8 cm/hour and a constant water content of 0.257 cm³/cm³ (0.8 of saturation) with non-saline water. At time zero,3g/l CaCl₂ was added to the leaching solution. The resultant transient changes of the salt concentration were measured at 7, 22, 37, 67, 82 cm in the column with resistivity probes, and with a conductivity cell at the exit of the column. The solid lines in fig.3 were calculated with a numerical model based on equations (9) and (10) for a finite column, having a flux boundary condition at the inflow. The values for α , Dap and θ_m/θ were obtained by curve fitting the measured concentration distribution at 22 cm. It is clear that with values of the parameters α , Dap and θ_m/θ as presented in fig.3, an excellent description is obtained of the very significant tailing observed during the experiment. Other experiments reported by Gaudet et al. (1976) show the same effect. They indicate an increase in percentage immobile water with decreasing water content in the sand.

The importance of the presence of immobile water on the position and shape of break through curves in clay loam (Van Genuchten and Wierenga, 1976) and sand (Gaudet et al. 1976) is further demonstrated in figures 4, 5 and 6. Figure 5 presents the calculated concentration effluent curves at 50 cm from the surface of a column leached at a Darcyan velocity of 5 cm/h at a constant water content of 0.24 cm³/cm³. The curves show the influence of the amount of immobile water on the relative concentration curves. Increasing the percentage of immobile water causes the chemical to appear earliear at 50 cm, while at the same time increasing the tailing. The influence of the dispersion coefficient on the shape

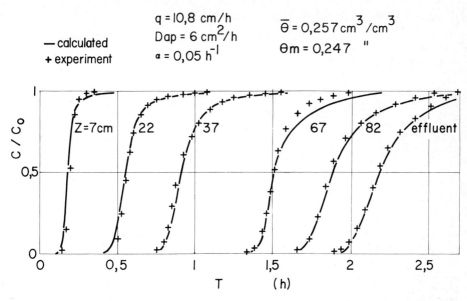

Fig. 3. Comparison between experimental and calculated concentration distribution curves obtained at various depths in a soil column, and at the outflow during a steady infiltration experiment in the laboratory, with a sudden charge of salt concentration at x = 0, t = 0. The computed profiles were obtained by numerical solution of the "Coats and Smith" scheme.

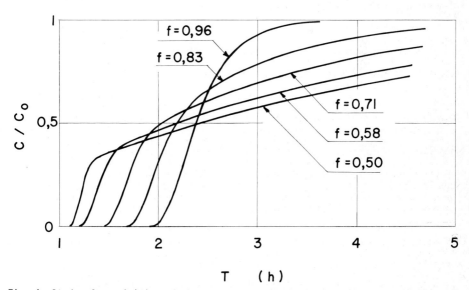

Fig. 4. Study of sensitivity of the parameters. Influence of the value of the mobile fraction of fluid on the concentration distribution curves computed in the column at z = 50 cm

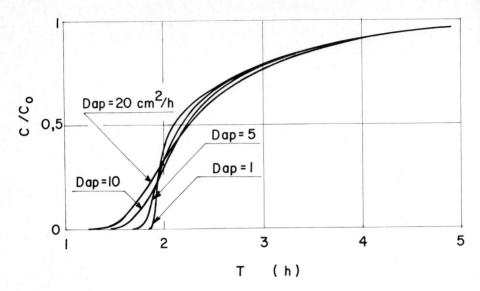

Fig. 5. Study of sensitivity of the parameters. Influence of the value of the dispersion coefficient on the concentration distribution curves computed in the column at z = 50 cm

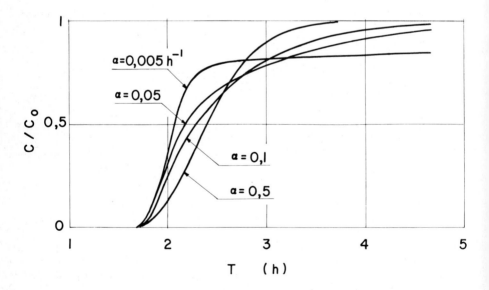

Fig. 6. Study of sensitivity of the parameters. Influence of the mass transfer coefficient on the concentration distribution curves computed in the column at z = 50 cm

and position of the calculated relative concentration curve at 50 cm is much
less, as evidence by fig.5. However, the diffusional mass transfer coefficient
α, has a significant effect.It influences both the position and the amount of
tailing of the relative concentration curve. Similar observations on the effect of
lateral diffusion on the movement of adsorbing chemicals through clay loam were
made before by van Genuchten (1974).

6. CONCLUSION

We have tried to review some of the problems that are encountered when one
uses the convective dispersion equation for describing solute movement through
soils. It is quite clear from this review that soil does not act as an ideal
porous medium, and that adsorption or precipitation and lateral diffusion can
greatly influence the rate at which chemicals move through soil. It is also evident that transient water flow conditions further complicate the matter. When
solutes move from the soil surface to the ground water table, the chemical and
physical properties of the porous medium change with depth, but also the water
regime. From a zone of transient infiltration near the surface, one may get
into a zone of relatively steady flow and water contents to finally reach the
saturated zone, which in turn may fluctuate up or down. Thus one may need not
just one but several models to describe to whole complex system of soil-water
and solute interactions during this transfer process. As a result it is very
questionable whether past analyses of water flow and groundwater recharge based
on tracer data in combination with the simple convective- dispersion equation
are valid. Much additional work needs to be done to determine order of magnitude
of the various chemical and physical parameters necessary, to predict solute
movement over any distance and time under field conditions.

REFERENCES

Anderson, L.J., and Sorel, T. (1974).6 Years Environmental Tritium in the Unsatu-
    rated and Saturated zones. Geological Survey of Denmark.

Bear, J. (1972). Dynamics of fluids in porous media. American Elsevier Publ. Co.,
    New-York, 764 pp.

Biggar J.W., and Nielsen, D.R. (1967). Miscible Displacement and Leaching
    Phenomenon. Irr. of Agric. Lands 11. 254-274.

Bresler, E. (1973). Simultaneous transport of solutes and water under transient
    unsaturated flow conditions. Wat. Res. Res. 9 : 975-986.

Coats, K.H. and D.B. Smith (1974). Dead and pore volume and dispersion in
    porous media. Soc. Petr. Eng. J. 4 : 73-84.

Davidson, J.M. and J.R. Mc Dougal, (1973). Experimental and predicted movement
    of three herbicides in a water-saturated soil. J. Envir. Qual.
    2 : 428-433.

de Josselin de Jong, G. (1958). Longitudinal and Transverse diffusion in
    Granular deposits. Trans. Amer. Geophys. Un. 39 : 67-74.

Deans, H.H. (1963). A mathematical model for dispersion in the direction of flow
    in porous media. Trans. A.I.M.E. 228.

Fried, J.J., and M.A. Combarnous (1971). Dispersion in porous media. Advan.
    Hydrosci. 7 : 170-282.

Gardner, W.R. and R.H. Brooks (1957). A descriptive theory of leaching.
    Soil Sci. 83 : 295-304.

Gaudet, J.P., Jegat H., VACHAUD G. (1975). Etude de la dynamique de la dispersion
    dans la zone non-saturée. Compte rendu des colloques ATP Hydrogéologie :
    Dispersion de fluides miscibles en milieux poreux. Grenoble 1975.

Gaudet, J.P., Jegat H., G. Vachaud and P. Wierenga (1976). Water and solute movement in non-saturated sand. Soil Sci. Soc. Amer. Proc. (submitted for publication).

Ghuman, B.S., Verma S.M., Prihar (1974). Effect of Application Rate, Initial Soil Wetness, and Redistribution Time on Salt Displacement by Water. Soil Sci. Soc. Amer. Proc. 39 : 7-10.

Kelstrup, N. (1974). Water Movement in the Unsaturated Zone. Proceedings of Isotopes Hydrology 1974. IAEA Symp. on use of isotopic techniques in Subsurface Hydrology. Vienne.

Lapidus, L. and N.R. Amundson (1952). Mathematics of adsorption in beds.VI The effect of longitudinal diffusion in exchange and chromatographic columns. J. Phys. Chem. 56 : 984-988.

Nielsen. D.R. and J.W. Biggar (1962). Miscible displacement :III Theoretical considerations. Soil Sci. Soc. Amer. Proc. 26 : 216-221.

Scheidegger A.F. (1954). Statistical Hydrodynamics in Porous media. J. of App. Phys. 25 : 997-1001.

van Genuchten, M. Th. Mass transfer studies in sorbing porous media (1974). Ph.D. thesis. New Mexico State University. Las Cruces. N.M.

van Genuchten, M.Th., J.M. Davidson, and P.J. Wierenga (1974). An evaluation of kinetic and equilibrium equations for the prediction of pesticide movement through porous media. Soil Sci. Soc. Amer. Proc. 38 : 29-35.

van Genuchten, M.Th., and P.J. Wierenga (1976). Mass transfer studies in sorbing porous media.
1. Analytical solutions. Soil Sci. Soc. Amer. Proc. (submitted for publication).

van Genuchten, M.Th., and P.J. Wierenga (1976). Numerical solution for convective dispersion with intra-aggregate diffusion and non-linear adsorption in Biosystems simulation in Water Resources and Waste Problems. North Holland/American Elsevier.

Villermaux,J. (1974) Deformation of chromatographic peakes under the influence of mass transfer phenomena. J. Chromatographic Sci. 12 : 822-831.

Villermaux, J. and W.P.M. van Swaay (1969). Modèle représentatif de la distribution des temps de séjour dans un réacteur semi infini à dispersion axiale avec zones stagnantes. Chem. Eng. Sci. 24 : 1097-1111.

Wierenga, P.J. , M.Th. van Genuchten and F.W. Boyle (1975). Transfer of boron and tritiated water through sandstone. J. Envir. Quality 4 : 83-87.

DISCUSSION

I found in your talk some antitheses in a sense that on a certain moment you said that the observed movement of the salt was nearly independent of moisture content. So, it was a very hopeful idea and then the further you went on, the more you showed us the complexity.
A question that arises to me is : For practical purposes : is it possible to measure directly salt movement and under what water regime we should measure in order to obtain the most reliable result ? (DE BOODT)

I was showing some data to show that the salt movement was underset by boundary conditions, independent of the initial water content, but not of the final water content. I think it is possible to measure the salt movement, but one has to be careful about the representativity of the measurements. It is not so simple as it was thought for many years to deduce simply the movement of water from the movement of the salt. Both are not related, certainly not linearly. It is not such a simple problem. I think one should be careful. If we measure the flow of salt, it may be different of the movement of water. It is not possible to deduce one from the other. It maybe possible in some cases, but not always.
(VACHAUD)

When I did some dispersion work, some years ago, we had great difficulties in matching viscosity and density curves from a laboratory experiment.
In real situations of course, matching is not so easy.
Could you give us some indication of the effects of viscosity and density differences, due to the presence of the salt, on the dispersion ? (PECK)

What I want to say is that one has to be careful not always to use the effluent curve for coming back to the flow inside of the column.
There is for example a good example of test where we had instabilities. We run an experiment with a pulse of salt at a very high concentration (5 gram/liter) and we have 2 stages.
First, the flow was stable for density contrast, but unstable for viscosity contrast, and at a given point as the light water was pushing the fresh water, it was unstable for density contrast but stable for viscosity contrast. So, if you take the concentration curves inside the column, the curve that we obtained in the first section was perfectly stable. At 37 cm we obtain a lot of instability. At the other hand, the outflow was perfectly stable. If you take your column of soil as a black box, and if you try only to take a convolution between the outflow and the inflow the mechanism seems to be perfect, but in fact you have to look inside. I have been quite careful about the density criteria we are using (DAGAN). In fact, from what I remember, we have that kind of effect mostly for very high water content, near to saturation.
As soon as you come to a very low water content, for example smaller than 2/3 of saturation, the permeability is small and the velocity is small and we have something almost stable. The viscosity and the density contrast are just fighting each other to get a stable solution. (VACHAUD)

What is the saturated value of θ ? (LOMEN)

About 30 % per volume. But it is not completely saturated. We make a difference between what we call the saturation which is the value that we would obtain if all the pores are saturated - and this is extremely complicated to obtain - and the "natural saturation", which is the highest water content you can obtain saturating the column by a natural process. If you do so, maybe there is saturation, but there is still at least 10 % of air. (VACHAUD)

Do you mean that the value 0.3 is the natural saturation ? (LOMEN)

Yes, because I think the porosity is something like 0.36 for our soil.
(VACHAUD)

The rate of values you determined experimentally, for the exchange between the mobile and the immobile phase, how do they compare with the diffusion coefficient of water ? (NEUMAN)

The diffusion coefficient is 6 cm^2/hour ; the rate is 0.005 hr^{-1}.
(VACHAUD)

I wonder if there is a way to compare the two, since you said that you had viewed it as a fick law. (NEUMAN)

It is a fick law, but not on a surface, that's the point.
It is a fick law for mass ; we don't know what is the surface of contact. This is the reason why when we write the law, we use θ. It is a mass exchange. (VACHAUD)

You express it as a mass exchange, but I wonder if you would express it as a diffusion process, using a fick law.
Let us say you could determine the surface of contact between the mobile and immobile phase.
We are talking about the diffusion process, where, instead of having just one concentration as we usually consider in our dispersion-convection equations, we only use one average concentration. Perhaps, if you would assume 2 average concentrations, one for the mobile, and another for the immobile phase, and perhaps you don't really have a mobile and an immobile phase, but a continuum...
This is just an idea in the air, would it be possible to use such a two-step concept ? (NEUMAN)

How could you then explain the leaching process, the desorption ?
(VACHAUD)

By diffusion. (NEUMAN)

Then again you introduce one more parameter. (VACHAUD)

Yes, a parameter which would take into account the surface of contact.
(NEUMAN)

This parameter alpha is a diffusion (unit time/surface). (VACHAUD)

If you could get a rough idea about that surface, you could make a comparison between the diffusion coefficient and your coefficient of transfer. (NEUMAN)

Then you have to introduce something like a tortuosity concept or anything else. (VACHAUD)

I'm interested in if you would use the approach on a groundwater system. Is it really necessary to use the complex set of partial differential equations, if you are only interested in the input-output behaviour of the system ? You said in your answer to Dr. Peck that the input-output behaviour is relatively simple. Maybe you could describe it with a lumped system.

Is it really necessary to look in great detail to the internal responses ?

(WHITEHEAD)

We have been working with a group of scientists in chemical engineering, and we have obtained simply - by direct lumped equations between input-output using a Laplace transform - the same kind of parameter.
This is correct, if you are sure - first of all - that your system is stable inside, and also if you are in a steady condition.
But if you come to a transient condition, which is the next step, you cannot do it anymore because your parameters are not linear. (VACHAUD)

You raised a number of situations, where you can separate the mobile from the immobile phase. There is one more thing which I think you did not mention and which I tend to think might be crucial in some situations we deal with. That is, normally we have assumed a random distribution of pores in a soil. In some cases this is a very poor assumption and there is a sort of structure in many soils. If you go to rocks of course, you consider fractured rock aquifers, then you have a lot of water in the interconnections of pores of certain sizes. And it seems from a lot of the information we have collected in understood soils, that there is a strong separation between mobile and immobile phases. Which we intended to interprete as due to an order in interconnection of pores. (PECK)

System Simulation in Water Resources, ed. G.C. VANSTEENKISTE
1976, North-Holland Publishing Company

SOIL WATER CONTENT AND POTENTIAL PROFILES IN RELATION
WITH THE PARAMETERS OF WATER BUDGET

O. COGELS and L.W. DE BACKER
Université Catholique de Louvain
Département de Génie Rural
Place Croix du Sud, 3
B 1348 Louvain-la-Neuve.

ABSTRACT

In the hydrological cycle, the soil layer of a small watershed is the
link between the surface and ground water systems. Taking this continuity into account, the water budget can be calculated in order to either quantify the water resources or to characterize the watershed status at a given moment, e.g. to determine the parameters of a prevision
model.

The theory of flows through porous media applied to some hydrological
concepts allows for the establishment of a model which involves the various soil water flow steps relating together precipitations, river flow,
evapotranspiration and groundwater recharge.

From these theoretical relationships between water budget terms, one can
deduce the necessary field parameters and data to be measured at each time step of the computation.

Such determinations imply the analysis and the treatment of experimental
functions and data mathematically suitable for use in a computer.

This methodology is applied to the KIPSTEEKBEEK watershed and allows for
commenting about its successive steps of procedure.

INTRODUCTION

The soil being a porous medium partially water saturated, its physical
properties are strongly dependent upon its water content.

The soil of a watershed is a compulsory path of the water between the
atmosphere and the groundwater. The taking into account of soil physical properties in water flow simulation will allow for an increase of the reliability of
the models (Holtan and Lopez, 1971).

Thus, a model of the watershed soil-water system is required as a valuable starting point of a full hydrological study. In multidisciplinary researches,
it bridges the gaps between meteorology, surface and groundwater hydrologies and
mathematics.

This paper presents a systematization of the water balance measurements
in relation with the soil physical parameters of a watershed. Observations can
be made on-line or off-line and be treated as given in the block diagram of
figure 1.

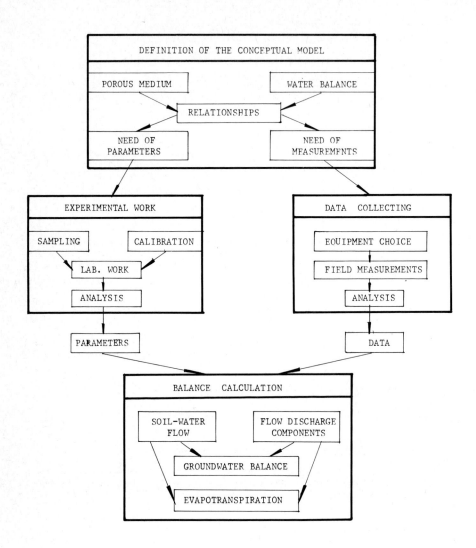

Figure 1 : Block diagram of the systematical observation of water balance.

DEFINITION OF THE CONCEPTUAL MODEL

The model results of the combination between the law of unsaturated flow through porous media and an expression of the water balance (Cogels, 1975).

1. LAWS OF UNSATURATED FLOW THROUGH POROUS MEDIA

Assuming that the flow is vertical and one dimensional, the general law of flow is :

$$\frac{\partial \theta}{\partial t} = - \frac{\partial v}{\partial z} \qquad\qquad 1$$

where θ is the volumetric water content $= \theta(z,t)$
      v is the flux $= v(z,t)$
      t is the time and z the depth from the soil surface.

For a time interval $\Delta t = t_2 - t_1$ and a soil layer $\Delta z = z_n - z_0$

$$\int_{z_0}^{z_n} [\, \theta(t_2) - \theta(t_1) \,]\, dz = \bar{v}_0 \,\Delta t - \bar{v}_n \,\Delta t \qquad\qquad 2$$

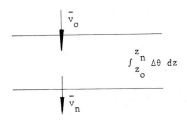

In equation (2), $\bar{v}_0 = 1/\Delta t \int_{t_1}^{t_2} v_0 \, dt$ is the input mean flux, and

$$\bar{v}_n = 1/\Delta t \int_{t_1}^{t_2} v_n \, dt \quad \text{is the output mean flux}$$

both directed positively downward.
The output mean flux can be calculated with the help of the generalized Darcy law :

$$\bar{v}_n = - K_n \,(\bar{\theta}) \;.\; \left(\frac{\overline{\Delta H}}{\Delta z}\right)_n \qquad\qquad 3$$

where

$$K_n \,(\bar{\theta}) = K_n \left(\frac{\theta(t_2) + \theta(t_1)}{2}\right) \qquad\qquad 4$$

is the unsaturated hydraulic conductivity of the soil at z_n and at the mean water content $\bar{\theta}$, $H = h + z$ is the total hydraulic head which is the sum of the suction head h and the gravimetric head z expressed in terms of length of water column and $\left(\frac{\Delta H}{\Delta z}\right)_n$ is the total head gradient at z_n.
Thus,

$$\left(\frac{\overline{\Delta H}}{\Delta z}\right)_n = \frac{1}{2} \left[\; \left(\frac{\Delta H}{\Delta z}\right)_{n,t_1} + \left(\frac{\Delta H}{\Delta z}\right)_{n,t_2} \;\right] \qquad\qquad 5$$

2. EXPRESSION OF THE WATER BALANCE

During the same interval of time Δt, the water balance illustrated in figure 2 and can be written in the following various terms :

$$P = R + L + P_u \qquad\qquad\qquad 6$$
$$\parallel$$
$$P_E + E_r$$
$$\parallel$$
$$I_E + F_s$$
$$\parallel$$
$$D + S$$
$$\parallel$$
$$\text{LEAKS} + W + B$$

with P is the total precipitation, R the surface run-off, L the subsurface flow, P_u the useful rainfall, P_E the effective rainfall, I_F the effective infiltration, E_r the rapid evaporation from the soil top layer, F_s the evapotranspiration out of the soil water storage, D the deep drainage from the soil, S the water storage in the soil, LEAKS the groundwater flow between aquifers, W the groundwater storage and B the base flow of the river. The river flow discharge O can therefore be expressed as :

$$O = R + L + B = C + B \qquad\qquad\qquad 7$$

3. RELATIONSHIPS BETWEEN THE WATER BALANCE TERMS

By an appropriate choice of boundary conditions at z_o and z_n, it is possible to define a soil profile representative of the watershed (Nielsen and al., 1973). Equation (6) can be applied to such a profile for which the following relationships with equation (2) can be written within the time interval $\Delta t = t_2 - t_1$:

$$I_E = \bar{v}_o \, \Delta t \qquad\qquad\qquad 8$$

$$D = \bar{v}_n \, \Delta t = - K_n \, (\bar{\theta}) \, . \, \overline{(\frac{\Delta H}{\Delta z})}_n \, \Delta t \qquad\qquad\qquad 9$$

$$S = \int_{z_o}^{z_n} [\, \theta(t_2) - \theta(t_1) \,] \, dz \qquad\qquad\qquad 10$$

Moreover, relationships must be defined in order to calculate independently the base flow B from the total flow discharge Q whose components are given equation (7).

In the case of on-line observation, one must use such relations or a groundwater model which will restitute the base flow from piezometric level measurements.

In the case of off-line observation, the separation of the flow discharge components can be done empirically by taking into account systematically the rainfall in the analysis of the hydrograms.

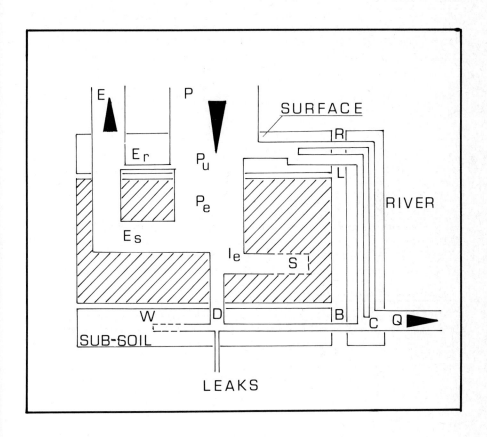

Figure 2 : Diagram of flows and storage of water in a watershed.

4. NECESSARY DATA

The evaluation of the water balance (Daian and Vachaud, 1972; Royer and Vachaud, 1974) requires an adequate treatment of field measurements in order to obtain the following data :

- Soil water profiles from z_o to z_n i.e. $\theta(t_1,z)$, $\theta(t_2,z)$

$$H(t_1,z) \ , \ H(t_2,z)$$

- Hydraulic gradients at the depth z_n of the representative profile

$$(\frac{\Delta H}{\Delta z})_{n,t_1} \qquad , \qquad (\frac{\Delta H}{\Delta z})_{n,t_2}$$

- Precipitation P
- River flow discharge Q.

5. NECESSARY EXPERIMENTAL PARAMETERS

Strongly dependent parameters are expressed by experimental relationships such as :

- K_n (θ), the hydraulic conductivity - water content curve at the depth z_n.
- h (θ) , the soil water content characteristic curve at the various depths in the soil profile.

THE COLLECTING AND ANALYSIS OF THE DATA AND THE EXPERIMENTAL FUNCTIONS

On the field :

Precipitation and flow discharge are measured with regular or automatic calibrated gauges.
Soil water suction h can be measured with the help of gypsum moisture resistance blocks in order to cover the greatest range of water content. The soil water content θ is related to the suction h through the soil water content characteristic curve h (θ).

In the laboratory :

Resistance blocks must be calibrated. Calibration is hastened by automatic weighing of a wet block during its drying due to natural evaporation and by interpretation of its pore size distribution. Pore size distribution of a soil or any porous sample is determined in the laboratory by mercury intrusion procedure. It allows for the establishment of the soil water content characteristic curve when taking into account the percentage of clay (Nagpal and al., 1972), and for the hydraulic conductivity - water content relationship calculated according to Quirck and Millington (1961) (Klock and al., 1969).
The analysis of the experimental data leads to the following empirical curves :

- Resistance block calibration curve :

$$h = a_o + a_1 \ r + a_2 \ r^2 + \ldots + a_n \ r^n \qquad 11$$

where r is the measured resistance at the given soil water suction h and a_i are the coefficients of the polynomial regression.

- Soil water content characteristic curves :

$$S_e (h') = 1 - (h')^{A+B/h'}$$ 12

$$\theta (h) = \theta_r + (f_e - \theta_r) S_e$$ 13

where $h' = h/h_{max}$ is the relative soil water suction

θ_r is the residual soil water content corresponding to h_{max}

f_e is the effective porosity or the water content θ at h = o

S_e is the effective saturation.

- Hydraulic conductivity - water content curve (Corey, 1957; Vachaud, 1968) :

$$K = K_o (S_e)^C$$ 14

where K_o is the saturated hydraulic conductivity.
The parameters K_o and C can be obtained directly from the A and B parameter
(equation 12) of the same sample.

APPLICATION OF THE METHOD

        The Service d'Etudes Hydrologiques of the Ministry of Public Works has
undertaken the measurements of rainfall, flow discharge and soil water suction
in the KIPSTEEKBEEK watershed located in the Schelde Basin on the left side of
the Dendre river in the loamy region of Belgium. The basin area covers about
1000 acres (435 ha) and the landscape is gently rolling.

        Two years of measurements have been treated according to the above me-
thodology. This has lead to the computation of the 10-day and monthly water balances by batch processing.

        The proposed empirical equations of the experimental curves have been
quite accurate in the case of loamy soils. Four resistance blocks are necessary
in each soil profile. Soil surface layer saturation is a factor which is not negligible in the mechanism of repartition of precipitation between infiltration
and surface flow. It has been shown that the run-off coefficient increases from
0 to 0,15 when the degree of saturation of the soil surface varies from 50 to
100 % respectively.

        It is advisable that measurements be made daily and automatically which
is rendered possible with the help of the LGR telemeasurement system presented
elsewhere in this symposium (Bazier and Persoons, 1975).

        Errors due to the inaccurate determinations of the parameters can be cor-
rected by identification procedure with the help of the calculated monthly evapotranspiration.

        Observation of the water balance in real time would allow for the adjust-
ment of the parameters of the physical prediction model in order to simulate the
surface flow.

CONCLUSION

        Good coordination between the various steps of the block diagram of fi-
gure 1 is of prime importance in all studies such as water balance.

        It is obvious that soil physical parameters play an essential role in
hydrological cycle study. They depend strongly upon the climactic conditions.
If one is to guarantee the continuity of the hydrological cycle, systematic
observation of the water balance is necessary in the elaboration and the utilization of any prediction model in natural environment. Further research should
lead to the establishment of a program of technical management of water resources in which flood predicting in large watersheds and basins would be included.
This is possible from observation and computation of the water balance terms in
small representative watersheds in order to determine the local parameters.

        In this program "observation - prediction" the terms of the balance
known at time k help to adjust the parameters of the prediction model terms at
time k + 1.

REFERENCES

BAZIER G. and E. PERSOONS, 1975 : Application of the LGR system of telemeasure-
            ment on flow predicting.
            2nd IFIP Working Conference.
COGELS O., 1975 : Systématisation de l'étude du bilan hydrique du sol de petits
            bassins versants.
            Mémoire fin d'études, Département Génie Rural, University of Louvain.
COREY A.T., 1957 : Measurement of water and air permeabilities in unsaturated
            soils.
            S.S.S.A. Proc., 21, p. 7-10.
DAIAN J.F. and VACHAUD G., 1972 : Méthode d'évaluation du bilan hydrique in situ
            à partir de la mesure des teneurs en eau et des succions.
            Isotopes and radiation in soil plant relationships including forestry.
            I.A.E.A. Proc., 1971, Vienne, p. 649-660.
HOLTAN H.N. and N.L. LOPEZ, 1971 : USDAHL-70 Model of watershed hydrology.
            Technical bulletin n° 1435, ARS, USDA.
KLOCK G.O., L. BOERSMA and L.W. DE BACKER, 1969 : Pore size distribution as mea-
            sured by the mercury intrusion method and their use in predicting
            permeability.
            S.S.S.A. Proc. 33, p. 12-15.
NAGPAL N.K., L. BOERSMA and L.W. DE BACKER, 1972 : Pore size distributions of
            soils from mercury porosimeter data.
            S.S.S.A. Proc. 36, n° 2, p. 264-267.
NIELSEN D.R., J.W. BIGGAR and K.T. ERH, 1973 : Spatial variability of field mea-
            sured soil-water properties.
            Hilgardia, vol. 42, n° 7, p. 215-259.
ROYER J.M. et G. VACHAUD, 1974 : Détermination directe de l'évapotranspiration
            et de l'infiltration par mesure des teneurs en eau et des succions.
            Bulletin des Sciences Hydrologiques, vol. 19, n° 3, p. 319-336.
VACHAUD G., 1968 : Contributions à l'étude des problèmes d'écoulement en milieux
            poreux non saturés.
            Thèse de doctorat, Grenoble.

DISCUSSION

You said the watershed was about 400 hectares ; I imagine that you made measurements at a nr. of points within this area. Could you tell us how many points, and how you handled problems of spatial variability ?   (PECK)

The measurements were made before, and were not programmed with our methods. We had measurements of moisture in three profiles, at 6 diff. depths, and data about the physical parameters at each depth. Different curves at each depth were computed, and we made an average to define representative profiles. But we did not treat the problem of space variability, because the parameters were first physically determined in the laboratory, and then they were corrected by an identification procedure. If we use such a method, we should place more measurement points, but since the measurements were not done with that objective, we were unable to study the spatial variability. (COGELS)

What kind of identification procedure did you use to correct your data ? Was it a global material balance of all the watershed ?   (NEUMAN)

We did the global study, with the monthly evapotranspiration. We have formulas for monthly evapotranspiration that are sufficiently correct. (COGELS)

Potential or actual evaporation ?   (NEUMAN)

Actual evaporation. For monthly evaporation we have sufficient information.
(COGELS)

What formulas did you use to caracterize monthly evaporation ?   (NEUMAN)

We used Turc's formulas.   (COGELS)

But that's potential... Besides, I wonder, after you performed your identification process, whether the relationships obtained did agree with the experimental relationships.   (NEUMAN)

We have identified only the relation at depth z_n between hydraulic conductivity and moisture content to calculate the downwards meanflow. (COGELS)

After you performed your calibration, however you obtained it, did you get more or less what you measured, or are you far away from it.   (NEUMAN)

There were differences. The physical determination of the parameters were done only with the available data, but I think we can make a finer determination.
(COGELS)

You measured a certain relationship between permeability and water content. When you calibrate your model on such generalities as you described here, I am suspecting what you get from the calibration would bear very little relation to what your actual measuring point was.
I wonder if this is something you actually saw.   (NEUMAN)

Concerning the actual conductivity, which value of K at z_n did you obtain ?
(VACHAUD)

After the identification, we obtained with this measurement methods a value of 10^{-5} cm/sec. (COGELS)

You are determining the flux value from the conductivity and the gradient. So you have to know the conductivity with water content. How did you determine the conductivity with water content ? At the laboratory ? (VACHAUD)

Yes, by the method of Wuirk-Millington. It has not been determined on the field. This was the only information we had. (COGELS)

So they only measured suction. (NEUMAN)

That is the problem dr. Peck spoke about : the representativity and the variability. About suction, I am still unaware of determining the suction from a gypsumblock. Years and years, people said that this was the worst way to determine the suction. Now we know that it is the best way. So we could discuss about the representativity of gypsum-blocks measurements for obtaining the suction. I wonder if this is a best sensor, a good sensor, or a bad. (VACHAUD)

That would be a very long discussion. (COGELS)

You averaged the water retention curves and you computed the potential moisture relation. Did you average these from different curves ? (PECK)

I did not average curves. I made an average of the results at each depth, but I did not define an average curve of a representative profile. In other words, I treated 3 profiles independently and averaged the results at each depth to define one profile. Then, at each point of this profile you can get K. You treat each curve separately and then you make the average. (COGELS)

Were you not doing that with a single profile ? I mean that there was a single relationship concerning moisture content. (NEUMAN)

We made measurements and for each point of the measurement, we used the calculated curve for the moisture retention. And then we averaged the moisture retention. (DE BACKER)

And then you weighted the locations equally in finding out the behaviour of the areas apart ? (PECK)

Somehow. (COGELS)

You have a watershed (400 ha) with plants and trees. Where is the root extraction in your balance equation ? (VACHAUD)

It is in the term of evapotranspiration. (COGELS)

Are you computing the flux at the soil surface also using Darcy ? (VACHAUD)

No, I did not utilize Darcy to compute the flux at the surface. I only did it at the lower boundary, because there it is possible. (COGELS)

Using Darcy's equation ? (NEUMAN)

Yes, but the assumption is not valid at the soil surface, you should have one more term : the root extraction. (VACHAUD)

I agree with you. If we take a gradient at the surface and we want to calculate the flux, it is not possible. I tried it inversely, but it did not work. (COGELS)

System Simulation in Water Resources, ed. G.C. VANSTEENKISTE
1976, North-Holland Publishing Company

SIMULATION OF INFILTRATION INTO
TILLED AND UNTILLED FIELD SOILS DERIVED FROM LOESS

W. Ehlers and R.R. van der Ploeg
Institut für Pflanzenbau und Pflanzenzüchtung
and
Institut für Bodenkunde und Waldernährung
Georg-August Universität Göttingen, Germany

ABSTRACT

A field study on infiltration and redistribution in tilled
and untilled loess (grey-brown podzolic) soils is made.
During one growing season the soil moisture tension is
recorded daily in various depths. In the field the relations between moisture content and moisture tension, and
between moisture tension and capillary conductivity are
determined. The unsaturated moisture flow equation is then
used to see if observed field behavior can be described
mathematically.

It is found that moisture tension values observed in the
tilled field soil agree well with simulated data. For the
untilled soil the agreement between theory and observation
is not so good. Due to a steady build-up of macrochannels
by earthworms, which are not destroyed by regular cultivation practices, part of the infiltrating water is
entering the untilled soil as noncapillary water. The unsaturated moisture flow equation does not account for noncapillary water. Another conclusion from the model is, that
a traffic pan in the tilled soil does inhibit rapid water
penetration down the profile during infiltration at high
rates. The agricultural significance of the simulated results in respect to aggregate stability, surface runoff
and erosion, soil aeration and trafficability is stressed.
The conclusions are supported by observations in the field.

INTRODUCTION

Grey-brown podzolic soils derived from loess represent a
productive base for the cultivation of sugarbeet and winter wheat
in Germany. But these soils suffer from a low infiltrability and
the danger of erosion at times, when the rain intensity is high.
The reason for this might be seen in a low aggregate stability and
a crust formation at the soil surface. This instability is the
consequence of a high silt content, a low organic matter content
and the absence of calcium carbonate. Furthermore, the regular
cultivated soils exhibit a traffic pan in 20-30 cm depth with low
porosity, which also can hinder rapid water infiltration (Ehlers,
1973).

Limited infiltration, surface runoff and soil erosion however are not observed on these soils, when intensive cultivation
is abandoned, and when crops are grown by use of the so called
zero-tillage method (Baeumer and Bakermans, 1973). Zero-tilled

soils have a lower porosity in the top layer (0-20 cm) as compared
to tilled soil, the aggregates are more stable and they are protected by a mulch cover. Also, the dense traffic pan (20-30 cm) is
loosened up by the activity of earthworms and plant roots in the
undisturbed soil (Ehlers, 1973, 1975a).

In order to find out about quantitative differences in the
moisture regime of tilled and untilled soils, a field experiment
was conducted in 1971 with different crops (wheat, beet, fallow)
(Ehlers 1975b,c; Ehlers and Van der Ploeg, 1975). The experimental
setup allowed the calculation of the soil moisture characteristic
and of the hydraulic conductivity function for different depths of
bare tilled and untilled soil (Ehlers and Van der Ploeg, 1975).

These data were taken for simulation of water infiltration
into tilled and untilled soil, on which we will report here. For
the simulation use is made of the unsaturated soil moisture flow
equation, which is solved numerically. The method which uses the
computer program CSMP, is described in Van der Ploeg (1974) and Van
der Ploeg and Benecke (1974). The approach is similar to the one
presented by Van Keulen and Van Beek (1971), who simulated water
movement in soils, layered by mechanical cultivation. But opposite
to the paper of Van Keulen and Van Beek, the hydraulic functions
needed for the simulation are actually derived from field measurements.

The aim of this investigation is to see, if with the aid of
the achieved hydraulic functions, infiltration processes in tilled
and untilled soil can be monitored comparable to results as they
have been measured in the field. Secondly, the simulation model is
used to elucidate the hindering effect of the traffic pan on rapid
water infiltration in tilled soil as it is often observed in the
field. For this purpose two hypothetical rainfall conditions will
be presented.

EXPERIMENTAL PROCEDURE

The experiment was conducted on a grey-brown podzolic soil
(hapludic Eutroboralf) derived from loess. The sequence of horizons
is sketched in Figure 1. The silty soil has a maximum clay content
of 27 weight percent ($<2 \mu$) in 60 cm depth ($B_{21(t)}$-horizon). The
composition of the A_{1p}-horizon is as follows: clay, 15 %; silt
(20-60 μ), 82 %; organic C, 1.3 %; pH, 6.7. The untilled plots had
been tilled for the last time in 1967.

The research site covered a nearly flat area of 0.1 ha, and
contained 6 plots (tilled-untilled, three crops). Mercury-type
tensiometers were installed in 10, 20, 30, 40, 60, 80, 100, 120,
150, and 180 cm depth, the first four having replicates. Tensions
higher than 0.8 atm were measured in the 10- and 30-cm depth with
osmotic tensiometers. Tensions were recorded daily, usually in the
morning hours. Soil samples for moisture determination were taken
with an auger down to 2 m depth twice a week, each sample in three
replicates. The gravimetric moisture content was converted to volumetric moisture content by bulk density values, which were determined from core samples. Core samples were also taken for the
determination of the moisture characteristic.

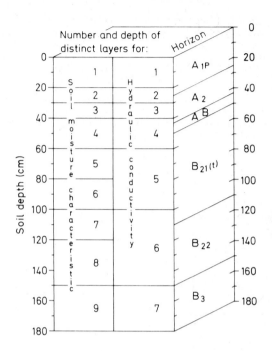

<u>Figure 1:</u> Sequence and depth of soil horizons
            and of layers as differentiated
            according to their hydraulic functions.

SIMULATION PROCEDURE

      To describe infiltration and redistribution, the unsatur-
ated moisture flow equation is used, which relates the volumetric
water content θ (cm3/cm3) in the soil to both time and space. For
one-dimensional vertical flow, the equation reads:

$$\partial\theta/\partial t = \partial(K\partial H/\partial z)/\partial z \tag{1}$$

in which t is time (days), K is the hydraulic conductivity (cm/day)
$\partial H/\partial z$ is the hydraulic gradient (cm/cm), and z is the depth (cm).
Equation (1) can be solved numerically with use of the computer
program CSMP (Continuous System Modeling Program). Details can be
found in Van der Ploeg (1974), Van der Ploeg and Benecke (1974) and
Van Keulen and Van Beek (1971). To do computational work with
equation (1), the hydraulic functions of the different layers of
either the tilled or the untilled soil have to be entered. Figure
1 shows number and depth of distinct layers, for which a soil
moisture characteristic and a hydraulic conductivity function were

assessed. These functions are calculated from data collected on
fallow plots.

As an example of these field-determined hydraulic functions
the moisture characteristics of the 20-30 cm layer of tilled and
untilled soil are presented in Figure 2. Two different sets of
curves are shown: one set of moisture characteristic curves is
determined in the laboratory, the other in the field (cp. experimental procedure). The laboratory desorption curve, which starts
from complete filling, is not used in the simulation, since it does
not reflect the moisture tension - moisture content relation under
field conditions. Therefore in the model, curves from field data
are used. Since only soil wetting periods are considered for the
simulation, hysteresis is not included.

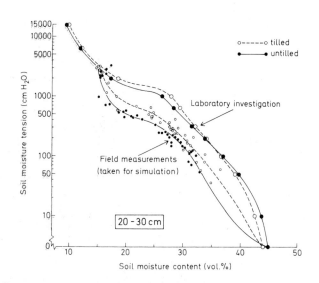

Figure 2: Field-determined and laboratory-determined
          soil moisture characteristics for the
          20-30 cm layer of tilled and untilled soil.

As another example, Figure 3 represents hydraulic conductivity functions, calculated for the 20-30 cm layer of tilled and
untilled soil. It may be noted, that in the tilled soil, which is
plowed every year, the conductivity is lower in the tension range
< 100 cm H_2O as compared to untilled soil. The reason for this
might well be that the vertical continuity of the larger pores in
the tilled soil is interrupted by the plowing (Ehlers, 1975a;
Ehlers and Van der Ploeg, 1975).

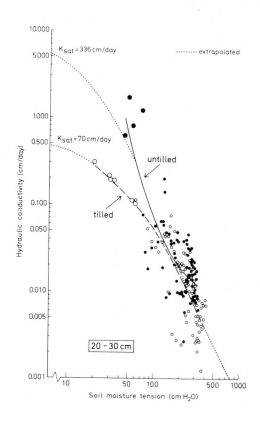

<u>Figure 3:</u> Unsaturated hydraulic conductivity as
related to moisture tension in the
20-30 cm layer of tilled and untilled
soil.

RESULTS AND DISCUSSION

        In Figure 4 simulation results for infiltration and redi-
stribution into tilled soil for either fallow or winter wheat are
presented. On June 9, during a heavy thunderstorm, a surface runoff
of 16 mm was assumed and subtracted from the total rainfall (59,4
mm). In the period free of rain, as indicated in the top of Figure
4, the evaporation and evapotranspiration rate was assessed as 2 mm
per day (Ehlers, 1975c). The simulation curves for moisture tension
in various depths may be compared with measured tensions, also
indicated in the figure. The agreement between theoretically derived
values and field observed tensions is good in the fallow soil and
reasonably good under winter wheat. On purpose a period with very

heavy rainfall was chosen in order to check the model under extreme conditions. Also, the amount of evaporation or evapotranspiration over the period is small as compared to the amount of precipitation.

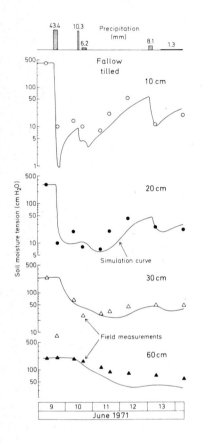

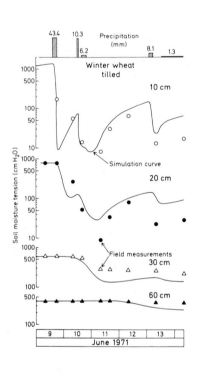

Figure 4: Simulated and field-measured tension values at various depths of the tilled fallow and wheat soil during a 5-day period.

On untilled soil (Figure 5) the agreement between theory and observations is not so good. In the upper soil depths simulated tensions drop too fast as compared to measured values, but in greater depths the opposite is true. Here the theoretically derived values remain high, although measurements indicate an instant reduction of the soil water tension. The reason is that due to a steady build-up of macrochannels by earthworms, part of the infiltrating water is entering the untilled soil as noncapillary water, since these channels are not destroyed by cultivation

practice (Ehlers, 1975a,b). The unsaturated soil moisture flow
equation does not account for the noncapillary infiltration.

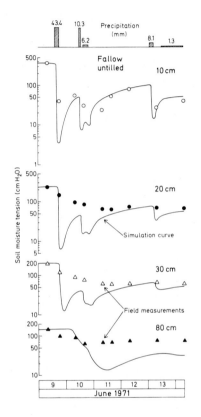
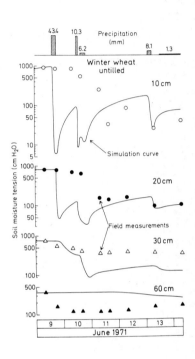

Figure 5: Simulated and field-measured tension
          values at various depths of the untilled
          fallow and wheat soil during a 5-day period.

        To demonstrate the difference in hydraulic behavior between
tilled and untilled soils, a number of hypothetical conditions were
simulated. Only capillary moisture flow will be considered. Figure
6 (top) presents profiles of moisture content, moisture tension and
hydraulic gradient in tilled and untilled fallow at various times
during a 20-days rain period with 2.4 mm per day. The tension profile as measured on June 9 was taken as initial condition. The graph
also includes the profile of total porosity, showing the presence
of the traffic pan in the tilled soil. Even after 20 days of rainfall with a cumulative infiltration of 48 mm, differences between
tillage treatments are negligible. Nevertheless the higher gradients in the top layers of tilled soil as compared to untilled
soil may be noticed. Furthermore the figure demonstrates an increase

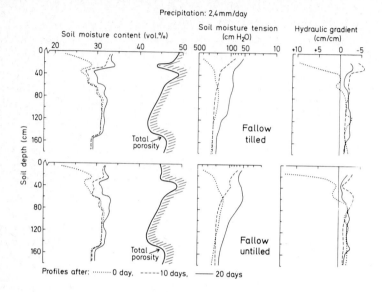

Precipitation: 2,4 mm/day

Profiles after: ········ 0 day, -----10 days, ——— 20 days

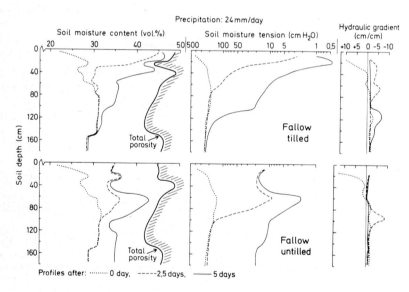

Precipitation: 24 mm/day

Profiles after: ········ 0 day, -----2,5 days, ——— 5 days

Figure 6: Simulated profiles of moisture content, moisture tension and hydraulic gradient in tilled and untilled fallow soil at different times during infiltration at low (2.4 mm/day) and high (24 mm/day) rain intensity. The total porosity profile is also shown.

of gradients within the $B_{21(t)}$- and B_{22}-horizon (50-150 cm depth) after 20 days, demonstrating the lower hydraulic conductivity of these horizons as compared to the A- and B_3-horizons.

When the hypothetical rain intensity is raised to 24 mm per day, differences between tillage treatments become more pronounced (Figure 6, bottom). In the top layers of tilled soil water contents are more increased and tensions are more reduced as compared to the untilled treatment. Hydraulic gradients indicate that after 5 days of rain with a cumulative infiltration of 120 mm, the wetting front of infiltration has reached a depth of 110 cm in the tilled soil, whereas in untilled soil the front has already left the profile because of a more rapid water penetration.

The computed water fluxes at various depths in tilled and untilled fallow at high rain intensities are shown in Figure 7. During the first days fluxes in tilled soil are always lower than fluxes in untilled soil at the same depth. The lag of time for the fluxes in tilled and untilled soil to become equal at a particular depth increases with depth.

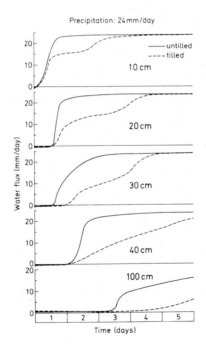

Figure 7: The water flux at different depths in tilled and untilled fallow soil during simulated infiltration at high rain intensities. Negative fluxes in 10 to 40 cm depth at begin of simulation indicate flux in upward direction.

The noted differences in flux and the hightened water storage in the top layers of tilled soil (Figure 6, bottom) are the result of the different hydraulic functions, induced by soil management practices. Because of only small differences in the slopes of the soil moisture retention curves (Figure 2) the main effect will be due to the differences in the hydraulic conductivity functions. These functions indicate smaller K-values of tilled soil not only in the 20-30 cm layer (Figure 3) but also in the 10-20 and 30-40 cm layer within the low tension range <100 cm H_2O (Ehlers and Van der Ploeg, 1975).

As a consequence of the high flux values in untilled soil the tensions are lower in the $B_{21(t)}$-horizon as compared to the tilled soil within the observation period of 5 days (Figure 6, bottom). In untilled soil the tensions of the $B_{21(t)}$-horizon are even lower than the tensions of the A_{1p}-horizon, expressing again the low conductivity of this B-horizon.

CONCLUSIONS

While infiltration is not markedly influenced by a traffic pan at low rain intensities, the striking effect of the pan can be demonstrated by simulation of higher rain intensities (Figure 6). Tensions become more reduced, and water contents are substantially increased in the top layers of tilled soil as compared to untilled soil, where a plow pan is not existent. The high degree of water saturation will facilitate the slaking of aggregates at the soil surface and hence will enhance the danger of surface runoff and soil erosion. During rainy periods aeration problems may arise on tilled soils, which were surmised in respect of the water uptake ability of wheat roots, growing in conventionally tilled plots (Ehlers, 1975c). Furthermore it may be deduced that the traffic-ability of the tilled soil becomes more reduced as compared to untilled soil. Field evidence on this is presented by Baeumer and Pape (1972), who reported on a field experiment with sugarbeet during a wet fall period.

Regarding the forementioned negative effects of a traffic pan one may consider, if on silty soils intense cultivation should be undertaken year after year. The no-tillage system, which complete-ly abandons mechanical cultivation, is not always practicable mainly because of the resistance of many perennial weeds to herbi-cides. And herbicide application is the only way of weed control, when mechanical means are out of question. Therefore persisting in the conventional tillage system one may conclude, that intense tillage should be restricted to periods when the soils have dried and are not susceptible to pan formation.

Within the common crop rotation with sugarbeet, winter wheat and winter barley favourable soil conditions for tillage will usually be met after the harvest of the cereals and not of the sugarbeet.

REFERENCES

Baeumer, K., and Bakermans, W.A.P. (1973). Zero-tillage. Advance. Agron. 25: 77-123.
Baeumer, K., and Pape, G. (1972). Ergebnisse und Aussichten des Anbaus von Zuckerrüben im Ackerbausystem ohne Bodenbearbei-tung. Zucker 25: 711-718.
Ehlers, W. (1973). Strukturzustand und zeitliche Änderung der

Wasser- und Luftgehalte während einer Vegetationsperiode
in unbearbeiteter und bearbeiteter Löß-Parabraunerde.
Z. Acker- und Pflanzenbau 137: 213-232.
Ehlers, W. (1975a). Observations on earthworm channels and infiltration on tilled and untilled loess soil. Soil Sci. 119:
242-249.
Ehlers, W. (1975b). Water regime in tilled and untilled loess soil:
I. Infiltration and redistribution. (submitted for publication, preprints available).
Ehlers, W. (1975c). Water regime in tilled and untilled loess soil:
III. Evapotranspiration and drainage in fields with winter
wheat and sugarbeet (submitted for publication, preprints
available).
Ehlers, W., and Van der Ploeg, R.R. Water regime in tilled and
untilled loess soil: II. Evaporation, drainage and unsaturated hydraulic conductivity of fallow soil. (submitted for
publication, preprints available).
Van der Ploeg, R.R. (1974). Simulation of moisture transfer in
soils: one-dimensional infiltration. Soil Sci. 118:349-357.
Van der Ploeg, R.R., and Benecke, P. (1974). Unsteady, unsaturated,
n-dimensional moisture flow in soil: a computer simulation
program. Soil Sci.Soc.Amer.Proc. 38: 881-885.
Van Keulen, H., and Van Beek, C.G.E.M. (1971). Water movement in
layered soils - a simulation model. Neth.J.Agric.Sci.19:
138-153.

DISCUSSION

Did you consider two different layers of the same soil ? The surface layer as uniform and the bottom layer also uniform ? Did you model the soil as lumped between the two layers, or have you assumed that there is a gradual change of the soil characteristics from the surface to the bottom ? (VACHAUD)

We have considered two different soils ; a tilled layered loess soil and an untilled layered loess soil. For each soil we used nine different soil moisture characteristics and seven hydraulic conductivity functions to model the infiltra-tion and the redistribution. The function were determined in the field and for the tilled and the untilled soil different functions were determined, and accord-ingly different functions were used in the models. (VAN DER PLOEG)

How did you determine the volumetric water content in the upper layer of the tilled soil ? (VACHAUD)

Moist samples of field soil of known volume were taken to the laboratory for this purpose. The mass of this known volume was determined after the sample had been dried to a constant weight at 105°C. The bulk density of the soil sample then can be determined. The volumetric moisture content of the soil sample then is obtained by multiplying the moisture content by weight with the bulk density value. (VAN DER PLOEG)

This might not be so easy, because the soil is not very cohesive after it has been ploughed. Already by taking samples from the field to the laboratory there is a chance that the density is changing. (VACHAUD)

Indeed this is a problem. In a previous publication Dr. Ehlers (Zeit-schrift fuer Pflanzenernaehrung und Bodenkunde, 1973 : 134, pp 193 - 207) has dis-cussed this problem and he has explained how he has handled it. (VAN DER PLOEG)

After considering the upper curves in your Figure 5 concerning the untilled soil, I do not understand why the tensiometers in the upper layers respond so slowly after the heavy rainstorm. (LOMEN)

We assume (and Dr. Ehlers has demonstrated it) that during the heavy rain-storm part of the infiltrating water is entering the soil through earthworm chan-nels and rootholes as noncapillary water. For these untilled loess soils the un-saturated moisture flow equation only partially may be used to describe the infil-tration. (VAN DER PLOEG)

As check for your model you use actual tensiometer values as obtained in the field. The model gives you a continuous soil suctiontime relation for every desired depth, but you have only a very limited amount of actual observations. Do you not have the feeling that you should have made more observations, and that you may have failed to register short-term fluctuations in the course of the soil suction, especially for the shallow soil depth. (VACHAUD)

For the shallow depths, say down to 20 cm, this may be the case. At present we are developing selfrecording tensiometers, so that in the future we can also record these daily fluctuations. (VAN DER PLOEG)

System Simulation in Water Resources, ed. G.C. VANSTEENKISTE
1976, North-Holland Publishing Company

TIME-DEPENDENT LINEARIZED MOISTURE FLOW SOLUTIONS FOR SURFACE SOURCES[1]

D.O. Lomen and A.W. Warrick
Departments of Mathematics and Soils, Water and Engineering
The University of Arizona
Tucson, Arizona U.S.A.

The increasing use of trickle and high-frequency irrigation, frequently with water of high salt content or sewage effluent, has intensified interest in obtaining wetting patterns from various types of surface sources. Questions arise as to the extent and time histories of wetting patterns when determining irrigation scheduling. Since most of the water movement in soil under trickle irrigation occurs in the unsaturated phase, we consider the following model.

The moisture flow equation for unsaturated soil is taken in the form

$$\partial\theta/\partial t = \nabla \cdot (K\nabla h) - \partial K/\partial z \qquad [1]$$

with θ the volumetric water content, t time, K the unsaturated hydraulic conductivity, "∇" the vector gradient operator, h the pressure head and z the depth with positive values in the downward direction. Use of the matric flux potential defined by Gardner (1958)

$$\phi = \int_{-\infty}^{h} K(h)dh, \quad K = K_0 \exp(\alpha h) \qquad [2]$$

and the assumption

$$d\theta/d\phi = \alpha/k, \quad k = dK/d\theta \qquad [3]$$

where k is a constant, give the linear differential equation

$$\partial\phi/\partial t = (k/\alpha)\nabla^2\phi - k(\partial\phi/\partial z) \qquad [4]$$

In general, the conductivity function K is not linearly related to θ; however if the moisture content varies over a limited range, the assumption is more realistic. In evaluating the acceptability of the assumptions, it is important

[1] Arizona Agricultural Experiment Station Paper No. 151. Support was through the Western Regional Project W-128 and Office of Water Resources Research, Department of Interior Project B-035-AZ.

to remember that there is a natural uncertainty in the input parameters due to spatial variability and to experimental error. Major advantages to be gained by the linearized solutions are numerical accuracy and convenience. Computational times are negligible compared to finite difference or finite element solutions. For the steady state case the left hand side of [4] is zero. Philip (1971) and Raats (1972) have given solutions for steady point and line sources on the soil surface.

Table 1 contains analytical solutions of [4] for point, line, strip, disc and ring sources. These solutions are for a "step input", that is, flow begins at a steady rate q at time t = 0 and are in terms of the dimensionless coordinates X, R, Z and T defined by

$$X = \alpha x/2, \quad Z = \alpha z/2, \quad R = \alpha r/2, \quad T = \alpha kt/4 \qquad [5]$$

The dimensionless Φ is given in terms of ϕ for each source in Table 1. In each case, a zero initial condition was assumed, i.e., $\Phi = 0$ for T = 0, and Φ was required to vanish at large distances away from the source. The boundary

Table 1. Linearized solutions for six types of surface sources.

Type and Location	Dimensionless Φ	Φ_B	Solution for a Step Input
Point (R = Z = 0)	$8\pi\phi/(\alpha q)$ (q is volume emitted per unit time)	$\dfrac{e^Z}{2\rho}\left\{e^{\rho}\,\mathrm{erfc}\!\left[\dfrac{\rho}{2\sqrt{T}}+\sqrt{T}\right]+e^{-\rho}\mathrm{erfc}\!\left[\dfrac{\rho}{2\sqrt{T}}-\sqrt{T}\right]\right\},\ \rho^2=R^2+Z^2$	$2\{\Phi_B - e^{2Z}\displaystyle\int_Z^{\infty} e^{-2Z'}[\Phi_B]_{Z=Z'}\,dZ'\}$
Line (Z = 0, X = 0, along Y-axis)	$2\pi\phi/q$ (q is volume emitted per unit time per unit length)	$\dfrac{e^Z}{2}\displaystyle\int_0^T \xi^{-1}\exp[-\xi-(X^2+Z^2)/4\xi]d\xi$	$2\{\Phi_B - \sqrt{\pi}\,e^{2Z}\displaystyle\int_0^{\sqrt{T}}\mathrm{erfc}[\xi+Z/2\xi]\exp[-X^2/4\xi]d\xi\}$
Strip (Z = 0, $-X_o \le X \le X_o$, along Y-axis)	$2\pi\phi/q$ (q is volume emitted per unit time per unit length)	$\dfrac{\sqrt{\pi}}{4X_o}e^Z\displaystyle\int_0^T \xi^{-1/2}\exp[-\xi-z^2/4\xi]\left[\mathrm{erf}\!\left(\dfrac{X+X_o}{2\sqrt{\xi}}\right)-\mathrm{erf}\!\left(\dfrac{X-X_o}{2\sqrt{\xi}}\right)\right]d\xi$	$2\left\{\Phi_B - \dfrac{\pi e}{2X_o}^{2Z}\displaystyle\int_0^{\sqrt{T}}\mathrm{erfc}[\xi+Z/2\xi]\left[\mathrm{erf}\!\left(\dfrac{X+X_o}{2\xi}\right)\right.\right.$ $\left.\left. -\,\mathrm{erf}\!\left(\dfrac{X-X_o}{2\xi}\right)\right]\xi\,d\xi\right\}$
Disc (Z = 0, $0 \le R \le R_o$)	$8\pi\phi/(\alpha q)$ (q is volume emitted per unit time)	$\dfrac{e^Z}{R_o}\displaystyle\int_0^{\infty}\dfrac{J_o(\xi R)J_1(\xi R_o)}{\sqrt{1+\xi^2}}\left[e^{-Z\sqrt{1+\xi^2}}\mathrm{erfc}[Z/2\sqrt{T}-\sqrt{T(1+\xi^2)}\,]\right.$ $\left. -\,e^{Z\sqrt{1+\xi^2}}\mathrm{erfc}[Z/2\sqrt{T}+\sqrt{T(1+\xi^2)}]\right]d\xi$	$2\{\Phi_B - e^{2Z}\displaystyle\int_Z^{\infty} e^{-2Z'}[\Phi_B]_{Z=Z'}\,dZ'\}$
Ring (Z = 0, R = R_o)	$2\pi\phi/q$ (q is volume emitted per unit time per unit length)	$\dfrac{e^Z}{4\sqrt{\pi}}\displaystyle\int_0^T \xi^{-3/2}I_o(RR_o/2\xi)\exp[-\xi-(R^2+R_o^2+Z^2)/4\xi]d\xi$	$2\{\Phi_B - \pi R_o e^{2Z}\displaystyle\int_0^{\sqrt{T}}\xi^{-1}I_o(RR_o/2\xi^2)\cdot$ $\cdot\exp[-(R^2+R_o^2)/4\xi^2]\mathrm{erfc}(\xi+Z/2\xi)d\xi\}$
Ring of Finite Width (Z = 0, $R_i \le R \le R_o$)	$2\pi\phi/q$ (q is volume emitted per unit time per unit length)	$\dfrac{e^Z}{\sqrt{\pi}(R_i^2-R_o^2)}\displaystyle\int_0^T \xi^{-3/2}\exp[-\xi-(R^2+Z^2)/4\xi]\cdot$ $\cdot\displaystyle\int_{R_i}^{R_o}\exp(-\eta^2/4\xi)\,I_o(R\eta/2\xi)\eta\,d\eta\,d\xi$	$2\{\Phi_B - \dfrac{\pi e}{2}^{2Z}\displaystyle\int_0^{\sqrt{T}}\xi^{-1}\exp(-R^2/4\xi^2)\mathrm{erfc}(\xi+Z/2\xi)\cdot$ $\cdot\displaystyle\int_{R_i}^{R_o}\exp[-\eta^2/4\xi^2]\,I_o(R\eta/2\xi^2)\eta\,d\eta\,d\xi\}$

Figure 1. Matric flux potential for a
point source (small times).

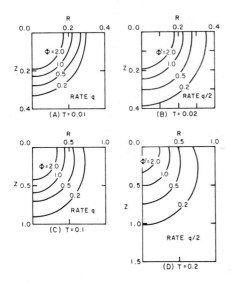

Figure 2. Matric flux potential for a
point source (large times).

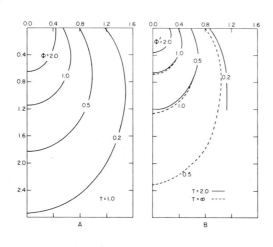

condition at the surface was that of
no vertical flow (except at the
source). The "buried" solution, Φ_B,
in each case is the solution of [4]
for an infinite space. For the
detailed derivations see Warrick
(1974a), Lomen and Warrick (1974)
and Warrick and Lomen (1974, 1975).

NUMERICAL RESULTS

In order to compare moisture
regimes for two flow rates from a
point source, lines of constant ϕ
are presented in Figure 1. The flow
rate in plots A and C is q, in plots
B and D is q/2. The times are chosen
such that the same amount of water
has been added in A as in B and C as
in D. The value of Φ' was taken as
$\Phi/2$. Thus, by [2] and Table 1, the
values of lines labeled 2, 1, 0.5
and 0.2 can be compared directly with each value corresponding to a constant pressure
head value.

To demonstrate the utility
of the linear solutions for a
time-varying source, we consider input of the form

$$q = q_0, \qquad 0 < T < T_1$$
$$= q_1, \qquad T_1 < T < T_2$$
$$\cdot$$
$$\cdot \qquad\qquad\qquad\qquad [6]$$
$$\cdot$$
$$= q_n, \qquad T_n < T$$

As [4] is a linear differential equation in ϕ, and is homogenous along with the
initial and boundary conditions, we can superimpose solutions corresponding to
different source strengths. From Table 1, we find for a point source

$$\begin{aligned}
\phi(R,Z,T) &= \alpha q_0/(8\pi) \cdot \Phi(R,Z,T), && 0 < T < T_1 \\
&= \alpha q_0/(8\pi) \cdot \Phi(R,Z,T) + \alpha(q_1-q_0)/(8\pi) \cdot \Phi(R,Z,T-T_1), && T_1 < T < T_2 \\
&\;\;\vdots \\
&= \alpha/(8\pi) \cdot \sum_{i=0}^{n} (q_i-q_{i-1})\Phi(R,Z,T-T_i), && T_0 = 0, \; q_{-1} = 0, \; T_n < T
\end{aligned}$$

$$[7]$$

Eq. [7] was used to simulate a "12 hour on--12 hour off" irrigation cycle. The input rate during the "on" half of the cycle was 2 liters/hr. Values of α, K_0 and k were taken as 0.04 cm^{-1}, 95 cm/day and 150 cm/day, respectively. Figures 3A and 3B show the pressure head distribution at the end of the wet and dry part of the cycle, respectively. At the end of the wet part of the cycle, the upper left-hand corner is at a pressure head greater than h = -46 cm. The region is roughly a quarter-ellipse extending 10 cm laterally and 15 cm deep. The driest part shown in Figure 3A is adjacent to the surface in the upper-right hand corner for which h is less than -121 cm. At the end of the "dry" part of the cycle (Figure 3B) the wettest portion is approximately spherical at a depth between 16 and 38 cm with h between -93 and 69 cm. For the outer edges of the plot (r = 50 cm and z = 50 cm), the pressure head is nearly the same in both 3A and 3B. Thus, fluctuations are damped with a constant moisture status obtained for large values of r and z.

Figure 3. Pressure head distributions for 12-hour on--12-hour off emissions from a point source.

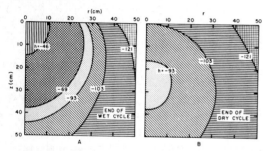

Figure 4. Matric flux potential for a surface line source.

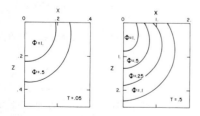

The solution of [4] for a surface line source along the y-axis is given on the second line of Table 1. Figure 4 shows equipotentials for T = .05 and T = .5. For many irrigation applications, the actual wetted surface area due to closely spaced emitters is that of a wetted strip of finite width. Assume the flux is uniform over strip $-X_0 \leq X \leq X_0$ and is infinite in extent along the y-axis. The solution for this configuration is given by line 3 of Table 1 and is presented in Figure 5.

Figure 5. Matric flux potential
for a surface strip source,
$-X_0 \leq X \leq X_0$.

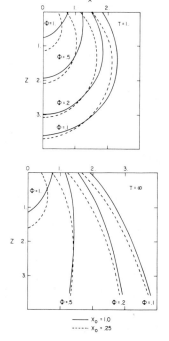

The strip sources have semi widths
X_0 = .25 and 1. As is to be expected, the
curves for the wider strip wet a shallower
and wider area for small times. These differences diminish with increasing depth.

For either the line or the strip source,
we can consider the effect of parallel
sources in the following manner. Consider
sources parallel to the y-axis and located
2L units apart, at X = 2jL, j = 0, ± 1,± 2...
Because we have a linear problem we may use
superposition to write the solution for an
infinite number of parallel surface sources
as

$$\sum_{j=-\infty}^{\infty} \Phi(X - 2jL,Z,T) \qquad [8]$$

where Φ is given by either line 2 (line) or
line 3 (strip) of Table 1. Figures 6A and
6B illustrate the use of [8] for an infinite
number of parallel lines (X_0 = 0) and parallel strips of width 0.5. Figure 6A is for
T = .1 while 6B is the limiting value as
$T \to \infty$. The centers of the lines and strips
are $2/\alpha$ units apart. The resulting wetting
patterns are symmetric about X = 0 and X = .5 so only the region $0 \leq X \leq .5$ is

Figure 6. Matric flux potential for an infinite
number of surface line and strip sources ($2/\alpha$
units apart).

shown. The wetting pattern
near X = 0 is essentially
unaffected by the presence of
the other sources, while
along X = .5 the soil is
much wetter, especially as
time increases.

Figure 7 compares the
solution for a disc of radius
R_0 = 1 with a point source.
The differences near the surface are considerable due to
the larger wetting area of the

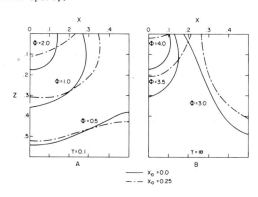

Figure 7. Matric flux potential
for a surface disc source
$0 \leq R \leq R_o$.

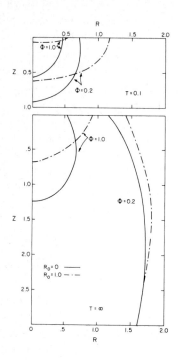

disc and continue for larger times. The
wetting pattern for the disc is shallower
than for the point, but these differences
vanish for large depths.

CONCLUSIONS

Table 1 presents analytical solutions
of [4] for six point source configurations.
An advantage of using the linear model is
that any combination of the solutions may
be added together to obtain the solution of
the resulting configuration. Two examples
of this were presented here in using [8] for
multiple line and strip sources. The analysis presented here assumes no plant-water
withdrawal. This has been done for the
one-dimensional, steady-state case (Warrick,
1974b) and Lomen and Warrick (1975) and
is currently being incorporated into a
two-dimensional model.

Another useful application of the
linear solutions is to serve as a check
for computer solutions of the nonlinear equations. Ben-Asher et al. (1975) has
compared a finite difference solution of [1] by Brandt et al. (1971) with the
linear solution given in Table 1 for a point source. For large times the two
methods give identical solutions. The degree of comparison at other times
depends on the depth and the other parameters.

REFERENCES

Ben-Asher, J., D.O. Lomen and A.W. Warrick. (1975) A comparison of linear and
        nonlinear solutions for time varying point and line water sources.
        Presented at the Amer. Soc. of Agron.; Agron. Abst. p. 114.

Brandt, A., E. Bresler, N. Diner, J. Ben-Asher, J. Heller and D. Goldberg. (1971)
        Infiltration from a trickle source: I. Mathematical models. Soil Sci.
        Soc. Amer. Proc. 35:675-682.

Gardner, W.R. (1958) Some steady-state solutions of the unsaturated moisture-flow equation with application to evaporation from a water table. Soil Sci. 85:228-232.

Lomen, D.O. and A.W. Warrick. (1974) Time-dependent linearized infiltration. II. Line sources. Soil Sci. Soc. Amer. Proc. 38:568-572.

Lomen, D.O. and A.W. Warrick. (1975) Solution of the one-dimensional linear moisture flow equation with implicit water extraction functions. (Submitted to Proc. Soil Sci. Soc. of Amer.).

Philip, J.R. (1971) General theorem on steady infiltration from surface sources, with application to point and line sources. Soil Sci. Soc. Amer. Proc. 35:867-871.

Raats, P.A.C. (1972) Steady infiltration from sources at arbitrary depth. Soil Sci. Soc. Amer. Proc. 36:399-401.

Warrick, A.W. (1974a) Time-dependent linearized infiltration. I. Point sources. Soil Sci. Soc. Amer. Proc. 38:383-386.

Warrick, A.W. (1974b) Solution to the one-dimensional linear moisture flow equation with water extraction. Soil Sci. Amer. Proc. 38:573-576.

Warrick, A.W. and D.O. Lomen. (1974) Linearized moisture flow solutions for point, line and strip sources. Proc. 2nd International Drip Irrigation Congress, pp. 228-233.

Warrick, A.W., and D.O. Lomen. (1975) Time-dependent linearized infiltration. III. Strip and disc sources. (Submitted to Proc., Soil Sci. Soc. of Amer.)

DISCUSSION

I would like to ask you about the ratio in computation times of 100 - 200. Are you telling about the specific program developped by Ben-Asher ? (NEUMAN)

Yes. (LOMEN)

The problem with that kind of equations is : is the computer program efficient ? I always liked a more efficient computer program for it. (NEUMAN)

Dr. Vachaud showed me some examples of differences between explicit and implicit schemes, and this has reached about 1 to 10. (LOMEN)

When we are working on mixed implicit - explicit schemes, it turns out that you can reduce the computer time in 2 and 3-dimensional problems, by really drastic amounts, from both explicit and implicit schemes. (NEUMAN)

Actually, the best use of these solutions would be to check out very complicated finite difference, finite element techniques as in fact I was showing here. You can stick in your linearizing assumptions or every assumption you need for the analytic solution in your numerical scheme, and have an excellent way of checking, because the chances of an error occuring here are very small. (LOMEN)

I think that another good point about your analytical solution is that analytical solutions are necessary to check finite differences finite elements programs. Number two is that you can generalize much more with an analytical solution. (NEUMAN)

Look at that curve : there is a function K which gives these curves. So you have an idea of what this particular K is there. We look at what the effects are and the parameters are much easier to obtain. (LOMEN)

I agree with you the great value of the analytical solution you put forward, but I don't think that we should overlook the limitations of this model. The hydrologic conductivity close to saturation is a tremendously important thing. You handled it as the most important part of the whole rank of conductivity. The whole thing is, whenever you are looking at real soils, you get away from this uniformity. In your example I think you had strip sources of a couple of centimeters, and depths of only a few centimeters. That may be far enough in some deep sands in some areas, but in many other you have to consider only a few tenths of centimeters to have drastic changes in soil particles. (PECK)

In Israël they found following results : if you look at what the scale is, there is a certain property of the soil for which I should be going, down a certain distance. We assume it to be uniform. So when you look at the finite difference scheme, that is actually computing the moisture content as you are going down. That actually computes the conductivity and diffusivity and then makes a prediction. It tries to follow the events, whereas the linearized solution does come very nicely along.
Real soils, are not very homogeneous, and we have here a homogeneous soil. All I'm saying is that we should be make some agreement. But I have disregarded the saturated zone in Arizona, as we are really down in the unsaturated area, while for most people in the world, that is not true. (LOMEN)

It is very helpful to get an analytical solution, because you can test your model, but you have also to be careful about the assumptions, which have been made for this intention. I don't think that the assumption that K varies exponentially with the suction from saturation is a valuable assumption for soil physics, because you always have a capillary friction and this is an important assumption. I wonder about the applicability, and I think your model is very good for testing, but with this assumption I should be careful in applying it to practice.   (VACHAUD)

In the last weeks we did some calculations without going into much detail. For start I rounded off the moisture characteristic in the wet end to the nearest centimeter, and I got results which looked a little curious, and I thought maybe I should take it a bit more accurate. When I took it to three digits - this is the potential when you reach a certain moisture around 5 to 25 cm - and to take 3 digits made an enormous difference.
In other words, rounding off to the nearest cm would have a very big effect on the behaviour.
It is remarkably sensitive in that way of the conductivity-potential relations.
(PECK)

I thought that your method could handle irregular soil geometrics.
(TAVARES)

I said complex, not irregular. For example for a particular irrigation, point sources around a tree, or a line irrigation with additional configurations here and there. There you can use superposition, but not for irregular geometrics.
(LOMEN)

Could you handle hill-sides, where you have a slope ?   (TAVARES)

No, these solutions only apply to infiltration from level surfaces.
(LOMEN)

System Simulation in Water Resources, ed. *G.C. VANSTEENKISTE*
1976, North-Holland Publishing Company

THE USE OF A HYBRID SIMULATION SYSTEM IN THE STUDY
OF SOIL IRRIGATION PROBLEMS

by

Bernard CAUSSADE

Institut de Mécanique des Fluides - Laboratoire associé au C.N.R.S.

2, rue Charles Camichel   31071   TOULOUSE CEDEX - FRANCE

and

Guy RENARD

Laboratoire d'Informatique pour la Mécanique

et les Sciences de l'Ingénieur du C.N.R.S.

B.P n° 30   91406   ORSAY - FRANCE

ABSTRACT

        Water transfers in a soil from the surface can be correctly described
by one equation based on the physics of flow in unsaturated porous media. It is
our purpose to present here a hybrid solution of this equation, which will be
applied to two processes : firstly non-stationary irrigation of a soil by means
of a continuous uniform watering and secondly to find a cyclic uniform watering
for impound a constant moisture soil at a given depth.

        Standard numerical approximation methods, analogical methods and
sophisticated simulation languages like, Continuous System Modeling Program
(CSMP), developed by IBM for its 360 and 370 series of machines, are today the
tools of research workers and engineers for solving these kinds of problems.

        Numerical methods generally permit a non linearities relatively easy
comput, but they require often expensive times and costs of compute. Analogical
methods, and chiefly, for some years, hybrid methods, are well adapted to study
these problems. But the major inconvenience of all these methods is to discreti-
sate the time and that involves constraints on the time step choice.

        These considerations have lead us to focus a new hybrid method based
on the connection of a digital computer with a resistance-capacitance network.
The network evolves during a space of time, its state is read, then the digital
computer computs the state which we should have obtained if the capacitances had
been evolved proportionaly to the non linearity. This state is taken into account
as the initial conditions of the next space time, and so on.

179

The advantages of this method are extremely accurate results and a very fast
compute velocity.
This hybrid method is applied to irrigation problems in homogeneous soils.
In a first case, the irrigation is considered uniform at the soil surface
(rain or watering) the limit condition at the surface is therefore a step or
a square wave and it's now possible to consider the moisture soil evolution in
a one-dimensional semi-infinite domain. We neglect hysteresis phenomenum but
it should be easy to take it into account.

In a second case, by means of these results we show how it's possible
to find a cyclic uniform watering for impound a constant percentage of water
at a given depth. An example shows the interest of this experimental parameter
optimization.

From the foregoing it is concluded that hybrid simulation is a strong
tool in the prediction of the behaviour of soil moisture under varying conditions.

BASIC FORMULATION OF WATER TRANSFERS IN UNSATURATED SOILS

This equation is based on Darcy's law and mass conservation of water.
In the unsaturated domain, it is known that Darcy's law is still generally valid,
but in the form :

$$V = - K \text{ grad } (h - z) \tag{1}$$

> h : the water pressure
> H = h-z : the hydraulic potential
> V : the Darcian velocity
> K : the hydraulic conductivity

The mass conservation law is :

$$\text{div } V = - \frac{\partial \theta}{\partial t} \tag{2}$$

where θ is the water content (volume of water/volume of soil)
if Φ is the Kirchhoff's potential defined by :

$$\Phi = \int_{-\infty}^{h} K(h) \, dh \tag{3}$$

and if K is given by :

$$K = K_o \cdot e^{\alpha h} \qquad \text{(Gardner)} \tag{4}$$

(α is a coefficient which depends on soil's nature)

and θ by :

$$\frac{K}{K_o} = (\theta/\theta_o)^3 \qquad \text{(Childs and Collis Georges)} \qquad (5)$$

combining these equations and if the boundary conditions are known, we are able to describe the transfer of water in the entire damain by an unique equation, written in two-dimensional plane flow case :

$$\frac{\partial^2 \phi}{\partial x^2} + \frac{\partial^2 \phi}{\partial y^2} - \alpha L \frac{\partial \phi}{\partial y} = \frac{\alpha L}{\phi^{2/3}} \frac{\partial \phi}{\partial \tau} \qquad (6)$$

THE HYBRID METHOD

Firstly consider the non linear diffusion equation :

$$\text{div } (b(\phi) \text{ grad } \phi) = a (\phi) \frac{\partial \phi}{\partial t} \qquad (7)$$

If we supposed that it's possible to apply it the Kirchhoff's transformation :

$$b (\phi) \cdot d\phi = d\Phi$$

equation (7) can be written :

$$\Delta \Phi = g(\Phi) \frac{\partial \Phi}{\partial t} \qquad (8)$$

where g is a function which depends on Φ and space coordinates.

We proposed a method based on the connection of a digital computer with a resistance-capacitance network. These two computers (the analog computer and the digital computer) are working successively. The network evolves during a space of time, its state is read, then the digital computer computs the state which we should have obtained if the capacitances has been evolved proportionaly to g (Φ). This state is taken into account as the initial conditions of the next time step.

Φ is the solution of (8)

Φ' the RC network reply

$\bar{\Delta}$ the operator of second derivatives for a node of the discretized field

λ the ratio between the real time and the time variable in the network

We can write :

$$\bar{\Delta}\Phi = h^2 g(\Phi) \frac{d\Phi}{dt} \qquad \text{for the discretized problem} \qquad (9)$$

$$\bar{\Delta}\Phi' = \lambda \cdot RC \frac{d\Phi'}{dt} \qquad \text{for the RC network} \qquad (10)$$

We considered the lapse of time : $(t, t+\delta t)$. At time t the capacitances are loaded at the known problem solution Φn : $\Phi' n = \Phi n$. At time $t+\delta t$ the network reply is $\Phi' n+1$, the question is : what is the solution $\Phi n+1$?

ε is the difference between Φ' and Φ with the equations (9) and (10) we obtained for all instants of the laps of time :

$$\lambda RC.d\Phi' = \bar{\Delta}\varepsilon dt + h^2 g (\Phi)d\Phi \qquad (11)$$

The integration of (11) between t and $t+\delta t$ gives :

$$\lambda RC(\Phi'_{n+1} - \Phi_n) = h^2 \left[G(\Phi'_{n+1} - \varepsilon_{n+1}) - G(\Phi_n) \right] + \int_t^{t+\delta t} \Delta\varepsilon \, dt \qquad (12)$$

with the follower approximation :

$$\int_t^{t+\delta t} \bar{\Delta}\varepsilon dt \simeq \frac{1}{2} \cdot \bar{\Delta}\varepsilon_{n+1} \delta t$$

it's possible to compute ε_{n+1} therefore Φ_{n+1} from equation (12) by means of an iterative "relaxation process" :

$$\overset{k+1}{\varepsilon}_{n+1} = \overset{k}{\varepsilon}_{n+1} + \omega. (\overset{k}{\varepsilon}_{n+1})$$

where ω is a coefficient of convergence and k the number of iteration.

We also show the possibility to take into account by this method more general equations involving terms of the form : $\frac{\partial\Phi}{\partial x}$ or $\frac{\partial\Phi}{\partial y}$

Consider this equation :

$$\Delta\Phi = g(\Phi)\frac{\partial\Phi}{\partial t} + f(\Phi)\frac{\partial\Phi}{\partial x} \tag{13}$$

Here we can also write :

$$\Sigma(\Phi_i - \Phi) = \bar{\Delta}\Phi = h^2 g(\Phi)\frac{d\Phi}{dt} + h^2 f(\Phi)\frac{d\Phi}{dx} \quad \text{for the discretized problem} \tag{14}$$

$$\Sigma(\Phi_i' - \Phi') = \bar{\Delta}\Phi' = \lambda RC\frac{d\Phi'}{dt} \qquad\qquad \text{for the RC network} \tag{15}$$

for a node i at all instants of the lapse of time we obtained :

$$\lambda RCd\Phi' = \bar{\Delta}\epsilon dt + h^2 g(\Phi_i)d\Phi + \frac{h}{2}.f(\Phi_i)(\Phi_{i+1} - \Phi_{i-1})dt \tag{16}$$

The integration of (16) between t and t+δt gives :

$$\lambda RC(\Phi'_{i,n+1} - \Phi_{i,n}) = h^2 \left[G(\Phi'_{i,n+1} - \epsilon_{i,n+1}) - G(\Phi'_{i,n}) \right]$$

$$+ \int_t^{t+\delta t} \bar{\Delta}\epsilon dt + \frac{h}{2} \int_t^{t+\delta t} f(\Phi_i)\left[\Phi_{i+1} - \Phi_{i-1}\right]dt \tag{17}$$

it is possible to compute ϵ_{n+1} therefore Φ_{n+1} from equation (17) by means of an iterative "relaxation process" as in the first example, with the following approximations :

$$\int_t^{t+\delta t} \bar{\Delta}\epsilon dt \simeq \frac{1}{2}\bar{\Delta}\epsilon_{n+1}\,\delta t$$

$$\int_t^{t+\delta t} f(\Phi_i).\left[\Phi_{i+1} - \Phi_{i-1}\right]dt \simeq \frac{\delta t}{2}\left\{ \left[f(\Phi_i)(\Phi_{i+1} - \Phi_{i-1})\right]_{n+1} \right.$$

$$\left. + \left[f(\Phi_i)(\Phi_{i+1} - \Phi_{i-1})\right]_n \right\}$$

These approximations can be justified by a judicious choice of the lapse of time duration.

THE HYBRID COMPUTER

The hybrid computer system is represented as shown in figure n° 1.

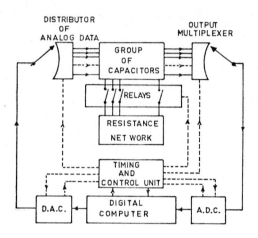

Figure n° 1 - THE HYBRID LOOP

For a lapse of time δt : the digital computer serves as a memory for
initial conditions, at the output of the digital to analog converter (DAC)
potentials are available for the capacitance network. After these operations,
the digital computer emits control pulses which activate during a lapse of time
δt, all the switches which permits the network evolution (relays)

The output multiplexer takes the analog informations on the network
nodes, gives them to an analog to digital converter (DAC), these digital informations are memorized by the digital computer.

The digital computer computes the solution and makes it available as
initial condition for the next lapse of time. And so on ...

APPLICATION OF HYBRID METHOD

We consider water infiltration in an homogeneous soil, at horizontal
surface of it continuous or cyclic watering is established. Thus it is possible
to study water flow in one-dimensional domain.

Results present here have been obtained with :

$$\delta y = 0,01$$
$$\delta \tau = 0,001$$

In all cases the initial water content is supposed uniform in the domain and corresponds to an initial potential : $\Phi = 0,05$

CONTINUOUS IRRIGATION

Irrigation is procuced by continuous watering or rain events. The initial and boundary conditions at soil surface corresponding to this case are :

$Y = 0$	$\Phi = 1$	$\forall \tau$
$0 < Y < \infty$	$\Phi = 0,05$	à $\quad \tau = 0$

In figure n° 2 potential evolutions at different depths are given for two cases corresponding to $\alpha L = 2,5$ and $\alpha L = 5$.

CYCLIC IRRIGATION

Then we have considered the cyclic irrigation problem. This problem of a great practical importance in agriculture is very complex, its treatment on modern computers is hard and request a long time of compute.

Intentionaly, we have simplified the problem. We neglect hysteresis phenomenum when water content changes and also water uptake by plant roots but in hybrid method, if experimental data are known, it was easy to take them into account. At last, initial conditions are such than soil water content is uniform, another arrangement is also easy to take into account.

In a first case we consider the boundary condition at the soil surface like a square wave.

The conditions are :

$0 < Y < \infty$	$\Phi = 0,05$	$\tau = 0$
$Y = 0$	$\Phi = 1$	$0 < \tau < \tau_1$
$Y = 0$	$\Phi = 0,05$	$\tau \geqslant \tau_1$

In figure n° 3 potential evolutions at different depths are given for two cases corresponding to $\alpha L = 2,5$ and $\alpha L = 5$.

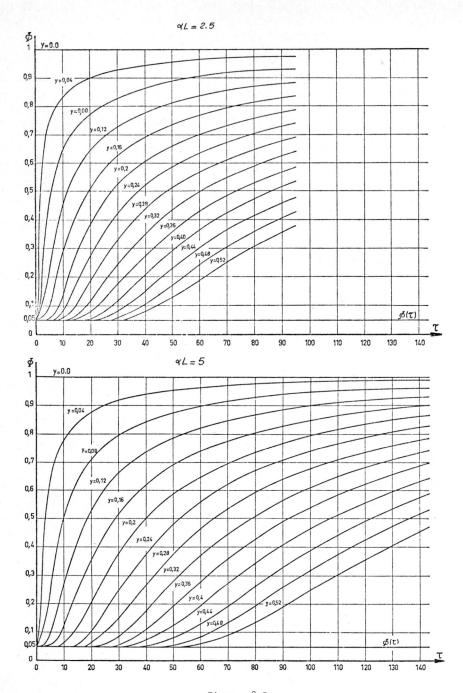

Figure n° 2

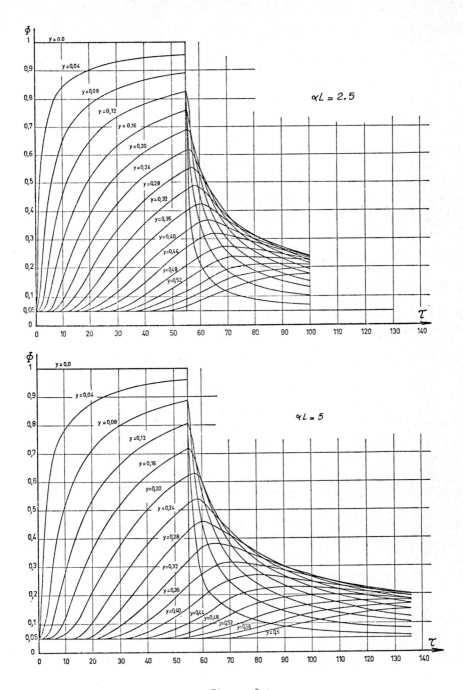

Figure n° 3

In a second case we consider a cyclic boundary condition at the soil
surface.

The conditions are :

$0 < Y < \infty$ $\Phi = 0,05$ $\tau = 0$

$Y = 0$ $\Phi = 1$ $2k\delta\tau < \tau < (2k+1)\ \delta\tau$ $k = 0,1,2, \ldots n$

$Y = 0$ $\Phi = 0,05$ $(2k+1)\delta\tau \leqslant \tau < (2k+2)\delta\tau$ $k = 0,1,2, \ldots n$

In figure n° 4 for $\alpha L = 2,5$ potential evolutions at different depths are given.

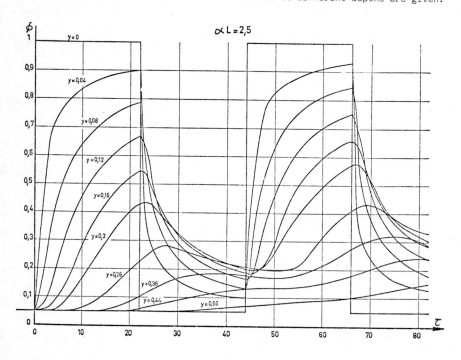

Figure n° 4

In agriculture we often look for maintain a constant water content at a given
depht, by means of irrigation, to give just necessary water at level with plant
roots because in many countries water is very rare and expensive.
For instance : what is the cycle of irrigation for maintain a potential,
Φ opt $= 2,5 \pm \varepsilon$ with $\varepsilon = 10$ %, at $y = 0,28$?

Figure n° 2 permits after the beginning of irrigation to know at what time
Φ = Φ opt   at y = 0,28. Results such those presented on figure n° 3 and
figure n° 4 gives the response time at the given depth when the boundary
condition at the soil surface change with the time.

Figure n° 5 shows the cyclic watering and the potential evolutions in the time
at y = 0,28. It is easy to verify then the potential remains in fixed limits
(± 10 %)

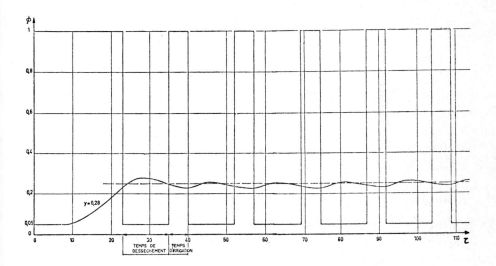

Figure n° 5

CONCLUSION

        Hybrid computer performances are very good at taking into account the
old technology.
        The capacitances present the advantage of arriving at a true time
derivative and that allows to free oneself of convergence problems so it's
possible to take large lapses of time. The speed of compute is very fast and
the accuracy is roughly of 10^{-3}.
        Some of the results presented in this paper shows the great interest
of the method for solving this kind of problems. It would be easy to change
boundary conditions for different values of coefficient αL to deduce some
criterium to draw nomograms of a strong interest in agriculture.

REFERENCES

M.MAALEDJ et L.MALAVARD - Compte rendu à l'Académie des Sciences de Paris
                            276 série A 1973 p. 1443

M. MAALEDJ et G. RENARD - Compte rendu à l'Académie des Sciences de Paris
                            277 série A 1973 p. 353

B.CAUSSADE, J.PAKLEZA, J.PIQUEMAL et G. RENARD
                            Compte rendu à l'Académie des Sciences de Paris
                            277 série A 1973 p. 543

B. CAUSSADE   "Simulation de phénomènes de diffusion non linéaires
                       par système hybride".
                       Thèse de Doctorat ès Sciences. Toulouse 20 février 1975

DISCUSSION

I wonder whether, in view of the fact that you made your Kirchoff transformation, and then neglected hysteresis entirely, whether you made some kind of comparison between your output and the output of a calculation that would include hysteresis and not impose these restrictions on the relationships between potential moisture and hydraulic conductivity in moisture. What is the effect of these approximation and assumptions that you made on the distribution of moisture contained in time, or on the variation of moisture at some fixed date with cyclic input ? (PECK)

For the thermal problem, we have compared an analytical solution with this method, with the following approximation.
The hybrid results are not obtained with a hybrid computer. In this case, we have simulated the network on a big computer.
In this case we have no errors. The difference between the results obtained in simulation and by numerical methods are roughly maximum 10^{-5}, 10^{-6}, with lapses of time, very large. It is possible to take, with boundary conditions as a step, lapses of time in a factor 1000. If you consider this method and the hysteresis phenomena, it is not a problem, because it is possible to take all the curves, all the nonlinearities, big or small. (CAUSSADE)

I did not quite understand when you said there is an advantage in speed of factor 100, computing speed. What do you compare with what ? (KARPLUS)

I compare the results obtained by this method, on the hybrid computer, and the results obtained with a numerical computer. In this method, we have no problem for convergence and stability, because the evolution in time is continuous. It is possible to take very large lapses of time, and the work to obtain the solution is very small. (CAUSSADE)

How many multipliers do you have in your system ? (KARPLUS)

It is a problem, actually. We have a model of 128 nodes, and in future we will have a bigger computer.   (CAUSSADE)

System Simulation in Water Resources, ed. *G.C. VANSTEENKISTE*
1976, North-Holland Publishing Company

THERMAL POLLUTION OF THE SCHELDT ESTUARY

G. Baron and S.J. Wajc
Dienst voor Chemische Ingenieurstechniek
en Industriële Scheikunde
Vrije Universiteit Brussel
Brussel, BELGIUM

ABSTRACT

The one dimensional non stationary intratidal model for heat transfer in an estuary is expressed by a linear parabolic partial differential equation with variable coefficients. A coordinate transformation brings it to a simpler form, for which an analytical solution is given, first for the case of an instantaneous discharge, then for the case of a continuous discharge.

The solution is implemented on a digital computer and used to investigate the temperature increase of the Scheldt estuary resulting from the continuous release of 4 000 MW of waste heat at a given location. The results show that the position of the maximum temperature increase oscillates with the tide, that its value is rather insensitive to the value of the effective diffusivity D, but sensitive to the value of the heat transfer coefficient to the surroundings q. The one dimensional stationary model predicts a higher temperature increase than this more realistic model.

INTRODUCTION

A serious controversy is now raging in Belgium around the planned expansion of the nuclear power station at Doel, north of Antwerp, on the Scheldt estuary. The electric utilities company about to run the plant, claims that the environment will suffer no harm, but a group of scientists have expressed their misgivings so convincingly indeed, that the public opinion was stirred and that the government asked a panel of experts to investigate the problem and report in due time.

The present paper, written on behalf of Prof. Dr. I. Elskens, one of the experts, describes the effect of the waste heat discharge on the temperature profile in the estuary. It is well known [1, 2, 3] that the global effect results from the interaction between the complex hydraulics of the estuary, the dispersion and the heat transfer to the surroundings. The relevant linear partial differential equation is solved here by a new more straightforward method. The results show that the maximum temperature is a sensitive function of the heat transfer coefficient, but is not strongly dependent on the effective diffusivity.

HYDRAULICS

The flow pattern in the Scheldt estuary is quite complex but constantly monitored, so that fairly accurate data are available to represent the water movement. The "Ministerie van Openbare Werken" regularly publishes the values of the wetted cross-sectional area Ω and of the local velocity u at different locations x along the estuary, as a function of the time t during one "mean tide" (the mean over one year). A so-called one dimensional non stationary intratidal model underlies these useful data [4].

In the present study, FOURIER-series were used to represent the averaged data in analytical form. The first two harmonics were sufficient to approximate these functions, even far from the estuary mouth (fig. 1) :

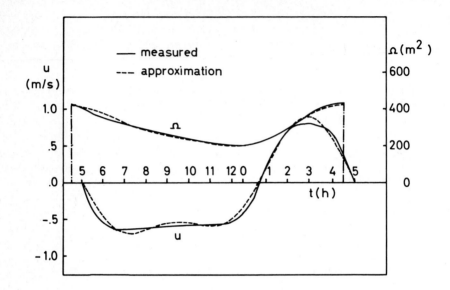

Fig. 1. FOURIER-series approximation of $u(x,t)$ and $\Omega(x,t)$
for a point at 129 km from the estuary mouth

$$u(x,t) = a_o(x) + \sum_{n=1}^{2} [a_n(x) \cos n\,\omega\,t + b_n(x) \sin n\,\omega\,t] \qquad (1)$$

$$\Omega(x,t) = c_o(x) + \sum_{n=1}^{2} [c_n(x) \cos n\,\omega\,t + d_n(x) \sin n\,\omega\,t] \qquad (2)$$

It should be noticed that Ω is measured and u is estimated from the conservation
law for water :

$$\frac{\partial \Omega}{\partial t} + \frac{\partial (\Omega u)}{\partial x} = v' \qquad (3)$$

where v' is the flow rate of affluents per unit length of estuary.

HEAT TRANSFER PHENOMENA

         For the sake of simplicity, let us suppose that the turbulent diffusivity D
is independent of x and t ; the energy conservation equation is then :

$$D\frac{\partial^2 T}{\partial x^2} = \frac{\partial T}{\partial t} + (u - D\frac{\partial \ln \Omega}{\partial x})\frac{\partial T}{\partial x} + (\frac{v'}{\Omega} + \frac{q}{h\,C_p\,\rho})(T - T_u) \qquad (4)$$

Remember that the concept of effective diffusivity hides our ignorance of the details of the mixing pattern and of the variability of the flow regime. For the
Scheldt estuary, the effective diffusivity D has been estimated by several independent methods [5] and values ranging from 100 to 300 m^2/s were reported.

         The heat transfer coefficient q was estimated from data on evaporation
ponds [6], on the cooling of the Thames [7] and on the German estuaries [8].
It varies between 20 and 80 W/m^2 °C.

The coefficient of the last term of (4):

$$B = \frac{v'}{\Omega} + \frac{q}{h \, C_p \, \rho}$$ (5)

therefore varies from $5 \cdot 10^{-7}$ to $20 \cdot 10^{-7} s^{-1}$, the first term being negligible.

SOLUTION METHOD

The linear partial differential equation (4) can be cast into a simpler form if the following coordinate transformation is used :

$$d \, \xi = dx - (u - D \frac{\partial \ln \Omega}{\partial x}) \, dt$$ (6)

$$d \, \tau = dt$$ (7)

For $D = 0$, the lines $d \, \xi = 0$ would simply be the trajectories of the water in the (x,t)-plane ; with $D \neq 0$ and

$\frac{\partial \ln \Omega}{\partial x} < 0$, it is still elementary to obtain the iso-ξ lines by integration of

$$\frac{dx}{dt} = u - D \frac{\partial \ln \Omega}{\partial x}$$ (8)

We will use the notation $x_\xi \, (t,t_1)$ for the value of x at time t_1, on the iso-ξ passing through the point (x,t).
Then (4) becomes

$$D \frac{\partial^2 T}{\partial \xi^2} = \frac{\partial T}{\partial \tau} + B(T - T_u)$$ (9)

Let us first suppose that a heat pulse Q is applied at line $t = 0$ in $x = \xi = 0$, under the following boundary conditions (far from the discharge point the temperature is equal to that of the surroundings, supposed to be uniform and constant) :

$$\xi = \pm \infty \qquad T = T_u$$ (10)

The solution of (9, 10) would then be :

$$T(x,t) = T_u = \frac{Q}{\Omega \, (0,0) \, 2 \, \sqrt{\pi \, D \, t}} \, e^{-\frac{[x_\xi \, (0,t) \,]^2}{4 \, D \, t} - B \, t}$$ (11)

In the case at hand, a constant flow of waste heat Q' is supplied to the river in $x = 0$, so that at any time t, the temperature profile carries the effects of all the infinitesimal heat pulses $dQ = Q' d \, \theta$ supplied since $t - \infty$:

$$T(x,t) - T_u = \frac{Q'}{2 \sqrt{\pi \, D}} \int_o^\infty \frac{e^{-\frac{[x_\xi \, (t,t-\theta) \,]^2}{} - B \, \theta}}{\Omega \, (0,t-\theta) \, \sqrt{\theta}} \, d \, \theta$$ (12)

To compute the value of the temperature T at given x and t, one computes the integral of (12) time upwards along the iso-ξ passing through that point for a sufficient number of tides, until the value of the integral no longer increases. Our computer program therefore essentially solves two ordinary first-order differential equations.

For a point around DOEL, the integral (12) has to be computed over 60 tides and this takes 20 seconds on the CDC 6500 of the VUB-ULB computer centre.
The generalization of our method to the case where D and B are functions of t but not of x is given in the appendix.

RESULTS

        For the sake of definiteness, let us suppose that the total electric power at Doel be expanded to 2000 MW, which would imply (with PWR) at waste heat flow of about 4000 MW.
For typical values of $D = 200$ m^2/s and $q = 50$ W/m^2°C, the temperature profiles at four characteristic moments of the tide appear as shown on fig. 2. They are steeper streamupwards than streamdownwards, due to the funnel-shape of the estuary and to the mean flow towards the sea. The maximum temperature increase varies between 2.45 and 2.58 °C but its position oscillates with an amplitude of some 15 km. At each turning of the tide, a small but sharp temperature peak is superposed in Doel, on an otherwise smooth profile. The boundary conditions (9) are now also verified : the estuary mouth, where $T - T_u$ is almost zero, is at 61 km from Doel and this may be considered as infinitely far.

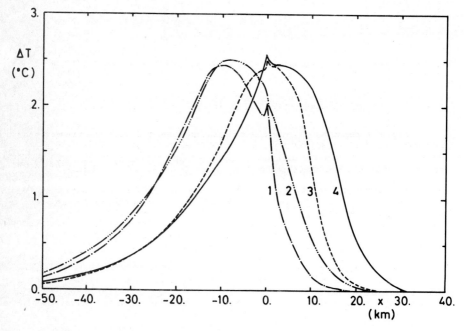

Fig. 2. Excess temperature profiles at four instants in a tide
        1. turning of the tide towards sea
        2. maximum velocity towards sea
        3. maximum velocity towards land
        4. turning of the tide towards land

        Figure 3 gives the temperature in Doel itself. The frequency of the oscillation is twice that of the tide, a reminder of the fact that the temperature peak passes the discharge point twice per tide.

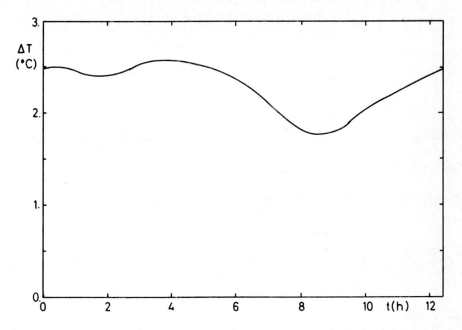

Fig. 3. Excess temperature in Doel over a full tide.

Figure 4 compares the maximum temperature computed with the present non-stationary intratidal model and the maximum temperature obtained with a stationary model
(the term $\frac{\partial T}{\partial t}$ is dropped from equ. 4).

Figure 5 shows the stationary temperature profile with the same values of D and q as in fig. 2. The alternating movement of the water effectively spreads the heat flow over a certain length of the river, so that the predictions of the stationary model are too pessimistic. The value of B (embodying the heat transfer coefficient) may reasonably be expected to vary between $7\ 10^{-7}$ and $15\ 10^{-7}s^{-1}$ so that the maximum temperature increase would vary between 3.32 and 2.26°C.

Figure 6 gives the effects on the maximum temperature of the diffusivity and of the heat transfer coefficient. It is surprising to see that the result is fairly insensitive to D in the range of reported values, from 100 to 300 m^2/s. The spreading due to the tidal movement is probably more important than the turbulent dispersion.

CONCLUSION

It remains now for the environmentalists, and more specifically the biologists, to say how the computed temperature increase and oscillation will affect the organisms living in the estuary. Besides, one might ask the meteorologists how the evaporation of about $1m^3/s$ of water (its latent heat carrying approximately one half of the heat transferred to the surroundings) will influence our already rainy weather.

198

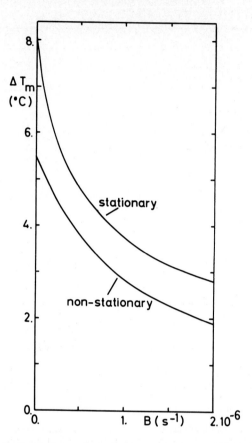

Fig. 4. Comparison of maximum excess temperatures computed
with the stationary and the non-stationary models

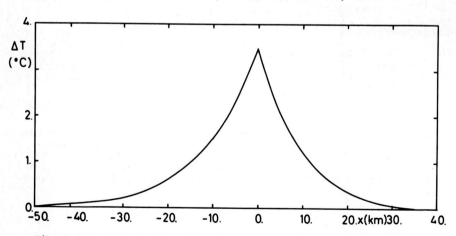

Fig. 5. Excess temperature profile computed with the stationary model

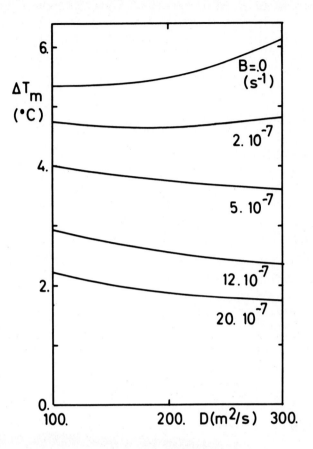

Fig. 6. Influence of D and B on the maximum excess temperature in Doel

APPENDIX

With D and B functions of t alone (not of x), equation (9) would be :

$$D(\tau) \frac{\partial^2 T}{\partial \xi^2} = \frac{\partial T}{\partial \tau} + B(\tau) (T - T_u) \qquad (13)$$

Let

$$d\sigma = D(\tau) d\tau \qquad (14)$$

$$A(\sigma) = A(\tau) = \frac{B(\tau)}{D(\tau)} \qquad (15)$$

Then (13) becomes

$$\frac{\partial^2 T}{\partial \xi^2} = \frac{\partial T}{\partial \sigma} + A(\sigma) (T - T_u) \qquad (16)$$

The solution corresponding to (10, 11) (effect of heat pulse Q at t = 0, x = 0) is
now :

$$T(x,t) - T_u = \frac{Q}{\Omega(0,0)\, 2\,\sqrt{\pi\,\sigma}}\; e^{-\dfrac{[\,x_\xi\,(0,t)\,]^2}{4\,\sigma} - \int_o^t B(\tau)\, d\,\tau} \qquad\qquad (17)$$

where

$$\sigma = \int_o^t D(\tau)\, d\,\tau \qquad\qquad (18)$$

The solution corresponding to (12) (effect of a continuous flow of waste heat Q')
would be :

$$T(x,t) - T_u = \frac{1}{2\sqrt{\pi}}\; \int_o^\infty \frac{Q'(t-\theta)\; e^{-\dfrac{[\,x_\xi\,(t,t-\theta)\,]^2}{4\,\sigma} - \int_{t-\theta}^t B(\tau)d\,\tau}}{\Omega\,(0,t-\theta)\,\sqrt{\sigma}}\; d\,\theta \qquad (19)$$

where

$$\sigma = \int_{t-\theta}^t D(\tau)\, d\tau \qquad\qquad (20)$$

There are physical reasons to expect D and B to vary indeed with time during one
tide, but until the effects of varying u and varying meteorological conditions,
for instance, are quantified, the extra sophistication of the more exact solutions
(17) and (19) will remain useless.

NOTATIONS

a_i, b_i, c_i, d_i		FOURIER coefficient (eqns (1) and (2))
h		average depth of estuary (m)
q		heat transfer coefficient ($W/m^2 {}^\circ C$)
t		time after high tide at estuary mouth (s)
u		local velocity (m/s)
v'		flow rate of affluents per unit length (m^2/s)
x		distance from Doel (positive towards land) (m)
A		(eqn. 15) (m^{-2})
B		(eqn. 5) (s^{-1})
C_p		specific heat (J/kg°C)
D		effective diffusivity (m^2/s)
Q		heat pulse (J)
Q'		waste heat flow (W)
T		local temperature (°C)
T_u		temperature of surroundings (°C)
ΔT	$= T-T_u$	temperature increase (°C)
ξ		(eqn. 6) (m)
σ		(eqn. 14) (m^2)

ρ specific mass (kg/m^3)

ω angular velocity (= .1406 10^{-3}s^{-1})

Ω wetted cross-sectional area (m^2)

REFERENCES

[1] Davidson, B., Shieh, Y.S. and Yih, S.M., (1975). Transient Analysis of Water
          Quality in the DELAWARE Estuary, Computer simulation of water resources
          systems, IFIP, North Holland Publ. Company, Amsterdam.

[2] Vichnevetsky, R., (1974). A.I.C.A., Vol. XVI, No.1, 1.

[3] Waterbouwkundig Laboratorium, Borgerhout, Thermische waterverontreiniging
          in de Westerschelde, Reports 295-4 (1974) and 295-5 (1975).

[4] Ministerie van Openbare Werken, Bestuur der Waterwegen, Brussel, Stormvloeden
          op de Schelde, Deel 4 (1966).

[5] Wollast, R. et al, (1973). Origine et mécanismes de l'envasement de l'estuaire
          de l'Escaut, Université Libre de Bruxelles.

[6] Perry, Ed., (1974). Chemical Engineers Handbook, 5th ed., Mc Graw Hill,
          New York.

[7] Water Pollution Research, (1964). Effects of Polluting Discharges on the
          Thames Estuary, Technical Paper 11, London, H.M. Stationary Office.

[8] Flugge, G. and Schwarze, M., (1974). Similarity Conditions for Thermal Hy-
          draulic Model Tests of Tidal Estuaries, 14th International Conference
          on Coastal Engineering, Kopenhagen.

DISCUSSION

*You said the temperature did not decrease much on the outgoing and incoming
tide. Can you explain that ? (WHITEHEAD)*

It takes about 60 tides before it has stabilized. So that, when you turn
on the plant today, you have to wait 1 month until the temperature profile has
stabilized. What the water actually does is push that peak up and down, and it
slightly deforms the profile. What you are doing during one tide, is only one
hundredth of what you needed to bring it to equilibrium.
There has been one experiment of a sudden injection of bromine 82, and there you
see that the peak, that is produced at one moment, travels with the tide, spreads
and also decreases. (WAJC)

*I've not seen any term taking into account the heat transfer between the
sea and the atmosphere. (VACHAUD)*

Yes, it has been showed on slide nr. 3. (WAJC)

Where did you take into account turbulent diffusion ? (VACHAUD)

In the water ? (WAJC)

In the air. (VACHAUD)

That's out of the limits of the system. What you see here is the heat
transfer coefficient to the surroundings. What the model actually says is : you
have water between two vertical planes. That water moves and the heat comes in
by thermal diffusivity and is transferred to the atmosphere. What the value of the
heat transfer coefficient is, depends indeed on the turbulence in the air, and the
humidity of the air. (WAJC)

*Did you have a sensible heat transfer coefficient ? You do not have a heat
loss. I cannot see that in it. Or is all that sucked up in your single heat transfer coefficient ? (PECK)*

Suppose that instead of water, you would have sand and on top of it : air.
So you have only "sensible" heat. Here it is more complicated because you have
evaporation at the same time. But there are scores of measurements, published in
the literature, for this type of situation. On the evaporation ponds on heat
transfer of the Thames and so on...
But there are lots of measurements that show that if you take all the heat transfer together, that is transfer of sensible heat and latent heat, and also radiation, (but radiation is negligible - not 1 % -), you have approximately half and
half - depending on the weather conditions - half transfer of sensible heat and
half of transfer of latent heat. Those values are available. (WAJC)

They are both hidden in your heat transfer coefficient ? (PECK)

Yes. (WAJC)

System Simulation in Water Resources, ed. G.C. VANSTEENKISTE
1976, North-Holland Publishing Company

THERMAL POLLUTION AND WATER QUALITY
IN AN INDUSTRIAL ESTUARY

G. Billen
Laboratoire d'Environnement
Université Libre de Bruxelles
and
Laboratorium voor Ekologie en Systematiek
Vrije Universiteit Brussel
Brussel, Belgium

J. Smitz
Groupe de Mécanique des Fluides Géophysiques
Université de Liège
Liège, Belgium

Contrarily to a widespread opinion, estuaries do not constitute the ideal environment for the cooling of thermal power plants, for at least three reasons :

i)   tide phenomena cause an important recycling of the cooling water, so that high temperatures can be reached even with important residual outflow. Taking into account those phenomena, Baron and Wajc (1975) have elaborated a mathematical model of the influence of the thermal discharge of two nuclear power plants of 1000 MWe at Doel on the temperature profile of the Scheldt estuary.

ii)   from an ecological point of view, an estuary is a very fragile ecosystem. Its role in the ecology of coastal marine systems is however very important.

iii) our estuaries are already submitted to an important domestic and industrial pollution, the effect of which would be enhanced by thermal discharge. This last aspect will be developped in the present paper for the special case of the Scheldt estuary.

Present state of organic pollution in the Scheldt estuary
_____

The Scheldt receives from Gent, from the Rupel and from
Antwerp an important organic load (about 150 T C/year according to
Wollast (1973)). This load provocates an important bacterial proli-
feration whose activity, at least in the summer, is far greater than
the reaeration capacity of the river. As a result, anaerobic conditions establish in the upstream part of the estuary (Rupel-Doel).

Other oxidants than oxygen are then used by heterotrophic bacteria for the oxidation of organic matter, according to the equations

$$CH_2O + H_2O \longrightarrow CO_2 + 4H^+ + 4e^-$$

$$4e^- + O_2 + 4H^+ \longrightarrow 2H_2O \tag{1}$$

$$2e^- + MnO_2 + 4H^+ \longrightarrow Mn^{++} + 2H_2O \tag{2}$$

$$5e^- + NO_3^- + 6H^+ \longrightarrow 1/2N_2 + 3H_2O \tag{3}$$

$$8e^- + NO_3^- + 10H^+ \longrightarrow NH_4^+ + 3H_2O \tag{3'}$$

$$1e^- + Fe(OH)_3 + 3H^+ \longrightarrow Fe^{++} + 3H_2O \tag{4}$$

$$Fe^{++} + HCO_3 \longrightarrow FeCO_3 + H^+ \tag{4'}$$

$$15/2e^- + SO_4^{--} + 3/4\ Fe^{++} + 8H^+ \longrightarrow 1/4\ Fe_3S_4 + 4H_2O \tag{5}$$

$$8e^- + SO_4^{--} + 9H^+ \longrightarrow HS^- + 4H_2O \tag{5'}$$

These processes are particularly intense when temperature is high
and discharge low.

Downstream, when salinity reaches a value of about 2 mg $CL^-/1$,
a great deal of suspension matter floculates and sedimentates, and
bacterial activity drops as well. A process of recuperation then
begins, under the influence of reaeration by the atmosphere and
mixing with unpolluted sea-water. The oxidants used in the upstream
zone by heterotrophic metabolisms are regenerated by turns, the last
stage of this process being the reapparition of oxygen.

Four experimental profiles of oxido-reduction species along the
Scheldt estuary in winter, spring summer and autumn are shown in
Fig. 1a,b,c,d. In February 1974, the mean heterotrophic activity
from the Rupel to Doel was about 1.4 μmoles C/1.hour, the stream

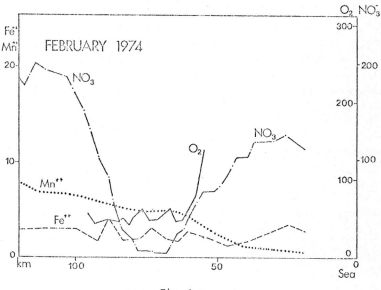

Fig. 1 a.

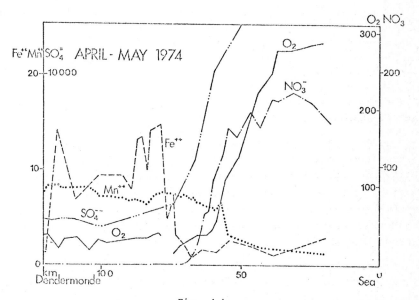

Fig. 1 b.

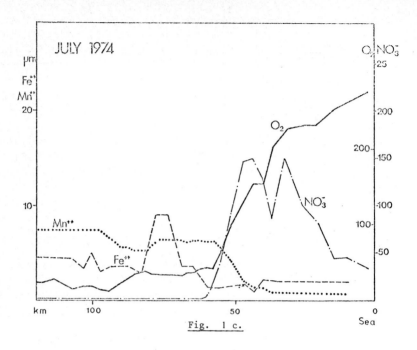

Fig. 1 c.

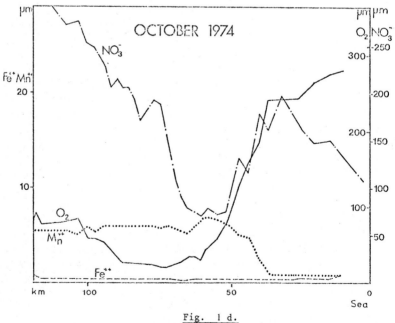

Fig. 1 d.

outflow was 130 m^3/sec.   Only nitrate was reduced, no reduced iron,
nor sulfides were produced.   In May 1974, (mean heterotrophic activity : 2.8 µmoles C/l.h. ; outflow : 35 m^3/sec.) and in July 1974
(mean heterotrophic activity : 3.6 µmoles C/l.h., outflow 40 m^3/sec),
all nitrate was already used before Dendermonde and all the heterotrophic activity proceeded at the expense of iron oxide or hydroxide
(rapidly reduced into Fe^{++} and insoluble $FeCO_3$) and sulfates (respectively about 200 and 500 µmoles/l sulfides were produced).   The
situation in October 1974 (heterotrophic activity : 2.5 µmoles/l.h ;
outflow 265 m^3/sec) was similar to this of February, but the reduction of nitrate was not completed.

These four profiles have been simulated by a mathematical
model the principles and resolution of which have been exposed in
details elsewhere (Billen and Smitz, 1975). Measured values of
heterotrophic activity along a longitudinal profile of the estuary
at the different seasons are introduced as a command parameter (no
deterministic model of bacterial activity itself is included).   The
concentration of the different chemical species involved in the oxidation reduction processes is affected by this bacterial activity,
viewed as an electron flux imposed to the system, by reaeration and
by hydrodynamic processes.   To portion out the heterotrophic activity between the different oxidants, the assumption is made that an
internal thermodynamic equilibrium is achieved between them ; this
imposes that five simultaneous equilibrium relations of the general
form $Eh = E_i^0 + RTln\frac{Ox_i}{Red_i}$ hold. As an exception, the rate of nitrate
production by equation (3') has been limited to a maximum value in
order to take into account the kinetics of nitrification.

The obtained profiles are shown in fig. 2 a,b,c,d.   It is seen
that the simulation of the experimental profiles of fig. 1 a,b,c,d
is quite good.

Effects of thermal discharges

Any temperature increase can aggravate the effects of organic
pollution of a stream by the conjugation of two processes :

i)   Increase of bacterial activity. Measurements of the seasonal
       variations of bacterial activity in the Scheldt allow to eva-
       luate empirically the effect of temperature on bacterial acti-
       vity in this environment by the relation :

$$\text{Activity } (t°) = \text{Activity } (t°_0) \; 10^{(t°-t°_0)/\theta} \qquad (1)$$

$$\text{with } \theta \text{ between } 16°C \text{ and } 20°C.$$

This include both a physiological effect of temperature on the
individual activity and a sociological effect on the community.

ii)   <u>Decrease of the reaeration capacity</u>. Reaeration rate is given
by the relation :

$$R = K(O_{2sat} - O_2) \qquad (2)$$

The value of the oxygen saturation concentration is very sensitive to temperature, as shown by the relation (Truesdel and
al., 1955) :

$$O_{2sat} = 1,5 \; 10^4 \; (33.5 + t°) \quad \text{in} \quad \mu \text{ moles/l} \qquad (3)$$

K increases slightly with increasing temperature according to
the relation (Truesdel and Vandyke, 1958) :

$$K(t°) = K(15°) + 0.015 \; (t°-15°) \qquad (4)$$

Using the results of the model of Baron and Wajc (1975) for
the temperature increase produced by the thermal discharge of two
nuclear power plants (2000 MWe) at Doel [*], the resultant heterotrophic activity was calculated according to equation (1). This
activity was then used to calculate the longitudinal profile of
oxidants, taking the relations (3) and (4) into account to evaluate
the reaeration. The results of these calculations applied on the
situations of February, May, July and October 1974 are shown in
figure 3 a,b,c,d. Comparizon with the corresponding profiles without
thermal discharge (fig. 2 a,b,c,d) shows the following effects :

(i) The reductive processes in the upstream part of the
estuary go farther : in February 1974, the thermal load considered would have provocate the reduction of iron and the production
of sulfides; in May and July 1974, it would have enhanced the
production of sulfide by a factor 1.5 and 2 respectively.
The water quality in the region of Antwerp would therefore become
much worse : the period during which the water is black and has
a smell of H_2S, presently restricted to the summer months, would
extend to almost he whole year.

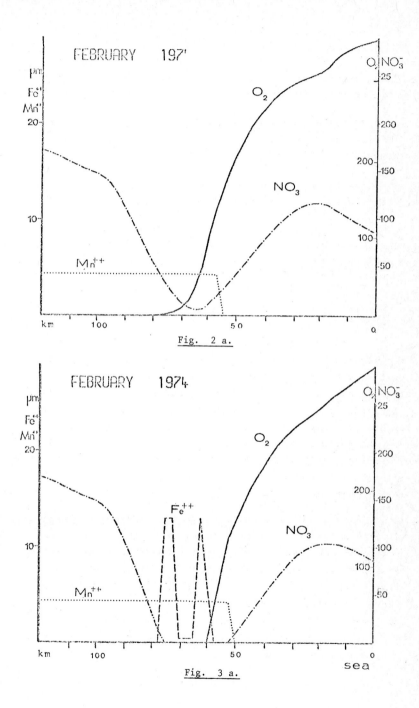

Fig. 2 a.

Fig. 3 a.

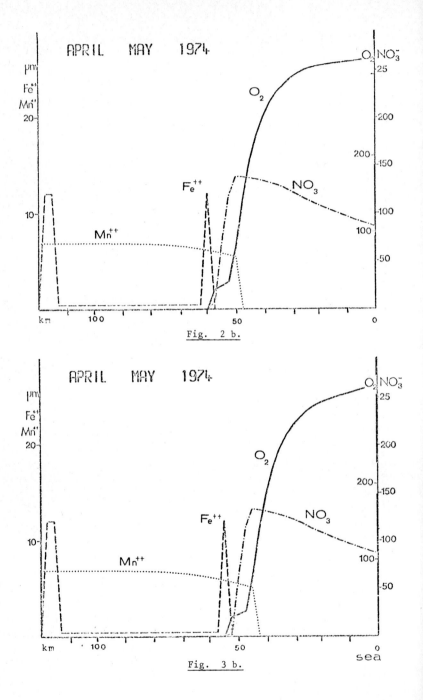

Fig. 2 b.

Fig. 3 b.

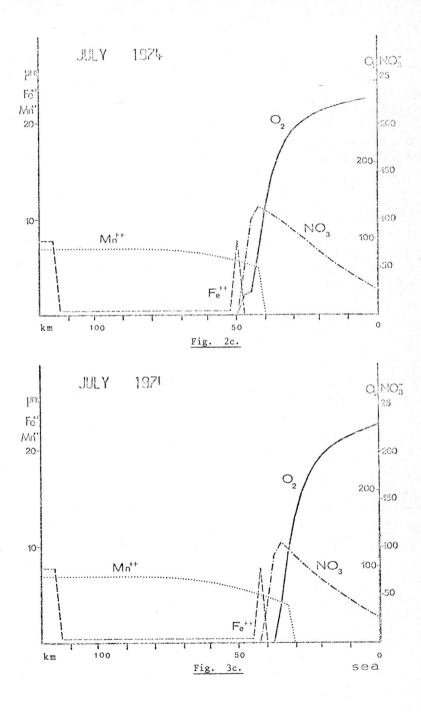

Fig. 2c.

Fig. 3c.

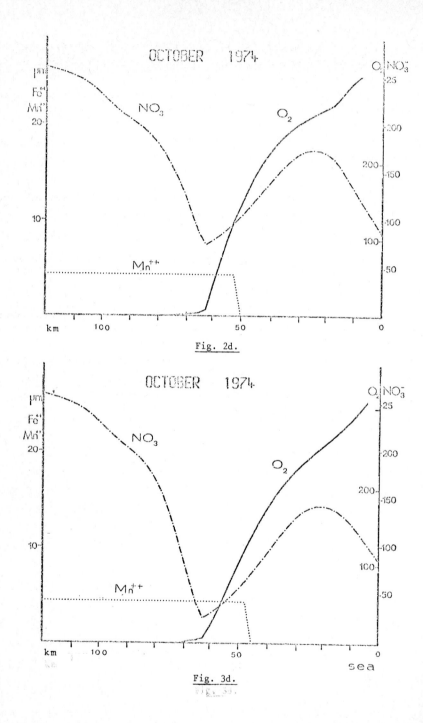

Fig. 2d.

Fig. 3d.

(ii)   The whole recuperation process, and in particular the reapparition of dissolved oxygen is rejected about   6 km downstream (February,May, October)   to 9 or 10 km   (July) downstream.
The polluted part of the estuary would then extend farther beyond the Netherlands frontier.

REFERENCES

BARON, G. and WAJC, S.   (1975)   Contribution of the nuclear power
         plants at Doel to the temperature profile in the Scheldt
         Estuary.   *Technical report*
         Belgian national R-D Program on the environment.

BILLEN, G. and SMITZ, J. (1975)   A mathematical model of microbial
         and chemical oxidation-reduction processes in the
         Scheldt Estuary.   Math. Modelsea
         International Council for the Exploration of the Sea   C(21)

TRUESDAEL, G.A. and VANDYKE, K.C. (1958)   The feect of temperature
         on the aeration of flowing water.
         Water and Waste Tr. J., 7,   9-11.

WOLLAST, R. (1973)   Origine et mécanisme de l'envasement de
         l'estuaire de l'Escaut.   Rapport de Synthèse.
         Recherches effectuées dans le cadre de l'étude de
         l'envasement de l'Escaut dirigée par le Laboratoire de
         recherches hydrauliques, Borgerhout, Ministère des
         Travaux Publics.

DISCUSSION

When the temperature increases 3 or 4 degrees centigrade, I expected that this would increase some of the bacterial activity and decrease some equilibrium concentrations of water and oxygen, but the effect that you showed is tremendous. What temperature level did you take in your computations ? *(WAJC)*

We are taking your stationary results. (SMITZ)

Anyhow, if the result would be only half of what you showed, it would be already quite interesting. If this moves down a few kilometers, it will probably cross the border. *(WAJC)*

Belgium could have serious problems with his neighbours ! The temperature profile is calculated without any Dutch power plant ; now they also intend to use that. (SMITZ)

Is the variability of the climate not more important than the heat production of a power plant ? *(DE MARSILY)*

The actual situation of two more loads has been included, but the influence is negligible. (SMITZ)

Another effect we did not take into account is the meanflow towards the sea. It varies from 40 to 400 m^3/sec. This year it reached 400, so that all these bacterials are washed out. But in my case, oddly enough it has hardly influenced the results of the temperature profile due to the plant, mainly because even a local flow rate of 400 m^3/sec is still only 2 à 3 % of the flow due to the tides. That is the mean effect, with heat transfer to the surroundings. *(WAJC)*

PART FOUR

ON THE USE OF DEDUCTIVE INFORMATION
IN QUALITY MODELS
OF WATER RESOURCES SYSTEMS

System Simulation in Water Resources, ed. G.C. VANSTEENKISTE
1976, North-Holland Publishing Company

A GROUNDWATER QUALITY MODEL OF THE RAYMOND BASIN[*]

Thomas M. Simundich
Computer Science Department
University of California, Los Angeles

INTRODUCTION

The quality of groundwater is as important to any water resources management plan which concerns itself with the beneficial uses of groundwater in domestic, industrial and agricultural applications as quantity. Therefore, it would
be desirable to establish a means for the quality prediction and control of a
groundwater system. Such a means is a mathematical model.

The method of applying mathematical modeling to complex systems such as
groundwater quality has gained impetus with recent advances in systems analysis,
operations research and computer technology. However, it is largely the impact
of computer technology which has expanded the spectrum of applying the techniques
of systems analysis and operations research in heretofore unsolved problem areas.

The advances in computer technology, however, do not overcome all the
problems inherent in groundwater quality modeling. The limitations of the mathematical modeling of groundwater quality systems fall under two categories. They
are:[6]

(1) Data limitations

(2) Model or structure limitations.

Data limitations develop when insufficient information is available to determine
values of critical parameters and inputs to a system. Model or structure limitations arise when one lacks sufficient insight into the structure of the system
and the interrelationships between the system parameters, variables and geometry
to represent accurately by means of a mathematical model the groundwater system
being studied. In general all groundwater quality models will suffer from both
data and structural limitations.

Therefore the objectives of this paper are to indicate for a particular
basin if there are any data limitations or model limitations which preclude the
utilization of a mathematical model of the groundwater quality as a tool for
water resource planning.

This discussion is confined to the modeling of the saturated zone of an
aquifer. The particular basin modeled is the Raymond Basin. The Raymond Basin
is located approximately 8 miles north of downtown Los Angeles and has the following features:

(1) The boundaries are well-defined.

(2) The Raymond Basin covers a small area (40 square miles).

(3) The basin has only one aquifer which is homogeneous and isotropic.

[*] The subject matter in this paper was supported in part by the National Science
Foundation under Grant GK 42774.

(4) A groundwater quantity model exists for the basin.

(5) The Raymond Basin hydrologic configuration allows simplification in
     the quality model governing equation.

GROUNDWATER QUALITY INDICATORS

Chemical, physical (taste, color, odor, etc.) and bacterial characteristics
of groundwater are factors in determining the quality of groundwater. Physical
characteristics of groundwater are difficult to model because of data limitations
and the complexity of the characteristics. There are bacteria in groundwater but
rarely in amounts greater than 15 ppm. Therefore, bacterial characteristics are
excluded from most groundwater studies. The chemical characteristics of groundwater are generally the modeled characteristics. There are five main reasons for
this:

(1) The chemical phenomena of groundwater are understood.

(2) Chemical analyses can be made in the field.

(3) Chemical analyses yield accurate data.

(4) Physical characteristics of groundwater are usually the results of
     chemical phenomena.

(5) Chemical characteristics are the most significant characteristic in
     evaluating the suitability of water for the greatest number of uses.

Throughout this paper - Total Dissolved Solids (TDS) is used as the indicator of
groundwater quality. There are three reasons for this choice:[3]

(1) TDS reflects the influence of the majority of dissolved constituents.

(2) TDS can be assumed to be chemically static, while individual ions are
     constantly being dissolved, precipitated and are reacting with other
     ions.

(3) TDS is the most significant chemical parameter in evaluating the
     suitability of water for the greatest number of uses.

EQUATIONS OF INTEREST

The general form of the equation which describes the two dimensional or
lateral flow of a tracer or indicator through a homogeneous, isotropic, porous
medium is indicated in the literature [1,5,12] to be

$$\frac{\partial C}{\partial t} = \frac{\partial}{\partial x_i}\left[(D_m + D_{i,k})\frac{\partial C}{\partial x_i} - V_i C\right] \tag{1}$$

where

x_i (i = 1,2) are the Cartesian coordinates.

D_m is the coefficient of molecular diffusion (L^2/T).

$D_{i,k}$ are the components of the second order tensor of dispersion (L^2/T).

C is the concentration of the tracer.

V_i is the average velocity (L/T).

t is time.

Diffusion [10] is a phenomenon arising from the random motion of the tracer particles in the fluid. Diffusion is characterized by the tracer particles moving from a higher concentration to a lower one. Dispersion [10] is a phenomenon arising from uneven fluid flow, that is, the tracer particles injected at a point in the fluid arrive at different points after an interval of time depending upon the tortuosity of the path taken. There are two types of dispersion to be considered longitudinal and transverse. Longitudinal dispersion (D_L) is in the direction of flow while transverse dispersion (D_T) is transverse to the direction of flow. Longitudinal dispersion is on the magnitude of 10 times that of transverse dispersion. For a homogeneous, isotropic medium the longitudinal and transverse dispersion have the following relation to the velocity of the fluid [1].

$$D_L = \alpha_L \, V_i \tag{2}$$

$$D_T = \alpha_T \, V_i \tag{3}$$

where α_L and α_T are the longitudinal and lateral dispersivities respectively of L dimension.

Considering the longitudinal dispersion to dominate the diffusion, D_m, and the other components of dispersion Eq.(1) reduces to

$$\frac{\partial C}{\partial t} = \frac{\partial}{\partial x_i} \left(D_{L_i} \frac{\partial C}{\partial x_i} \right) - \frac{\partial (V_i C)}{\partial x_i} \qquad i = 1,2 \tag{4}$$

DISPERSION

The effect of the first term on the right hand side of Eq.(4) is influenced greatly by the dynamic hydraulic gradient rather than the near static gradient. The steepening of the gradient by pumping or localized recharge is the largest contributing factor. However a groundwater quality model for an aquifer is based on general gradients (macrogradients), which describe the movement of water through the entire aquifer, rather than microgradients that describe the effects of local dynamic hydrology [9]. Hence the effects of dispersion are not included in the model.

The sensitivity of Eq.(4) to typical field values of the dispersivity is given with the following example. Consider the following one dimension version of Eq.(4).

$$\frac{\partial C}{\partial t} = D_L \frac{\partial^2 C}{\partial x^2} - V_x \frac{\partial C}{\partial x} \tag{5}$$

with the following idealized initial and boundary conditions

$$C(x,0) = 0 \qquad x > 0$$

$$C(0,t) = C_0 \qquad t \geq 0 \tag{6}$$

$$C(\infty,t) = 0 \qquad t \geq 0$$

The solution [8] of Eq.(5) with the above conditions is

$$\frac{C}{C_0} = \frac{1}{2} \operatorname{erfc}\left(\frac{x - V_x t}{2\sqrt{D_L t}}\right) + 1/2 \exp\left\{\frac{V_x x}{D_L}\right\} \operatorname{erfc}\left[\frac{x + V_x t}{2\sqrt{D_L t}}\right] \tag{7}$$

Taking typical values of D_L and V_x for a basin as

$$V_x = 200 \text{ft/yr}$$

$$D_L = 2000 \text{ft}^2/\text{yr}^*$$

After 10 years assuming the same field conditions the dispersion front from $C/C_0 = .95$ to $C/C_0 = .05$ will be 780 ft. This is small when compared to a typical grid spacing of $\Delta x = 500$ when the field is discretized. Therefore small errors are accumulated if dispersion is neglected. A more rigorous analysis for an aquifer by Robson [11] yielded the same conclusion.

THE MODEL

The equation utilized as the basis of groundwater quality model for the Raymond Basin is

$$\frac{\partial (V_i C)}{\partial x_i} + \frac{\partial C}{\partial t} = S \ (x_i, t) \tag{8}$$

where S is the rate of gain or loss of concentration due to local sources or sinks.

When Eq.(8) is applied to describe the TDS concentrations of the groundwater in a saturated zone of an aquifer it may be given the interpretation that dissolved solids in the saturated zone of the aquifer move from one area to another by convection, that is, an ion can be associated with the same drop of water as the water moves laterally through the aquifer. Also the local inputs are a major contribution to the accumulation of TDS throughout the aquifer.

The October 1969 water level contour map for Raymond Basin shows that the equipotential lines (i.e., contours of equal water heads) in the northern region are quite close to being parallel. In the southern region of the basin the water movement is negligible. Therefore, unidirectional flow might be assumed. Therefore, Eq.(8) becomes

$$\frac{\partial (V_x C)}{\partial x} + \frac{\partial C}{\partial t} = S(x, t) \tag{9}$$

To utilize Eq.(9) on the Raymond Basin, the basin is divided into 9 strips as shown in Fig.(1). It is assumed that in each strip that the water in the saturated zone moves parallel to the strips and does not cross the strip boundaries. The velocity of the water, however, is not uniform throughout the length of the strips. Each strip, then, can be solved independently.

The nine strips are sufficiently narrow to justify the above assumption. Dividing the basin into fewer strips makes the assumption of questionable validity, and dividing the basin into more strips will add to the computation needed to simulate the model. Further, there are insufficient data on the parameters of the system and inputs to substantiate more strips. However, the 9 strips are sufficient to give an overall groundwater description of the Raymond Basin.

---
*It is interesting to note that the estimates for the dispersivity of a porous media varies by two orders of magnitude from a sand column experiment [2] to a field experiment [7].

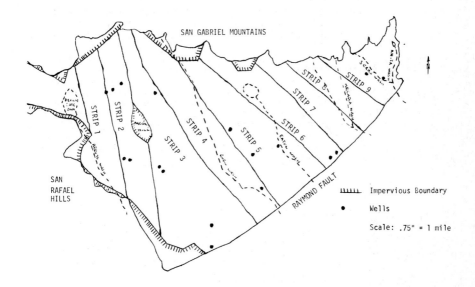

Figure 1

In order to implement Eq.(9) as a model and simulate the behavior of the basin the following steps are carried out:

(1) Discretization of Basin

The basin has been divided into nine strips (See Fig. 1). These strips vary in length from 2 miles to 6 miles with a hundred nodes per strip. Eq.(9) is approximated by finite differences for computer implementation. The space discretization size Δx varies from 105 ft. to 315 ft. depending on the length of the strip. The time discretization size Δt is .125 year.

(2) A Precise Description of Boundaries

The North, East and West boundaries of the Raymond Basin are mountains which are considered to be impervious to water flow. Likewise, the Southern boundary of the basin is a fault which is likewise considered impervious to water flow. Therefore the boundary conditions on the strips are:

$$\frac{\partial C}{\partial x} = 0$$

(3) A Determination of the Velocity of Subsurface Flow (V_x)

The velocities were computed from Raymond Basin groundwater study by
Weber S. Tyson [4]. The velocities were not uniform in respect to
time. But the variation was rather small and the average values were
used in the study.

(4) A Determination of the Initial Conditions

The initial conditions shown in Fig. 2 should not be viewed as exact
representations. The lines in Fig. 2 are not contour lines of equal
ionic concentrations of TDS, but are demarcations of areas where the
particular concentration may lie. These areas are hypothetical and
constructed by general descriptions of the conditions in the basin.
The values of the area in TDS concentrations were taken from the
nearest averaged well analysis taken during the 1955-60 period,

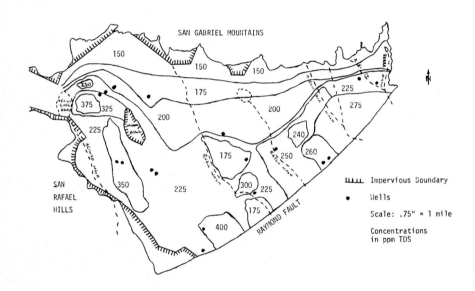

Figure 2

(5) A Determination of Sources or Sinks

The principle sinks of TDS concentration are surface water runoffs
near the mountains diluting the saturated zone by natural recharge.
Also surface water running through the basin in deep canyons helps
wash and dilute the TDS content in the saturated zone. These areas
are well defined for placing the appropriate sinks to the nodal
finite difference equations. The values of these sinks were determined so as to reflect the correct trend indicated by the averaged
well analysis taken during the 1960-65 period.

Less physically defined were the sources of TDS concentration increase
which most likely is caused by irrigation water returns, and percolation of domestic waste water to the saturated zone from cesspools.
Therefore the sources were defined so as to align the results with
the trend.

For the entire basin the term S includes the changes of concentration
due to precipitated waters (rain) percolating into the saturated zone.
During Fall and Spring the changes in concentration due to rain is
considered zero. During the summer, Dry Season, S is a source adding
25 PPM/year, TDS from the concentration. Therefore over a time period
the groundwater will become more concentrated with dissolved salts
due to the fact that Southern California in general has a dry climate.

(6)   Simulation

Eq.(9) with the required data and boundary conditions are simulated
on a hybrid computer. The groundwater quality change of the Raymond
Basin after a five year simulation is presented in Fig. 3.

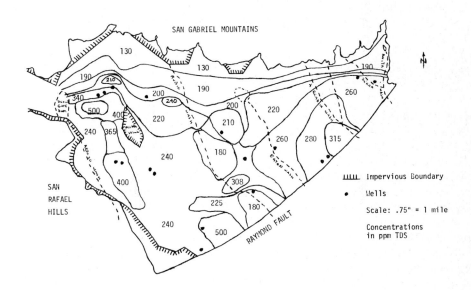

Figure 3

RESULTS

Fig. 3 shows the results of the groundwater TDS quality simulation of
Raymond Basin after five years. Throughout the basin there is an increase of TDS
concentration except near the mountains. This is a trend shown in the data which
is probably caused by decreasing water tables in turn caused by a preponderance
of dry seasons over wet seasons.

The 900 nodes of the present model appear to be adequate in minimizing the numerical errors inherent in the discretizing process. This conclusion was reached since there did not appear an undue amount of dispersion of concentration fronts in the simulation.

The subsurface lateral water movement for the simulation time period is generally of small significance for most of the basin. Water movement, however, is of significance near the mountains and in the eastern portion of the basin. Hence, it can be concluded that the local inputs dominate in the major portion of the area in the model. That is, the sources and sinks of TDS concentration of a nodal area change the TDS quality character of the water in that area more so than water of different TDS concentration moving into that nodal area from another nodal area.

Since the inputs to the model are only generally known it can be concluded that the groundwater TDS quality model of Raymond Basin yields simulation results of a general nature. That is, the simulation will not forecast water quality at individual wells or well fields. It should, however, be capable of predicting a trend in the overall groundwater TDS quality of Raymond Basin.

As a result of the modeling exercise it appears that the data limitations rather than model limitations are the biggest hindrance in the development of an accurate groundwater quality model for the Raymond Basin. The existing data were collected to comply with a civic ordinance rather than for modeling.

Figure 1 shows the location of wells yielding the most recent groundwater TDS quality analyses of the Raymond Basin. There are only 18 wells and their distribution is poor. Other shortcomings are:

(1) Samples were taken at various seasons.

(2) Samples were taken over a long period of time, but with few in any one year.

(3) There are gaps of five years or more in some well analysis histories.

(4) Samples were taken from wells with unknown perforation intervals making it impossible to determine which part of the aquifer was represented in the sample.

(5) Several wells are privately owned and their availability for sampling is at the convenience of the proprietor.

(6) Samples were taken at some wells with the pump being turned on just long enough to acquire a sample. At other wells the pumps may have ran for several hours. Thus there was no uniformity of taking the samples.

(7) In some strips a few wells are available in others no data is available.

Hence, data on the areal and temporal variations of groundwater TDS quality are inadequate for precise modeling.

Ideally, there should be monthly data available on the groundwater quality from the wells, to be more realistic, seasonal readings could suffice. Also a history of TDS quality of waste waters discharged or used locally should be accumulated. A complete history of the TDS quality or surface runoff water should be made.

Further a study is needed to evaluate the period of time it takes for surface water to percolate to the saturated zone so as to be able to correctly place a source or sink in the model with the correct temporal relation to the cause. Also it appears that some of the system inputs should be stochastic rather than deterministic.

CONCLUSIONS

From the modeling experience it can be concluded for the groundwater quality model of the Raymond Basin that

(1) The data limitations are the biggest constraint in developing an accurate model. Particularly in a determination of the aggregate source term.

(2) Some of the model inputs should be considered to be stochastic rather than deterministic.

(3) Distributed inputs dominate in a groundwater quality model for a near term period (less than 30 years).

(4) In general water TDS quality data are not adequately monitored to enable an accurate verification of the model.

The study in this paper is only a beginning. It has provided a framework and a guide line of how to improve it. It is hoped that this study will stimulate the people in the field and bring success in the near future.

REFERENCES

Bear, J. "On the Tensor Form of Dispersion in Porous Media," J. Geophysics Research, 66 (4), 1961, pp. 1185-1197.

Bruch, J. C., "Two-Dimensional Experiments in Porous Media," Water Resources Research, June 1970, pp. 791-800.

California Department of Water Resources, "Progress Report on Water Quality Prediction Procedure for the Costal Plain of Orange County," Office Report, October 1967.

California Department of Water Resources, "Raymond Basin Ground Water Study," Office Report, August 1969.

DeJosselin De Jong, G. and Bossen, M. J., "Discussion of Paper by Jacob Bear, 'On the Tensor Form of Dispersion in Porous Media'," J. Geophys. Research, 66 (10), 1961, pp. 3623-2624.

Drobny, N. L., "Water Resources Systems Analysis - An Overview," 4th American Water Resources Conference, Proceedings, New York, 1968, Urbana, Illinois, American Water Resources Association, 1968, pp. 534-558.

Grove, D. B. and Beetam, "Porosity and Dispersion Constant Calculations for a Fractured Carbonate Aquifer Using Two-Well Tracer Methods," Water Resources Research, Vol. 7, No. 1, February 1972, pp. 128-134.

Harleman, D. R. F. and Rumer, R. R., "Longitudinal and Lateral Dispersion in an Isotropic Proous Medium," J. Fluid Mech., 16 (3), July, 1963, pp. 385-394.

Hassan, A. A. and Motokane, "Mathematical Modeling of Groundwater Quality," Tech. Memo No. 50, State of California Department of Water Resources, March 1973.

Perkins, T. K. and Johnston, O. C., "A Review of Diffusion and Dispersion in Porous Media," J. Soc. of Petroleum Engr., March 1963, pp. 70-84.

Robson, S. G., "Feasibility of Digital Water Quality Modeling Illustrated by Applications at Barstow, California," U.S. Geological Survey, No. 46-73, February 1974.

Scheidegger, A. E., "General Theory of Dispersion in Porous Media," J. Geophys. Research, 66 (10), 1961, pp. 3273-3278.

DISCUSSION

You neglected the dispersion coefficient. I will make the same assumption this afternoon. You seem to be quite satisfied about this assumption ? I did it but I don't think I was allowed to. You stated that several people would accept that dispersion may be neglected. I'm aware of the contrary that some people pretend that the values of the dispersion coefficient are so high in nature, that perhaps you may neglect convection and advection with regard to dispersion. (DE MARSILY)

I am aware of this point also. Much of the early dispersion experiments which influenced my modeling effort were sand column experiments. These experiments yielded small dispersitivities. Later field experiments have given dispersitivities 100 times those of the sand column experiments. However even in these later dispersion values the concentration spread is small.

A very general question is whether or not to neglect dispersion. You cannot solve it now, I think, in theory and have a general answer. For example you have a 1-dimensional case and your transition zone varies with the square root of the travel distance. So it means that, when you look at the relative value of the transition zone, you have 1 1x that means that when the travel distance increases, the relative value of the transition zone decreases. It means that for large basins, in general, you may very well neglect dispersion. Of course it will depend on the strengths of the sources, that means on the scale of your phenomena, and there, there is no answer right now. You have to examine every case, case by case. There is no way, now, to solve the most important problem we are faced with : the change of scale problem, which is the only problem that prevents the development of dispersion theory. (FRIED)

One of the reasons for choosing this basin was, according to your statement in the abstract, that a quantity model exists for this basin. Do you feel that this model was useful ? (VAN DER BEKEN)

The quantity model of the basin was employed to yield the velocity terms in the quality model. (SIMUNDICH)

What we want to say is : you can not rely on regressive modeling. How can you draw conclusions from it ? For example : one of the assumptions that strike me is the statement in the beginning that the aquifer is homogeneous and isotropic. How can you say that, you don't even have a representative indication ? (NEUMAN)

I relied on statements to this effect made by the California Department of Water Resources. (SIMUNDICH)

It is not possible that some of the inaccuracies arise from the use of TDS ? Because every soil will behave differently in respect to adsorption.
(DE BOER)

An assumption made is that the TDS remains constant in regards to adsorption. (SIMUNDICH)

System Simulation in Water Resources, ed. G.C. VANSTEENKISTE
1976, North-Holland Publishing Company

MODELING OF THE SALT TRANSPORT
IN MULTILAYERED AQUIFERS

M. Besbes, E. Ledoux, G. de Marsily
Centre d'Informatique Géologique
Ecole Nationale Supérieure
des Mines de Paris
Fontainebleau, France

ABSTRACT

The transport of a dissolved species in an aquifer may be described by the theory of dispersion. However, the application of this theory to a general case creates such numerical difficulties that it seems necessary to simplify the theory in order to apply it to practical problems.

After a brief look at the theory of dispersion, a particular simplification for multilayered aquifers will be presented, and an application given for a large aquifer system near Kairouan, Tunisia.

Another example of simplification will be given for the problem of storage of waste in an aquifer over a long period of time.

I - TRANSPORT OF DISSOLVED SPECIES: THEORY OF DISPERSION

A) Three physical mecanisms seem to play an important role in the transport of a dissolved species in porous media:
- convection,
- adsorption-desorption,
- dispersion.

The theory of dispersion can take into account those three mecanisms.

1) Convection

Convection represents the transport of the solute in accordance with the mean movement of filtration of water in the porous media; convection is determined by the knowledge of the mean pore velocity of the flow, therefore by the effective porosity of the medium.

2) Adsorption-desorption

Sorption is the interaction of the solution with the solid phase. It is given by a relationship between the concentration of the species in the liquid phase, and in the solid phase. It will be shown that, under certain assumptions, adsorption acts as a delay on convection, by reducing the apparent pore velocity.

3) Dispersion

Dispersion takes into account the molecular diffusion of the species in the fluid phase, and the mecanisms of mixing due to the circulation of the fluid. It is generally represented by one or more coefficients, the value of which depends on the nature of the dissolved species, the structure of the porous media and the magnitude of the pore velocity of the fluid.

The splitting up of the mecanism of transport into three terms (convection, sorption, dispersion) is already a model. Their distinction and their relative independence are not always easy to see, and depend, among other things, upon the scale of observation used. The magnitude of the dispersion coefficient, for instance, is linked to the precision with which the pore velocity distribution is described. Also sorption may depend upon the size of the representative elementary volume (REV) used to define the concentration. This importance of the scale of observation makes it necessary to determine coefficients in the field with experiments of the same order of magnitude as the phenomenon that will be studied.

B) General equations

The system of equations given to represent the theory of dispersion in porous media expresses the conservation of the mass of the fluid and of the solute in a representative elementary volume:

$$\text{div} (D\rho_f \text{ grad } \frac{C}{\rho_f}) - \text{div} (VC) = \frac{\partial}{\partial t} (\varepsilon C + (1-\varepsilon)\rho_s F)$$

$$V = -\frac{k}{\mu} (\text{grad } p + \rho_f \text{ grad } z)$$

$$\text{div} (\rho_f V) = \frac{\partial (\varepsilon \rho_f)}{\partial t}$$

$$\rho_f = \rho (C,p)$$

$$\mu = \mu(C)$$

$$F = F(C)$$

with p = pressure of the fluid,
C = concentration, mass per unit volume, in the fluid phase,
F = concentration, mass per unit mass, in the solid phase,
V = Darcy's velocity of the fluid,
ε = effective porosity,
ρ_f = mass per unit volume of fluid,
ρ_s = mass per unit volume of solid,
k = intrinsic permeability of the porous medium,
μ = fluid viscosity,
D = dispersion coefficient (or dispersion tensor).

This equation is generally written using the pore velocity instead of Darcy's velocity, so that the dispersion coefficient introduced here is different by a factor ε from the usual dispersion coefficient. We prefer this form, however, because Darcy's velocity is a well known parameter, and the importance of porosity is easier to see in this equation.

By solving this system of equations, it is possible to determine, in each location of the porous medium, and for all time, the concentration in the fluid phase, and the velocity of the flow.

C) Boundary conditions

The most usual boundary conditions may be described by knowing the density of mass flux of the dissolved species on the boundary. This density is given by:

$$Q = [VC - D\rho_f (\text{grad } \frac{C}{\rho_f})]\vec{n}$$

This shows that this condition needs data both on Darcy's velocity V and on concentration C.

Some special cases of interest are:

1) Flow line

The velocity is tangent to the boundary, and the density of mass flux is

$$Q = - D\rho_f \; \overline{(\text{grad} \; \frac{\vec{C}}{\rho_f})} \; \vec{n}$$

This is the case, for instance, of the contact between an aquifer and the bedrock. The mass flux by convection is zero on the boundary, but the diffusion may either be neglected, or evaluated with an analytical expression (model in one dimension, for instance).

2) Line of equal head

This is the case, for instance, of the contact between an aquifer and the sea bottom, if the pressure is hydrostatic in the sea.

There are two possibilities:
- the concentration is supposed to be uniform on each side of the boundary, i.e. there is no dispersion through the boundary; therefore:

$$\frac{\partial C}{\partial n} = 0$$

The density of mass flux in this case is given by:

$Q = VC$ if water flows towards the sea
         C: concentration in the porous medium,

$Q = VC_0$ if water comes from the sea,
         C_0: concentration in the sea.

- the concentration of the species coming into the sea is assumed to be instantly mixed and homogenized with the sea. The density of mass flux is then:

$$Q = [VC - D\rho_f \; (\text{grad} \; \frac{C}{\rho_f})_{\text{boundary}}] \qquad \text{if water flows towards the sea}$$

$$Q = [VC_0 - D\rho_f \; (\text{grad} \; \frac{C}{\rho_f})_{\text{boundary}}] \qquad \text{if water comes from the sea}$$

In the latter case, there may be retrodiffusion of the species in the opposite direction of that of flow; this may become non negligeable if the velocity if very low.

II - MODELLING OF MULTILAYERED AQUIFERS

A large sedimentary basin may often be described as a succession of aquifers and aquitards (strata of low permeability) or aquicludes (very low permeability). The number of layers identified may vary with the precision of the geological survey.

We may then assume that:
1) flow is in two dimensions in the aquifers,
2) flow is in one dimension in the aquitards.

It may be shown that the higher the permeability ratio between aquifers and aquitards, the better this assumption holds.

The model consists therefore of a succession of aquifers, interconnected by leakage. This approach is sufficient for modelling large sedimentary basins, and makes it unnecessary to deal with a complete three-dimensional approach, more difficult and expensive.

A) Simplification of the transport equation

When modelling a large multilayered system, only the regional balance of salt will at the beginning be studied, without aiming at precise values of the concentration. Therefore, to apply the theory of dispersion, the following assumptions are made:
1) The mass per unit volume of the fluid, ρ_f, and the viscosity μ, do not depend on the concentration (assumption of a tracer). This implies that the presence of the solute does not modify the flow.
2) Dispersion is neglected with respect to convection.
3) The adsorption isotherms are linear, and the equilibrium between the fluid and the solid phase is reached immediately.

The relation between F and C may then be written:

$$F = K_d C \qquad \text{with } K_d = \text{distribution coefficient}$$

With these assumptions, the transport equation writes:

$$e \left[\frac{\partial}{\partial x} (V_x C) + \frac{\partial}{\partial y} (V_y C) \right] + Q_h + Q_b + Q = - e \, \varepsilon R \, \frac{\partial C}{\partial t}$$

$$\frac{\partial}{\partial x} \left(T \frac{\partial h}{\partial x} \right) + \frac{\partial}{\partial y} \left(T \frac{\partial h}{\partial y} \right) + q_h + q_b + q = S \frac{\partial h}{\partial t}$$

with   e   = aquifer thickness,
        h   = head in aquifer,
        C   = concentration in an aquifer,
        V_x, V_y = Darcy's velocity in the two directions of an aquifer plane
        $R = 1 + \frac{1-\varepsilon}{\varepsilon} \rho_s K_d$ = delay coefficient (sorption),
        T   = transmissivity in an aquifer,
        S   = storage coefficient in an aquifer,
        q   = flow per unit area withdrawn or injected in an aquifer,
        q_h = flow per unit area between the aquifer and the upper aquitard,
        q_b = flow per unit area between the aquifer and the lower aquitard,
        Q   = density of mass flux of the species withdrawn or injected in an aquifer
        Q_h = density of mass flux of the species exchanged between the aquifer and the upper aquitard,
        Q_b = density of mass flux of the species exchanged between the aquifer and the lower aquitard.

1) Determination of the flow between aquifer and aquitards q_h and q_b

Let us considerer a layer of porous medium, of thickness l, permeability K and specific storage S. Initially, this layer is at equilibrium with a hydrostatic head H_0. Suddenly, one side of the layer is brought to the head H_1, while the other is kept at the head H_0. The resulting flow is one-dimensional and orthogonal to the side of the layer.

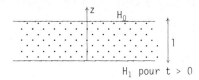

$$H_1 \text{ pour } t > 0$$

The flow per unit area inside the layer is given by:

$$Q = K\frac{H_1-H_0}{l}\left[1 + 2\sum_{n=1}^{\infty} \text{Cos}\,\frac{n\Pi z}{l}\,e^{\frac{-n^2\Pi^2 Kt}{sl^2}}\right]$$

with K = permeability of the layer,
      s = specific storage,
      l = thickness of the layer.

This gives for z = 0 $Q_1 = K\frac{H_1-H_0}{l}\left[1 + 2\sum_{n=1}^{\infty} e^{\frac{-n^2\Pi^2 Kt}{sl^2}}\right]$

      for z = l $Q_2 = K\frac{H_1-H_0}{l}\left[1 + 2\sum_{n=1}^{\infty} (-1)^n\,e^{\frac{-n^2\Pi^2 Kt}{sl^2}}\right]$

i.e. $Q_1 = \Delta H\,f(t)$
                  $Q_2 = \Delta H\,f'(t)$ with $\Delta H = H_1 - H_0$

Let us consider now the more general problem where the side z=0 is brought to the head h(t) which varies with time. According to the linearity of the equation, one can write:

$$Q_1 = \int_0^t \frac{\partial h}{\partial t}\,f(t-\tau)\,d\tau$$

$$Q_2 = \int_0^t \frac{\partial h}{\partial t}\,f'(t-\tau)\,d\tau$$

Coming back to the multilayered system, let us consider two aquifers, 1 and 2, overlying and underlying an aquitard. We want to determine the flow q_b per unit area at the boundary between aquifer 1 and the aquitard.

aquifer 1

q_b aquitard

aquifer 2

The flow is generated by the variations in the heads $h_1(t)$ and $h_2(t)$ in each aquifer. Accordingly, the flow q_b will be the sum of:

$$Q_1 = \int_0^t \frac{\partial h_1}{\partial t}\,f(t-\tau)\,d\tau$$

and $Q_2 = \int_0^t \frac{\partial h_2}{\partial t}\,f'(t-\tau)\,d\tau$

$$q_b = Q_1 + Q_2$$

In a similar way, the flow q_h at the upper boundary of an aquifer can be evaluated.

In conclusion, the flow exchanged between an aquifer and an aquitard depends, through a convolution equation, upon the record of the heads in the aquifer.

Computation of the convolution integrals Q_1 and Q_2

The time interval (o,t) is divided into several time-steps. The convolution integrals are discretized and computed step by step, taking into account the variations of the heads h_1 and h_2. In principle, this would require, at each time-step, a summation over all the previous time-steps, i.e. the storage in the core of the value of the head at each time-step and in each point. However, in this case, the special form of functions f and f' does not require this storage.

Let us expend function f, at the order 2, for instance:

$$f(t) \simeq f^*(t) = 1 + 2\,e^{-kt} + 2\,e^{-4kt}$$

with $k = \dfrac{\Pi^2 K}{s1^2}$

If we assume that we know the value of the convolution integral at time t:

$$I(t) = \int_0^t \frac{\partial h}{\partial t}\,f^*(t-\tau)d\tau = \int_0^t \frac{\partial h}{\partial t}\,d\tau + \int_0^t \frac{\partial h}{\partial t}\,2e^{-k(t-\tau)}d\tau + \int_0^t \frac{\partial h}{\partial t}\,2e^{-4k(t-\tau)}d\tau$$

$$I(t) = I_1(t) + I_2(t) + I_3(t)$$

Then, the value of $I(t+\Delta t)$ can easily be determined, taking into account the properties of f :

$$I(t+\Delta t) = I_1(t+\Delta t) + I_2(t+\Delta t) + I_3(t+\Delta t)$$

$$= \int_0^t \frac{\partial h}{\partial t}\,d\tau + \int_t^{t+\Delta t} \frac{\partial h}{\partial t}\,d\tau + e^{-k\Delta t}\int_0^t \frac{\partial h}{\partial t}\,2e^{-k(t-\tau)}\,d\tau +$$

$$+ \int_t^{t+\Delta t} \frac{\partial h}{\partial t}\,2e^{-k(t+\Delta t-\tau)}d\tau + e^{-4k\Delta t}\int_0^t \frac{\partial h}{\partial t}2e^{-4k(t-\tau)}d\tau +$$

$$+ \int_t^{t+\Delta t} \frac{\partial h}{\partial t}\,2e^{-4k(t+\Delta t-\tau)}\,d\tau$$

$$I(t+\Delta t) = I_1(t) + e^{-k\Delta t}\,I_2(t) + e^{-4k\Delta t}\,I_3(t) + \int_t^{t+\Delta t} \frac{\partial h}{\partial t}\,f^*(t+\Delta t-\tau)d\tau$$

This gives a recurrent algorithm to compute the convolution integrals, needing only to store the heads at the given time-step.

2) Determination of the mass flux of the dissolved species exchanged between aquifers and aquitards

The transport of salt at the upper and lower boundary of an aquifer comes mainly from the flow of water by leakage.

```
Concentration   ....................    aquifer
      C         ....................
                ....................
Concentration   ————————————————————    aquitard
      C         ————————————————————
       sp       ————————————————————
```

The flow q at a boundary between aquifer and aquitard has been determined in the previous paragraph. The mass flux of the dissolved species depends upon the direction of this flow:

$$Q = q \ C \quad \text{if water flows from the aquifer to the aquitard,}$$
$$Q = q \ C_{sp} \text{ if water flows from the aquitard to the aquifer.}$$

We assume that the salinity in the aquifer and in the aquitard may be described by only one concentration, i.e. that any amount of salt is instantly diluted in the entire porous medium, when moving from an aquifer to an aquitard, or vice-versa.

Denoting Q_h and Q_b the mass flux of the dissolved species at the upper and lower boundary of an aquitard, the principle of mass conservation gives:

$$Q_h + Q_b = \frac{d \ C_{sp}}{dt} \ 1 \ \varepsilon_{sp} \ R_{sp}$$

with 1 = thickness of the aquitard,
      ε_{sp} = effective porosity of the aquitard,
      R_{sp} = sorption coefficient in the aquitard.

This last relation gives the concentration C_{sp}.

B) Numerical solution

The numerical solution of the flow and transport equations in a multi-layered system was done using a finite difference approximation on a set of nesting square meshes of variable size.

Each aquifer is represented by a layer of square meshes. The basic grid consists of squares of size 8a. Each of these squares can be divided into four smaller squares of size 4a. If this division is repeated three times, the result is a set of nesting squares of size 8a, 4a, 2a and a. Such a method makes it possible to obtain a finer discretization in some areas of the aquifers, where a large amount of information is available or where precise results are needed.

On a given vertical line, each aquifer may have a different grid than the other, according to the amount of available data, and to the magnitude of the exploitation.

The equations of flow and of transport are discretized on this grid. This generates two separate systems of equations, where the unknowns are heads on one hand, and concentration on the other.

The time space of the simulation is divided into several time-steps. For each time-step, the two linear systems are solved successively by an iterative technique (point successive overrelaxation), giving the values of the unknowns assigned at the center of the meshes.

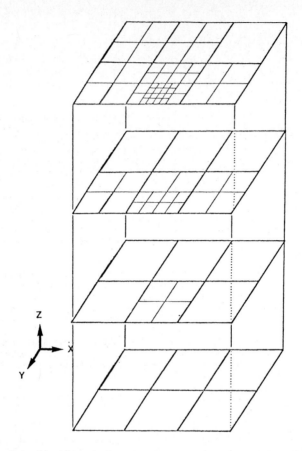

The discretization of the transport equation generates errors due to numerical dispersion. These errors do not shift the average movement of a pollution wave, but generate a spreading of the wave, the overall balance being respected.

C) Conclusion: Use of multilayered models

On such a model, one can represent the overall transfer of water and of dissolved salts over a large sedimentary basin. The aim of the model is not to predict with great precision the concentration of salts at each point of the aquifers, but to help to understand the regional mechanisms of the transport of salts, in order to detect the areas where the risks are particularly important. Accordingly, in our opinion, mechanisms like dispersion may be neglected, as they require measurements of parameters very difficult to obtain at such a scale.

However, at a local scale, modelling which takes into account dispersion may be considered in the areas where the simplified overall model shows a possible high risk.

III - MODELLING OF THE AQUIFERS OF THE KAIROUAN BASIN

A) Description of the aquifer system

The alluvial plain of Kairouan occupies over 3.000 km^2. This sink-hole basin is filled with plio-quaternary dedrital deposits. Sedimentation is lenti-cular, with alternation of strata of coarse sands and marls, and all the transi-tion facies. The thickness is over 500 m.

Two main aquifers may be distinguished (Fig.1): the upper watertable aquifer, and a lower aquifer exploited by wells. Most of the recharge of these aquifers comes from the floods of two main rivers flowing through the plain: "oueds" Zeroud and Merguellil. Evaporation is the only natural outlet of the basin. It takes place mainly in the "sebkhas" (brackish lakes) of the north and east boundaries, which also receive the running water of the "oueds".

The piezometric chart (Fig.2) shows the hydraulic mechanism of the underground reservoirs. Upstream, the lower aquifer is recharged by the upper aquifer, and this downward flow is easy. Downstream, to the east and the north, the lower aquifer is confined, and the flow is upward from the lower aquifer to the upper one. The loss of head between the two aquifers becomes high, showing a less easy vertical connection.

The spatial distribution of the salt concentration of the underground waters is good evidence of this mechanism. The horizontal gradient of salinity is much higher in the upper aquifer: from 1 g/l upstream, in the recharge area, to more than 7 g/l downstream, where evaporation occurs. In the lower aquifer, this gradient is much lower: from 1,5 g/l upstream to 3 g/l downstream.

Upstream, the easy flow downward into the recharge area, from the upper aquifer to the lower, keeps a good quality in the water of both, whereas down-stream, the existence of an aquitard between the two aquifers makes it possible to observe a high difference of salinity.

B) May the quality of the water of the confined aquifer become lower with development ?

The agricultural development of the plain will largely increase the demand of water in the near future. This will generate development of the lower aquifer, where the well capacities are much higher, and where the water quality downstream is better.

In modifying the hydrodynamical regimen of the aquifer system, there may also be a modification in the present equilibrium of salinity. There is a risk of intrusion of water of poor quality from the upper aquifer to the lower, downstream, if the hydraulic gradient becomes directed downwards. On the other hand, upstream, in areas where the recharging water is of good quality, there may be an improvement of the quality of the water in the lower aquifer, if the rate of recharge of this aquifer is increased.

A realistic hypothesis of development was considered, based on an increa-se in pumpage in the lower aquifer. The simulation of this hypothesis over 20 years was performed, using program SAMMIR, and giving the distribution of head at the end of each year. The transport of salt was also determined, using the method described earlier in this paper. The following assumptions were made:

- The concentration in the upper aquifer is supposed not to vary with time. Only the variations of the concentrations in the lower aquifer are conside-red. Fig.3 and 4 show this constant concentration in the upper aquifer, and the initial concentration in the lower.

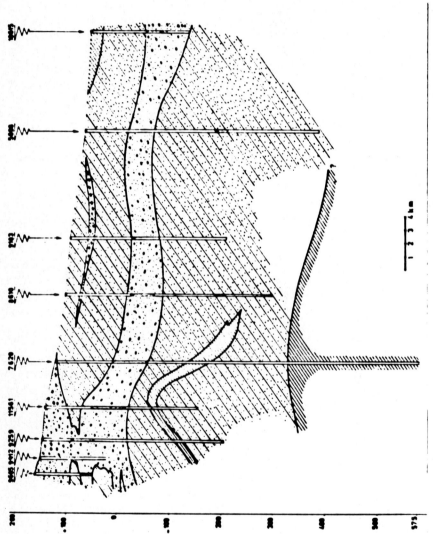

FIG.1 - Example of cross-section in the Kairouan aquifer
showing the different aquitards and aquifers

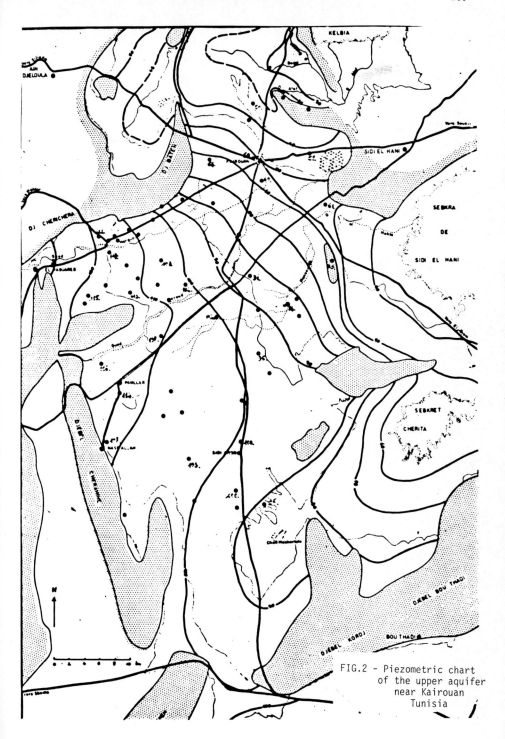

FIG.2 - Piezometric chart
of the upper aquifer
near Kairouan
Tunisia

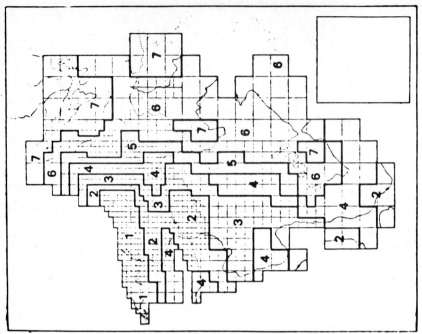

Fig.3 - Present salinity (G/1) of the upper aquifer

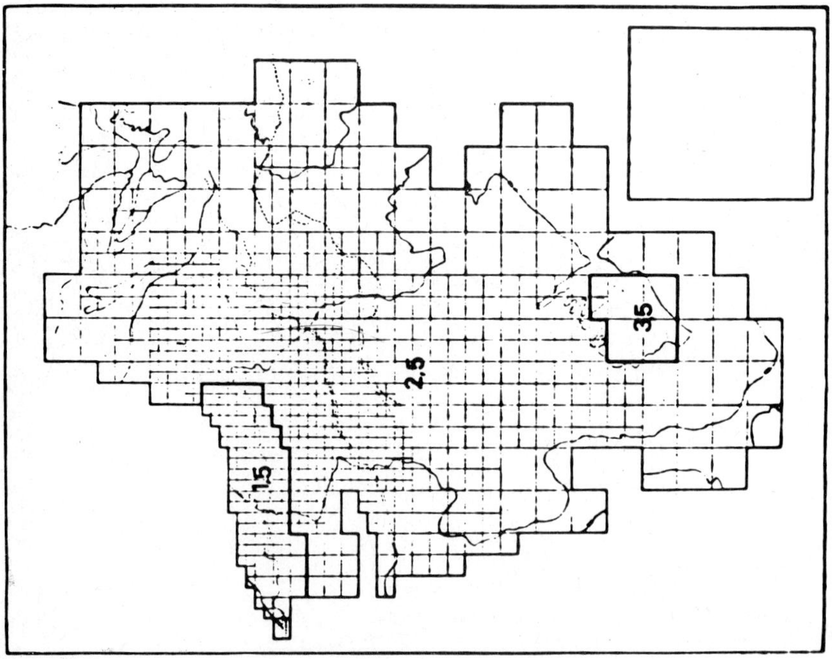

Fig.4 - Present salinity (g/1) of the lower aquifer

- The initial concentration in the aquitard between the two aquifers is supposed to be equal to that of the upper aquifer.
- Sorption, which is unknown, is supposed to be null.

These assumptions seem to be on the safe side. Furthermore, assumptions
had to be made on the magnitude of the volume of the porous medium in the lower
aquifer, where mixing would occur between water flowing from the aquitard and the
existing water of the aquifer. Two trials were made:

a) Thickness of the aquifer 100 m, effective porosity 10%. The variation of concentration of salt is then very low.

b) To be safer, we tried a thickness of 50 m, and an effective porosity
of 5%, which is equivalent also to 25 m and 10%.

The variations in concentrations are then more important, but they
remain acceptable: in the area south from Kairouan, there is a constant increase
in salinity, but after 20 years, it never goes beyond 0,5 g/l, which is an acceptable long term result and of the same order of magnitude as the uncertainties on
the data used in this computation: thickness and porosity of the lower aquifer,
initial concentration in the water of the two aquifers.

On the other hand, there is a favorable dilution of the water in the
lower aquifer, in the north-western part of the plain, in the area where the upper
aquifer is recharged with very good quality water from oued Merguellil. This
water flows towards the lower aquifer as the drawdown in this aquifer increases.

Fig.5 shows the variations in salt content over the whole lower aquifer:
negative values represent a dilution, and positive values an increase in salinity.
These variations are given in 0,1 g/l.

Taking into account the fact that our assumptions for this computation
were rather pessimistic, these variations in salinity were found acceptable, and
the hypothesis of development considered was found realistic.

IV - AN EXAMPLE OF COMPUTATION OF THE RISING VELOCITY OF AN OBNOXIOUS SUBSTANCE STORED IN A DEEP LAYER

We consider the storage of an obnoxious species in the underground.

The substance is supposed to be injected in a deep permeable strata
confined by a layer of very low permeability. We assume, however, that there is
small hydraulic gradient upwards between the permeable strata and the ground surface, allowing a small amount of leakage to take place through the confining
layer.

The aim of this research was to study which were the parameters enabling
to confine the obnoxious substance over a very long period of time. We tested
different values of the:
- depth of the permeable strata,
- hydraulic gradient,
- permeability of the confining layer, supposed to be homogeneous up to the
  ground surface,
- effective porosity of the confining layer,
- sorption coefficient of the confining layer,
- dispersion coefficient of the confining layer.

The following simplifications were assumed:

- The flow of water through the confining layer will be vertical, directed upwards, with a constant Darcy's velocity.

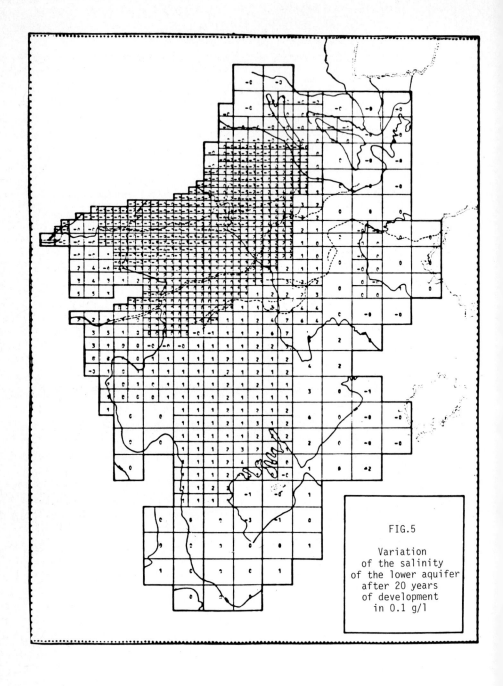

FIG.5

Variation
of the salinity
of the lower aquifer
after 20 years
of development
in 0.1 g/l

- The transport of the obnoxious species will not modify this velocity (tracer assumption), i.e. ρ_F and μ are constant.
- There is a linear adsorption isotherm between the obnoxious species and the particles of the confining layer.

With these assumptions, the general transport equation writes:

$$D_z \frac{\partial C^2}{\partial z^2} - V_z \frac{\partial C}{\partial z} = R \, \epsilon \, \frac{\partial C}{\partial t}$$

with D_z = longitudinal dispersion coefficient in the vertical direction,
   C = concentration in mass per unit volume in the fluid phase,
   V_z = Darcy's velocity in the direction z,
   R = delay coefficient due to sorption: $R = 1 + \frac{1-\epsilon}{\epsilon} \rho_s \, Kd$
   ϵ = effective porosity,
   ρ_s = mass per unit volume of the solid phase,
   K_d = distribution coefficient.

If the obnoxious substance has a natural radioactive decay, it is only necessary to substract $\frac{0,69}{T} \epsilon RC$ from the left hand side of this equation, T being the half life of the substance. This makes the concentration decay both in the fluid and in the adsorbed phase.

This equation was discretized with finite differences using meshes of small size, to limit the influence of numerical dispersion. The resulting tridiagonal linear system is solved at each time-step by direct matrix inversion. The discretization was done with backward differences in the direction of the velocity, and implicitly with respect to time.

The boundary conditions were:

- $C = C_0$ constant with time, at the boundary between the deep permeable strata and the confining layer;
- $\frac{\partial C}{\partial z} = 0$ at the ground surface, assuming that the obnoxious substance would be swept off when coming to the ground surface and would not accumulate.

The following table shows some results obtained with a given set of values of the different parameters. We assumed here:

- a depth of 500 m for the storage,
- no radioactive decay,
- a dispersion coefficient having the value $D_z = \alpha \, V_z$

   V_z = Darcy's velocity
   α = 10 m.

this is equivalent, if we use the usual dispersion coefficient, to a dispersivity of 10 m.

Distribution coefficient Kd, ml/g	Darcy's velocity m/s	Effective porosity %	Time of arrival at the surface of 1% of C_0 years	Time of arrival at the surface of the concentration C_0 years
0	10^{-8}	1	6	40
		10	60	400
	10^{-9}	1	60	400
		10	600	4.000
	10^{-10}	1	600	4.000
		10	6.000	40.000
10	10^{-8}	1	15.000	100.000
		10	14.000	90.000
	10^{-9}	1	150.000	1.000.000
		10	140.000	900.000
	10^{-10}	1	$1.5 \cdot 10^6$	10^7
		10	$1.4 \cdot 10^6$	$9 \cdot 10^6$
100	10^{-8}	1	150.000	1.000.000
		10	140.000	900.000

These results show without question the overwhelming importance of adsorption with respect to the other geologic parameters as far as the confining of the obnoxious substance is concerned.

Such a one-dimensional model including dispersion could be used for solving a pollution problem in a dangerous area of a multilayered system. But, generalizing it in three dimensions to a complete sedimentary basin seems to be a heavy procedure. Therefore, we prefer looking at the risks of pollution in large systems on a simplified model, such as the one presented in paragraph II, keeping a more detailed approach for particular zones only.

REFERENCES

ARMISEN, P., BESBES, M., LEDOUX, E., LEVASSOR, A., de MARSILY, G., POITRINAL, D. (1975). Sammir: un programme mathématique de simulation des aquifères multicouches en mailles irrégulières sur ordinateur. Congrès Intern. d'Hydrogéologie, Porto-Alegre, 23-27 Mars 1975.

BEAR, J. (1972). Dynamics of fluids in porous media. American Elsevier, New-York, London, Amsterdam.

BESBES, M. (1975). Etude hydrogéologique de la plaine de Kairouan par modèle mathématique. Rapport interne CIG-Ecole des Mines de Paris.

CAZAILLET, O. (1974). Ecoulement des fluides à travers les semi-perméables. Application aux modèles hydrogéologiques. Rapport interne CIG-Ecole des Mines de Paris.

FRIED, J.J. (1972). Etudes théoriques et méthodologiques de la dispersion en milieu naturel. Thèse de Doctorat d'Etat es Sciences Physiques, Bordeaux.

HOUPEURT,A. (1955 à 1957). Eléments de mécanique des fluides dans les milieux
          poreux. Revue de l'Institut Français du Pétrole, Vol. X, n°4 à Vol. XII
          n°3.

MARSILY, G. de (1971). Mathematical models for hydrologic processes. VIII Intern.
          Sedimentological Congress, Heidelberg, published in "Computer applica-
          tion in the Earth Sciences", Plenum Press, 1972, edited by D.F. MERRIAM

DISCUSSION

*Some of the changes in your aquifers are due to actual movements of salt
between the different aquifers. Is it a large percentage ? (NEUMAN)*

Transport of salt between the aquifers and also transport in the horizontal direction in the lower aquifer are taken into account. But the increase in
salinity, and the decrease of salinity in some areas, are mainly due to vertical
flow. (DE MARSILY)

*With respect to the transfer function in the aquitards, how much did you
consider ? How much back did you remember what was happening in the aquifer ?
(NEUMAN)*

In fact to apply the convolution relation here, you would need to memorize
the variation of the drawdown in each aquifer. (DE MARSILY)

How many time steps back did you memorize ? (NEUMAN)

Not any. If you look at the particular form of the transfer function here,
you see that you have a sum of exponentials. Instead of using the sum of them from
1 to infinity, we used only a first few terms of this sum. Then you make this convolution equation with each exponential term, without having to store in your computer anything. Because, if you want to compute :

$$F(t) = \int_0^t f_1(\tau) \, e^{-\tau} \, d\tau,$$ suppose you have computed this integral from 0

to t, you can find a recursive relationship between $F(t+\Delta\tau)$ and $F(t)$, and you only
need to have just the past variation of f_1. So you don't have to store a large
number of time steps. But the assumption that you make is that you may limit your
summation of exponential terms to a few terms. (DE MARSILY)

*Did you have a lot of data limitations that I experienced ? Are there a lot
of well samples taken in that area ? (SIMUNDICH)*

Very little. Actually we also applied the same technique to another aquifer,
and there were no data of water quality at all. However, the same question had to
be answered. We assumed that in one layer - the first - (supposing that the pollution would come down from this first layer) - the initial concentration was 1.
This concentration in the first layer was supposed not to vary with time, and the
value "1" was an arbitrary reference value. Then you can predict in the deeper
layer, which percent of the initial concentration of the first layer you may reach
in the future, in addition to what is already present. This means that we don't

know the initial concentration in the deeper layer, but we compute the increase
in salinity with reference to what the initial concentration was in the first
layer, even if you don't know it. But you can make assumptions.
For instance, suppose in this case we found an increase of 5 % of what were the
salinity in the upper layer. We did not know it, but we assumed it was between
10 and 15 g per liter, so 5 % of it would be only 0.05 to 0.075 g/liter. This would
be the increase, and that is an acceptable increase. So the risk of pollution of
the deeper aquifer could be estimated. I don't think we made a mistake in having
our estimates this way. (DE MARSILY)

*If you know the answer, why do you perform this ? You assume the increase,
but that is your answer. (VACHAUD)*

No, I assume that the reference initial concentration in the first layer
is 1, and I compute what happens after 20 years in the deeper layers in terms of
percentage of this reference concentration. (DE MARSILY)

*But the result that you obtain will depend on this assumption ! You assumed
the increase of 5 % per year. If you assumed 1 % you get another answer, and you
need 50 years to know if your assumption was correct. I mean that you obtain what
you assume. (VACHAUD)*

The point is : is that 5 % assumed or is it computed ? (PECK)

On which basis could it be calculated, without data ? (VACHAUD)

The 5 % is computed. It is an increase of salinity in the deeper layers,
refered to the constant concentration of the first layer. This result is obtained
by solving the transport equation in the domain, using the estimated parameters
of the aquifers, and the initial concentration : $C = 1$ in the first layer, $\forall\, t$
$$C = 0 \text{ in each other layer, for } t=0$$
I don't suggest to do so in each situation, but I intend to show that you may in
this way evaluate the risks of pollution of some aquifers even with a formidable
lack of data, if you have to make a decision concerning the development of the
aquifer system. (DE MARSILY)

System Simulation in Water Resources, ed. G.C. VANSTEENKISTE
1976, North-Holland Publishing Company

TRANSPORT FEASIBILITY OF
WASTEWATER IN A GULF-COAST ESTUARY

Jerry R. Rogers, Ph.D.
Department of Civil Engineering
University of Houston
Houston, Texas

ABSTRACT

A high nitrogenous wastewater is discharged to a Louisiana (USA) river
above an abundant dissolved oxygen lake source and the river confluence
with the Gulf of Mexico where the tidal influence is significant. A
transport feasibility study of discharging on the larger monthly ebb
tides in conjunction with treatment and storage ponds was initiated.

Seasonal flow patterns of freshwater advective flows were estimated from
flow depths over an upstream saltwater barrier and streamflow gage information. U.S. Corps of Engineers velocity-discharge measurements indicated a rapid decline in tidal ebb velocity with upstream river distance,
which was a major disadvantage to the transport feasibility concept.

The simplified mathematical modeling approach for water quality of the
U.S. Environmental Protection Agency was adopted for multiple waste
sources in the estuary.

INTRODUCTION

In southwestern Louisiana (U.S.A.), the Calcasieu River has a tidal
influence from its confluence with the Gulf of Mexico to an upstream saltwater
barrier at river distance 70 km (43.5 miles). This section has a large concentration of petroleum-chemical plants and other industries below the city of
Lake Charles, Louisiana. Discharges from industries and municipalities oscillate
in the river with the tides, but ultimately pass southward in a 12.2m(40 ft.)
deep navigation channel past the Intracoastal Waterway barge crossing and along
the edge of Calcasieu Lake and into the Gulf of Mexico (see Fig. 1). A portion
of channel water spills into Calcasieu Lake at its northern edge and at other
wind-driven entrance sections. Little daily or hourly coordinated data is
available on general flow circulation, velocities, and actual water quality, but
maximum utilization of existing data will be presented in later sections of this
paper.

STANDARDS AND WASTE ALLOCATION MODEL

Louisiana water quality criteria (1973) contained a minimum dissolved
oxygen level of 4.0 mg/l for the lower Calcasieu River and a maximum temperature
standard of 35°C. Waste load allocations were made for the river utilizing
estuary multiple waste modeling of the U.S. Environmental Protection Agency
(1971) (1972). The model values summarized in Fig. 1 were adopted by Roy F.
Weston, Inc. for the Louisiana Health Administration (1974). The Calcasieu River
model had three sections based on velocities and two sections based on dispersion
coefficients, E. A model assimilative capacity of 15,850 kg/day (35,000 lbs./day)
was estimated. Industrial and municipal waste load allocations were based on
this assimilative capacity.

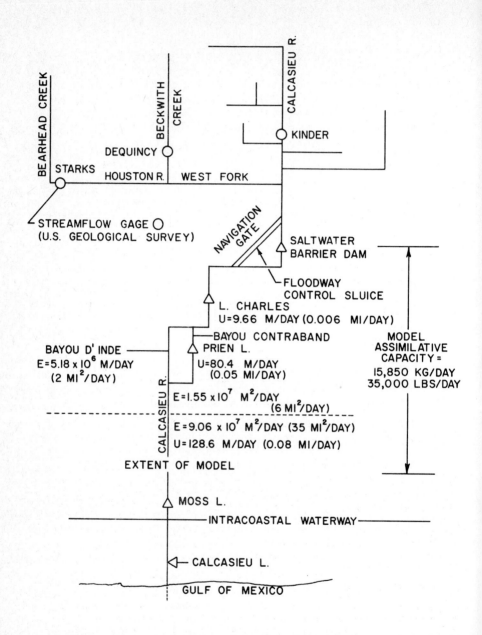

Fig. 1. Calcasieu River, Louisiana (USA) to Gulf of Mexico

DISSOLVED OXYGEN CONDITIONS

The dissolved oxygen pattern shown in Fig. 2 may be typical of the ebb and flood tidal patterns near high nitrogenous or carbonaceous waste discharges. Note the dissolved oxygen sag below the stream standard of 4.0 mg/1 for the ebb tides and the different profiles for the flood tides. More coordinated stream surveys and data collection should reflect these same patterns with more data points.

MODEL PARAMETERS AND DISPERSION COEFFICIENTS

A graphical estimate of the dispersion coefficient, E, is based on the postulated exponential relationship:

$$c = c_o e^{UX/E}$$ Eq. (1)

where:

 c = water quality level some time after the initial concentration, c_o
 U = stream velocity
 X = distance downstream
 E = dispersion coefficient

Taking natural logarithms of Eq. (1):

$$\ln c = (U/E)X + \ln (c_o)$$ Eq. (2)

If the slope of a semi-logarithmic plot of $\log_{10}$ c vs. x is adjusted to the natural logarithm base by the factor 2.3 when a linear plot is obtained:

$$E = \frac{U}{2.3x(\text{slope})}$$ Eq. (3)

The graphical estimate of dispersion coefficient is shown in Fig. 3.

The velocity term, U, is highly dependent upon the critical discharge level, Q, utilized for the model, (U=Q/A), since the cross-sectional area of the 12.2m (40 ft.) deep channel can be estimated. Assuming a channel 122m (400 ft.) wide and 3.05m (10 ft.) – 30.5m (100 ft.) sections on either side of the main channel, an area of $1510m^2$ (16220 $ft.^2$) is obtained. A flow of 28.3m^3/s (1000cfs) yielded a velocity of 1620m/day (1.01 miles/day) and $E=3.91\times10^7 m^2$/day (15.1 $miles^2$/day). A flow of 2.26m^3/s (79.9 cfs) provided a velocity estimate of 128.5m/day (0.08 miles/day) and $E=3.09\times10^6 m^2$/day (1.19 $miles^2$/day). In general, the higher flow gave water quality parameters similar to those reported in the literature while the low flow (2.26m^3/s) (79.9 cfs) provided quality parameters which were too low. Therefore, the low flow estimate for the model should be obtained as carefully as possible from streamflow information.

DEOXYGENATION COEFFICIENTS

The estimate of deoxygenation coefficient shown in Fig. 4 was 0.212/day at 20°C for a streamflow of 28.3 m^3/s (1000 cfs) and velocity of 1620m/day (1.01 miles/day). Adjusting this to 35°C for the critical conditions of the model:

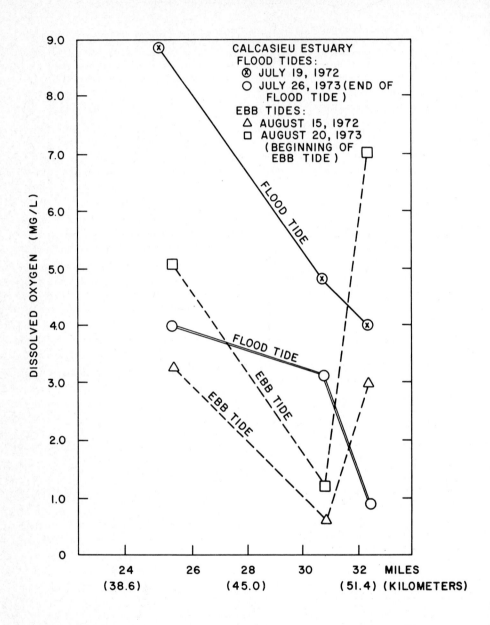

Fig. 2. Dissolved oxygen vs. river distance

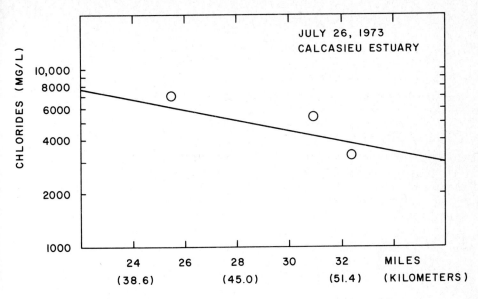

Fig. 3. Graphical estimate of dispersion coefficient (E)

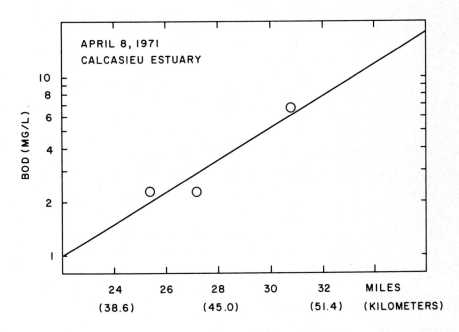

Fig. 4. Graphical estimate of deoxygenation coefficient (K_d)

$$k_{d_{35}} = k_{d_{20}} \ (1.047)^{35-20} = 0.423/\text{day}$$

These levels fall within the 0.2-0.5/day range for BOD reaction coefficients for tidal rivers and estuaries of the U.S.E.P.A. (1971).

NITROGENOUS DEOXYGENATION COEFFICIENTS

Limited nitrate-nitrogen data has been plotted in Fig. 5. Adopting the hint in Eckenfelder (1970):

"The nitrification rate should be converted to terms of oxygen."

and writing the reaction of the conversion from ammonia to nitrate:

$$2NH_3 + 4\tfrac{1}{2}O_2 \longrightarrow 2NO_3 + 3H_2O$$

leads to:

Rate O_2 = (4.5 x 32)/(2 x 62) Rate NO_3 = (1.16) Rate NO_3

Applying a velocity of 1620m/day (1.01 miles/day) to data from Fig. 5:

$$k_n = 2.25/\text{day}$$

which is higher than the 0.1-0.25/day range for nutrient reaction coefficients for tidal rivers and estuaries of the U.S.E.P.A. (1971) and the 0.28/day level for the Potomac Estuary reported by O'Connor and Thomann (1971) and the 0.1/day rate used by Sparr and Hann (1973). Other literature on nitrogenous material kinetics include DeMarco, et al (1967) and Downing, et al (1964).

VELOCITIES FOR REAERATION AND TRANSPORT

Velocities in rivers or estuaries reflect the dissolved oxygen transfer capability. The standard reaeration formulas usually contain a term on velocity and depth. Only a small sample of velocity data was available for the Calcasieu estuary from the U. S. Army Corps of Engineers District Office in New Orleans. Table 1 contains this data listed by river distance. The maximum ebb and flood tide velocities were measured for September 21, 1973 with data for river distance 4.82 km (3.0 miles) being the nearest data to the entrance at Calcasieu Pass. This is important to utilize and understand the information available on predicted tidal current data from the U. S. Department of Commerce (1973). These tables are available one year in advance and could be used in setting up water quality sampling programs in estuaries to anticipate profiles such as that found in Fig. 2. Obviously, the freshwater advective flows and wind conditions have an impact on these predicted tidal currents. In Table 1, the Corps of Engineers measurement of 1.525m/s (5.0f/s) is slightly higher than the predicted ebb current of 1.44m/s (4.73f/s) due to the freshwater advective flow. The flood tide measured velocity of 1.1m/s (3.6f/s) is slightly lower than the predicted level of 1.22m/s (4.0f/s) which is to be expected due to the freshwater flow downstream.

Since the feasibility of transport of wastewater downstream to the high dissolved oxygen lake source, Lake Calcasieu, or to the Gulf of Mexico was being investigated, the velocities measured were plotted vs. river distance as shown in Fig. 6. Note the rapid decrease in velocity with upstream distance; the maximum velocity at distance 4.82 km (3.0 miles) of 1.525m/s (5.0f/s) dropped off to 0.672 m/s (2.2f/s) at distance 24.1 km (15 miles), about a 44 percent decrease. This decrease in velocity indicated a long transport time for upstream wastewater

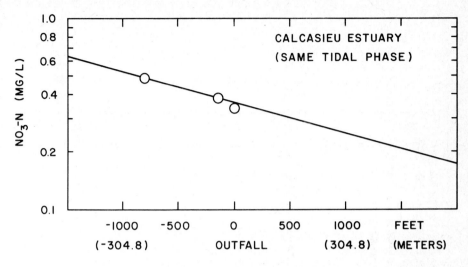

Fig. 5. Graphical estimate of nitrogenous deoxygenation coefficient (K_n)

TABLE 1

CALCASIEU CHANNEL VELOCITIES VS. RIVER DISTANCE

(From Data of U.S. Army Corps of Engineers District - New Orleans)

DATE	APPROX. RIVER DISTANCE		DISCHARGE,	VELOCITY, f/s		PREDICTED TIDAL CURRENT AT CALCASIEU PASS		
	mile	km	cfs	Max.	Mean	KNOTS	f/s	m/s
Sept. 21, 1973	3	4.02	14,000 at salt water barrier up-stream (396 m³/sec)	5.0E 3.6F		2.8E 2.4F 0.5E 0.3F	4.73E 4.0 F 0.84E 0.56F	1.440E 1.220F 0.256E 0.171F
" "	4	6.42	" "	4.4E 2.2F				
" "	15	24.1	" "	2.2E 1.2F				
March 4, 1973	23.1	37.2	24,100 (682m³/sec)	1.4	0.87	2.4E 1.3F 0.9E 0.9F	4.07E 2.19F 1.52E 1.52F	1.242E 0.668F 0.463E 0.463F

E = Ebb Tide,   F = Flood Tide

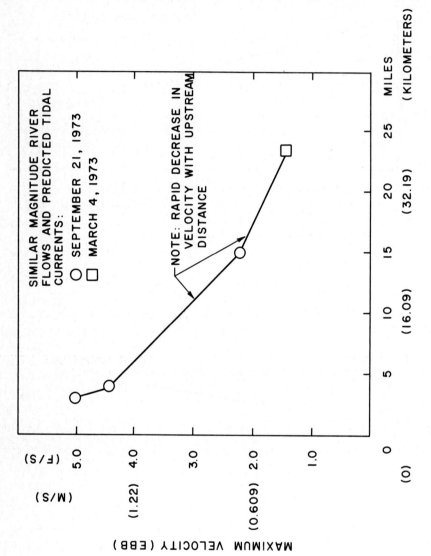

Fig. 6. Maximum Ebb velocity vs. river distance

to Lake Calcasieu and ended the prospect of taking advantage of this assimilative capacity on the ebb tide from wastewater storage ponds. However, the concept is still available for those discharges closer to an estuary mouth. Dr. Ken Shumate with Roy F. Weston, Inc. suggested the use of a relationship with predicted tidal current information:

$$\frac{\text{Velocity upstream}}{\text{Water Surface area upstream}} = \frac{\text{Velocity at pass (predicted)}}{\text{Water surface area upstream from the pass}}$$

which could be used for order of magnitude estimates for upstream velocities for reaeration or transport studies.

SEASONAL FLOWS

The final portion of the study involved an analysis of seasonal flows below Lake Charles. The monthly minimum streamflow data and drainage area adjustments are shown in Table 2. The 1972 summer monthly flows were fairly low at 750, 511, 513, 494, 354 cfs for April, June, July, August, and September, respectively. The 1973 summer season was a wet period in that the same months listed above had 3730, 1183, 684, 893, and 1135 cfs flows. For perspective on flow magnitudes, the section on MODEL PARAMETERS compared two model flows below Lake Charles - one of 28.3m^3/s (1000 cfs) magnitude and the other of 2.26m^3/s (79.9 cfs). The 1972-1973 monthly minimum flows are larger than the lower model flow, and local inflow below Lake Charles has not been added to these estimates. Therefore, the lower model flow of 2.26m^3/s (79.9 cfs) may be somewhat conservative.

To obtain a better estimate of the duration of dependable wet season flows, data from the largest drainage area gage (at Kinder) was analyzed with results shown in Table 3 for 1971-1973. The number of days of flow greater than 28.3m^3/sec (1000 cfs)(for the majority of the month) indicated a wet season from November through May. If the definition of dependable flow included the flow greater than 19.8m^3/sec (700 cfs), the wet season might be extended until August, although flows during the summer months of June-August fluctuate widely.

The purpose of this seasonal analysis was related to holding pond capacity considerations and wastewater releases during the wet season on the ebb tide. There would be some dilution advantage from a water quality stand point, primarily from November through possibly June.

Another measure of flow past Lake Charles could be obtained from depths over the floodway control sluice and the typical weir flow formula such as that found in Richey, et al (1961):

$$Q_{cfs} = CLH^{3/2}$$

where:

L = crest length
H = depth over the weir
C = 3.1 to 3.6

Typical depths are supposed to range from 0.122 m (0.4 ft.) to 0.305 m (1.0 ft.) (e.g., the depth was 0.122 m (0.4 ft.) on August 14, 1974). Since the control sluice is 122 m (400 ft.) wide, the weir formula for a 0.061 m (0.2 ft.) depth (which might occur during drought periods) would yield:

$$Q = 10.5m^3/sec \ (372 \ cfs)$$

TABLE 2

MONTHLY MINIMUM DRY SEASON ADVECTIVE STREAMFLOWS NEAR LAKE CHARLES

	DRAINAGE AREA (SQUARE MILES) At Gage	Adjusted to L. Charles	April		June		July		Aug.		Sept.	
			\			1972 FLOWS (cfs)						
a. Calcasieu R. near Kinder, La.	1700	2125	589	736	404	504	407	509	390	487	274	343
b. Beckwith Creek near De Quincy	148	296	6.3	12.3	3.5	7	2.5	5	2.1	4.2	5.4	10.8
c. Bearhead Creek near Starks	177	354	0.7	1.4	0	0	0.1	0.2	1.2	2.4	0	0
1972 Subtotal L. Charles Saltwater Barrier			603	750	408	511	410	513	393	494	279	354
1973 Subtotal L. Charles Saltwater Barrier			2925	3730	933	1183	540	684	708	893	894	1135

1973 FLOWS (cfs)

TABLE 3

DURATION OF DEPENDABLE WET SEASON FLOWS AT KINDER

	Days of Flow > 1000 cfs. (28.3m^3/sec)											
	Oct.	Nov.	Dec.	Jan.	Feb.	Mar.	Apr.	May	June	July	Aug.	Sept.
1971	19	18	18	27	23	31	9	17	0	0	8	9
1972	2	7	31	31	28	31	8	16	8	2	0	0
1973	9	22	31	31	28	31	30	31	29	5	15	26
Ave.	10	15.6	26.6	29.6	26.3	31	15.6	21.3	12.3	2.3	7.6	11.6

$\longleftarrow$ Dependable $\longrightarrow$
Flow > 1000 cfs.(28.3 m^3/sec)

	Days of Flow > 700 cfs (19.8m^3/sec)											
	Oct.	Nov.	Dec.	Jan.	Feb.	Mar.	Apr.	May	June	July	Aug.	Sept.
1971	20	30	21	30	24	31	15	23	1	0	16	10
1972	7	11	31	31	28	31	20	22	10	12	6	0
1973	9	27	31	31	28	31	30	31	30	20	30	30
Ave.	12	23.6	27.6	30.6	26.6	31	21.6	25.3	13.6	10.6	17.3	13.3

$\longleftarrow$ Dependable Flow > 700 cfs. (19.8m^3/sec) $\longrightarrow$

Local inflow below Lake Charles would need to be added to this flow estimate.
Finally, the navigation gate near the control sluice is only open from October 1
to March 1; therefore, it would not normally be a factor during the low flow
period, but would pass flows during the winter, wet season.

SUMMARY AND CONCLUSIONS

    This paper reviewed the considerations of transport feasibility of
wastewater in an estuary, including stream standards, water quality coefficient
estimation (e.g., dispersion, deoxygenation, nitrification coefficients), velocities for reaeration estimation and transport feasibility, and seasonal flow
estimates from upstream gage information or from the weir flow formula. Since
the upstream velocities are so small during the tidal cycle, the quick wastewater transport feasibility concept (to the high dissolved oxygen lake source
or to the Gulf of Mexico) was rejected. However, the concept does have potential
for those discharges near the mouth of estuaries, and the use of predicted
tidal current information should be utilized in water quality sampling programs
or transport design considerations.

ACKNOWLEDGMENTS

    The New Orleans Corps of Engineers district transmitted flow and
velocity information through the assistance of Larry Dement and Cecil Soileau.
Dr. Ken Shumate, Doug Diehl, Jack Piskura, and others at Roy Weston, Inc.,
consulting engineers, provided much valuable advice and ideas. Many others in
the Lake Charles area contributed in local data aspects and their assistance was
appreciated.

REFERENCES

    DeMarco, J., et al (1967). "Influence of Environmental Factors on the
        Nitrogen Cycle in Water," J. American Water Works Association, May.
    Downing, A., et al (1964). "Nitrification in the Activated Sludge Process,"
        J. Institute of Sewage Purification.
    Eckenfelder, W. (1970). Water Quality Engineering for Practicing Engineers,
        Barnes and Noble, Inc., p. 48.
    Louisiana Stream Control Commission (1973). Water Quality Criteria,
        Baton Rouge, Louisiana.
    O'Connor, D. and R. Thomann (1971). "Water Quality Models: Chemical,
        Physical, and Biological Constituents, " Espey, W. and G. Ward (Editors),
        Estuarine Modeling: An Assessment, U. S. Environmental Protection
        Agency, Washington, D.C., p. 154.
    Richey, C., et al (1961). Agricultural Engineers Handbook, McGraw-Hill, N.Y.
    Sparr, T. and R. Hann (1973). "Nitrogen Modeling in the Houston Ship Channel,"
        Texas A & M University, presented to Environmental Engineering Technical
        Group, Texas Section - American Society of Civil Engineers.
    U. S. Department of Commerce (1973). Tidal Current Tables-1973. Atlantic
        Coast of North America, National Ocean Survey, Washington, D.C.
    U. S. Environmental Protection Agency (1971). Simplified Mathematical
        Modeling of Water Quality, March.
    U. S. Environmental Protection Agency (1972). Addendum-Simplified Mathemati-
        cal Modeling of Water Quality, May.
    Roy F. Weston, Inc. (1974). Water Quality Management Plan - Calcasieu River
        Basin, Louisiana Health and Social and Rehabilitation Services
        Administration, New Orleans, Louisiana, March.

DISCUSSION

*I think the model completely depends on the type of river you deal with.
For example with the Scheldt it does not happen. (WAJC)*

Remember we have a salt-water barrier upstream and that is the boundary
condition. That is the obvious reason why for this particular case, we have very
little freshwater flow. (ROGERS)

I think that the width of your river must be fairly constant. (WAJC)

It is a navigation channel. (ROGERS)

It is not at all the case for the Scheldt, which is an old river. (WAJC)

This was very new to me. It is some of the first work I've done in this
area. I do think it is very informative and it does show a lot of transferability
from concepts such as nitrogen cycle and things of this type.

*Did you have to make a balance between the importance of the influence of
the concentration gradient and the influence of the flow ? (COTTENIE)*

There is a dilution importance. One conclusion I found from my study is
that I believe that the model was a little conservative in the dilution water that
they use. They use very small velocities, and I believe there is really higher
flow because of the gating information flow I looked at. I did feel that the
value of flow is a little bit larger, as I used in the Roy Weston model. (ROGERS)

System Simulation in Water Resources, ed. G.C. VANSTEENKISTE
1976, North-Holland Publishing Company

MODELING OF MINERAL CONTENT VARIATIONS
IN NATURAL WATERS

F. DE TROCH
Laboratorium voor Hydraulica
Rijksuniversiteit Gent
Gent, Belgium

A. DHAESE and A. COTTENIE
Laboratorium voor Analytische en Agrochemie
Rijksuniversiteit Gent
Gent, Belgium

ABSTRACT

The content of mineral compounds and its variations in a
waterway were studied in function of actual and antecedent flow. The simulation model worked out for this purpose makes use of an "Antecedent flow index" (AFI) and
needed a time correction.

Thus it was possible to fit a water quality prediction
model. The concentration changes with flow variations
are explained in function of specific retention and release
phenomena taking place during soil leaching.
Interaction of fertilizer applications was introduced as
time correction.

INTRODUCTION

The use of surface water for urban distribution makes necessary the choice
of the least polluted stream basins and the protection and control of their quality. Furthermore the interaction between the flow of a river and the concentration of different dissolved and suspended constituants was studied in order to
establish water quality prediction models, including the knowledge of the way in
which the concentration of different compounds varies with flow variations.

GENERAL ASPECTS

The salt content of soil water is the result of physico-chemical interaction between solid and liquid phase, which is a function of the properties of the
adsorbing complex and of the specific behaviour of the ions involved, especially
of the cations. When percolation occurs, a dynamic system of ion exchange, retention and release takes place and in conditions of high rainfall a considerable
run-off simultaneously transports dissolved and suspended matter towards the river
beds.

Due to the complexity of all these phenomena, the final input of dissolved
matter into a waterway, its relationship with the flow and the speed of concentration changes in function of flow variations have to be studied, by means of a mathematical model which simulates the measured concentrations.

MATHEMATICAL MODEL

It has been recognized by several authors (Durum, 1953 ; Ledbetter &
Gloyna, 1964) that the concentration C of a mineral constituent in solution may
be related to the mean daily streamflow Q by the following basic equation :

$$C = aQ^b \qquad (1)$$

with a and b constants to be determined by regression.

In order to verify this relationship for the ZWALM-river (a confluent of the SCHELDE, some twenty kilometers upstream of Gent), every fortnight from July 1970 till December 1973, water samples were taken for chemical analysis. Though also trace elements were determined, the major ion-concentrations measured were : chlorides, sulphates, bicarbonates, sodium, potassium, calcium and magnesium. The total mineral load was calculated as the sum of the major elements-concentrations. Were also determined : nitrates, phosphates and $KMnO_4$-consumption.

A simple linear regression of the logarithms of the concentrations C of these elements versus the mean daily discharges, as suggested by eq.(1), did not give satisfactory results.

It appeared that, as already suggested by Ledbetter & Glovna, b in eq.(1) is not a constant, but may be a function of the water discharges of the days before the sampling day and of the discharge Q at the sampling day itself.

The following expression for b was then adopted :

$$b = a_o + a_f.\ln(AFI) + a_q.Q^n \qquad (2)$$

where : AFI : "Antecedent Flow Index"

a_o, a_f, a_q and n : constants to be determined.

As eq.(1) can be written $b = \dfrac{\ln C - \ln a}{\ln Q}$ $\qquad (3)$

the parameters a_o, a_f and a_q can be found by a multiple linear regression of b versus $\ln(AFI)$ and Q^n. Therefore, an expression for AFI needs to be chosen and a value of n must be determined. An approximative value of the exponent n was calculated by means of a simple linear regression of $\ln b$ versus $\ln Q$.

For the expression of AFI, several formulae (analoguous to the antecedent precipitation index in hydrology) were tested. The best results were obtained by putting :

$$AFI = \sum_{i=1}^{3} \frac{Q_{j-i}}{i} \qquad (4)$$

where : Q_{j-i} = mean daily discharge at the i-th day before the sampling day (j)

i = number of the day preceding the sampling day.

After calculating the values of $\ln(AFI)_j$ and Q_j^n for every sampling day j the multiple linear regression mentioned before provided the parameters a_o, a_f and a_q. The introduction of these parameters allowed a first approach to the C-Q relationship :

$$C_{1,j} = a Q_j^{\left[a_o + a_f.\ln(AFI)_j + a_q.Q_j^n \right]} \qquad (5)$$

with j indicating the sampling day.

For every major constituent, a deviation appeared to be time linked and periodical (see fig. 1).

If C_j = concentration of the constituent measured at sampling day j, the percentic deviation of the calculated concentration with regard to the measured one is :

$$\Delta_j \% = \frac{C_j - C_{1,j}}{C_j} \times 100 \qquad (6)$$

and could be formulated as a mathematical expression of the form :

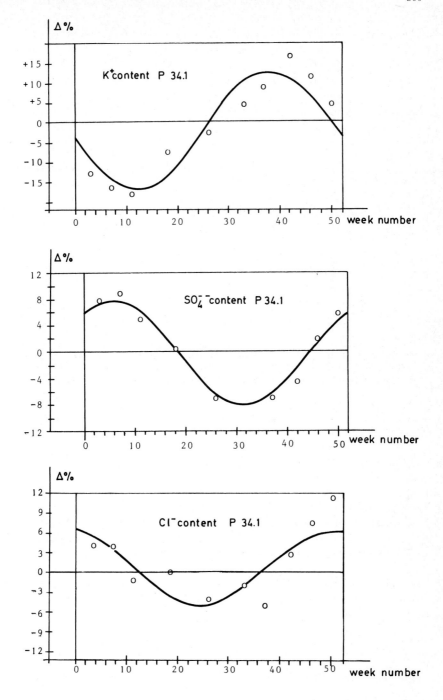

Fig 1 Percentic deviation Δ% in function of week number t_i

$$\Delta\% = A \cdot \cos\left[\frac{\pi}{26} (t_i + \psi)\right] + B \qquad (7)$$

where : t_i = the number of the week of the year
A, B, ψ : constants calculated by regression.

Hence, this expression for $\Delta\%$ was introduced as a correction factor for $C_{1,j}$ in order to calculate the final C-Q relationship :

$$C_{2,j} = \frac{100}{100 - \Delta\%} \cdot C_{1,j} \qquad (8)$$

In figure 2 some examples of the relationship of the concentrations C with the mean daily discharge Q, the antecedent flow index AFI and the week of the year t_i are shown.

Figure 3 illustrates the obtained results, showing the measured and the calculated concentrations for some elements under study. The efficiency r^2 of the model was calculated as : (Watt & HSU, 1970)

$$r^2 = \frac{U_o - U}{U} \qquad (9)$$

with

$$U_o = \sum_{j=1}^{n} \left(\frac{C_j - \bar{C}}{C_j}\right)^2$$

$$U = \sum_{j=1}^{n} \left(\frac{C_j - C_{2,j}}{C_j}\right)^2 \qquad (10)$$

$$\bar{C} = \frac{1}{n} \cdot \sum_{j=1}^{n} C_j$$

In order to limit the number of data, these figures, as well as the following discussion, are based on the results of a single sampling point (P 34.1 at Nederzwalm).

DISCUSSION

1. Concentration variations as a result of flow variations

In order to specify the behaviour of different mineral components in a simulation model, a numerical measure has to be established.

The dilution effect may be estimated by calculating the ratios of the concentrations corresponding for instance with two flow values of 200 and 2000 l per sec. and for a given AFI-index, frequently being of the order of 1000 1/s.

Table 1 gives such calculated ratios
$$R = \frac{C_{1, Q = 2000}}{C_{1, Q = 200}}$$ where C_1 = calculated concentrations

The R values show quite large differences, from 3.83 in the case of NO_3 to 0.31 in the case of PO_4.

R values smaller than 1 mean a dilution of the component with increasing flow, whereas R values higher than 1 correspond with an enrichment. The latter

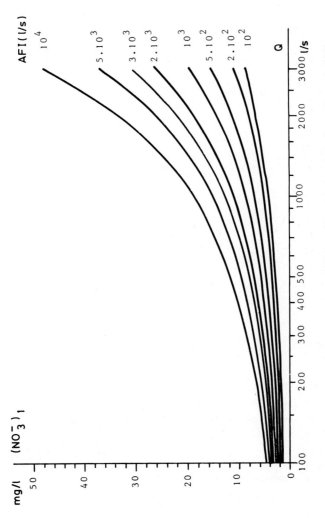

Fig 2a Nitrate content in function of flow Q and AFI

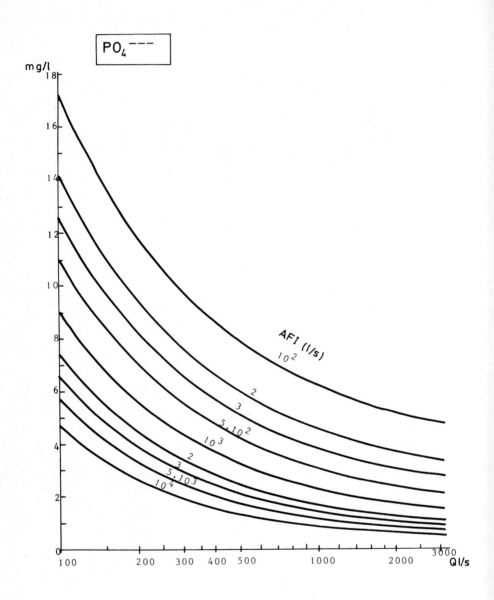

Fig 2b PO_4^{---} content in function of flow Q and AFI

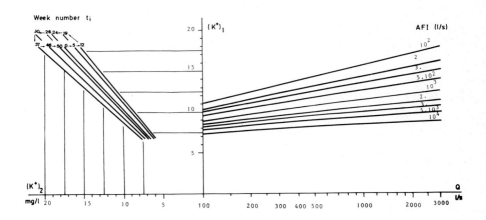

Fig 2c K^+ content in function of flow Q, AFI and week number t_i

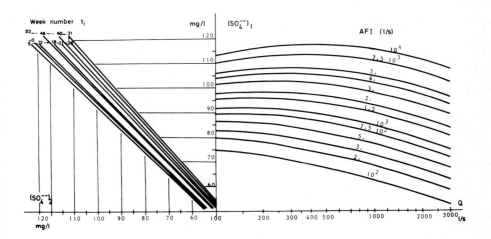

Fig 2d SO_4^{--} content in function of flow Q, AFI and week number t_i

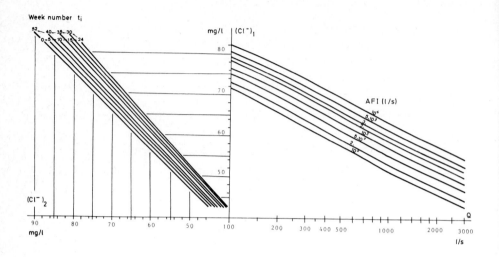

Fig 2e: Cl content in function of flow Q, AFI and week number ti

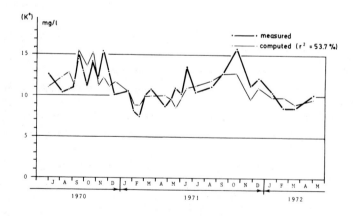

Fig 3a Comparison of measured and computed K⁺content P 34.1

phenomenon, as caused by leaching, contrasts with the dilution always observed in the case of local discharges of waste water.

Table 1. Dilution effect, expressed by the ratio $R = \dfrac{C_{1, Q = 2000}}{C_{1, Q = 200}}$

Element	AFI = 1000 1/s			AFI = 500 1/s		
	$C_{1,Q = 2000}$	$C_{1,Q = 200}$	R	$C_{1,Q = 2000}$	$C_{1,Q = 200}$	P
NO_3^- mg/l	14.1	3.7	3.83	10.9	3.1	3.54
$KMnO_4$ " consumption	5.8	3.4	1.71	7.0	3.9	1.81
K^+ "	12.2	9.9	1.24	13.5	10.6	1.28
SO_4^{--} "	78.9	91.8	0.86	71.2	85.5	0.83
Cl^- "	51.6	71.5	0.72	49.8	69.8	0.71
Ca^{++} "	93.8	140.0	0.67	85.3	132.0	0.65
Mg^{++} "	11.7	18.0	0.65	10.8	17.0	0.63
Total mineral load (meq/l)	14.4	22.7	0.64	13.4	21.5	0.62
HCO_3^- mg/l	266	462	0.58	242	432	0.56
Na^+ "	21.6	48.0	0.45	20.9	46.9	0.44
PO_4^{---} "	1.76	5.67	0.31	2.44	7.1	0.34

2. Relative content variations

The interaction between flow and content may also be represented for each compound by the ratio of its percentage into the total mineral load, as stated at different flow values.

Table 2 gives such results obtained with flow figures of 2000 and 200 1/sec and an AFI-index of 1000 1/sec.

The following different situations may be encountered :

$\alpha = 1$: negligible flow influence on the relative presence of the compound or element

$\alpha < 1$: in this cases the element fraction decreases with increasing flow

$\alpha > 1$: the percentage of a dissolved compound into the total mineral load increases with increasing flow.

From table 2 it can be seen that increasing flow has the following effect :

- decrease of percentic part of Na and HCO_3
- negligible increase of relative presence of Ca, Mg and Cl
- considerable increase of SO_4, K and NO_3.

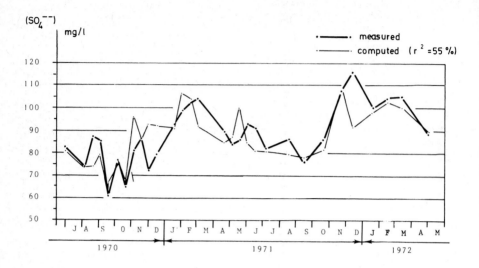

Fig. 3b: Comparison of measured and computed SO_4^{--} content P 34.1

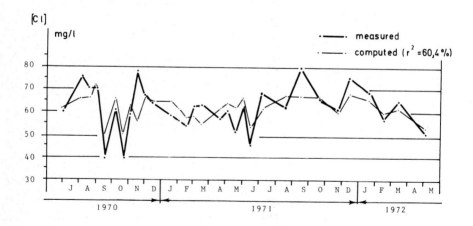

Fig. 3c: Comparison of measured and computed Cl^- content P 34.1

Table 2. Interactions between flow and percent   distribution of dissolved ions

	C_1 for Q = 200 1/s	%	C_1 for Q = 2000 1/s	%	$\alpha = \dfrac{\% \text{ for Q = 2000 1/s}}{\% \text{ for Q = 200 1/s}}$
NO_3^-	0.06	0.3	0.23	1.6	5.33
K^+	0.25	1.1	0.31	2.1	1.91
SO_4^{--}	1.92	8.4	1.67	11.4	1.36
Cl^-	2.03	8.8	1.46	9.9	1.13
Ca^{++}	7.10	30.9	4.75	32.3	1.05
Mg^{++}	1.50	6.5	1.00	6.8	1.05
Total mineral load	23	100	14.70	100	1.00
HCO_3^-	7.54	33	4.30	29.3	0.89
Na^+	2.09	9.1	0.96	6.5	0.71

C_1 = calculated concentrations in milli-eq. per litre

% = percent   part of each component in the total.

3. Classification of elements in the order of their leaching

The concentration of most elements shows to be directly related to the AFI-index and indirectly to the flow Q (fig. 2). The latter is to be considered as a dilution effect, which is however not observed for potassium , nitrates and $KMnO_4$ consumption. Furthermore, phosphate-concentrations are indirectly proportional with the AFI-index.

In order to explain these phenomena one should consider the following facts :

The quantities of elements present in a waterway originate from run-off and leaching, the latter practically being the only acting transport in low AFI-situations.

Slowly leaching water-nearly contains the "equilibrium concentrations" of elements, this means low concentrations of elements which are strongly retained by the soil. With regard to compounds which are easily leached, such as nitrates, the percolating water may contain higher amounts, thus enriching the receiving water.

When AFI is high the equilibrium concentration may not be reached, so that the percolation water remains relatively poor especially in elements which are slowly leached.

In any case, at constant flow, the influence of AFI upon concentration in the waterway will be highest with regard to elements which are easily leached.

The concentration variations as influenced by a 100 fold increase of AFI (10^2 to 10^4 1 per sec.) is given in table 3. This classification gives the comparative velocity with which the elements are released from the soil by leaching.

Table 3. Concentration variations in function of AFI

Element (mg/1)	Q = 2000 1/sec			Q = 500 1/sec
	AFI		ratio (1)/(2)	ratio (1)/(2)
	$10^2$1/s (2)	$10^4$1/s (1)		
NO_3^-	5	32	6.4	4.5
SO_4^-	56	113	2	1.7
Mg^{++}	9	17	1.9	1.6
Ca^{++}	70	130	1.7	1.8
HCO_3^-	200	380	1.6	1.7
Na^+	19	24	1.3	1.2
Cl^-	46	58	1.25	1.2
K^+	17	9	0.5	0.57
$KMnO_4^-$ consumption	11	3	0.3	0.36
PO_4^{---}	5.2	$\pm$ 0.1	0.02	0.01

4. Concentration variations in function of time

As already mentioned calculated concentrations are not only a function of flow and AFI, but also of time. The latter influence would be negligible if a more or less constant input of urban waste would be the main source of mineral compounds and no periodical deviation between simulated and measured values would be observed in function of time t_i.
However, in practice, there is a pronounced periodical relationship between 'Δ% and t_i, which is specific for each compound (fig. 1).

Since a considerable flow increase only results in a limited concentration decrease for most elements and even in an enrichment for some others, the main mineral charge of this waterway must be ascribed to release from the soil.

The periodicity of Δ% variations might be the result of time linked interactions such as fertilization and its element-specific nature may be the result of selective retention and release by the soil.

The concentrations corresponding with Δ% = 0 (without any time correction) are to be considered as the net-concentration, caused by a leaching process where an ideal soil-solution equilibrium is acting as a steady-state phenomenon, and where only the flow Q and AFI are the operating parameters.

Every deviation from this situation must be explained in function of variations in soil content, heterogeneity and external input, which is normally time linked.

- If Δ %> 0 the percolation and run-off water carries higher mineral contents and provides a positive contribution to the mineral charge of the receiving waterway
- If Δ% < 0 the percolation and run-off water contains smaller amounts of minerals than the initial soil water, as a consequence of exhaustion by plant uptake or earlier leaching and contributes to a dilution of the receiving waterway.

CONCLUSIONS

From this study it appears that the mineral load of a waterway can be simulated, taking into account at least three interacting factors : the flow (Q), the antecedent flow conditions (AFI) and the time of the year (t_i). Satisfactory correspondence between calculated and measured concentrations were obtained introducing these variables. Thus it was possible to fit a water quality prediction model.

The different considered mineral constituents are subject to quite large variations, which proved to be specific for each of them. These variations could be explained by means of soil physico-chemical phenomena.

REFERENCES

Durum (1953). Relationships of the mineral constituents in solution to streamflow, Saline River near Russell, Kansas. Trans. Amer. Geophys. Union, Vol. 34, nr. 3 - 1953 pp. 435-442.
Ledbetter & Gloyna (1964). Predictive Techniques for Water Quality Inorganics. Proceed. Amer. Soc. Civil Engrs., SA-div. Vol. 90 nr. SA1-Feb 64 pp. 127-151.
Watt & Hsu (1970) Continuous Basin Snowmelt Runoff Simulation. Hydrology Symposium nr. 8 (1970) Vol. 2, Nat. Research Council of Canada, Subcommittee on Hydrology.

DISCUSSION

The thing I was not clear about was, whether in evaluating the parameters of that model you'd actually use the same data that you are comparing the model with. I think you said you collected the data in the period 1971-1973. So when you are comparing your data with your comparison there, that's really evaluating the parameters and fitting the model to that set of data, is that correct ? I think the point was : If you obtained your parameters in 1971, did you use the same parameters in 1972 against those of 1972 ? (PECK)

The parameters were obtained from all the data together and the figures show the correspondance between calculated and measured values over the same period. (COTTENIE)

Do I understand that you have calibrated your model, but did not use it to predict ? (NEUMAN)

Indeed, the model has not yet been used for practical prediction. (COTTENIE)

This is the real test on the validity of the model. You showed us the comparison between modeled prediction of nitrate and observed nitrate. It seems to be remarkably better than for other elements. (BECK)

Indeed, for nitrate, a better correspondance was observed than for some other elements. The elements which are most easily released by the soil correspond best. For others the retention by the soil is quite important and not perfectly predictable. However one must consider also the order of magnitude for each element. (COTTENIE)

Would it be because it depends on a longer time history of what has been happening in the soil ? (BECK)

When a soil is percolated and when you have a high AFI-index, that means a high rainfall during three days past ; you have quite an important percolation. You may have 2 contradictory effects : for elements which are easily released by the soil, the concentrations will be increased in the river. Elements which are difficultly released are diluted in the percolating water, and finally for these ones, a dilution effect may be observed. So there is a quite different behaviour in function of the type of element. That's the reason why we showed the listing of elements in function of their leaching, when the soil is percolated. (COTTENIE)

How did you determine the number of days in the AFI-index ?
Was this a matter of judgement ? (VAN DER BEKEN)

We took 3 days. One could take a longer period of course, but the practical test made us decide on 3 days. (COTTENIE)

The measurements have been taken every fortnight. You could perhaps use an index with a decreasing importance given to the days before the sampling day.
I would use for instance 14 flows of the preceedings days.
And from a conceptual point of view ? (VAN DER BEKEN)

If you take the antecedent flow index in analogy with the antecedent precipitation index in hydrology, and an expression that takes into account the influence of the days before, in decreasing degree, after some 5, 6 days, the importance of these factors becomes very small. So, we limited it to 3 days. (DHAESE)

System Simulation in Water Resources, ed. G.C. VANSTEENKISTE
1976, North-Holland Publishing Company

NUMERICAL SOLUTION FOR CONVECTIVE DISPERSION
WITH INTRA-AGGREGATE DIFFUSION
AND NON-LINEAR ADSORPTION

M. Th. van Genuchten
Department of Civil Engineering
Princeton University
Princeton, New Jersey

P. J. Wierenga
Department of Agronomy
New Mexico State University
Las Cruces, New Mexico

ABSTRACT

A simulation model is presented for the dispersion of a chemical in an aggregated sorbing porous medium. The model considers concentrations in terms of mobile (dynamic) and immobile (stagnant) regions of the liquid phase. Sorption processes are assumed to be instantaneous. The occurence of hysteresis between the equilibrium adsorption and desorption isotherms is also considered.

Numerical results show that intra-aggregate diffusion is the main mechanism causing tailing in the effluent concentration profiles. Hysteresis in the equilibrium isotherms appears to have less effect on the calculated results than was suggested in earlier studies, provided intra-aggregate diffusion is taken into account.

INTRODUCTION

Numerous attempts have been made in the last few decades to quantitatively describe solute movement in soils. Most mathematical studies have been concerned with either the simple convective-dispersive equation (Lapidus and Amudson, 1952; Brenner, 1962), or with modifications of this equation in attempts to include adsorption (Kay and Elrick, 1967; Lindstrom et al., 1967) or decay (Cassel et al., 1974). Recent studies have revealed many asymmetrical effluent concentration curves, deviating from the nearly symmetrical ones predicted with the convective-dispersive equation. These deviations were contributed principally by kinetic effects (Giddings, 1962; Lindstrom and Boersma, 1973), non-linear adsorption (deVault, 1943; Davidson et al., 1972), hysteresis in the equilibrium adsorption-desorption isotherms (Swanson and Dutt, 1973; van Genuchten et al., 1974) and by intra-aggregate diffusion (Green et al., 1972; van Genuchten and Wierenga, 1975). Analytical models have been derived for some of these phenomena, for example for kinetic adsorption (Lindstrom and Narasimhan, 1973), while for other phenomena for example, hysteresis, numerical models were necessary (Swanson and Dutt, 1973; van Genuchten and Wierenga, 1974).

All of these previous studies have been concerned with only one phenomenon. To the author's knowledge no attempts have been made to include all of the physical and chemical effects given above in one model. The purpose of this paper is to present a numerical simulation program, which includes the effects of intra-aggregate diffusion, non-linear adsorption and hysteresis.

PREVIOUS STUDIES

We refer the reader to several literature reviews for studies of dispersion
in porous media: Perkins and Johnson (1963), Fried and Combarnous (1971),
Biggar and Nielsen (1967) and Gershon and Nir (1969). Many studies have used
the convective-dispersive equation:

$$\frac{\partial C}{\partial t} = D \frac{\partial^2 C}{\partial z^2} - v_o \frac{\partial C}{\partial z}$$
(1)

where C is the concentration (meq/cm^3), D is the dispersion coefficient
(cm^2/day), v_o is the pore-water velocity (flux divided by the volumetric water
content ; cm/day), z is the distance (cm) and t is time (days). Solutions of
equation (1) were summarized by Coats and Smith (1964), Gershon and Nir (1969)
and by Bear (1972). These solutions predict nearly sigmoid or symmetrical
effluent concentration profiles. Recent studies have been concerned with the
deviations between the predicted (symmetrical) curves and the observed asymmetrical concentration effluent curves (Green et al., 1972; van Genuchten et al., 1974).
Coats and Smith (1964), Villermaux and van Swaay (1969) and Bennet and Goodridge
(1970) each modified equation (1) to account for the asymmetry (or tailing),
noted in effluent curves. These different studies included diffusion or
mass transfer from mobile (dynamic) liquid regions into immobile (stagnant)
regions. The differential equations used by these authors are the following:

$$\theta_m \frac{\partial C_m}{\partial t} + \theta_{im} \frac{\partial C_{im}}{\partial t} = \theta_m D \frac{\partial^2 C_m}{\partial z^2} - v_m \theta_m \frac{\partial C_m}{\partial z}$$
(2)

$$\theta_{im} \frac{\partial C_{im}}{\partial t} = \alpha (C_m - C_{im})$$
(3)

where the subscripts m and im refer to dynamic and stagnant regions, respectively,
and where v_m is the average pore-water velocity (cm/day) in the dynamic region
of the soil. Equation (2) assumes that average concentrations can be assigned
to the mobile and immobile regions (C_m and C_{im} respectively). Equation (3)
further states that a diffusional exchange of material is present between the
two liquid regions, the rate of exchange being proportional to the difference in
concentration between dynamic and stagnant regions. The proportionality constant α in this first-order mass transfer process is referred to as the mass
transfer coefficient (1/day). The model given by equations (2) and (3) compared favorably with the experimental data of Coats and Smith (1964) and Villermaux and van Swaay (1969). Hence they provide an excellent starting point for
modelling a medium with intra-aggregate diffusion.

In order to include adsorption in the transport equations, van Genuchten
and Wierenga (1975) modified equations (2) and (3) and obtained the following
set of differential equations:

$$\theta_m \frac{\partial C_m}{\partial t} + \theta_{im} \frac{\partial C_{im}}{\partial t} + f\rho \frac{\partial S_m}{\partial t} + (1-f)\rho \frac{\partial S_{im}}{\partial t} = \theta_m D \frac{\partial^2 C_m}{\partial z^2} - \theta_m v_m \frac{\partial C_m}{\partial z}$$
(4)

$$\theta_{im} \frac{\partial C_{im}}{\partial t} + (1-f)\rho \frac{\partial S_{im}}{\partial t} = \alpha (C_m - C_{im})$$
(5)

where S_m and S_{im} represent adsorption in the dynamic and stagnant regions, respectively (meq/g soil), while ρ is the bulk density (g/cm^3). The parameter f
characterizes the distribution of the adsorption sites into readily accessible
sites (f) and sites located in the stagnant region of the soil (i.e. around
blind pores and inside aggregates). Figure 1 gives a schematic representation

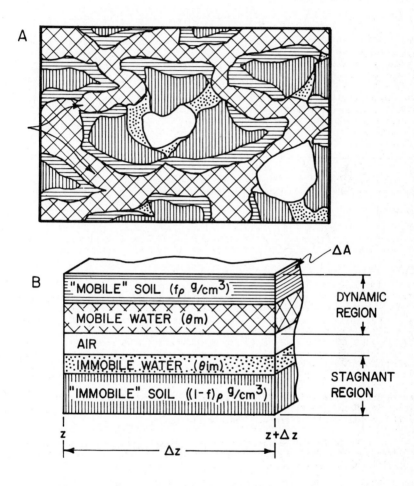

Figure 1.   Schematic diagram of unsaturated aggregated
porous medium. (A) Actual model. (B) Simplified model. The shading patterns in A
and B represent the same regions.

of a sorbing medium with intra-aggregate diffusion. The reader is referred to
the original paper of van Genuchten and Wierenga (1975) for an extensive discussion of equations (4) and (5). Several studies on the movement of chemicals
through sorbing porous media have assumed equilibrium between sorbed and solution concentrations, and have used the Freundlich relation to describe this
equilibrium (equation 6),

$$S = K C^N \qquad (6)$$

where K and N are empirical constants. Differentiation of equation (6) with
respect to time gives:

$$\frac{\partial S}{\partial t} = K N C^{N-1} \frac{\partial C}{\partial t} \qquad (7)$$

Equation (7) applies to both the mobile and immobile regions of the soil. Substitution in equations (4) and (5) results in:

$$\left[\theta_m + f\rho KNC_m^{N-1} \right] \frac{\partial C_m}{\partial t} + \left[\theta_{im} + (1-f)\rho KNC_{im}^{N-1} \right] \frac{\partial C_{im}}{\partial t}$$

$$= \theta_m D \frac{\partial^2 C_m}{\partial z^2} - v_m \theta_m \frac{\partial C_m}{\partial z} \qquad (8)$$

$$\left[\theta_{im} + (1-f)\rho KNC^{N-1} \right] \frac{\partial C_{im}}{t} = \alpha(C_m - C_{im}) \qquad (9)$$

In this study we will use the following initial and boundary conditions to describe a pulse input of solute into a semi-infinite medium of zero initial
concentration:

$$\lim_{z \to 0+} \left[v_m C_m - D \frac{\partial C_m}{\partial z} \right] = \begin{cases} v_m C_o & 0 < t < t_1 \\ 0 & t \geq t_1 \end{cases} \qquad (10)$$

$$\lim_{z \to \infty} [C_m(z,t)] = 0 \qquad (11)$$

$$C_m(z,0) = C_{im}(z,0) = 0 \qquad (12)$$

The solution of equations (8) - (12) for linear adsorption (N=1) was
obtained by van Genuchten and Wierenga (1975), and can be formulated in the
following dimensionless form:

$$c_m(x,T) = \begin{cases} c_1(x,T) & T < T_1 \\ c_1(x,T) - c_1(x,T-T_1) & T \geq T_1 \end{cases} \qquad (13)$$

$$c_{im}(x,T) = \begin{cases} c_2(x,T) & T < T_1 \\ c_2(x,T) - c_2(x,T-T_1) & T \geq T \end{cases} \qquad (14)$$

$$c_1(x,T) = G(x,T)e^{\frac{-\bar{\alpha}T}{\beta R}} + \frac{\bar{\alpha}}{R} \int_0^T G(x,\tau)H_1(T,\tau)d\tau \qquad (15)$$

$$c_2(x,T) = \bar{\alpha} \int_0^T G(x,\tau) H_2(T,\tau) d\tau \tag{16}$$

$$G(x,T) = 1/2 \, \mathrm{erfc}\left(\sqrt{\frac{P}{4\beta RT}} \; (\beta Rx - T)\right)$$

$$- \; 1/2 \left(1 + Px + \frac{PT}{\beta R}\right) e^{Px} \mathrm{erfc}\left(\sqrt{\frac{P}{4\beta RT}} \; (\beta Rx + T)\right)$$

$$+ \left(\frac{PT}{\pi \beta R}\right)^{1/2} \exp\left(\frac{-P}{4\beta RT} (\beta Rx - T)^2\right) \tag{17}$$

$$H_1(T,\tau) = e^{-(u+v)} \left\{ -\frac{I_0(\xi)}{\beta} + \frac{I_1(\xi)}{1-\beta} \left(\frac{u}{v}\right)^{1/2} \right\} \tag{18}$$

$$H_2(T,\tau) = e^{-(u+v)} \left\{ \frac{I_0(\xi)}{1-\beta} + \frac{I_1(\xi)}{\beta} \left(\frac{v}{u}\right)^{1/2} \right\} \tag{19}$$

$$\xi = 2(uv)^{1/2} \qquad u = \frac{\bar{\alpha}\tau}{\beta R} \qquad v = \frac{\bar{\alpha}(T-\tau)}{(1-\beta)R} \tag{20}$$

with the different dimensionless variables defined as:

$$c_m = C_m/C_o \qquad\qquad c_{im} = C_{im}/C_o \tag{21}$$

$$T = v_o t/L = v_m t \phi/L \qquad\qquad x = z/L \tag{22}$$

$$P = v_m L/D \qquad\qquad \phi = \Theta_m/\Theta \tag{23}$$

$$\beta = \frac{\Theta_m + \rho f K}{\Theta + \rho K} = \frac{\Theta_m}{\Theta} \frac{R_m}{R} \qquad\qquad \bar{\alpha} = \alpha L/(v_m \Theta_m) = \alpha L/q \tag{24}$$

$$R_m = 1 + \frac{\rho f K}{\Theta_m} \qquad\qquad R = 1 + \frac{\rho K}{\Theta} \tag{25}$$

The solutions given here for linear adsorption hold only when no hysteresis is present between the equilibrium adsorption and desorption isotherms. Recent studies however, have revealed the possibility of such a hysteresis (adsorption and desorption isotherms are not "single-valued"). Swanson and Dutt (1973), Hornsby and Davidson (1973) and van Genuchten et al (1974) each encountered hysteresis in the equilibrium isotherms. In these studies the coefficients K and N in equation (6) were found to depend on the sorption direction, i.e., on whether adsorption ($\partial S/\partial t > 0$) or desorption ($\partial S/\partial t < 0$) occured. The presence of a non-single-valued adsorption-desorption process results in more tailing and asymmetry in the effluent concentration curves (Davidson et al., 1972; Hornsby and Davidson, 1973; van Genuchten et al., 1974, van Genuchten and Wierenga, 1974).

NUMERICAL SOLUTION OF EQUILIBRIUM ADSORPTION

No analytical solutions are available for equations (8) and (9) when adsorption and desorption do not follow the same equilibrium relation, or when the adsorption isotherm is not linear ($N \neq 1$). A S/360 CSMP (Continuous System Modeling Program) simulation model may be used under such circumstances as will be presently demonstrated. The CSMP-simulation language has been shown to be very powerful in recent studies of transport processes in soils, e.g. unsaturated water movement van Keulen and van Beek, 1971 ; Bhuiyan et al., 1971), solute movement (Frissel et al., 1970), pesticide movement (van Genuchten et al, 1974) and heat transfer (wierenga and de Wit, 1970; Westcot and Wierenga, 1974). General discussions of the simulation of transport processes in soils were presented by De Wit and van Keulen (1972), Beek and Frissel (1973) and by van Genuchten and Wierenga (1974). Simulation of these transport processes involves dividing the soil into a number of layers or compartments of a given thickness. For each time step the flow of water, heat or solute is calculated over the compartmental boundaries by means of well-known mass transfer equations. Upon computing these flow rates, the computer updates (integrates) for each time step the net gain of material in each layer using one of the available intergration subroutines.

Since detailed descriptions of CSMP-programs for one-dimensional transfer problems can be found in the literature cited above, only the central equations in the dynamic part of the model will be presented here. A schematic representation of the dynamic part of the model is given in Fig. 2, while a listing of the program is given in Table 1. Fig. 2 shows the main variables of the model associated with every layer. The column consists of NL such layers. Each layer is schematically divided, as suggested by Fig. 1b, into four parts: mobile and immobile liquid, and "mobile" and "immobile" soil. The effects of air are ignored in Fig. 2. Equilibrium exists between the mobile liquid concentration and the mobile sorbed concentration (CM and SM respectively), and between the immobile liquid concentration and the immobile sorbed concentration (CIM and SIM respectively).

We first rewrite equations (8) and (9) in the following difference form:

$$\theta_m \Delta z \left(1 + \frac{f \rho K N C_m^{N-1}}{\theta_m} \right) \frac{\Delta C_m}{\Delta t} + \theta_{im} \Delta z \left(1 + \frac{(1-f)\rho K N C_{im}^{N-1}}{\theta_{im}} \right) \frac{\Delta C_{im}}{\Delta t}$$

$$= \left(\theta_m D \frac{\Delta^2 C_m}{\Delta z^2} - q \frac{\Delta C_m}{\Delta z} \right) \Delta z \tag{26}$$

$$\theta_{im} \Delta z \left(1 + \frac{(1-f)\rho K N C_{im}^{N-1}}{\theta_{im}} \right) \frac{\Delta C_{im}}{\Delta t} = \alpha [C_m - C_{im}] \, \Delta z \tag{27}$$

Define further the following variables:

$$\text{MOBS} = \theta_m \Delta z C_m \tag{28a}$$

$$\text{IMMOS} = \theta_{im} \Delta z C_{im} \tag{29a}$$

$$\text{RM} = 1 + f \rho K N C_m^{N-1} / \theta_m \tag{30a}$$

$$\text{RIM} = 1 + (1-f)\rho K N C_{im}^{N-1} / \theta_{im} \tag{31a}$$

$$\text{SFLW}_i = \theta_m D_c \frac{(C_{m_{i-1}} - C_{m_i})}{\Delta z} + q C_{m_{i-1}} \tag{32a}$$

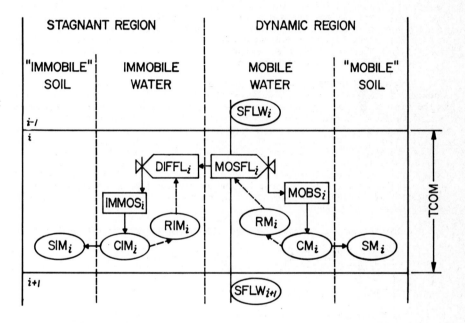

Figure 2. Schematic representation of CSMP-model for one-dimensional transfer through a sorbing porous medium, with intra-aggregate diffusion and adsorption.

$$\theta_m D_c = \theta_m (D - 1/2 v_m \Delta z) \tag{33a}$$

or in CSMP (see also Table 1):

$$MOBS = MWC*TCOM*CM = MOWAT*CM \tag{28b}$$

$$IMMOS = IMWC*TCOM*CIM = IMWAT*CIM \tag{29b}$$

$$RM = 1 + F*RHO*KM*NM*CM**(NM-1)/MWC$$
$$= 1.+ MOSOIL*KM*NM*CM**(NM-1)/MOWAT \tag{30b}$$

$$RIM = 1. + (1-F)*RHO*KIM*NIM*CIM**(NIM-1)/IMWC$$
$$= 1. + IMSOIL*KIM*NIM*CIM**(NIM-1)/IMWAT \tag{31b}$$

$$SFLW_i = APDIF*(CM_{i-1}-CM_i)/TCOM+FLUX*CM_{i-1} \tag{32b}$$

$$APDIF = MWC*D - FLUX*TCOM/2 \tag{33b}$$

The variables MOBS and IMMOS (equations 28a and 29a) represent the amount of material stored in the mobile and immobile liquid regions of each compartment, RM and RIM are the "mobile" and "immobile" retardation factors (see also equation 25), while $SFLW_i$ represents the flow of material over each compartmental boundary, which is composed of a dispersive flux

$$\left(- \theta_m D \frac{\partial C_m}{\partial z} \right)$$

and a massflow (qC_m). The variable D_c, defined by equation (33a), includes corrections for numerical dispersion. An extensive discussion of D_c is given by van Genuchten and Wierenga (1974).

Substitution of equations (28a) - (33a) in equations (26 and 27) gives:

$$RM\frac{\Delta MOBS}{\Delta t} + RIM\frac{\Delta IMMOS}{\Delta t} = SFLW_i - SFLW_{i+1} \tag{34}$$

$$RIM\frac{\Delta IMMOS}{\Delta t} = \alpha(CM-CIM)\Delta z \tag{35}$$

Equations (34) and (35) define the rate of change of the material stored in both liquid regions: $\Delta MOBS/\Delta t$ and $\Delta IMMOS/\Delta t$, respectively. Denoting these rates by MOSFL ("MObile Salt FLow") and DIFFL ("DIFfusion FLow"), we obtain (ALPHA = α):

$$DIFFL = ALPHA * (CM - CIM)/RIM * TCOM \tag{36}$$

$$MOSFL = (SFLW_i - SFLW_{i+1} - DIFFL * RIM)/RM \tag{37}$$

From these rates, we can finally calculate the variables MOBS and IMMOS:

$$MOBS = \int_0^t MOSFL \, dt \tag{38a}$$

$$IMMOS = \int_0^t DIFFL \, dt \tag{39a}$$

or in CSMP:

TABLE 1. S/360 CSMP program for simulation of one-dimensional transfer through an aggregated, sorbing porous medium.

```
TITLE  SOLUTE MOVEMENT THROUGH AGGREGATED SORBING MEDIUM
/      REAL PIM (30),SFLW(31),SM(30),SIM(30),IMS(30),IIS(30)
/      REAL MOSFL(30),RM(30),RIM(30),NM(30),NIM(30),KM(30),KIM(30),PM(30)
/      REAL CM(30),CIM(30),MOBS(30),IMMOS(30), DIFFL(30)
/      EQUIVALENCE (MOBS1,MOBS(1)),(IMMOS1,IMMOS(1)),(DIFFL1,DIFFL(1))
/      EQUIVALENCE (MOSFL1,MOSFL(1)),(IMS1,IMS(1)),(IIS1,IIS(1))
FIXED I,NL,TT
INITIAL
NOSORT
PARAMETERS CO=10.,T=2.,KADS=0.616,ALPHA=0.2,RMOB=0.6,FREQ=0.6,FLUX=10.
PARAMETERS WC=0.40,D=30.,N=0.792,RHO=1.25,TCOM=1.0,NL=30,AB=2.3
       MWC=WC*RMOB
       IMWC=WC*(1.-RMOB)
       MOWAT=MWC*TCOM
       IMWAT=IMWC*TCOM
       MOSOIL=TCOM*FREQ*RHO
       IMSOIL=TCOM*(1.-FREQ)*RHO
       APDIF=D*MWC -0.5*FLUX*TCOM
       DEPTH=NL*TCOM
       DO 2 I=1,NL
       NM(I)=N
       NIM(I)=N
       KM(I)=KADS
       KIM(I)=KADS
       PM(I)=1.
       PIM(I)=1.
       IMS(I)=1.E-06
    2  IIS(I)=1.E-07
DYNAMIC
NOSORT
       TT = T/DELT
       T1-TT*DELT
       CIW = FCNSW(TIME - T1,CO,(T - T1)*CO/DELT,0.)
       DO 5 I=1,NL
       CM(I)=AMAX1(1.E-06,MOBS(I)/MOWAT)
       CIM(I)=AMAX1(1.E-07,IMMOS(I)/IMWAT)
       SM(I)=RHO*KM(I)*CM(I)**NM(I)
    5  SIM(I)=RHO*KIM(I)*CIM(I)**NIM(I)
       IF(TIME.LT.T) GO TO 9
       DO 9 I=1,NL
       IF(PIM(I)) 7,7,6
    6  IF(DIFFL(I).GT.0.) GO TO 7
       PIM(I)=-1.
       KIM(I)=KADS*CIM(I)**(N-N/AB)
       NIM(I)=N/AB
    7  IF(PM(I)) 9,9,8
    8  IF(MOSFL(I).GT.0.) GO TO 9
       PM(I)=-1.
       KM(I)=KADS*CM(I)**(N-N/AB)
       NM(I)=N/AB
    9  CONTINUE
       DO 10 I=1,NL
       RIM(I)=1. + IMSOIL*KIM(I)*NIM(I)*CIM(I)**(NIM(I)-1.)/IMWAT
   10  RM(I)=1. + MOSOIL*KM(I)*NM(I)*CM(I)**(NM(I)-1.)/MOWAT
       SFLW(1)=FLUX*CIW
       DO 12 I=2,NL
   12  SFLW(I) = CM(I-1)*FLUX + APDIF*(CM(I-1)-CM(I))/TCOM
       SFLW(NL+1)=CM(NL)*FLUX-APDIF*(2.*CM(NL)-3.*CM(NL-1)+CM(NL-2))/TCOM
```

TABLE 1 Continued

```
        DO 15 I=1,NL
    DIFFL(I)=ALPHA*(CM(I)-CIM(I))*TCOM/RIM(I)
15  MOSFL(I)=(SFLW(I)-SFLW(I+1)-RIM(I)*DIFFL(I))/RM(I)
    MOBS1=INTGRL(IMS1,MOSFL1,30)
    IMMOS1=INTGRL(IIS1,DIFFL1,30)
******************      PRINT OUT      ******************************************
    A = IMPULS(0.,PRDEL)
    IF(A*KEEP.LT.1.) GO TO 23
    WRITE(6,18)TIME
18  FORMAT(1H ,///,T5,'MOBILE CONCENTRATION VERSUS DEPTH, PRINTED FOR
    $EVERY LAYER (MICROGRAM PER CC MOBILE WATER) AT',F5.2,T110,'DAYS')
    WRITE (6,19) (CM(I), I=1,NL)
19  FORMAT(1H ,15F8.4)
    WRITE (6,20) (CIM(I),I=1,NL)
20  FORMAT(1H ,35HIMMOBILE CONCENTRATION VERSUS DEPTH/(15F8.4))
    WRITE(6,21) (SM(I),I=1,NL)
21  FORMAT(1H ,28HADSORPTION PER G MOBILE SOIL/(15F.4))
    WRITE(6,22) (SIM(I),I=1,NL)
22  FORMAT(1H , 30HADSORPTION PER G IMMOBILE SOIL/(15F8.4)
23  CCO=(15.*CM(NL)-10.*CM(NL-1)+3.*CM(NL-2))/(8.*CO)
    VVO=FLUX*TIME/DEPTH*WC)
    NMNL=NM(NL)
    RMNL=RM(NL)
    PMNL=PM(NL)
    PIMNL=PIM(NL)
METHODS RKS
TIMER FINTIM=30.,OUTDEL=0.05,PRDEL=1.0
FINISH VVO=7
PRINT VVO,CCO,PMNL,PIMNL,RMNL,NMNL,APDIF,MOWAT,MOSOIL,IMWAT,IMSOIL
PRTPLT CCO(0.,1.0,VVO,PMNL,PIMNL)
END
STOP
ENDJOB
```

$$MOBS1 = INTGRL(IMS1,MOSFL1,30) \tag{38b}$$

$$IMMOS1 = INTGRL(IIS1,DIFFL1,30) \tag{39b}$$

The integrals in equations (38) and (39) are updated each time step and for every layer. The variables MOBS1 and IMMOS1 represent the updated arrays of the amounts of chemicals in the two liquid regions of all layers [MOBS(1,...,NL) and IMMOS(1,...,NL), respectively]. IMS1 and IIS1 represent the arrays MOBS1 and IMMOS1 at time zero, while MOSFL1 and DIFFL1 represent the arrays MOSFL(1,...,NL) and DIFFL(1,...,NL). The third argument in both INTGRL-statements gives the number of integrations to be performed per time increment, and is equal to the number of layers (NL). Several integration methods are available to perform the integrations of equations (38) and (39), ranging from a simple rectangular method (METHOD RECT) to the fifth order predictor-coorector-modifier method of Milne (METHOD MILNE). A list of the available integration subroutines is given in the CSMP manual (IBM, 1972). In this study the integrals were updated with the fourth order Runge-Kutta method (METHOD RKS). The main advantage of this method over the rectangular method is a correct evaluation of the retardation factors RM and RIM. These factors depend on the concentrations CM and CIM and have to be evaluated about halfway in the integration interval $(t,t+\Delta t)$. With the rectangular method these factors are evaluated at time t, while the Runge-Kutta method evaluates them toward the end of the indicated integration interval. Inaccurate calculations of RM and RIM are immediately reflected in an inaccurate material balance during the computations. The program in Table 1, which uses

Runge-Kutta integration, shows an accurate balance; only about 0.2% of the material was lost during the simulations. An additional advantage of the Runge-Kutta method is its unconditional stability. Some minor oscillations, however, may occur whenever D_c becomes negative.

The retardation factors RM and RIM may depend on the sorption direction, i.e., whether adsorption or desorption occurs. The possibility of hysteresis in the adsorption-desorption isotherms is included in the program listed in Tabel 1. The modeling techniques for this problem are the same as those discussed in examples 1 and 2 of van Genuchten and Wierenga (1974), and will not be repeated here.

The following boundary conditions were used:

$$SFLW_1 = FLUX * CIW \qquad\qquad (z=0) \qquad\qquad (40)$$

with

$$CIW = \begin{cases} 1 & Time \le T \\ \\ 0 & Time > T \end{cases} \qquad\qquad (41)$$

$$SFLW_{NL+1} = FLUX*C_{NL} - APDIF*(2.*CM_{NL}-3.*CM_{NL-1} + CM_{NL-2})/TCOM \qquad (42)$$

The boundary condition at z=0 (equations 40 and 41) follows directly from equation (10), while the condition at z=L (equation 42) has been shown to duplicate very closely the results of a semi-infinite profile (van Genuchten and Wierenga, 1974). Equation (42) assumes that only mobile liquid leaves the basale plane of the column. The effluent concentration hence can be calculated upon extrapolation of CM to the end of the column (z=L). Denoting the exit concentration by $CM_{NL+1/2}$, we have:

$$CM_{NL+1/2} = CM_{NL-1} + \frac{3}{2} \Delta z \left. \frac{\partial CM}{\partial z}\right|_{NL-1} + \frac{9}{8} \Delta z^2 \left. \frac{\partial^2 CM}{\partial z^2}\right|_{NL-1} \qquad (43)$$

Using central differences for $\partial CM/\partial z$ and $\partial^2 CM/\partial x^2$, equation (43) reduces to:

$$CM_{NL+1/2} = (15.*CM_{NL} - 10.*CM_{NL}-1 + 3.*CM_{NL-2})/8 \qquad (44)$$

MODEL VERIFICATION

The CSMP-model discussed in this paper has been verified under several analytical and experimental conditions. When no adsorption occurs, i.e. KADS=0 in Table 1, the simulation model reduces to a numerical solution of equations (2) and (3). A comparison of the results obtained with the analytical solution of equations (2) and (3) (given by equations 13 - 20, with R=1 and $\beta=\phi$) and the CSMP-solution is given in Table 2, and shows excellent agreement. Approximately the same results were obtained with layer thicknesses (Δz) of 0.5 and 1.0 cm, respectively. Hence excessively small layers were not necessary during the simulations.

Table 2 also gives the numerical results for a finite column. For this purpose boundary condition (42) in Table 1 was replaced by equation (45) below, in order to obtain the numerical solution for a finite column (van Genuchten and Wierenga, 1974).

$$SFLW_{NL+1} = FLUX * CM_{NL} \qquad\qquad (45)$$

Table 2. Comparison of analytical and numerical results for the movement
through a non-sorbing medium. The numerical results are given for a semi-
infinite and a finite medium. Results were plotted versus pore volume (T),
and were obtained with the following parameters: $D=30$ cm^2/day, $q=10$ cm/day,
$\phi = 0.6$, $\theta=0.4$, $\alpha=0.2$ 1/day, $L=30$ cm and $T_1=2$ days.

T	Semi-infinite medium			Finite medium	
	Analytical	Numerical		Numerical	
		$\Delta z=.5$	$\Delta z=1.0$ -	$\Delta z=.5$	$\Delta z=1.0$
0.375	0.010	0.011	0.013	0.011	0.017
0.500	0.132	0.132	0.132	0.152	0.153
0.625	0.365	0.364	0.361	0.394	0.391
0.750	0.541	0.541	0.540	0.563	0.563
0.875	0.635	0.635	0.636	0.650	0.650
1.000	0.690	0.690	0.691	0.702	0.702
1.125	0.731	0.731	0.731	0.741	0.741
1.250	0.766	0.766	0.766	0.775	0.775
1.375	0.796	0.796	0.796	0.804	0.804
1.500	0.822	0.822	0.822	0.829	0.829
1.625	0.845	0.845	0.845	0.851	0.851
1.750	0.865	0.865	0.865	0.870	0.870
1.875	0.882	0.882	0.882	0.887	0.887
2.000	0.895	0.895	0.894	0.899	0.897
2.125	0.839	0.838	0.837	0.829	0.826
2.250	0.636	0.637	0.640	0.611	0.613
2.375	0.439	0.440	0.441	0.417	0.419
2.500	0.331	0.331	0.331	0.317	0.317
2.625	0.275	0.275	0.275	0.265	0.265
2.750	0.237	0.237	0.237	0.229	0.229
2.875	0.207	0.207	0.207	0.200	0.200
3.000	0.181	0.181	0.181	0.174	0.174
3.125	0.158	0.158	0.158	0.152	0.152
3.250	0.138	0.138	0.138	0.132	0.132
3.500	0.105	0.105	0.105	0.100	0.100
3.750	0.079	0.079	0.079	0.076	0.076
3.875	0.069	0.069	0.069	0.066	0.066
4.000	0.060	0.060	0.060	0.057	0.057

The CSMP-solution in Table 1 with N=1 was also compared with the analytical solution presented by equations (13) - (20) for a sorbing medium. Numerical results (not given here) compared excellently with the analytical results. Deviations between the two solutions were of similar magnitude as those given in Table 2 for the non-sorbing medium.

Effluent curves calculated with the numerical model are further compared with the experimental data of van Genuchten et al. (1976) for the movement of the herbicide 2,4,5,-T (2,4,5-Trichlorophenoxyacetic acid) through aggregated unsaturated Glendale clay loam. Fig. 3 shows the equilibrium adsorption and desorption isotherms of this herbicide and soil. The adsorption isotherm is described by the following Freundlich equation:

$$S_{ads} = 0.616 \ c^{0.792} \tag{46}$$

The desorption curves are given by:

$$S_{des} = K_{des} \ c^{0.344} \tag{47}$$

The coefficient K_{des} during desorption is a function of the maximum concentration, C_{max}, before desorption is initiated (van Genuchten et al. (1976):

$$K_{des} = 0.616 \ C_{max}^{0.448} \tag{48}$$

The adsorption-desorption process is clearly non-single-valued (hysteretic) and is programmed in Table 1 in the same manner as was done by van Genuchten and Wierenga (1974).

Figure 4 gives observed and calculated effluent curves of 2,4,5-T for experiment 2-4 of van Genuchten et al. (1976). The solid line represents the analytical solution (equations 13-20), assuming no hysteresis in the equilibrium isotherms and using a linearized adsorption constant K_{ads} of 0.426. This value was obtained directly from the adsorption isotherm in Fig. 3, as discussed earlier (van Genuchten et al, 1976). The dashed and dashed-dotted lines in Fig. 4 represent simulation results, using the non-linear equilibrium adsorption isotherm (N=0.792), with and without hysteresis (AB = 2.3 and 1.0 respectively in Table 1). The coefficients in the numerical and analytical solutions, except for K_{ads}, N_{ads}, K_{des} and N_{des}, were obtained by curve fitting as explained elsewhere (van Genuchten et al. 1976).

The three curves in Fig. 4 each describe the data points fairly accurately. From this we may conclude that a slight non-linearity in the equilibrium adsorption isotherm has only a minor influence on the calculated results (solid versus dashed-dotted line). It is furthermore evident that hysteresis in the equilibrium isotherms is less important than was suggested in several earlier studies, e.g. in those of Swanson and Dutt (1973), van Genuchten et al. (1974) and van Genuchten and Wierenga (1974). The results of this study clearly suggested that the heavy tailing in Fig. 4, both during break through and elution of the chemical, can be fully explained by intra-aggregate diffusion alone.

In conclusion, it is clear from Fig. 4, that an analytical solution could have been used in the first place. The effects of non-linear adsorption and hysteresis appear to be minor compared to the effects of intra-aggregate diffusion. This result, however, could only be obtained after carefully weighing the different tailing-causing phenomena in one integrated numerical model. Hence numerical methods can be very valuable tools for studying complex systems, even if they eventually verify that an analytical approach is sufficient for the problems being considered.

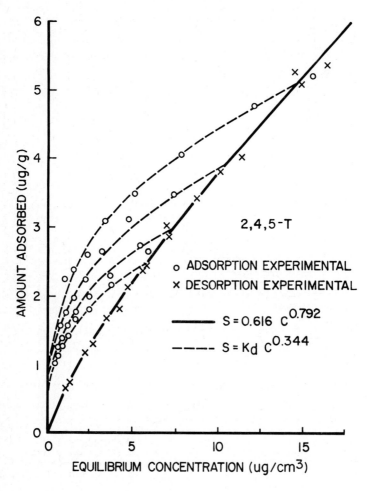

Figure 3.   Equilibrium adsorption and desorption data
for 2,4,5-T in Glendale clay loam (van Genuchten,
et al., 1976).

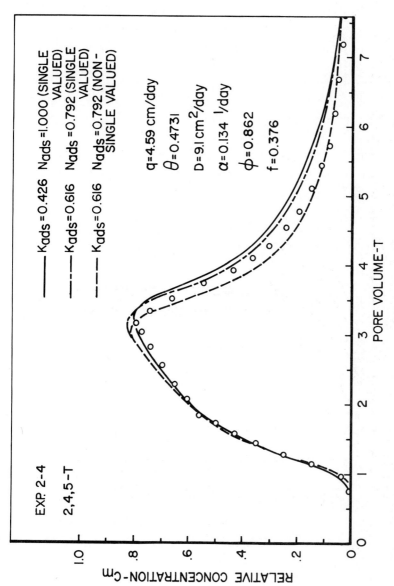

Figure 4. Observed and calculated 2,4,5-T effluent curves for experiment 2-4. The open circles represent observed data points (van Genuchten, et al., 1976).

REFERENCES

Bear, J. (1972). Dynamics of fluids in porous media (American Elsevier Publ. Co. New York).

Beek, J., and Frissel, M.J., (1973). Simulation of nitrogen behavior in soils (Centre For Agric. Publ. and Document. Pudoc. Wageningen).

Bennet, A., and Goodridge, F., (1970). Hydrodynamic and mass transfer studies in packed adsorption columns: I. Axial liquid dispersion (Trans. Instn. Chem. Engrs. 48:232-244).

Bhuiyan, S.E., Hiler, E.A., van Bavel, C.H.M., and Aston, A.R., (1971). Dynamic simulation of vertical infiltration into unsaturated soils (Water Res. Res. 7: 1597-1606).

Biggar, J.W., Nielsen, D.R., (1967) Miscible displacement and leaching phenomenon. In. Hagan, R.M., Haise, R.R., and Edminster, T.W. (eds), Irrigation of agricultural lands. (Agronomy 11:254-274, Am. Soc. Agron., Madison, Wisconsin).

Brenner, H., (1962). The diffusion model of longitudinal mixing in beds of finite length.Numerical values (Chem. Eng. Sci. 17:229-243).

Cassel, D.K., van Genuchten, M.Th., and Wierenga, P.J., (1974). Simulation of chloride and nitrate movement through Gardena very fine sandy loam (Proceeding 1974 Summer Simulation Conference, Houston, July 9-11, 1974:263-270).

Coats, K.H., and Smith, B.D., (1964). Dead end pore volume and dispersion in porous media (Soc. Petr. Eng. J. 4:73-84).

Davidson, J.M., Mansell, R.S., and Baker, D.R., (1972). Herbicide distributions within a soil profile and their dependence upon adsorption-desorption (Soil and Crop Sci. Soc. Florida Proc. 32:36-41).

DeVault, D., (1943). The theory of chromatography (J. Am. Chem. Soc. 65:532-540).

DeWit, C.T., van Keulen, H., (1972). Simulation of transport processes in soils (Centre for Agric. Publ. and Document. Pudoc. Wageningen).

Fried, J.J., and Combarnous, M.A. (1971). Dispersion in porous media (Advan. Hydrosci. 7:170-282).

Frissel, M.J., Poelstra, P., and Reiniger, P., (1970) Chromatographic transport through soils. III. A simulation model for the evaluation of the apparent diffusion coefficient in undisturbed soils with tritiated water (Plant and Soil 33:161-176).

Gershon, N.D., and Nir, A., (1969). Effects of boundary conditions of models on tracer distribution in flow through porous mediums (Water Res. Res. 5:830-839).

Giddings, J.C., (1963). Kinetic origin or tailing in chromatography (Anal. Chem. 35:1999-2002).

Green, R.E., Rao, P.S.C., and Corey, J.C., (1972). Solute transport in aggregated soil: tracer zone shape in relation to pore-velocity distribution and adsorption (Proc. 2nd Symp. Fundamentals of Transport Phenomena in Porous Media. IAHR-ISSS. Guelph. August 7-11, 1972. Vol. 2:732-752).

Hornsby, A.G, and Davidson, J.M., (1973). Solution and adsorbed fluometuron concentration distribution in a water-saturated soil: experimental and predicted evaluation (Soil Sci. Soc. Amer. Proc. 37:823-828).

IBM Corporation, (1972). System/360 Continuous System Modeling Program (360A-CX-16X), User's Manual (Data Processing Division, 122 East Post Road, White Plains, New York).

Kay, B.D., Elrick, D.E., (1967). Adsorption and movement of lindane in soils (Soil Sci. 104:314-322).

Lapidus, L., and Amundson, N.R., (1952). Mathematics of adsorption in beds. VI. The effect of longitudinal diffusion in ion exchange and chromatographic columns (J. Phys. Chem. 56:984-988).

Lindstrom, F.T., and Boersma, L., (1973). A theory on the mass transfer of previously distributed chemicals in a water-saturated sorbing medium: III. Exact solution for first order kinetic sorbtion (Soil Sci. 115:5-10).

Lindstrom, F.T., Haque, R., Freed, V.H., and Boersma, L., (1967). Theory on the movement of some herbicides in soils (Env. Sci. Tech. 1:561-565).

Lindstrom, F.T., and Narasimhan, M.N.L., (1973). Mathematical theory of a kinetic model for dispersion of previously distributed chemicals in a sorbing porous medium (S.I.A.M.J. Applied Math. 24:496-510).

Perkins, T.K., and Johnson, O.C., (1963) A review of diffusion and dispersion in porous media (Soc. Petrol Eng. J. 19:70-84).

Swanson, R.A., and Dutt, G.R., (1973) Chemical and physical processes that affect atrazine movement and distribution in soil systems (Soil Sci. Soc. Amer. Proc. 37:872-876).

van Genuchten, M. Th., Davidson, J.M., and Wierenga, P.J., (1974). An evaluation of kinetic and equilibrium equations for the prediction of pesticide movement through porous media (Soil Sci. Soc. Amer. Proc. 38:29-35).

van Genuchten, M.Th., and Wierenga, P.J., (1974). Simulation of one-dimensional solute transfer in porous media (N. Mex. Agr. Exp. Sta. Bull. 628).

van Genuchten, M.Th., and Wierenga, P.J., (1975). Mass Transfer studies in sorbing porous media. I. Theoretical development (Soil Sci. Soc. Amer. Proc: Submitted).

van Genuchten, M.Th., Wierenga, P.J., and O'Connor, G.A., (1976). Mass Transfer studies in sorbing porous medium. III. Experimental evaluation with 2,4,5-T (Soil Sci. Soc. Amer. Proc: Submitted).

Van Keulen, H., and van Beek, C.G.E.M., (1971). Water movement in layered soils. A simulation model (Neth. J. Agr. Sci. 19: 138-153).

Villermaux, J., and van Swaay, W.P.M., (1969). Modèle répresentatif de la distribution des temps de sejour dans un reacteur semi-infini a dispersion axiale avec zones stagnantes (Chem. Eng. Sci. 24:1097-1111).

Westcot, D.W., and Wierenga, P.J., (1974). Transfer of heat by conduction and vapor movement in a closed soil system (Soil Sci. Soc. Amer. Proc. 38:9-14).

Wierenga, P.J., and de Wit, C.T., (1970). Simulation of heat transfer in soils (Soil Sci. Soc. Amer. Proc. 34:845-848).

DISCUSSION

What kind of material did you use ? (PROPFE)

For these studies, it was a clay loam soil. We used two size fractions : a fraction which passed through a 2 mm sieve, and a fraction which passed through a 6 mm sieve. (WIERENGA)

You did the determination on the saturated soil ? (PROPFE)

In these experiments we used unsaturated soil. The reason is that field soils are almost never saturated, exept below the water table. During infiltration of irrigation or rainwater there may be saturation near the soil surface for a short period, but generally this period is very short. Thus much of the solute transfer is in non-saturated soil. In our experiments the water content was about 47 % by volume, while the saturated water content is approximately 52 %. On the other hand the saturated hydraulic conductivity is about 30 - 40 cm/day, while in the experiment reported here we used a flux of only 4.5 cm/day. (WIERENGA)

We have heard yesterday from Dr. Vachaud that when you go down with the water content, the immobile phase increases very much. (PROPFE)

This is probably correct. However, in our experiments we could not test this. We obtained unsaturated conditions by controlling the flux at the surface of the columns and by applying a constant suction through a fritted glass porous plate at the lower end of the column.

By reducing the flux and increasing the vacuum at the lower end, one may further desaturate the column. However, use of small fluxes (e.g. less than 1 cm/day) causes the experiment to last too long, while on the other hand the suction at the lower end of the columns was limited to 400 cm H_2O, the air entry value of the fritted glass plates. Thus our experiments were limited to volumetric water contents varying between 40 and 52 %. With sandy soils it is possible to vary the water content over a wider range. (WIERENGA)

You have 4 or 5 coefficients. How many of them were determined by curve fitting ? (VAN DER PLOEG)

The mass transfer coefficient α, **the** fraction of adsorption in the dynamic region f, and the fraction mobile water ϕ, were determined by curve fitting. Values for these parameters are not known, and up to now we do not even know the order of magnitude for different soils. We have done one set of experiments for one particular soil. Dr. Vachaud is working with a sandy soil, and we hope that others will try to determine values for these parameters for other soils and experimental conditions. The solution presented here contains, in dimensionless form, four parameters. This is two more than the convective dispersion equation for sorbing media. On the other hand this provides a means for separating some of the phenomena which usually are included in the apparent dispersion coefficients determined on the basis of column effluent data. (WIERENGA)

The sorption problem would probably be quite important in analysing data from aquifers ? (VACHAUD)

Yes, sorption may indeed be very important when dealing with aquifers, because sorption causes a delay in the appearance of the chemical when moving through a porous medium. This delay may be particularly important in non-saturated sandy materials. For example with an adsorption coefficient of only 0.1, a water content of 0.10 cm^3/cm^3 and a density of 1.7 one obtains a value for the retardation factor R in equation 25 of 2.7. This means that the rate of convective mass transfer is only about 0.4 times the rate of mass transfer without adsorption. (WIERENGA)

Even under saturated conditions. If one has an aquifer with an adsorption coefficient of 0.3 or 0.4, it is important. (VACHAUD)

Yes. (WIERENGA)

System Simulation in Water Resources, ed. G.C. VANSTEENKISTE
1976, North-Holland Publishing Company

ESTIMATING THE EFFECT OF A LAND USE
CHANGE ON STREAM SALINITY IN
SOUTH-WESTERN AUSTRALIA

A.J. Peck
Division of Land Resources Management
CSIRO
Wembley, Western Australia

ABSTRACT

A method is developed for estimating the effect of a change in land
use on the salinity of a gaining stream. It is assumed that the
discharge of groundwater is increased, but there is a negligible
change of surface run-off. Input data for the calculation are the
initial streamflow and salinity, the increase of groundwater recharge
(assumed equal to the increased discharge), and the salinity of
discharging groundwater. The method developed takes no account of the
details of distribution and transport of solute in the soil so that
the predicted change in stream salinity should be regarded as a first
estimate with uncertain accuracy. Such an estimate is valuable in
classifying areas where the salinity change will be negligible, large
or intermediate so that data should be collected for the operation of
a more accurate model.

INTRODUCTION

It has been known for more than 50 years that agricultural development
of areas of southern Australia has affected stream salinity. For example, Fig.
1 shows the increase in salinity of the Blackwood River at Bridgetown, W.A.
during this century. More recently, significant differences between the chloride
balances of farmed and forested catchments in south-western Australia have been
demonstrated by Peck and Hurle (1973).

The Darling Range area includes major surface water catchments for
south-western Australia. Forest vegetation in this area is subjected to many
pressures, and it is important to estimate the impact of possible changes in
land use on stream salinity. Some of the changes are clearing for agriculture,
horticulture, softwood plantations, or services (electricity and roads), strip

mining for bauxite, and intensive logging for wood chips. In addition to these
human activities, jarrah dieback disease (Phytophthora cinnamomi) is spreading
rapidly with severe effects on many plants of the forest ecosystem.

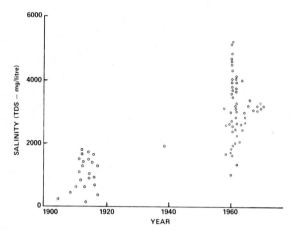

Fig. 1.   Records of salinity (Total Dissolved Solids
estimated from electrical conductivity or Cl
analysis) of the Blackwood River at Bridgetown,
W.A.   Data from Wood (1924) and the W.A.
Department of Agriculture. Wood suggests that
some increase may have taken place before the
first analyses.

To the extent that the hydrologic effects of a land use change can be
described quantitatively, the leaching of solutes from the soil into a stream may
be represented by water and solute transport equations. With some simplifications,
such an approach has been developed by Konikow and Bredehoeft (1974). Pikul et al.
(1974) have reported a useful simplification for modelling soil water movement,
and models of the associated solute transport have been developed by Bredehoeft
and Pinder (1973) and Schwartz and Domenico (1973).

Stephenson and Freeze (1974) applied a sophisticated method to model
the movement of soil water in a section of a catchment. They concluded that
widespread application of detailed soil water models is unlikely for some time
due to the general lack of data characterizing the soil, the high cost of acquiring
this data, and the capacity of present-day computers. Thus there exists a need
for models which rely on readily available input data, and modest computer capacity
to provide numerical first approximations to salt and water transport through
soil. Such a model is likely to play a continuing role in defining areas where
data should be collected for the operation of a more accurate simulation.

DEVELOPMENT OF A SIMPLIFIED MODEL

The method is developed from one described by Pinder and Jones (1969) and applied by Peck and Hurle (1973). These authors used data on solute concentrations in streams to estimate the contribution of groundwater discharge to total streamflow. In the present application, stream salinity is estimated from groundwater discharge.

Let Q_g, Q_r, and Q_s $[L^3 T^{-1}]$* represent initial fluxes of groundwater, surface runoff and streamflow respectively. Then neglecting changes of storage of water within the stream itself, which will be reasonable over a sufficiently long period, we have

$$Q_g + Q_r = Q_s. \qquad (1)$$

If the solute concentrations in groundwater, surface runoff, and streamflow are c_g, c_r and c_s $[M L^{-3}]$ respectively, then we have, with the same assumption on storage within the stream,

$$Q_g c_g + Q_r c_r = Q_s c_s. \qquad (2)$$

Let a change of land use increase the water fluxes by δQ_g, δQ_r and δQ_s. Then

$$Q_g + \delta Q_g + Q_r + \delta Q_r = Q_s + \delta Q_s. \qquad (3)$$

If the solute concentrations of the increased flows of groundwater and surface runoff are c_g' and c_r', and c_s'' is the solute concentration in the stream then

$$Q_g c_g + \delta Q_g c_g' + Q_r c_r + \delta Q_r c_r' = (Q_s + \delta Q_s) c_s''. \qquad (4)$$

By eliminating the variables Q_g, Q_r and δQ_s from equations (1) to (4), the increase in stream salinity Δc_s $[M L^{-3}]$ resulting from the change of land use is expressed by

$$\Delta c_s = c_s'' - c_s = \frac{\delta Q_g (c_g' - c_s) - \delta Q_r (c_s - c_r')}{Q_s + \delta Q_g + \delta Q_r}. \qquad (5)$$

The assumptions of negligible changes in storage of water or solute within the stream itself will be adequately met by considering a period of one year, so that the concentrations will be flow-weighted yearly averages.

One of the major applications of this method is to estimate the effect of proposed bauxite mining ventures on the salinity of streams in the Darling Range. Current mining practice is to prevent surface runoff from mined areas to minimize stream turbidity, and there is no evidence of significant surface runoff

*Dimensions are indicated in square brackets using the symbolism M = mass, L = length, T = time.

from the bauxitic soil before mining. Thus we neglect the terms involving δQ_r in equation (5). This is a reasonable approximation in other applications too, provided that

$$\left| \delta Q_r \right| << \left| \delta Q_g (c'_g - c_s)/(c_s - c'_r) \right| \qquad (6)$$

and

$$\left| \delta Q_r \right| << \left| Q_s + \delta Q_g \right|. \qquad (7)$$

The expression for Δc_s then becomes

$$\Delta c_s \simeq \delta Q_g (c'_g - c_s)/(Q_s + \delta Q_g). \qquad (8)$$

Assuming that Q_s and c_s have been measured by stream gauging and sampling, values of c'_g and δQ_g for a particular area and change of land use are needed to estimate the resultant Δc_s.

CONCENTRATION OF SOLUTES IN DISCHARGING GROUNDWATER

Pinder and Jones (1969) estimate the solute concentration in the groundwater which discharges into a gaining stream from water samples taken during a period of baseflow. In our present symbolism this method may be used to estimate c_g. If the change of land use causes a relatively small disturbance to the leaching of salt from the soil, then it is also reasonable to approximate c'_g by the baseflow stream salinity.

In situations where the change of land use greatly changes the amount and pattern of soil water movement, c'_g may be estimated from

$$c'_g = (S/W) \exp(-Gt/W) \qquad (9)$$

where S [$M L^{-2}$] is the mass of solute, and W [$L^3 L^{-2}$] the volume of water stored in the soil below unit area of land, G [$L^3 L^{-2} T^{-1}$] is the rate of groundwater discharge per unit of catchment area, and t [T] is the leaching time. This equation is supported by some field and laboratory leaching data (Pillsbury et al. 1965; Mulqueen and Kirkham 1972), but it is uncertain how accurate it may be in a complex field situation (Peck 1973).

INCREASE OF GROUNDWATER DISCHARGE

An increase of groundwater discharge results from a change of land use which increases groundwater recharge within the catchment area. The discharge will lag behind recharge in time depending on spatial separation of the input and output sites, hydraulic characteristics of the aquifer material, and other factors. There may also be losses of water to plant roots so that the increased discharge of groundwater into the stream may be less than the increased recharge beneath the area of changed land use.

If the input-output lag and transmission losses of water are to be estimated, then it will be necessary to measure soil characteristics in some detail. But this data is not usually available, and it is costly to collect. For this reason, both the lag and the transmission losses are neglected in the development of this first approximation method. That is, we assume that at all times following a change of land use

$$\delta Q_g = A_c \delta G \qquad (10)$$

where A_c $[L^2]$ is the area of changed land use, and δG $[L^3 L^{-2} T^{-1}]$ is the increased groundwater recharge. This is assumed to be known from independent observation or calculation.

THE PREDICTIVE EQUATION

From equations (8) and (10), the equation which may be applied to estimate a change in stream salinity is

$$\Delta c_s \simeq A_c \delta G \ (c_g' - c_s)/(Q_s + A_c \delta G). \qquad (11)$$

In a small catchment area of relatively unform rainfall it is convenient to introduce an increased recharge factor α, and a runoff factor β defined by

$$\alpha = \delta G/P \qquad \beta = Q_s/PA_w$$

where P $[L^3 L^{-2} T^{-1}]$ is the rainfall, and A_w is the catchment area. Then substituting for δG and Q_s in equation (11) leads to

$$\Delta c_s \simeq \gamma (c_g' - c_s)/(1+\gamma) \qquad (12)$$

where

$$\gamma = (\alpha/\beta)(A_c/A_w). \qquad (13)$$

MORE SELDOM SEEN CATCHMENT

Strip mining for bauxite began in this small catchment (area 386 ha) near Jarrahdale, Western Australia in 1969, and by mid 1974 a total of 38.9 ha of previously forested land had been cleared (G. White, Alcoa of Australia, personal communication). For the purpose of this example it is assumed that the mining operation took place at one instant in time rather than continuously, and the effects of a revegetation program are neglected. Clearly these assumptions will tend to an overestimate of the actual impact of mining in this catchment.

Rainfall in the catchment averages 1270 mm yr^{-1} and streamflow 211 mm yr^{-1}; the flow-weighted average NaCl concentration (from Cl analysis) in the stream is 136 mg l^{-1}, and the 90th percentile value of all stream salinity measurements is 180 mg l^{-1} (Anon. 1972). This latter value is used as an estimate

of c'_g although there is evidence that bauxite mining in the Darling Range can
cause significant hydrologic changes (Anon. 1974). There are no data on amounts
of salt and water storage in this catchment so equation (9) cannot be used.
Neither are there data on the effect of bauxite mining operations on groundwater
recharge in this area, but Peck and Hurle (1973) estimated that farming in a
climatically similar catchment increased recharge by 430 mm yr^{-1}. For the purpose
of the example, this value is assumed to apply in the mined catchment.

TABLE 1

A Summary of Data Used in the Two Examples

Catchment Name	Area A_w(ha)	Rainfall P(mmyr^{-1})	Streamflow Q_s(m^{3}yr^{-1})	Salinity c_s(mgl^{-1})	Area changed A_c(ha)	Increased Recharge δG(mmyr^{-1})	Groundwater Salinity c'_g(mgl^{-1})
More Seldom Seen	386	1270	8.14x10^5	136	38.9	430	180*
Wights Brook	93.8	1390	2.87x10^5	400	75	430	3500+

* 90th percentile of samples of stream salinity used to estimate groundwater
  salinity.

+ Groundwater salinity estimated from storages of soluble salts (S = 15 kgm^{-2})
  and water (W = 4.3 m^{3}m^{-2}) in the soil profile.

The values of the parameters are listed in Table 1. Substitution in
equations (12) and (13) leads to

$$\Delta c_s \simeq 7 \text{ mg } l^{-1}.$$

Such a small change cannot be detected by time-series analysis of
the stream salinity data (D.H. Hurle, personal communication, 1975).

APPLICATION TO WIGHTS BROOK CATCHMENT

This is a forested experimental catchment of area 93.8 ha near Collie,
Western Australia. After a suitable calibration period, the catchment will be
cleared for agriculture. For this example, it is assumed that the area to be
cleared will be 75 ha.

Peck and Hurle (1973) estimated that the change of land use from forest
to pasture in a nearby catchment increased recharge by 430 mm yr^{-1} so this value
is used in the present calculation. Measurements during 1974 are used as
estimates of long term averages of rainfall (1390 mm yr^{-1}) and streamflow (306 mm

yr^{-1}). The flow-weighted salinity (Total Dissolved Solids estimated from electrical conductivity) is approximately 400 mg l^{-1}, and the 90th percentile salinity is 1230 mg l^{-1}.

In this catchment core samples from five bore holes, which penetrate to basement rock, provide data to estimate salt and water storage in the soil: $S = 15$ kg m^{-2}; $W = 4.3$ m^3 m^{-2}. Substituting in equation (9), the maximum value of c_g' is found to be 3500 mg l^{-1}. This value is preferred to the 90th percentile of stream salinities since the increased recharge over 80% of the catchment is a major change. This change will increase W so that our estimate of c_g' is likely to be too large. Neglecting the decay of c_g' (with time constant $W/G \approx 10$ yrs), and substituting the values summarized in Table 1 into equations (12) and (13) leads to

$$\Delta c_s \approx 1600 \text{ mg } l^{-1}.$$

An increase of this magnitude over the initial value of 400 mg l^{-1} would be readily detectable. This field experiment should be a good test of the usefulness of the model.

DISCUSSION

The accuracy of predictions from any model is determined by the assumptions and approximations made in model development, and by the accuracy of input data. In this case the neglect of any change in surface runoff, or of any water lag or loss between recharge and discharge areas all tend to overestimate the increase of stream salinity. Moreover, the neglect of any increase in W in estimating c_g' by equation (9) will also tend to an overestimate of Δc_s. Therefore it is tempting to suggest that predictions based on equations (9) and (11) will tend to be biassed towards overestimation of the change Δc_s. However, such a suggestion should be treated with some caution since it is conceivable that disturbance of the groundwater system may bring about the leaching of highly saline aquifers, and c_g' may be underestimated.

Limitations of the model have not been determined by the formal process of comparison of field data with predictions. Until this is done the predictions must be considered as first estimates with uncertain accuracy. The method is reported now because there is no practical alternative for application to the problems which are faced today. Collection of field data to test the model has begun, but results will not be available for several years.

ACKNOWLEDGEMENTS

I acknowledge background discussions with my CSIRO colleagues, the

cooperation of staff of several W.A. Government Departments and of Alcoa of
Australia (W.A.) Ltd., and an improvement to the model suggested by Mr. R.H.B.
Hebbert, Department of Civil Engineering, University of W.A.

REFERENCES

Anon. (1972). Streamflow records of Western Australia 1939 to 1970.
        Public Works Department of W.A.

Anon. (1974). Project 3 report to Steering Committee on the effects of
        bauxite mining in the Darling Range. Geological Survey, W.A.
        Department of Mines.

Bredehoeft, J.D., and Pinder, G.F. (1973). Mass transport in flowing
        groundwater. Water Resour. Res. 9, 194.

Konikow, L.F., and Bredehoeft, J.D. (1974). Modelling flow and chemical
        quality changes in an irrigated stream-aquifer system. Water Resour.
        Res. 10, 546.

Mulqueen, J., and Kirkham, D. (1972). Leaching of a surface layer of sodium
        chloride into tile drains in a sand-tank model. Soil Sci. Soc. Am. Proc.
        36, 3.

Peck, A.J. (1973). Analysis of multidimensional leaching. Soil Sci. Soc. Am.
        Proc. 37, 320.

Peck, A.J., and Hurle, D.H. (1973). Chloride balance of some farmed and forested
        catchments in southwestern Australia. Water Resour. Res. 9, 648.

Pikul, M.F., Street, R.L., and Remson, I. (1974). A numerical model based on
        coupled one-dimensional Richards and Boussinesq equations. Water Resour.
        Res. 10, 295.

Pillsbury, A.F., Johnston, W.R., Ittihadieh, F., and Dann, R.M. (1965). Salinity
        of tile drainage effluent. Water Resour. Res. 1, 531.

Pinder, G.F., and Jones, J.F. (1969). Determination of the ground-water component
        of peak discharge from the chemistry of total runoff. Water Resour.
        Res. 5, 348.

Schwartz, F.W., and Domenico, P.A. (1973). Simulation of hydrological patterns
        in regional groundwater flow. Water Resour. Res. 9. 707.

Stephenson, G.R., and Freeze, R.A. (1974). Mathematical simulation of subsurface
        flow contributions to snowmelt runoff, Reynolds Creek watershed, Idaho.
        Water Resour. Res. 10, 284.

Wood, W.E. (1924). Increase of salt in soil and streams following the
        destruction of the native vegetation. J. Roy. Soc. West. Aust. 10(7),
        35.

DISCUSSION

There was a paper about long term water quality changes by Ackermann in a publication of the American Geophysical Union, several years ago. They discuss 4 cases from the middle of the USA : Lake Michigan, Chicago's drinking water source, having data from before 1900 ; the Mississippi river ; the Ohio river ; and another river in that region. The idea was to look at long-term changes in water quality, and they noted similar increases in salinity or chlorides for certain rivers in the central part of the USA. They did not only look at chlorides, but also at nitrates, sulfates and similar parameters, but I feel more and more that all of our countries ought to be doing this kind of long term statistical study by moving averages of water quality parameters, and if the increase over time is significant, going back to find cause-effect relationships. From a planning standpoint, you try to project this into the future and estimate influences over time. This is a very interesting subject area, and more and more we need to look at preliminary baseline studies going back to their planning role with all the data we have collected. (ROGERS)

I don't know the situation in other countries, but in Australia there is a lot of data hidden away in files. Thus information is not readily accessible, but it is there. (PECK)

You have a lot of salt in your soil profiles. How deep are they ?

(WIERENGA)

On average about 20 meters, but we have found some more than 45 meters to basement rock. It is a laterite profile. Hydrologically, there is an upper layer of sandy gravel about 0.5 m deep overlying a much less permeable sandy clay which continues to the igneous basement. (PECK)

What are the solutes in the soil ? (WIERENGA)

The ionic composition of the soil solutes is essentially the same as that of seawater, almost certainly, the source of the salts is cyclic deposition in the rainfall. (PECK)

System Simulation in Water Resources, ed. G.C. VANSTEENKISTE
1976, North-Holland Publishing Company

MODEL EXPERIMENTS ON SALT DISPLACEMENT MECHANISMS
IN AN UNSATURATED LAYERED POROUS MEDIUM

H.T. Propfe
Leichtweiss-Institut für Wasserbau
Technische Universität Braunschweig
Braunschweig, West Germany

Abstract

The displacement of a salt slug with capillary rising and infiltrating water in a homogenous and a layered porous medium was studied
in laboratory experiments under unsaturated conditions and numerically calculated.
A time dependent dispersion coefficient described the observed maximum solute concentration reasonably well for the infiltration experiments.
In the experiments with an interlayer and in the capillary rise
experiments with high suctions the relative contribution of the
several transfer mechanisms to the total salt displacement changed
in relation to decreasing flow velocities and stagnant volumes.

Introduction

In the frame of research conducted on the problem of salinization
during irrigation in the arid zones, studies were made on the movement of water and solutes in the soil. Preliminary results are
presented here.
Interest in the phenomenon of simultaneous transfer of water and
solutes has significantly grown in recent years due to the ever
growing importance of irrigation and drainage in the arid zones and
the increasing skill in modelling complex physical systems. There is
no lack of different modelling systems of miscible displacement in
the literature. Mostly, the experiments are carried out under simplified conditions like constant flow velocity, water saturation and
a homogenous profile. An exception is the modelling system described
by BRESLER and HANKS (1969) which considers varying velocities, and
a mathematical system described by DAGAN (1967) which takes a varying density in one direction into consideration. Mathematical models
often describe with reasonable agreement the downward displacement
in the soil under unsaturated conditions. Under very unsaturated
conditions often greater discrepancies are observed due to the lack
of complete information about the influence of the soil structure.
There is still no satisfactory concept about the different flow velocities in the soil. KISSEL (1973) showed in displacement experiments
that in an undisturbed soil core 60 per cent of the soil solution do
not participate in convection. Discreapancies in modelling and field
experiments are often explained with the incomplete mixing of the
soil solution and with the influence of inhomogenities in the soil
profile.
In these simulation experiments studies were made dealing with the

influence of inhomogenities in the profile on the displacement
mechanisms of water and solutes in a non-sorbing medium under unsaturated conditions, in order to evaluate the several transport
mechanisms of a salt solution in a non-homogenous profile.

Experimental

Displacement studies were carried out in plexiglass columns (200 mm
high and 32 mm inner diameter) which were filled with air dried
quartz sand of high purity. The sand was delivered by V.Busch, Quarz-
werk in Schnaittenbach, West Germany in precision classifications.
The sand was purified with 10 per cent HF and washed with distilled
water to an E.C. of 2.5 μS and then oven dried. A control column was
packed homogenously with air dried quartz sand (0.04-0.15 mm) and in
another column a thin interlayer (normally 2 cm thick) of a finer
material (0.01-0.06 mm) was included for investigation. During the
filling of the column with the air dried sand there was introduced
a salt slug in a height of 18 mm. The slug contained 2 ml of a salt
solution with 7 mg LiCl and 42 mg $Sr(NO_3)_2$. These salts were selected
as nearly all other elements were still detectable in the sand in traces.
One end of the column was closed with a ceramic plate, the other end
was open. The salt slug was displaced by distilled water which was
delivered through the ceramic plate in the direction of gravity or
with the capillary rising water. During the displacement a constant
water level was held by a Mariotte-bottle. The experimental series
were carried out with various water levels (from 0 cm to -50 cm of
water). At the end of the run the sand column was destructed and
sectioned in approx. 15 g portions. The quartz sand was extracted
with distilled water (1 : 10) and Li and Sr were measured with an
atomic absorption spektralphotometer. The chlorid concentration was
also determined. Only the results for the displacement of Li are
shown as chlorid showed the same behaviour. Little differences in
the concentration of Sr were observed due to precipitation.
Additional terms which describe chem.effects and sorption(FRISSEL
1974) were not considered here.

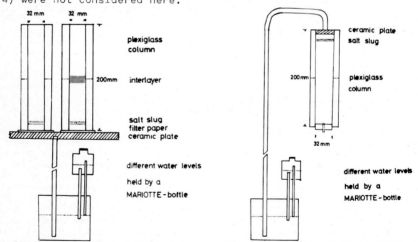

Fig. I Sketch of the experiments   Fig. II Sketch of the infiltra-
        with capillary rising   tion experiments
        water

Results and discussions

For the characterization of the used material Figure III shows a plot
of the pressure head versus soil moisture content for the wetting
and drying.

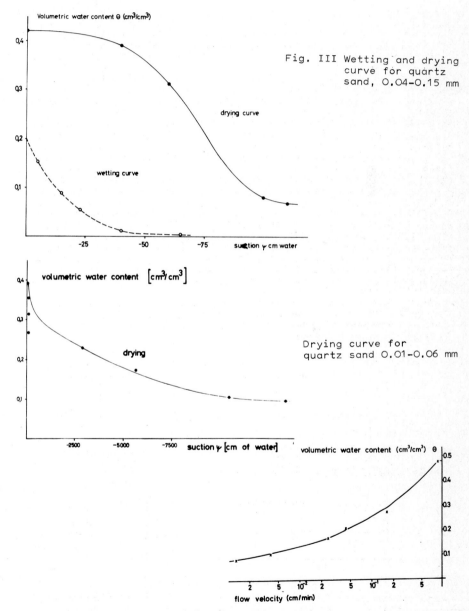

Fig. III Wetting and drying
curve for quartz
sand, 0.04-0.15 mm

Drying curve for
quartz sand 0.01-0.06 mm

Fig. IV Average pore water velocity as a function of the volumetric
moisture content for quartz sand 0.04-0.15 mm

The average pore water velocity $\overline{v}_L$ shown in Figure IV, was determined in quartz sand (0.04 - 0.15 mm) with the equation:

$$\overline{v}_L \;=\; \frac{Q}{\Theta \cdot t} \tag{1}$$

where is

      Q the liquid water flux per unit area of medium (cm^3/cm^2)
      Θ the volumetric water content (cm^3/cm^3)
      t the time (min)

It can be assumed that under the conditions and flow velocities chosen in the experiments the transfer of solute by molecular diffusion makes no significant contribution to the total salt displacement. This can be proved by calculating the decrease of the initial concentration caused only by the effect of molecular diffusion in the absence of flow of water ($v_L = 0$). Values for the moleculardiffusion for unsaturated **soils** are reported by PORTER, KEMPER and JACKSON (1960) for chlorid: D = $4.8 \cdot 10^{-5}$ cm^2/min, for barium in sand by DIESTEL (1974): D = $3 \cdot 10^{-6}$ cm^2/min and by other authors in the same order of magnitude. Calculations with the value D = $5 \cdot 10^{-5}$ cm^2/min show that the initial concentration c_0 decreases in a time of 1500 min (~1 day) to the value of c_{max}/c_0 = 0.98. This substantiates the concept that the transfer of solute by molecular diffusion did not significantly change the dispersion profiles in the experiments. As therefore the dominant transport mechanism is convection, a close relationship should exist between the water content of the column and the amount of water above the observed depth of the peak salt concentration.

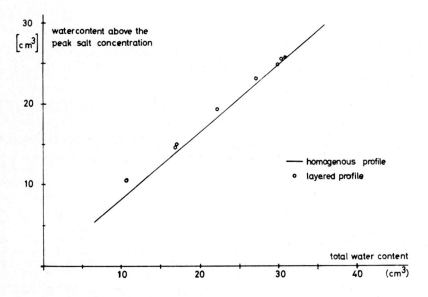

. Fig. V Observed relationship between the total water content and the amount of water above the peak salt concentration

This relationship was found to be linear for the infiltration experiments and the experiments with capillary rising water in homogenous columns. The experiments with an interlayer showed an increasing discreapancy with decreasing moisture content. In other experiments it was found that the lines of best fit for finer and coarser materials showed different slopes, as it was expected from the different tortuosities. These results are not shown.
From the slope of the line in Figure V it can be seen that the peak salt concentration lags behind the water front. That means that the average pore water velocity determined with the equation 1 is too high.
From Figure V a conversion factor of 0.925 for the average pore water velocity was determined to describe the lag of the observed salt maximum.The numerical calculations for the dispersion of the salt slug were carried out with the equation developed by KIRKHAM and POWERS (1972)

$$C/C_0 = \frac{1}{2} \left[\left(erf \frac{x+x_0-v\cdot t}{2\ (D\cdot t)^{1/2}} \right) - \left(erf \frac{x-v\cdot t}{2\ (D\cdot t)^{1/2}} \right) \right] \tag{2}$$

in a system with moving coordinates:

$$x_1 = x - v\cdot t$$
$$t_1 = t$$

as the solution for the one-dimensional dispersion equation:

$$\delta C/\delta t_1 = D(\delta^2 C/\delta x_1^2) \tag{3}$$

Where is

    D the apparent dispersion coefficient (cm^2/min)
    x_0 the initial height (cm) of the salt slug
    x the water penetration depth (cm) calculated with the equation, described by WARRICK (1972)

$$x = \int_0^t v\ (0,t)\ dt/\Theta \tag{4}$$

where is

    v the flow velocity (cm /min)
    Θ the volumetric water content (cm^3/cm^3)

Results of the infiltration experiments

It took only 25 min in the infiltration experiments to attain a constant flow rate. A nearly linear distribution of the moisture was observed at the end of the experiments. Figure VI compares the measured and calculated dispersion profiles for the infiltration case in a homogenous profile at certain times with a constant suction of approximatly -10 cm of water. The maximum observed concentration drops from 2.65 mg LiCl/g sand (2.85 mg LiCl/ml solution) to 1.45 mg LiCl/g sand (1.57 mg LiCl/ml solution) in the period of 330 min. As the salt is displaced downward,the solute is being dispersed in the

sense that the maximum concentration reduces by about 45 per cent
during 330 min.

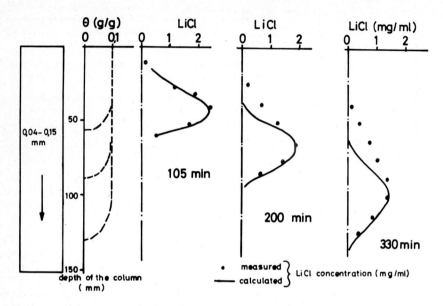

Fig. VI Measured and calculated salt concentration and the moisture
        content for the downward displacement of a salt slug at
        approx. -10 cm of water

A decrease of the maximum salt concentration and the spread of the
dispersion profiles was also reported by GHUMAN et al. (1975) for
infiltrating water into initially dry soil. But he reported that the
maximum salt concentration occurs at the waterfront. It is apparent
from Figure VI that the maximum does not coincide with the wetting
front. Probably this can be explained by the lack of complete solute
mixing since most of the infiltrating water moves through the larger
water-filled capillaries. This was discussed previously by MILLER et
al. (1965) and WARRICK (1971).
The observed depth of the peak salt concentration and the measured
profiles are described reasonably well with a time dependent dispersion coefficient D. D increases in the narrow range of 0.0015 cm²/min
to 0.002 cm²/min. Only the increasing "tailing" of the curves is not
described by the calculation. DIESTEL (1975) and WARRICK (1971) and
COREY (1970) reported the same behaviour of the dispersion coefficient D: an increase with time and travelled distance.
The results for the layered profile are shown in Figure VII. During
the downward displacement a higher salt content in the interlayer was
observed due to the higher solution content. By calculating the salt
concentration per ml solution an in-crease in salt concentration
occured at the boundary between the finer and coarser material below
a moisture content of approximately 12 per cent.
It is assumed that a mechanical sieving effect is responsible for the
salt accumulation. Due to the difference in the matrix potential some

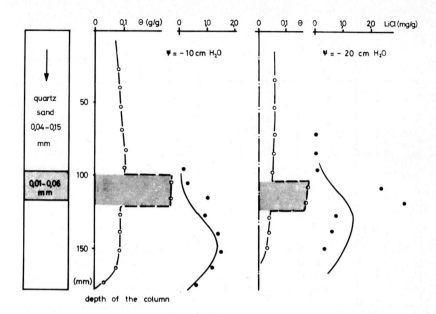

Fig. VII Measured and calculated salt concentration for the downward
          displacement of a salt slug through an interlayer of finer
          material

of the water filled capillaries in the finer material do not have a
direct connection with the capillaries in the coarser material.
During the process the accumulated salt is leached out of the interlayer.

Results for the experiments with capillary rising water

The same results as for the infiltration experiments were observed in
the experiments with capillary rising water: the peak salt concentration lagged behind the wetting front and the shape of the dispersion
profiles altered due to the change in suction as it is shown in
Figure VIII.
In contrast to the infiltration experiments the peak salt concentration was observed at a lower depth. This can be explained by the decrease of the moisture content in the upper part of the column. But
the described linear relationship between the water content in the
column and the amount of water above the peak salt concentration
still holds. This substantiates the postulate that only convection
took place. The decrease of the water content with depth caused a
drastic decrease of the flow velocity and a reasonable asymmetry of
the dispersion profiles.

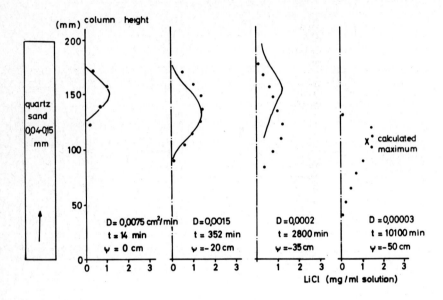

Fig. VIII Measured and calculated salt concentration for the dis-
          placement of a salt slug with capillary rising water at
          4 different suctions

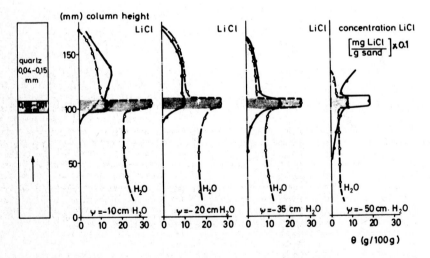

Fig. IX Measured salt concentration and moisture content for the
        displacement of a salt slug through an interlayer of a finer
        material at 4 different suctions

In the experiments with the interlayer the salt accumulation was
also observed due to the higher water content of the interlayer as it
is shown in Figure IX.
Below a water content of approx. 12 per cent a salt accumulation
above the concentration of the displacing fluid is observed. At very
high suctions the concentration of the salt solution in the finer
material exceeds the initial concentration of the salt slug. See
Figure X. During the operation the displacing fluid leaches the salt
out of the interlayer. It is assumed that this is not a convective
mechanism, as the stagnant volumes at the boundary between the finer
and coarser material do not participate significantly at the convective flow. The dispersion curves could not be calculated by the
simple described equations.

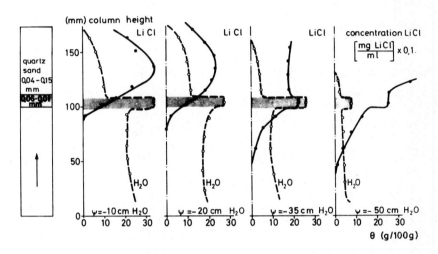

Fig. X Measured salt concentration (mg/ml solution) and moisture
        content for the displacement of a salt slug through an inter-
        layer of a finer material

Summary and conclusions

Considerations about various transfer mechanisms indicate that most
of the salt is transported by convection. Diffusion does not contribute to the transfer of solute in the sense that the movement of solute against the direction of mass flow plays a significant role.
But the experimental results show that the contribution of various
transfer mechanisms to the total mass transport changes due to the
influence of soil structure and water content. The experimental results show that the influence of soil structure increases with decreasing water content. It is concluded that in relatively simple
porous media, as pure quartz sand and in natural soils, regions exist
where the soil solution is nearly stagnant. These regions may be
macroscopic (for example layers and horizons) or microscopic (for
example small aggregates of finer material). Stagnant volumes which do
not significantly participate in the mechanism of convection act as
salt sinks, as it is shown in the experiments with the interlayer.

It is not clear by which mechanism the salt is leached out of these
volumes. From the small dimensions of these volumes it can be assumed
that diffusion may play a dominant role here. From these considerations it can be assumed that these spaces act as salt sources.
The rigorous application of the longitudinal dispersion equation describes the phenomena of solute transfer exactly. But variations in
the boundary conditions which may be caused by changing flow velocities or stagnant volumes lead to discrepancies which make predictions impossible. For the prediction of the unsaturated flow phenomena
additional source and sink terms must be considered which describe
the influence of the soil structure.

Literature cited

Bresler, E.,R.J. Hanks, (1969), Numerical method of estimating simul-
    taneous flow of water and salt in unsaturated soil, Soil Sci.Soc.
    Amer. Proc., 33, 827-832
Corey,J.C., R.H.Hawkins, R.F.Overmann, R.E.Green, (1970), Miscible
    displacement measurements within laboraty columns using the gamma
    photoneutron method, Soil Sci. Soc. Amer. Proc., 34, 854-858
Dagan,G., (1967), Hydrodynamic dispersion in a non-homogenous porous
    column, Journal of Geophysical Research, 72, 4075-4080
Diestel,H., (1975), this book
Frissel,M.J., P.Reiniger, (1974), Simulation of accumulation and
    leaching in soils, Wageningen
Ghuman,B.S., S.M.Verma, S.S.Prihar, (1975), Effect of application
    rate, initial soil wetness, and redistribution time on salt dis-
    placement by water, Soil Sci. Soc. Amer. Proc., 39, 7-10
Kirkham,D., W.L.Powers, (1972), Advanced soil physics, Wiley-Inter-
    science, New York, London
Kissel,D.E., J.T.Ritchie, Burnett,E., (1973), Chloride movement in
    undisturbed swelling clay soil, Soil Sci. Soc. Amer. Proc.,
    37, 21-24
Porter,L.K., W.D.Kemper,R.D.Jackson and B.A.Stewart. , (1960),
    Chloride diffusion in soils as influenced by moisture content.
    Soil Sci.Soc.Amer.Proc.24, 460-463
Warrick,A.W.,J.W.Biggar and D.R.Nielsen, (1971),Simultaneous
    solute and water transfer for an unsaturated soil.Water
    Resources Research 7, 1216-1225.

Acknowledgement

The work reported here was carried out in the frame of a research
project which is part of the "Sonderforschungsbereich 150- Water
Balance, and Soil Use" of the Technical University of Braunschweig.
The author wishes to express his thanks to Prof. Dr. G. Schaffer,
the leader of this research project and to the financing agency, the
Deutsche Forschungsgemeinschaft.

DISCUSSION

Were the samples in all the tests shown initially dry ? (VACHAUD)

I have also performed experiments with prewetted samples. However, here I have discussed only experiments with initially dry samples. (PROPFE)

Did you get a similar effect with prewetted samples ? (VACHAUD)

Yes, also in the prewetted samples salt accumulated at the discontinuity, but to a lesser degree than in the initially dry samples. The reason for this is that solutes cannot accumulate in those spaces which are already filled with water through the prewetting procedure. (PROPFE)

System Simulation in Water Resources, ed. G.C. VANSTEENKISTE
1976, North-Holland Publishing Company

MODEL EXPERIMENTS ON SALT DISPLACEMENT MECHANISMS
IN UNSATURATED POROUS MEDIA UNDER TEMPERATURE GRADIENTS

H. Diestel
Leichtweiss-Institute for Water Research
Technical University Braunschweig
Braunschweig, Fed. Rep. of Germany

ABSTRACT

The mechanisms leading to the salinization of a soil from a high water
table are investigated. It is shown that the accretion of salt in a salinizing capillary zone is initially caused by convective salt transport.
In a subsequent phase, an enrichment due to evaporation takes place. Only
in an advanced stage of salinization, molecular diffusion plays a role in
the downward displacement of salt immediately under the salt accumulation
near the surface. It is shown that salt sieving, thermal diffusion, gravitative descent and molecular diffusion (with the exception mentioned) do not
become effective as salt displacement or accumulation mechanisms in the
salinization of a soil with a high water table. Some aspects of the mathematical treatment of this process are discussed.

1. INTRODUCTION

The aim of the work reported here was to determine the contribution of
various salt displacement mechanisms to the salinization of a homogeneous soil
with a high water table. This information is considered useful for the development
of refinements of agricultural practices presently used under conditions of salinization hazard, including irrigation and drainage practices and reclamation procedures, as well as for the development of mathematical models to describe the process
of salinization from a high water table.

This paper is a continuation and extension of a previous paper by the
author (Diestel 1974). The shortness of space often precludes a full description
and discussion. A complete and detailed treatise of the work reported here and in
Diestel (1974) can be found in Diestel (1975).

2. EXPERIMENTAL INFORMATION

The two experimental runs discussed here were carried out in a lysimeter
of 1 cbm volume. Water and salt contents were determined from samples obtained
with augers introduced through lateral holes. Temperatures were recorded continuously with mercury thermographs. The arid climatic conditions were simulated with
infrared radiators and a warm wind generator. The medium used was sand, 0.08 –
0.2 mm, of a very high quartz content. The salt used was $BaCl_2 . 2 H_2O$.

In the run designated in the following as run 1, constant temperature gradients and a constant evaporation rate were maintained. The distribution of temperatures and of evaporation rates with depth is given in Diestel (1974). The
groundwater level was constant in 36.2 cm depth. The evaporation rate of 0.1 mm/h
which prevailed in this run is about 1/5 of the evaporation rate which would have
prevailed during the day if the lysimeter would have been set up under arid conditions. This can be deduced from the work of Sleight (1917). Thus, conditions prevailed which favoured non-convective displacement mechanisms. The water and salt
contents measured through the unsaturated zone during run 1 are given in Diestel
(1974). In the run designated in the following as run 2, the temperatures shown in
Fig. 1 prevailed in various depths.

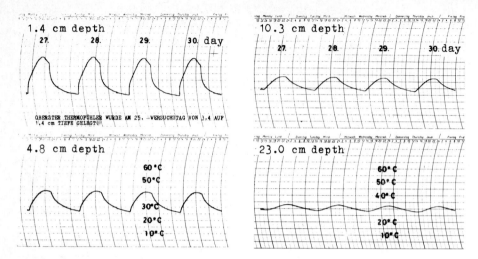

Fig. 1. Daily temperature waves in various depths, run 2.

The absolute magnitude as well as the change with time of soil temperatures in an arid location are very similar (C.W. Rose 1968). The water level varied between 62 and 65 cm depth. The average daily evaporation was 0.6 mm/day. Sleight (1917) determined 3.3 mm/day during the summer months for a very dimilar sand with the groundwater at 61 cm, again 5 times the rate of the experiment. The samples were taken at midnight. The measured water and salt contents for run 2 are shown in Figs. 2 and 3, respectively, as a function of depth and time.

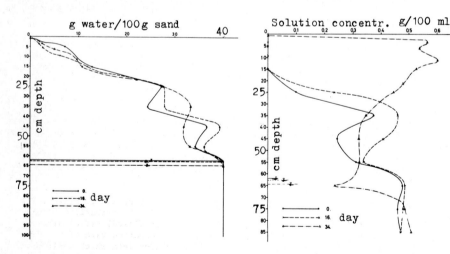

Fig. 2. Water contents, run 2.   Fig. 3. Salt contents, run 2.

The coefficients of molecular diffusion for barium chloride in this sand were determined as a function of temperature, moisture content and concentration. They are given in Diestel (1974). The measurements shown in that paper were complemented by additional measurements near zero concentration. At the concentrations prevailing in the unsaturated zone during the initial rise of salt from the groundwater (0 - 0.5 g/100 ml), the diffusion coefficients are zero.

3. SALT DISPLACEMENT MECHANISMS

3.1. The rise of salt from the groundwater level

As mentioned above, the coefficient of molecular diffusion is zero for the concentrations, temperatures and moisture contents prevailing in the unsaturated zone above the groundwater level and below the region of salt accumulation. Even if an experimental error in the determination of the diffusion coefficients at these low concentrations is taken into account, and values are obtained by interpolation between the lowest "reliable" concentration and zero concentration, (as was done in Diestel 1974), calculations of the convective and diffusive fluxes reveal that, at these pore water velocities, molecular diffusion is absolutely negligible in comparison to convection (Diestel 1975). Therefore, the upward advance of salt is a phenomenon of convection under the influence of hydrodynamic dispersion. It is to be noted that the evaporation rates were lower than field evaporation rates.

It can be seen from the data that whereas the water content is relatively unchanged during the course of both experiments, the concentrations gradually rise. There is a lag of the rise of salt behind the rise of water. There are two reasons for this lag. In the unsaturated zone under evaporation, a certain fraction of the water rises in the continuously liquid phase, and a certain fraction with a phase-changing mechanism, undergoing evaporation and condensation cycles. The two-phase mechanism is more rapid than the one-phase mechanism (Philip and de Vries 1957, D.A. Rose 1963). The classical concept of hydrodynamic dispersion is valid for the phenomenon of the distortion of the initially piston shaped leading edge of a body of water entering a medium which already has the same moisture content as the one prevailing at and behind this leading edge. In the case discussed here, capillary, salty, continuously liquid water advances from the groundwater surface into a medium which has a salt free moisture content decreasing with distance. (Diestel 1974, 1975).

The second reason for the lag of the rise of salt behind the rise of water is salt immobilization. A part of the barium present in the sand could not be removed from the sand with the barium extraction method used. With this extraction method, only barium chloride and barium carbonate could be extracted, not barium sulphate. Barium silicate was probably not present. The amount of undetermined barium was inversely proportional to temperature and proportional to moisture content and concentration, as shown in Fig. 4. That means that the rate of removal of salt from the displacement process, up to the time where salt accumulation near the surface began, increased with depth. This also lead to a time lag of the rise of salt behind the rise of water. Salt is "filtered" out of the continuously liquid water as it rises.

It is noteworthy that whereas the capillary zone under the higher temperatures and constant temperature gradients of run 1 is only 30 cm high and does not have a salt free region, the capillary zone under the lower temperatures and changing temperature gradients of run 2 is twice as high and exhibits a salt free region during the first 16 days of the experiment. It can be shown with the well-known equation of capillary rise that the difference in absolute temperatures does not explain this difference in zone height. Likewise, it can be shown that the higher friction losses which occur under the higher flow velocities of run 1 do not lead to this difference. Calculation with the equation of Krischer (1956)

$$H' = \frac{2\sigma}{r(l_2 g + B)} \qquad\qquad B = \frac{8\,\eta\,V}{r^4\,\pi} \qquad\qquad \text{Eq. 1}$$

gives capillary rise heights differing by only 0.002 cm for a radius of 0.003 cm
and pore velocities of 10 .10^{-6} and 5 . 10^{-6} cm/sec, corresponding to runs 1 and 2.
The packing of the sand for run 2 was slightly less dense than for run 1, resulting
in possibly larger capillaries. The fraction of immobilized salt and its distribution (see Sec. 4) is very similar for the 8. and 19. day of run 1 and for the
16. day of run 2. Therefore, only the c h a n g e in temperature lead to the higher
zone and to the salt free region of run 2. This finding adds weight to the mechanism of rise of water postulated above. In the run with changing temperature gradients, water evaporated during the noon hours, condensed during the cooling period
and rose as capillary water during the night. It evaporated during the following
evaporation period from a higher point than the day before. Thus, additional to the
processes taking place under constant temperature gradients, an upward displacement
of condensed water takes place under changing temperature gradients. After equilibrium is reached, a higher capillary zone is established.

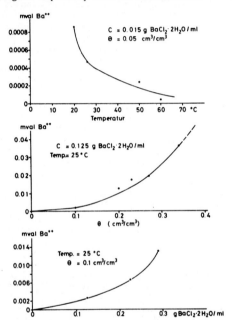

Fig. 4. Undetermined Ba^{++} = f(temp.,θ,conc.)
ordinate : meq. undetermined barium per cm^3 sand
abscissa : solution concentration

It follows from the above that the magnitude of the temperature fluctuation has
a direct influence on the amount of salt and water rising from the water table.
It would be interesting to take a close look at reports of the beneficial effects
of mulching. This practice improves soil structure and soil fertility, and reduces
evaporation and thus salt accumulation. However, it is doubtful whether in all
cases its costs can be justified exclusively with a reduction of salinization.
Mulching reduces the magnitude of the temperature fluctuations, and thus also the
rate of rise of "two-phase-water". Under certain conditions the total stress on
the plant root, in which the moisture tension and the concentration are complementary, may be lower in an unmulched than in a mulched field.

3.2. Salt accumulation and/or redistribution due to evaporation, salt sieving, molecular and thermal diffusion, and gravitative descent

Above 20 cm depth in run 1 and above 35 cm depth in run 2, a strong increase in the concentration of the soil solution has taken place. The primary cause of this increase is evaporation. However, salt accumulation in a given depth can also take place due to diffusion and salt sieving. As the amount of water evaporating in different depths is known for run 1 (Diestel 1974), the concentration profile of the 81. day lends itself to a quantitative analysis of the contribution of these mechanisms to the accumulation of salt in the profile depths near the soil surface. The estimates for this analysis will be explained with reference to Table 1.

Table 1 : Accumulation due to evaporation and molecular diffusion

Depth, cm	5	10	15
1. Water quantity evaporating per day, ml/m^2	158	75	40
2. Concentration, g/ml (Fig. 3)	0.007	0.006	0.0045
3. Accumulation by evaporation, Nr. 1.Nr. 2, g/m^2 on the 81. day	1.11	0.45	0.18
4. Difference in conc. grad. above and below the plane, g/ml/cm	0.018	0	0
5. Diffusion coefficient on th 81. day, $cm^2/sec. 10^{10}$	11.06	6.20	0
6. Accumulation by molec. diffusion on the 81. day, g/m^2	0.017	0	0
7. [Nr. 6 : (Nr. 3 + Nr. 6)].100, %	1.50	0	0
8. Film thickness, Å	11 250	18 070	25 470
9. Daily accumulation by evaporation "under arid conditions", (Nr. 3.2), g/m^2	2.22	0.90	0.36
10. Accumulation by molecular diffusion "under arid conditions", (Nr. 6.100), $g/m^2/81.$ day	1.7	0	0
11. [Nr. 10 : (Nr. 9 + Nr. 10)].100, %	43.4	0	0

The calculation of the values for row 1 is explained in Diestel (1974). Rows 2 and 3 are self-explanatory. Above any plane considered, the concentration gradient is higher than below the plane. The amount of salt accumulated during one day in this plane by molecular diffusion is equal to the difference between these gradients, multiplied by the diffusion coefficient and by 86400 sec/day (Rows 4 - 6). The diffusion coefficients are calculated from the data in Diestel (1974), corrected near zero concentration. The film thicknesses in row 8 are rough estimates, obtained by dividing the volumetric moisture content by the surface area of the sand (80000 $cm^2/100$ g sand). From Section 2 it follows that, with a distribution of evaporation rates with depth as in run 1, the total amount of salt accumulated in any plane, under the assumption that the lysimeter would have been set up under arid conditions, can be estimated by dividing the amounts of row 3 by 24 hours/day, and by multiplying them by 10 evaporation hours per day and the factor 5 (row 9). In the field, moisture contents would rarely exceed 20 gravity % or be below 7.5 gravity %, and thus not lead to a change in the diffusion coefficient. Field temperatures would, however, lead to a tenfold increase of the diffusion coefficient (Diestel, 1974). Favoring molecular diffusion, it is assumed that concentrations can prevail in the field which lead to a tenfold increase of the diffusion coefficient, thus leading to values 10 x 10 = 100 times larger than in row 6 (row 10).

With this information, an estimate can be made of the contributions to the increase in salt concentration in the plane at 5, 10 and 15 cm depth, for run 1 as

well as for field conditions. For run 1, molecular diffusion contributed 1.5 % to
the total salt increase in 5 cm depth, its contribution was zero (row 7). Thus,
under these conditions, evaporation was the cause of the "bulging out" of the concentration profiles above 20 cm depth. In the immediate vicinity of the dry sand
cover, downward redistribution through molecular diffusion played a very minor
role. Under field conditions, the redistribution through molecular diffusion can
be expected to reach the order of magnitude of the primary accumulation due to
evaporation, but this also only in the vicinity of the surface (row 11).

Sleight (1917) has shown that with the same groundwater level, the evaporation from a fine sandy loam is higher than from a sand. The accumulation due to
evaporation will accordingly be higher in a normal field soil. The diffusion coefficients in non-sandy soils available in the literature are of the order of magnitude of the diffusion coefficients determined here. Therefore, the relative contribution of molecular diffusion to salt displacements taking place in the soil
profile will not be higher under field conditions.

Salt accumulation due to salt sieving will occur when salt movement has to
take place through water wedges and films which are so thin that the influence of
the electric double layer extends through a substantial part of the film or wedge.
This distance is 10 - 100 Å according to Tschapek (1964), 20 - 300 Å according to
Nielsen et al (editors, 1972). The accompanying cation, in this case Ba^{++}, will
then also accumulate to a certain extent. The effective thickness of these films
and wedges can only be calculated approximately (Kemper 1961 a, b). But already the
very rough thickness estimates of row 8 in Table 1 show that under the conditions
of these experiments, salt sieving is highly unlikely to occur. The smallest film
thickness estimated is still 37.5 times larger than 300 Å. No information is available to make a general statement about the role of salt sieving in the salinization
of a field profile. Nielsen et al (editors, 1972) state that "the significance of
salt sieving in soilwater systems has not yet been established". The admittedly
rather speculative statement shall be made here that from the evidence available
here and in the literature, it is likely that during the salinization of a soil
under field conditions, salt sieving will lead to salt accumulations that are
absolutely negligible compared to the primary accumulation due to evaporation and
the secondary accumulation due to molecular diffusion. (See also Bresler and
Laufer, 1974).

The contribution of thermal diffusion to salt movement during salinization
will now be dealt with. Payton and Turner (1962) and Tanner (1927) determined
Soret (or Ludwig-Soret)-coefficients of Barium chloride. Their data complement
each other to a curve giving Soret-coefficients between 0.00465 and 0.0037 degree^{-1}
for concentrations between 0.001 and 0.052 g/ml. As thermal diffusion is, the same
as molecular diffusion, a manifestation of Brownian motion, it can safely be assumed
that the influence of the electric double layer, of the tortuosity of the diffusion
path and of the moisture content on the coefficient of thermal diffusion is the same
as on the coefficient of molecular diffusion. When concentration and temperature
gradients are active, the total diffusion flux is

$$J = -D_1 \frac{\partial C}{\partial x} - D_T \frac{\partial T}{\partial x}$$

Eq. 2[*]

(Lykow 1958). When both processes are equal in magnitude and opposite in direction,
J = 0. This relation allows the calculation of the thermal diffusion coefficient
from the molecular diffusion coefficient :

$$S = \frac{D_T}{D_1} = - \frac{\partial C/\partial x}{\partial T/\partial x} = - \frac{\partial C}{\partial T}$$

Eq. 3

---

[*] Explanation of symbols in Section 5

The total diffusion flux is thus also given by

$$J = - D_1 \frac{\partial C}{\partial x} - D_1 . S . \frac{\partial T}{\partial x} \qquad\qquad \text{Eq. 4}$$

and the proportion of molecular to thermal diffusion

$$\frac{\partial C}{\partial x} : S \frac{\partial T}{\partial x} \qquad\qquad \text{Eq. 5}$$

After conversion of the Soret coefficients into the units g/ml/degree, a calculation of this proportion is possible with the concentration and temperature gradients in various depths of the profile. At the end of run 1, substantial temperature and concentration gradients prevailed in the zone near the surface. For the 81. day, Table 2 gives the corresponding calculations for 2.5, 5 and 10 cm depth.

Table 2 : Thermal and molecular diffusion

Depth, cm	Conc. g/ml	Soret coeffic. degr.$^{-1}$	Soret coeff.S g/ml/deg.	Temp.grad. degr/cm	$S \frac{\partial T}{\partial x}$	Conc. grad. g/ml/cm	% molec.	% thermal
2.5	0.0513	0.00370	0.000190	1.16	0.00022	0.018	99	1
5	0.0073	0.00418	0.000031	0.40	0.000012	0.00077	98	2
10	0.0060	0.00424	0.000025	0.25	0.000006	0.00028	98	2

Example 2.5 cm depth : 0.018 : (0.00022 + 0.018) = 0.99
The proportion of molecular diffusion is thus 99 %.

It can be seen that the thermal diffusion flux is very small compared to the molecular or "concentration diffusion" flux. From Table 1 it can be seen that the molecular or "concentration" diffusion itself played a very minor role in the same depths and time. Therefore, thermal diffusion did not become effective as a displacement mechanism on the 81. day of run 1. Under arid field conditions, temperature gradients very similar to those of run 2 prevail, as already stated in Section 2. In 5 cm depth, a temperature gradient of 1.6 degr/cm prevails during noon time. Favoring thermal diffusion, 5 degr/cm shall be assumed. With a Soret coefficient of 0.000037 g/ml/degr. (Payton and Turner, Tanner), the following calculation yields the thermal diffusion flux :

$$D_T = D_1 . S = 11.06 \times 10^{-8} \times 37 \times 10^{-6} = 409 \times 10^{-14} \text{ g/cm sec degr.}$$

$$J = 409 \times 10^{-14} \times 5 = 2045 \times 10^{-14} \text{ g/cm}^2 \text{ sec.}$$

If it is now assumed that this large temperature gradient prevails for ten hours per day, and that immediately under the 5 cm depth the temperature gradient is zero, two assumptions which again favor thermal diffusion, a daily accumulation of salt of 0.0074 g ensues for this plain per square meter. This quantity is now added to the accumulation quantities for the 5 cm plain in table 1 (rows 9 and 10). It is 0.2 % of the total daily accumulation in this plain.

It follows that thermal diffusion does not become effective as a salt displacement mechanism in a salinizing soil profile.

The question will now be dealt with whether the salt enrichment of the soil solution during salinization can lead to such high densities that a gravitative descent of solution begins. An analysis of the data for the 81. day of run 1 is useful in this context. The main calculations and results of this analysis are given in Table 3.

Table 3 : The gravitative descent of soil solution

Depth, cm	4.50	6.75	10.00	13.75	16.20
1. Hydraulic cond.,cm/ sec.10^4	0.119	0.663	1.921	5.203	12.525
2. Darcy flux $cm^3/cm^2/$ sec.10^9	1 725	2 175	2 614	2 950	3 075
3. Grad.total pot.,cm wat./cm	−0.14	−0.03	−0.01	−0.006	−0.0025
4. Grad.grav. pot.,cm wat./cm	1.0	1.0	1.0	1.0	1.0
5. Grad. of rest pot., cm wat./ cm	−1.14	−1.03	−1.01	−1.006	−1.0025
6. Rest. pot. cm water	−32.0	−29.7	−26.3	−22.6	"−20.00"
7. Rest pot. dyne/cm^2	−30 920.96	−28 814.94	−25 503.37	−21 915.45	"−19 384.4"
8. Equil. gravit. pot.,dyne/ cm^2	+30 920.96	+28 814.94	+25 503.37	+21 915.45	+19 384.4
9. Prev. grav. pot., cm water	31.70	29.45	26.20	22.45	20.00
10. Equil. density g/ml	0.9953	0.9984	0.9933	0.9961	"0.9890"
11. Density of the so- lution,g/ml	0.9860	0.9900	0.9895	0.9895	0.9890

In row 1, the hydraulic conductivities, calculated with the method of Millington and Quirk (1961) and modified by Kunze et al (1968) are given. Rows 2 and 3 give the Darcy fluxes in the various depths, and the gradient of the total potential obtained with Darcy's law from rows 1 and 2. Rows 4 and 5 give the gradient of the gravitational potential and of the "rest potential". This "rest potential" gradient is obtained by subtracting the gradient of the gravitational potential from the gradient of the total potential. It is mainly a matrix potential gradient. The absolute values of this rest potential are obtained graphically from the gradients and listed in row 6. The rest potentials in dyne/cm^2 (row 7) are calculated with the acceleration of gravity and the density of the solution. Row 8 gives the gravitational potential that would be in equilibrium with the rest potential. The gravitational potentials which actually prevailed are listed in row 9. In row 10, the density is given which would allow an equilibrium between the prevailing gravitational potentials and the rest potential. It is calculated by dividing the values of row 8 by the product of the values of row 9 and the acceleration due to gravity. It can be seen from rows 10 and 11 that the densities prevailing at this late stage of salinization did not suffice to allow a gravitative descent of the solution. (The densities for the prevailing temperatures and concentrations in row 11 are from Landolt and Björnstein 1969). Gravitational potentials of about 100 cm or less are common in the field where a salinization hazard from a high water table exists. In such a situation, matrix potentials of several hundred cm prevail during the salinization period.

Calculations analogous to those of Table 3 reveal that gravitative descent can normally not lead to a displacement of salt in a salinizing field profile.

4. THE MATHEMATICAL TREATMENT OF THE PROCESS OF SALINIZATION

The question of the mathematical treatment of the salinization of a soil from a high water table is of special interest at this Symposium. The phase of the upward rise of salt under disregard of the immobilization of salt and under consideration of the fraction of continuously liquid water has been treated by Diestel (1974). In the same paper, a possibility is shown to treat mathematically the phase in which salt moves up by hydrodynamically dispersed convection, and simultaneously moves down by molecular diffusion. Immobilization of salt is again neglected, but the increase with time of the concentration at the surface is considered. It follows from Section 3 that for practical purposes, a mathematical treatment of the following processes would be of interest : the rise of water in the continuously liquid phase and by the phase-changing mechanism, the immobilization of salt and the accumulation due to evaporation. All other salt displacement mechanisms can neglected. Downward diffusion is "uninteresting" in the sense that drainage design, irrigation timing and dosage, and cultural practices should aim at avoiding the primary salinization, not the secondary distribution of the accumulated salt.

A complete mathematical model of the three processes mentioned can not be presented here. It is hoped, however, that the fragmentary data and discussion given in Diestel (1974, 1975) and here will provide some useful information and a stimulus to a participant of this Symposium to work out such a model.

Hydrodynamic dispersion coefficients for run 1 were determined by Diestel (1974) by matching the concentration curves as they were measured to the corresponding hydrodynamic dispersion equation

$$\frac{\partial C}{\partial t} = D_h \frac{\partial^2 C}{\partial (x - v_1 t)^2} \qquad\qquad \text{Eq. 6}$$

The solution of this equation for this case is :

$$C = 0.5 \cdot C_o (\text{erfc} \frac{x - v_1 t}{2\sqrt{D_h\ t}}) \qquad\qquad \text{Eq. 7}$$

(Kirkham and Powers 1972). The immobilization of salt is neglected, and the matching factors found in that way decrease with time and distance from the water level. It is problematic to define the significance of these "hydrodynamic dispersion matching factors". Immobilization of salt can be treated by including a corresponding term in Eq. 6 respectively in the miscible displacement equation. Much work has been done in this direction (Lapidus and Amundson 1952, Banks and Ali 1964, Lindstrom and Boersma 1973, among others). This approach is mathematically cumbersome and also problematic when, as is the case here, the moisture content is variable with distance, condensed water plays a role, and immobilization varies with temperature, moisture content and concentration as shown in Fig. 4. The primary aim here was not to work out a fitting mathematical model, but to arrive at coefficients which allow a description of the complicated process described above, a practically relevant but rather deviate variant of the classical, simple hydrodynamic dispersion case, with the hydrodynamic dispersion equation. This is considered useful, as, with the exception of those of Todd and Kemper (1972), no dispersion coefficients for the process discussed here have been determined. To calculate the diffusion flux at a given point, Todd and Kemper multiply the concentration gradient with the dispersion coefficient $D_d = D_p + D_h$. Diestel (1975) argues that it would be correct to use the D_p.

Barium did not behave like an ideal tracer, as it showed an interaction with the medium. But the dependence of this interaction on various parameters was known, as well as the absolute amount of salt immobilized in the unsaturated zone. With this information, the solute-medium interaction was "reversed" and concentration distributions found to which the hydrodynamic dispersion equation could be matched. The approach shall be demonstrated for the 19. day of run 1. In Fig. 5, the measured salt distribution is plotted to the left of the vertical. From the area of this plot, the amount of salt which is not immobilized is obtained, in this case 420 g. The amount of salt expected above the waterlevel is 600 g (from the amount of capillary water, the amount of evaporated water and the concentration of the groundwater). The difference, 180 g of salt, are immobilized. An "immobilization factor" is plotted with the information of Fig. 4 to the right of the vertical. It is equal to 1 at the water level, where the temperature is lowest and the moisture content and the concentration highest. The distribution of the immobilized salt in the unsaturated zone is obtained by planimetering. (The procedure is described in detail in Diestel 1975).

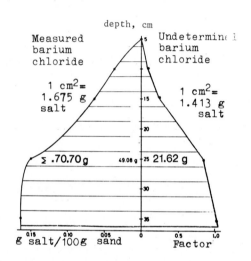

Fig. 5. 19. day, run 1 : measured and undetermined salt

Dividing the total amount of determined and immobilized salt in each depth by the moisture contents, "ideal tracer concentrations" are calculated. These concentrations are brought to the basis 1 at x = 0 for convenience. It is questionable whether exactly this concentration distribution actually would have arisen if an ideal tracer would have been used. This actual distribution could only have been calculated if all the processes of precipitation, sorption and desorption would have been known and taken into account in their calculation. Their r e l a t i v e d i s t r i b u t i o n with time and depth is, however, supposedly much closer to the distribution which an ideal tracer would have had than the one of the measured concentrations. And it is the distribution of C with t and x which determines the value of D_h, not the absolute values of C. When x, as in Diestel (1974), is taken as equal to zero in 25 cm depth, and the constant D_h is allowed to vary, a reasonable match between the "ideal tracer concentrations" and Eq. 7 is obtained. This can be seen in Fig. 6.

It is interesting to note that the trend in the dispersion coefficients is reversed when the immobilization is taken into account. The hydrodynamic dispersion coefficients grow with time and distance from the water level (Fig. 7). If the

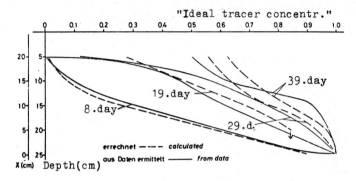

Fig. 6. Application of Eq. 7 to run 1

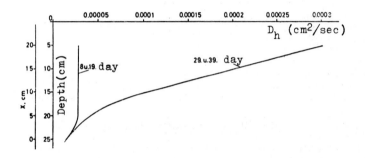

Fig. 7. D_h as a function of depth and time, run 1

coefficient D_h in Eq. 6 is an unambiguous index of the degree of dispersion of the advancing body of fluid, then this can be taken as a proof of the increase with time of the pore spectrum in which capillary water moves. This is to be expected : in a given depth, capillary water initially is present only in the capillaries in which a rapid rise took place. A fraction of the moisture content derives from water which has risen changing phases. This fraction is reduced, however, as capillary water in slower capillaries also reaches the upper region of the unsaturated zone. As this capillary water arrives at a given height, the pore spectrum participating there in capillary transport increase. An increase of D_h with time is also found by Propfe (1975).

Another example shall be given of the usefulness of this type of mathematical analysis. For the average pore velocity of run 2 ($5.3 \cdot 10^{-6}$ cm/sec), a dispersion coefficient of $20 \cdot 10^{-6}$ cm^2/sec can be estimated from Fig. 7 and from Fig. 4 of Diestel (1974). Now, the C-x-curve resulting from convection during evaporation can be calculated. For the 16. day of run 2, this C-x-curve is shown in Fig. 8 as a dashed line, with x = 0 in 45 cm depth for graphical convenience. 10 hours evaporation per day are assumed. The measured C-x-curve is also shown (solid) as well as the curve which results by adding the immobilized salt to the measured salt (dotted and dashed).

All concentrations are brought to the basis 1 at the water level. This analysis allows a separation of the amounts of salt rising during the evaporation hours

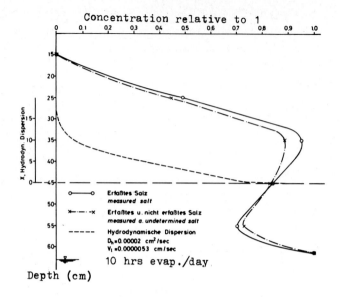

Fig. 8. C-x-curves from 16 x 10 = 160 hours (Eq. 7),
        and measured after 16 x 24 = 384 hours, run 2.
        D_h-value extrapolated from conditions of constant evaporation (run 1)

and during the night. Obviously, the rise of salt during evaporation would only
lead to the distribution shown by the dashed line. Estimates independent of this
analysis with the convective flux and by evaluation of Fig. 3 show, in fact, that
only slightly more than half of the salt which is above the depth of 30 cm on the
16. day was transported there during the daytime hours. The rest rose with capillary water during the night (Diestel 1975).

     It is noteworthy here that for another variant of "classical" hydrodynamic
dispersion, the downward displacement of a salt slug in a homogeneous and layered
porous medium, a more rigorous solution of Eq. 6 satisfactorily describes the observed data (Propfe 1975). In this section, a mathematical analysis was performed
by matching processed data to equations which are accepted as a common language
and definition for the hydrodynamic dispersion phenomenon. In a similar way, miscible displacement data match the miscible displacement equation if D_d, mathematically a constant, is allowed to vary (Biggar and Nielsen 1967, Bresler 1973).
Such procedure is useful, and the dispersion coefficients determined in such a way
do have a physical meaning, as was shown above. However, an unambiguous model to
describe the salinization from a high water table would inherently have to account
for two-phase water rise, salt immobilization, and a variable D_h.

5. SYMBOLS USED

C   = Concentration [g/ml, unless otherwise indicated]

C_o = Initial concentration [g/ml, unless otherwise indicated]

D_1 = Coefficient of molecular diffusion in pure solution [cm^2/sec]

D_p = Coefficient of molecular diffusion in a porous medium [cm^2/sec]

D_h = Coefficient of longitudinal hydrodynamic dispersion [cm^2/sec]

D_d $\quad = D_p + D_h =$ Dispersion coefficient [cm^2/sec]

D_T $\quad =$ Coefficient of thermal diffusion [g(sec cm degree)$^{-1}$]

erfc(x) $\quad =$ Complementary error function $= \dfrac{2}{\sqrt{\pi}} \displaystyle\int_x^\infty e^{-\xi^2} \, d\xi$

g $\quad =$ Acceleration due to gravity $= 980$ cm^2/sec

H' $\quad =$ Maximum height of capillary rise [cm]

J $\quad =$ Flux of solved particles [g/cm^2 medium/sec]

r $\quad =$ Radius of a capillary [cm]

S $\quad =$ Soret (Ludwig-Soret)-coefficient [degree^{-1}, g/ml/degree]

T $\quad =$ Absolute Temperature [$^\circ$K]

t $\quad =$ Time [seconds, unless otherwise indicated]

V $\quad =$ Liquid flux through the capillary (r . v_1) [cm^3/sec]

v_1 $\quad =$ Average velocity of liquid water in pores [cm/sec]

x $\quad =$ Distance [cm]

η $\quad =$ Viscosity [Poises]

θ $\quad =$ Volumetric moisture content [cm^3 liquid/cm^3 medium]

π $\quad = 3.1416$

ρ_1 $\quad =$ Density of the liquid [g/ml]

σ $\quad =$ Surface tension of the liquid [dyne/cm]

6. ACKNOWLEDGEMENTS

The work reported here was carried out in the frame of a research project which is part of the Sonderforschungsbereich 150 (Water Balance and Soil Use) of the Technical University of Braunschweig. The author wishes to express his thanks to Prof. Dr. G. Schaffer, the leader of the research project, and to the financing agency, the Deutsche Forschungsgemeinschaft.

7. REFERENCES

Banks, R.B. and I. Ali (1964). Dispersion and adsorption in porous media flow, J. Hydraul. Div., Proc. ASCE Vol. 90, No. HY 5 (Paper 4022) : 13 - 31.

Biggar, J.W and D.R. Nielsen (1967). Miscible displacement and leaching phenomenon, Irrigation of Agric. Lands. Agron. Monogr. 11. Amer. Soc. Agron : 254 - 274.

Bresler, E. (1973). Solute Movement in Soils, In : Arid Zone Irrigation, Ed. B.Yaron et al. Springer Verlag pp. 165 - 175.

Diestel, H. (1974). Salt displacement mechanisms in the unsaturated zone under evaporation, Preliminary results, Mitt. Deutsche Bodenk. Ges. 20 : 347 - 361.

Diestel, H. (1975). Der Anteil verschiedener Salzverlagerungsmechanismen bei der Versalzung eines Sandes mit oberflächennahem Grundwasser, Schriftenreihe des Sonderforschungsbereiches 150 der Technischen Universität Braunschweig, Selbstverlag.

Bresler, E. and A. Laufer (1974). Anion exclusion and coupling effects in non-steady transport through unsat. soils. II. Soil Sci. Soc. Amer. Proc. 38 : 213 - 218.

Kemper, W.D (1961 a). Movement of water as affected by free energy and pressure
    gradients, I. Application of classic equations for viscous and diffusive
    movements to the liquid phase in finely porous media, Soil Sci. Soc.
    Amer. Proc. 25 : 255 - 260.

Kemper, W.D. (1961 b). Movement of water as affected by free energy and pressure
    gradients, II. Experimental analysis of porous systems in which free ener-
    gy and pressure gradients act in opposite directions, Soil Sci. Soc. Amer.
    Proc. 25 : 260 - 265.

Kirkham, D. and W.L. Powers (1972). Advanced Soil Physics, Wiley-Interscience, 534pp.

Kunze, R.J., G. Uehara and K. Graham (1968). Factors important in the calculation
    of hydraulic conductivity, Soil Sci. Soc. Amer. Proc. 32:760 - 765.

Landolt and Björnstein (1969). Zahlenwerte und Funktionen etc. 6, Ausgabe, Vol. II
    5a.

Lapidus, L. and N.R. Amundson (1952). Mathematics of adsorption in beds. I. Phys.
    Chem. 56 : 984 - 988.

Lindstrom, F.R and L. Boersma (1973). A theory on the mass transport of previously
    distributed chemicals in a water saturated sorbing porous medium, III,
    Exact solution for first-order kinetic sorption, Soil Sci. 115 : 5 - 10.

Lykow, A.W. (1958). Transporterscheinungen in kapillarporösen Körpern. 275 pp.
    Akademie Verlag Berlin.

Millington, R.J. and J.P. Quirk (1961). Permeability of porous solids, Trans. Farad.
    Soc. 57 : 1200 - 1206.

Nielsen, D.R , R.D. Jackson, J.W. Cary and D.D. Evans (Editors) (1972). Soil water,
    Amer. Soc. Agron./Soil Sci. Soc. Amer. Madison, 175 pp.

Payton, A.D. and J.C.R. Turner (1962). Soret coefficients and heats of transport
    of some salts of alkaline earth metals in water at 25°C, Transact. Farad.
    Soc. 58 : 55 - 59.

Propfe, H. (1975). Model experiments on salt displacement mechanisms in an unsatu-
    rated layered porous medium, Article in this book.

Rose, C.W. (1968). Water transport in soil with a daily temperature wave, I. Theory
    and experiment, Austr. J. Soil Res. 6 : 31 - 44.

Sleight, R.B. (1917). Evaporation from the surfaces of water and river-bed materials
    J. Agric. Res. 10 : 209 - 262.

Tanner, C.C. (1927). The Soret effect, Trans. Farad. Soc. 23 : 75 - 95.

Todd, R.M. and W.D. Kemper (1972). Salt dispersion coefficients near an evaporating
    surface, Soil Sci. Soc. Amer. Proc. 36 : 539 - 543.

Tschapek, M. (1963). The ion sieving phenomenon in soils, Z. Pflanz-enern. Düng.
    Bodenk. 102 : 193 - 203.

Krischer, O. (1956). Die wiss. Grundlagen der Trocknungstechnik, Springer Verlag.

DISCUSSION

*You did the experiments with barium chloride. Is barium exchanged from the
soil or is it adsorbed. How did you determine the adsorption coefficient ?
(WIERENGA)*

There is one slide which I showed with the amount of undetermined barium.
I call it "undetermined" because I want to evade the decision of whether it is
precipitated or adsorbed. I have made a series of experiments to find an extraction
method with which I can extract as much barium as possible from the sand. Even with
this method not all of the barium put into the lysimeter and into the diffusion
cells could be recovered. However, from the data obtained for the diffusion cells,
which were subjected to different moisture contents, temperatures and concentrations,
the dependence from these variables of the difference between the amount of barium
put in and the amount of barium recovered could be determined. (DIESTEL)

*And what you have in that figure, the concentration distribution with time,
was it chlorideor barium ? (WIERENGA)*

Barium. (DIESTEL)

Did you try it with chloride too ? (WIERENGA)

I determined chloride too. But the sand which I used was unpurified and
already had a chloride content before the start of the experiments. (DIESTEL)

*But you should have some time delay to do this, to know the amount of water
that will assure that you have a material balance, because you determined the total
barium in the soil. (WIERENGA)*

I have a total material balance for barium, but not for chloride. What I
could have done is make a chloride analysis of the sand before filling it into the
lysimeter. (DIESTEL)

*So you have a total material balance for barium. But why didn't you recover
all of it ? You must have had an adsorption. (WIERENGA)*

In the sand I verified that I have many elements and a certain clay content.
I have an exchange capacity of 1.5 milliequivalents per 100 gram sand. What I am
interested in are the dynamics of the salt. I did not worry about whether the immobilization was caused by precipitation or adsorption. What I want to know is whether
the amount of immobilized salt is proportional to concentration, moisture content
and temperature. And you saw in Fig. 4 that the curves look like typical sorption
curves. But I doubt that only sorption is involved. I did not go into the problem
very deeply, because I felt that the problem of the sorption of barium on quartz
sand is not that much of general interest. (DIESTEL)

*But you need to know it if you want to describe mathematically what is
going to happen. (WIERENGA)*

I needed "ideal tracer concentrations". I had the choice of two procedures
to obtain them : either introduce a sorption term into the hydrodynamic dispersion
equation, or "correct" the concentration curves obtained as original data. I chose
the latter procedure. I will explain it with reference to Fig. 5.

In this slide the measured salt distribution is plotted to the left of the vertical.
From the area of this plot, the amount of salt which is not immobilized is obtained,
in this case 420 g. The amount of salt expected above the waterlevel is 600 g (from
the amount of capillary water, the amount of evaporated water and the concentration
of the groundwater). The difference, 180 g of salt, are immobilized. An "immobilization factor" is plotted with the information of Fig. 4 to the right of the vertical. It is equal to 1 at the water level, where the temperature is lowest and the
moisture content and the concentration highest. The distribution of the immobilized
salt in the capillary zone is obtained by planimetering. Dividing the total amount
of determined and immobilized salt in each depth by the moisture contents, "ideal
tracer concentrations" are calculated. These concentrations are brought to the
basis 1 at x = 0. I matched the hydrodynamic dispersion equation to the concentrations, "corrected" for immobilization. I am not very happy about this procedure,
but the other alternative, the inclusion of a sorption of immobilization term into
the hydrodynamic dispersion equation, would have been cumbersome and problematic,
because the moisture content is variable with distance, condensed water plays a
role, and immobilization varies with temperature, moisture content and concentration. (DIESTEL)

PART FIVE

ON THE USE OF DEDUCTIVE INFORMATION IN QUALITY MODELS INVOLVING BIOSYSTEMS

System Simulation in Water Resources, ed. G.C. VANSTEENKISTE
1976, North-Holland Publishing Company

MATHEMATICAL MODEL OF AN INDUSTRIAL RIVER

J.C.J. Nihoul
Institut de Mathématique
Liège, Belgium
Institut de Géophysique
Louvain-La-Neuve, Belgium

J. Smitz
Institut de Mathématique
Liège, Belgium

Industrial and urban discharges in rivers have created major problems in most developed countries. In a first stage, river waters have become unfit to drink without elaborated epuration processes. Then continued harrying of the rivers ecological balances , simultaneously feeding nutrients and poisons into the system, has progressively perverted the conditions of life and produced denatured, sometimes entrophicated waters, diserted by fish and human recreation activities.

Still continuous import of fresh rain water, obstinate autoepuration wherever possible, reoxygenation by stormy weather and the ineluctable slow evacuation of polluted waters towards the sea succeeded in maintaining an apparently acceptable situation to those who were prepared to pay a price for urban and industrial developments.

But industry needs water too, if only for cooling, and although this is low quality water in most cases, there must be enough of it and it cannot be too degraded.

Polluted rivers may also create Public Health problems and more severe regulations, coinciding with new environmental public demands, intersected with industrial concerns to denounce the barbarous exploitation of rivers and call for control and management of river systems.

Management is a very popular word nowadays and, although different people may define it differently, everybody feeds that it includes choices and decisions motivated by some optimal utilization
of the system allowing the necessary compromises between the requirements of increasing industrialization and affluent society and the
necessity to preserve the valuable natural resources.

The management of a river depends on the manager's ability to
predict the system's behaviour, its response to perturbations, alte-
rations induced by man or nature. The prediction of course needs
not - and cannot hope to - reproduce all the details of the natural
system. Efficiency requires rapid answers and this, in turns,
restricts the analysis to the cogent features of the system.

The predictive understanding of the dynamics of the system's
essential organs is prerequisite to any management program.

The foundation of any management decision is always some model
idea of the system's functioning.

Whether this can be based on intuitive experience, reduced
scale models of the river or mathematical models rooted in extensive
data banks depends on the complexity of the system, the number of
its aspects and components which, guided by the management objectives, one addresses to.

The model of a river can thus be more or less sophisticated
according to one's interest in navigation, water quality defined by
temperature, dissolved oxygen or more variables, ecology, etc...

This is the reason why in the past different models, often
sponsored by different organizations, have been developed dealing,
one with river flows, one with water temperature and cooling potential, one with biological oxygen demand, etc..

These models have served their purpose by answering each the
specific management question asked to it.

One realizes now, however, that these models, disconnected as
they were in most cases, cannot solve the multidisciplinary problems
of modern river management. Wind and rain conditions, flow rates,
water temperature, oxydo-reduction processes, turbidity, turbulence,
sediments deposition and erosion, primary and secondary productions
and bacterial activities are closely interrelated and in the present
state of rivers pollution all equally important.

In addition surface waters cannot be dissociated from underground
waters the quantity and quality of each reflecting on the other.
Then the river can no longer be considered in itself, independently
of its affluents and the whole hydrous balance of the river basin.

What is needed finally is a comprehensive interdisciplinary
river basin model.

Fig. 1. (Nihoul 1972) shows the mathematical model now being
developed by the Geophysical Fluid Mechanics Groups of Liège and
Louvain Universities for the River Meuse and its basin. Interactions between subsets of the general model are emphasized.

The hydrodynamic submodel (hydrometeorology and hydrology) includes the calculation of the filling capacities and the characteristic times of response of possible barrages as well as the simulation of their potential role in maintaining water quantity and quality all along the river.

A special attention is paid to the evaluation of evapotranspiration fluxes which are very badly approximated in previously existing models and specialized studies of micro-turbulence are conducted to this effect.

The surface waters quality model is not - as it is often in
previously existing models - restricted to temperature, dissolved
oxygen or BOD. Following the work done for the Scheldt estuary
(e.g. Math. Modelsea 1975) a complete micriobial and chemical oxydo-
reduction kinetics is included in the evolution equations.

The model also contains the determination of the concentration
of nutrients, toxic metals, pesticides and pathogenic germs in the
tributaries and their evolution along the river. The study is supported by a comprehensive data bank constituted in the last five
years by the Institute of Hygiene and Epidemiology and the Institute
for Chemical Research in connection with the general inventory of
pollutants commanded by the National Environment Program, Sea
Project (e.g. Math. Modelsea 1975).

Finally the model is not regarded simply as a scientific tool
providing information and alternatives for management decisions ;
the economy of water resources and needs is taken into account and
simulation exercises include operational research and optimal control.

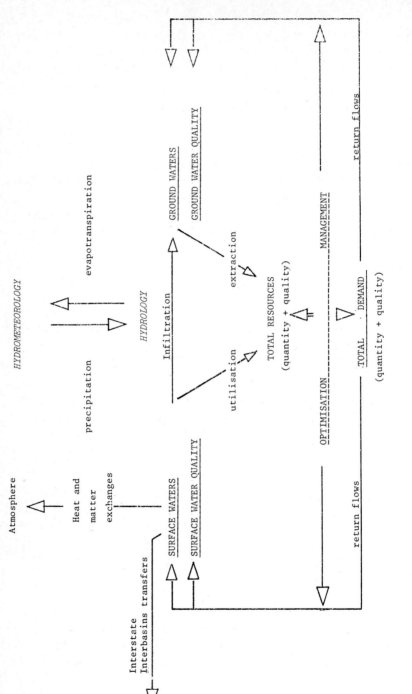

Fig. 1.

MATHEMATICAL   MODEL
of NATURAL   TEMPERATURE

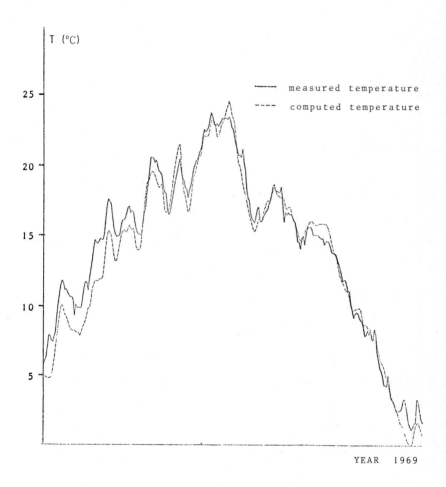

Fig. 2

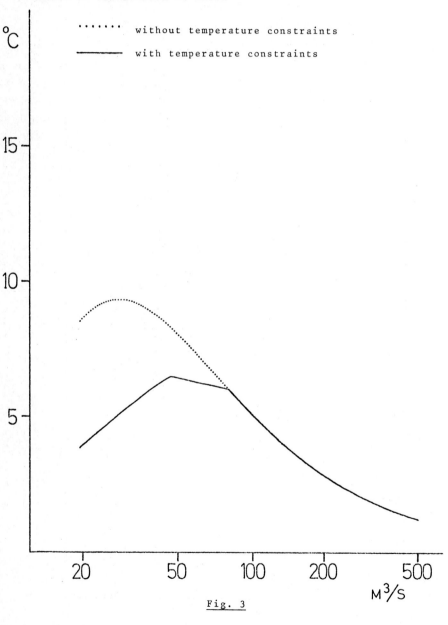

Fig. 3

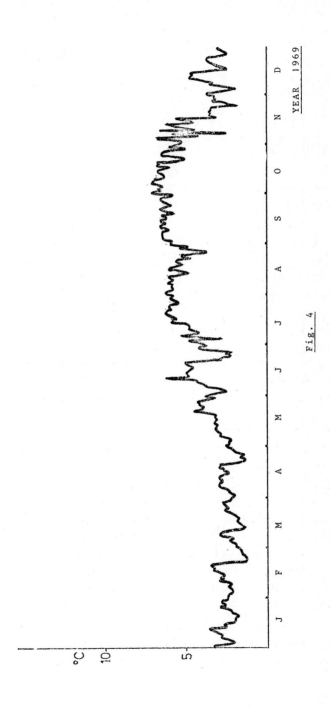

EXCESS OF TEMPERATURE AT LIEGE

YEAR 1969

Fig. 4

Applications of the model's predictions to restricted management problems are critically followed and subsequent modifications
of the basin's conditions are fed back into the equations. A per-
manent dialogue between research and applications, modellers and
users is maintained to continuously adjust the model and increase
its accuracy.

Emphasis is put, in the surface quality model, on the profile
of temperature along the river and its annual variations. Indeed
heat is the omnipresent pollutant and temperature elevations affect
the quality of the water (depletion of oxygen, inconvenience to
fish survival, increase in bacterial activity,...) as much as its
industrial quality (reduction of cooling capacity,...).

Extremely interesting and indicative results have however been
obtained by preliminary modelling investigations. The simulation of
the natural temperature given by the model is presented at fig. 2
(Smitz 1975). The different thermal fluxes are calculated from data
collected at meteorological stations. The predictive capabilities
of the model will still be increased by an ultimate calibration
using data measured directly on the site. The temperature excess
(with respect to the natural temperature) is also computed and, as
illustration, fig. 3 shows the excess of temperature at a point si-
tuated immediately upstream of Liège City, assuming thermal discharges of 1720 MW at Tihange (nuclear power plant 860 MWe) and 920 MW
at Les Awirs (classical power plant 660 MWe) and taking into account
regulation constraints bearing on the maximum temperature excess in
the zone of mixing and on the maximum river temperature.

The calculations show a cumulative effect of the two power
plants, which leads to a temperature excess of 8-9 °C at Les Awirs,
and 6-7 °C at Liège. This cumulative effect is maximum for river
outflow values of about 45-50 m^3/s. This situation is essentially
the consequence of the relative location of the two power plants and
of Liège ; it may create serious problems for downstream users of
cooling water during four or five months every year, as described at
fig. 4. which shows the result of simulation of annual variation of
excess temperature at Liège (Smitz 1975).

Preliminary investigations have suggested implantation schemes
of barrages in order to increase the lowest water outflow, which is
at the present time about 20-30 m^3/s, up to 50 m^3/s.

This value was also recommanded by industries, and particularly by electric production industry.

It is now established that this outflow value will lead to the maximum cumulative effect of excess temperature (fig. 2) and the benefit in cooling capacity for the first power plant (Tihange) will be balanced by equivalent loss for the power plants located around Liège ; moreover, this maximum excess temperature profile along the river may affect strongly the regeneration capacities (G. Billen & J. Smitz, 1975). Taking into account existing industrial and domestic utilization of the river, the proposed increase of the lowest outflow will lead to an improvement out of proportion with the required investment, and in some cases, to a degradation of the water quality.

This study shows clearly that any particular project elaborated to improve water quantity or quality is hazardous and meaningless without a complete understanding of the dynamics of the considered system, and that any management decision,which generally conduces here to irreversible situations, must be supported by multiobjectives optimization schemes obtained from the general model of the river basin.

References
_____

G. Billen & J. Smitz (1975), "Thermal pollution and water quality in an industrial estuary", Biosystems simulation in water resources and waste problems. North Holland Publ. Comp.

Math. Modelsea (1975), Fisheries Improvement Committee, International Council for the Exploration of the Sea C(21).

Nihoul J.C.J. (1972), Modèle Mathématique de la Meuse et du Bassin, Rapport préparé pour l'Economie Régionale Wallonne.

Smitz J. (1975), Modèle Thermique de Rivière, Ph. D. Dissertation. Liège University, in preparation.

DISCUSSION

I would like to know some details about the way you simulated some hydro-
logical aspects of your model.
How did you model for example infiltration and evaporation ? (NEUMAN)

This work has been done by the Louvain University, and I can say that the
scale is the scale of the whole basin. We take into account underground levels of
water. (SMITZ)

What is your time scale ? (NEUMAN)

I do not know. (SMITZ)

Did you use, remote sensing infrared measurements from planes to measure
the evolution of temperature of the estuary ? (FRIED)

Not systematically. (SMITZ)

Do you have a program ? (FRIED)

A big program was proposed. Now we are waiting. (SMITZ)

This has been done for the Scheldt, but the result was very poor. It was
very expensive also.
It was done for thermal pollution of a power station – smaller than the one we
mentioned – and the result was not very good.
We do not have much clear weather, this is one of the problems, and these rivers
are heavily industrialized, which creates another problem. We also do not have
data of the years before. (WAJC)

System Simulation in Water Resources, ed. G.C. VANSTEENKISTE
1976, North-Holland Publishing Company

SPATIAL STRUCTURATION OF DIFFUSIVE PREY-PREDATOR BIOLOGICAL POPULATIONS :
SIMULATION OF THE HORIZONTAL DISTRIBUTION OF PLANKTON IN THE NORTH SEA

D.M. Dubois and Y. Adam
Université de Liège
Institut de Mathématique
Liège, Belgium

ABSTRACT

Space and time variations of plankton populations are described by a mathematical model taking into account prey-predator interactions, advection by
residual currents and dispersion by eddy diffusion. The numerical simulations show off a spatial structuration which matches some observations in
situ.

INTRODUCTION

The spectral analysis of the spatial organization of phytoplankton populations exhibits two main classes of behaviour depending on the range of spatial
scale. Below 5 km, the phytoplankton behaves as a passive scalar [Platt et al.
(1975)] , (i) from zero to 100 m, the spatial variability of phytoplankton is controlled by turbulence and its spectrum is similar to the spectrum of homogeneous
and spatially isotropic turbulence according to Kolmogorov's theory, (ii) from
100 m to 5 km, the coherences between chlorophyll and temperature are high.
An experimental investigation of the spatial pattern of zooplankton was given by
Fasham et al. (1974). Beyond 5 km and until 100 km, the phytoplankton dynamics in
promoting patchiness, i.e. mesoscale spatial heterogeneity,dominates over that of
the physical diffusive processes in eroding it.

Most theoretical models describing the evolution of biological populations
only deal with time fluctuations. Kierstead and Slobodkin (1953) proposed one
equation describing plankton blooms by adding diffusion to the usual growth term.
The possibility of spatial variations is then accounted for by the apparition of
a critical length : for volumes of water smaller than a critical volume, plankton
populations die out, while they are able to grow in larger volumes.

While Kierstead and Slobodkin started with only one equation describing
both phyto- and zooplankton populations, the prey-predator interactions between
these two populations can be taken into account in using a prey-predator model.

Steele (1974) thinks that spatial heterogeneity in plankton populations
could be explained by a stochastic treatment of the Lotka-Volterra equations in
adding diffusion terms. Dubois (1975b) showed that these inhomogeneities can be
reproduced by a deterministic theoretical model in taking into account diffusivity
and advection.

The numerical simulation of the horizontal structuration of a patch of
phyto- and zooplankton populations was made in the Southern Bight of the North
Sea. During its drift in the Southern Bight, the horizontal structuration of the
patch is given by a growing circular disc which loses its centre and breaks into
segments. In other words, the initial patch transforms into a series of patches
as observed experimentally by Wyatt (1973).

In order to take into account of a saturation in the grazing rate of the
prey by the predator a more sophisticated interaction between the prey and the
predator is considered.

Theoretical considerations and numerical simulations of this system are given in view of obtaining some information of the importance of the interaction term on the spatial structuration of the two biological populations : a stable solution is obtained in imposing also a saturation in the growth term of the prey.

The non linear prey-predator equations with diffusion have got up to now no analytical solution. A numerical solution is thus necessary if one wants to get an idea of the evolution. Special numerical integration schemes have been developped from well-known existing ones (Crank-Nicholson's method for the unidimensional case, Peaceman-Rachford's alternating directions implicit method for the bidimensional problem) to take the non linear interaction terms into account. Both improvements are of the predictor-corrector type. Although the numerical methods are implicit (to increase numerical stability), the algorithms are very fast. This feature is particularly useful when one wants to simulate a wide range of theoretical situations.

THE MATHEMATICAL MODEL

As plankton can be considered as small organisms of identical size embedded in a turbulent flow [Pielou (1969)], their number is sufficiently large so that only statistical properties can be possibly studied. The characteristic time of ecological response is of the order of

$$\omega^{-1} = (k_1 \, k_3)^{-\frac{1}{2}}$$

where k_1 and k_3 are respectively the rates of natality-mortality of phytoplankton and herbiborous zooplankton. From experimental values, one finds that the characteristic time is of the order of a few days. Hence, if we average the evolution equations over a time which is short compared to the characteristic time of ecological response but still cover several tidal periods we smooth out the effects of oscillation and fluctuations of the sea without affecting significantly the process under study.

Let $\underline{u}$ and N_i be the average velocity (residual currents) and weighted depth average concentration of species i at position $\underline{r}$ and time t, respectively. The general equation of the horizontal distributions of species i can be written [e.g. Dubois (1975a)] :

$$\frac{\partial N_i}{\partial t} + \underline{u} \cdot \nabla N_i \; = \; < F_i > + \; \nabla \cdot (K \; \nabla N_i) \tag{1}$$

where $< F_i >$ is the average ecological interaction term of species i with the other species and K an eddy diffusivity. The second term in the first member represents advection due to residual currents and the second term in the second member the turbulent lateral diffusion.

Explicit expression of the interaction term $< F_i >$ is now given in the case of prey-predator plankton populations.

For the phytoplankton, one can write

$$< F_1 > \; = k_1 N_1 - k_2' \, \{1 - \exp [- \delta (N_1 - N_1')] \} \, N_2 \tag{2}$$

where N_1 and N_2 are respectively phyto- and zooplankton biomasses expressed in their organic carbon content per unit volume (mg C m^{-3}), k_1 the rate of growth of phytoplankton. The coefficient of N_2 is a modification of an expression due to Ivlev (1945) and represents the rate of ingestion per unit concentration of grazer at phytoplankton concentration, k_2' is the maximum rate of ingestion attainable by the zooplankton, δ is a constant defining the rate of change of ingestion with food concentration and N_1' is the concentration of phytoplankton at which feeding begins. The growth of phytoplankton is related to temperature, sunlight intensity and nutrient concentration. Averaging over the depth H and over time, k_1 can be written [O'Connor et al. (1973)] :

$$k_1 = K_1 \ T \ e \ f(K_e \ H)^{-1} \ [\exp(- \ \alpha_1) - \exp(- \ \alpha_o) \ ] \ \frac{N}{(K_N + N)} \tag{3}$$

where K_1 is the slope of the maximum growth rate versus temperature, T the temperature, e the base of the natural log, K_e the extinction coefficient, H the depth, f the fraction of daylight, N the nutrient concentration, K_N the half saturation constant for the nutrient N, $\alpha_1 = \alpha_o \exp(- \ K_e H)$ with $\alpha_o = \frac{I_{av}}{I_s}$ where I_{av} is the mean daily incident solar radiation and I_s the optimal light intensity. It may be noted that the extinction coefficient is an important component in the growth rate expression which is related to a number of physical and biological variables : turbidity due to the inorganic composition of the water and the self-shading of the growing phytoplankton. This last effect can be taken into account using the correlation developed by Riley (1963), i.e.

$$K_e = K'_e + 0.008 \ N_1 + 0.054 \ N_1^{2/3} \ ,$$

where K'_e is the extinction coefficient without the phytoplankton related extinction and N_1 is the phytoplankton chlorophyll α content (in mg m^{-3}).

For the herbivorous zooplankton, the interaction function $< F_2 >$ is written :

$$< F_2 > = - \ k_3 \ N_2 + \beta \ k'_2 \ \{ 1 - \exp [- \ \delta(N_1 - N'_1) \ ] \} \ N_2 \tag{4}$$

where k_3 is the rate of decay of zooplankton as a function of temperature and predation of the higher trophic levels and β is the ratio of phytoplankton carbon ingested to zooplankton carbon produced (utilization coefficient). In first approximation k_3 can be expressed as a linear function of temperature, i.e. $k_3 = k'_3 T + k''_3$

Substituting equations (2) and (4) in equation (1) for i = 1,2, the master equations for phyto-zooplankton horizontal structuration are written :

$$\frac{\partial N_1}{\partial t} + \underline{u}.\nabla N_1 \quad = K_1 \ T \ e \ f(K_e \ H)^{-1} \ [\exp(- \ \alpha_1) - \exp(- \ \alpha_o) \ ] \ \frac{N}{K_N + N}$$
$$- \ k'_2 \ \{ 1 - \exp [- \ \delta(N_1 - N'_1) \ ] \} \ N_2 + \nabla.(K \ \nabla N_1) \tag{5}$$

$$\frac{\partial N_2}{\partial t} + \underline{u}.\nabla N_2 \quad = -(k'_3 \ T + k''_3) \ N_2 + \beta k'_2 \ \{ 1 - \exp [- \ \delta(N_1 - N'_1) \ ] \} \ N_2$$
$$+ \ \nabla.(K \ \nabla N_2) \tag{6}$$

When the behaviour of phyto- and zooplankton populations are only considered on a few weeks, parameters like T, f and I_{av} do not change drastically.

In assuming that k_1 is a constant, equations (5) and (6) are written

$$\frac{\partial N_1}{\partial t} + \underline{u}.\nabla N_1 \quad = k_1 \ N_1 - k'_2 \ \{ 1 - \exp [- \ \delta(N_1 - N'_1) \ ] \} N_2 + \nabla.(K \ \nabla N_1) \tag{7}$$

$$\frac{\partial N_2}{\partial t} + \underline{u}.\nabla N_2 = -k_3 N_2 + \beta k_2' \{1 - \exp[-\delta(N_1 - N_1')]\}N_2 + \nabla.(K \nabla N_2) \quad (8)$$

If the physical mechanism of patchiness is assumed working in the linear region of the grazing, the term $\exp[-\delta(N_1 - N_1')]$ can be developed in series. Equations (7) and (8) become

$$\frac{\partial N_1}{\partial t} + \underline{u}.\nabla N_1 = k_1 N_1 - k_2 N_1 N_2 + \nabla.(K \nabla N_1) \quad (9)$$

$$\frac{\partial N_2}{\partial t} + \underline{u}.\nabla N_2 = -k_3 N_2 + \beta k_2 N_1 N_2 + \nabla.(K \nabla N_2) \quad (10)$$

where $k_2 = k_2' \delta$

The ecological interactions are then identical to those described in the Lotka-Volterra prey-predator model.

These equations exhibit a non-zero stationary solution uniformly distributed in space (with $\underline{u} = 0$)

$$N_{10} = \frac{k_3}{\beta k_2} \quad (11)$$

$$N_{20} = \frac{k_1}{k_2} \quad (12)$$

For small fluctuations of populations around (N_{10}, N_{20}), analytical solutions of equations (9) and (10) are given in the one-dimensional case [Dubois (1975d)]. The stationary spatial structuration is characterized by a wavelength given by

$$\lambda_c = 2\pi (\frac{2K}{\omega})^{1/2} \quad (13)$$

where $\omega = (k_1 k_3)^{1/2}$

is the frequency of the ecological response.

Equations (9) and (10) were simulated on computer in one and two spatial dimensions without advection. The basic mechanism of a spatial structuration of prey-predator was well exhibited. Three fundamental "laws" for the space and time behaviour of this structuration were deduced [Dubois (1975c)] :

a) the creation of a prey-predator wave ;
b) the propagation of this wave with constant intensity and velocity ;
c) the annihilation of two meeting waves.

A remarkable property is that this wave looks like an all-or-none response (active wave), the prey behaving like an activator and the predator like an inhibitor (with a refractory period during which the generation of a new wave cannot occur). In two dimensions, the wave exhibits a ring structure the radius of which increases with time.

Taking into account the transport by advection due to the residual circulation [the residual currents are computed as described in [Nihoul and Ronday (1975)], equations (9) and (10) are integrated on computer to simulate the spatial structuration of a patch of prey-predator plankton populations in the Southern Bight of the North Sea (see figures 1a - b - c). During its drift in the Southern Bight, the horizontal structuration of the patch is given by a growing circular disc which loses its centre (ring structure) and breaks into segments. Due to advection, the highest densities lie in a series of areas surrounding the empty region. In other words, the initial patch transforms into a series of patches sur-

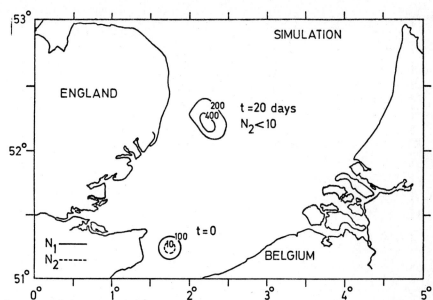

Fig. 1a. Initial repartition (t = 0) of prey N_1 and predator N_2. The numerical
simulation shows that the spatial repartition of prey-predator populations 20 days later is identical with and without saturating grazing.
(concentrations are given in mg C m^{-3})

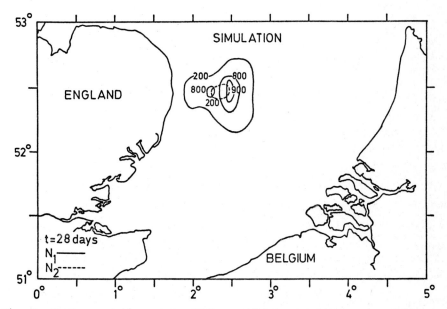

Fig. 1b. Further evolution, at t = 28 days, without saturating grazing. Notice
two maxima for the prey patch and the growth of the predator population
in the centre of the patch.

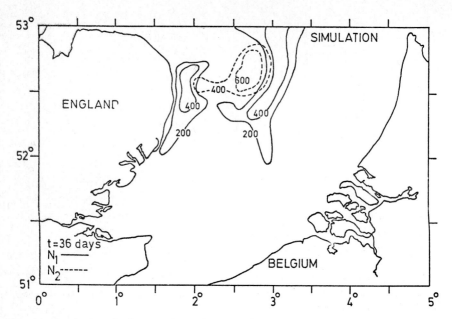

Fig. 1c. Further evolution, at t = 36 days, without saturating grazing. The ini-
         tial prey patch transformed into two separate patches. Notice the replace-
         ment of prey population in the centre of the initial patch by the preda-
         tor population. This figure shows clearly the physical mechanism of the
         spatial structuration of prey-predator plankton populations.

rounding an empty region (initial patch). The same succession of events was observed experimentally in following patches during a few weeks [Wyatt (1973)].

        If the grazing is saturated, $\exp[-\delta(N_1 - N_1')]$ drops in equations (7)
and (8). One obtains

$$\frac{\partial N_1}{\partial t} + \underline{u}.\nabla N_1 = k_1 N_1 - k_2' N_2 + \nabla.(K \nabla N_1) \tag{14}$$

$$\frac{\partial N_2}{\partial t} + \underline{u}.\nabla N_2 = (-k_3 + \beta k_2') N_2 + \nabla.(K \nabla N_2) \tag{15}$$

Equation (15) shows that the zooplankton is no more feedbacking with the phytoplankton and its behaviour is essentially due to a balance between its decay rate
and grazing, i.e. $(-k_3 + \beta k_2')$. Temperature and predation on zooplankton can become command parameters for the survival of plankton populations. When k_3 is
greater than $\beta k_2'$, the zooplankton population decreases and as a consequence the
quantity of phytoplankton increases indefinitely. One can then assist to the phenomenon of "red tide" for patches where these dramatic conditions hold.

        In view of studying the effect of the saturation of the grazing on the be-
haviour of the prey-predator system, equations (7) and (8) are now integrated on
computer starting with the same initial conditions as in the integration of equations (9) and (10) (see figure 2).

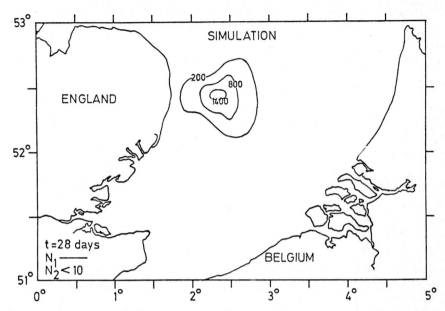

Fig. 2. Continuation of fig. la, at t = 28 days, with saturating grazing. Notice
the very high concentration of prey population and the absence of predator
population (this figure is to be compared with fig. lb without saturating
grazing). The prey will continue to increase indefinitely while the predator will disappear completely. To stabilize the ecological system·the
growth term for the prey can no longer be taken as a constant.

After a decay of the phytoplankton, we assist to its "explosive" growth and a decay of the zooplankton population. The behaviour is exactly the same as described
by equations (14) and (15) : no more feedbacking between phyto- and zoo-plankton
populations occurs.In this case, diffusion is no longer sufficient to compensate
the unstable ecological interactions described by equations (7) and (8). A stabi-
lisation of the solution can be obtained by taking into account phenomena like the
variation of the extinction coefficient and nutrient concentration with the concentration of phytoplankton. A logistic law can be used to approximate the growth
rate k_1 [Dubois (1975e)] :

$$k_1 = k_1' \left(1 - \frac{N_1}{N_1''}\right) \qquad (16)$$

where N_1'' is the maximum concentration of living phytoplankton in the sea.

THE NUMERICAL INTEGRATION METHODS

As the non linear prey-predator equations have received up to now no analytical solution, a numerical integration is necessary. Classical numerical schemes
do not deal with non linear interaction terms, so that special algorithms are to
be derived for the solution of the complete equations. We are bound to use implicit schemes for the sake of numerical stability and to solve linear algebraic
systems, for the sake of computational speed.

THE ONE-DIMENSIONAL PROBLEM

An improvement of the Crank-Nicholson scheme can be found in a paper by Lees (1970) ; the modified scheme can cope with non linear diffusion equations. Another possible improvement is to use higher accuracy approximations for the second derivatives [Adam (1974)]. The fully improved Crank-Nicholson scheme can be written for any of the state variables (say α) :

$$N_{\alpha,i}^{n+1} - N_{\alpha,i}^n = \frac{\tau}{2} (\mathcal{H}_{\alpha,i}^{n+1} + \mathcal{H}_{\alpha,i}^n) + I_i^{n+\frac{1}{2}} (N_\alpha, N_\beta) \quad \alpha = 1,2 \; ; \; \beta = 1,2 \quad (17)$$

where $\mathcal{H}_{\alpha,i}$ denotes an approximation of $\dfrac{\partial^2 N_\alpha}{\partial x^2}$ at the grid point i, and $I_i^{n+\frac{1}{2}} (N_\alpha, N_\beta)$ an approximation of the interaction term at an intermediate time $(n + \frac{1}{2})\tau$.

A usual approximation $\mathcal{H}_{\alpha,i}$ of $\dfrac{\partial^2 N_\alpha}{\partial x^2}$ is

$$\mathcal{H}_{\alpha,i} \sim \frac{1}{h^2} (N_{\alpha,i+1} + N_{\alpha,i-1} - 2 N_{\alpha,i}) + 0(h^2) \quad (18)$$

where h is the grid interval.

Instead of substituting $\mathcal{H}_{\alpha,i}$ in equation (17), we can substitute a linear combination of $\mathcal{H}_{\alpha,i+1}$, $\mathcal{H}_{\alpha,i}$, $\mathcal{H}_{\alpha,i-1}$ without increasing the complexity of the resultant set of linear equations ; such a substitution yields a more accurate discretization of the diffusion term. For instance, Collatz (1970) proposes :

$$\frac{\partial^2 N_\alpha}{\partial x^2} \sim \frac{1}{12} (\mathcal{H}_{\alpha,i+1} + 10 \, \mathcal{H}_{\alpha,i} + \mathcal{H}_{\alpha,i-1}) = \frac{1}{h^2} (N_{\alpha,i+1} + N_{\alpha,i-1} - 2 N_{i-1}) \quad (19)$$

Combining (17) and (19), we get the system of linear equations in the unknowns $N_{\alpha,i}^{n+1}$:

$$\frac{1}{12} (N_{\alpha,i+1}^{n+1} + 10 \, N_{\alpha,i}^{n+1} + N_{\alpha,i-1}^{n+1}) - \frac{1}{12} (N_{\alpha,i+1}^n + 10 \, N_{\alpha,i}^n + N_{\alpha,i-1}^n)$$

$$(20)$$

$$= \frac{\tau}{2h^2} (N_{\alpha,i+1}^{n+1} + N_{\alpha,i-1}^{n+1} - 2 N_{\alpha,i}^{n+1}) + \frac{\tau}{2h^2} (N_{\alpha,i+1}^n + N_{\alpha,i-1}^n - 2 N_{\alpha,i}^n)$$

$$+ \frac{1}{12} (I_{i+1}^{n+\frac{1}{2}} + 10 \, I_i^{n+\frac{1}{2}} + I_{i-1}^{n+\frac{1}{2}})$$

which also reads

$$N_{\alpha,i+1}^{n+1} (1 - \frac{6\tau}{h^2}) + N_{\alpha,i}^{n+1} (10 + \frac{12 \, \tau}{h^2}) + N_{\alpha,i-1}^{n+1} (1 - \frac{6\tau}{h^2})$$

$$= N_{\alpha,i+1}^n (1 + \frac{6\tau}{h^2}) + N_{\alpha,i}^n (10 - \frac{12 \, \tau}{h^2}) + N_{\alpha,i-1}^n (1 + \frac{6\tau}{h^2}) \quad (21)$$

$$+ I_{i+1}^{n+\frac{1}{2}} + 10 \, I_i^{n+\frac{1}{2}} + I_{i-1}^{n+\frac{1}{2}}$$

As to the values of $I_i^{n+\frac{1}{2}}$ they are 'predicted' or extrapolated in the following way.

Let $N_{\alpha,i}^{n-1}$ and $N_{\alpha,i}^{n}$ be the values of N_α at times $(n-1)\tau$ and $n\tau$ respectively. A linear extrapolation yields the approximate value of $N_{\alpha,i}$ at $(n+\frac{1}{2})\tau$

$$N_{\alpha,i}^{n+\frac{1}{2}} = \frac{3}{2} N_{\alpha,i}^{n} - \frac{1}{2} N_{\alpha,i}^{n-1} + O(\tau) \tag{22}$$

The values of the interaction terms are then simply

$$I_{1,i}^{n+\frac{1}{2}} = k_1 N_{1,i}^{n+\frac{1}{2}} - k_2 N_{1,i}^{n+\frac{1}{2}} N_{2,i}^{n+\frac{1}{2}} \tag{23a}$$

$$I_{2,i}^{n+\frac{1}{2}} = -k_3 N_{2,i}^{n+\frac{1}{2}} + k_4 N_{2,i}^{n+\frac{1}{2}} N_{1,i}^{n+\frac{1}{2}} \tag{23b}$$

The set of equations (21) are easily solved by the Thomas' direct inversion technique :

$$N_{\alpha,i} = E_i N_{\alpha,i+1} + F_i \qquad \text{for } i = n,1 \tag{24a}$$

with

$$E_i = - \frac{1 - \frac{6\tau}{h^2}}{(1 - \frac{6\tau}{h^2}) E_{i-1} + (10 + \frac{12\tau}{h^2})} \tag{24b}$$

$$F_i = \frac{1}{(1 - \frac{6\tau}{h^2}) E_{i-1} + (10 + \frac{12\tau}{h^2})} [- (1 - \frac{6\tau}{h^2}) F_{i-1} + (N_{\alpha,i+1}^{n} + N_{\alpha,i-1}^{n})(1 + \frac{6\tau}{h^2})$$
$$+ N_{\alpha,i}^{n}(10 - \frac{12\tau}{h^2}) + I_{i+1}^{n+\frac{1}{2}} + I_{i-1}^{n+\frac{1}{2}} + 10 I_i^{n+\frac{1}{2}}] \tag{24c}$$

for $i = 2,n$.

The algorithm cannot begin in the same way because one only knows the values $N_{\alpha,i}^{o}$, $\alpha = 1,2$; the technique is the following

1) compute the value $N_{\alpha,i}^{\frac{1}{2}}$ using

$$N_{\alpha,i+1}^{\frac{1}{2}} (1 - \frac{6\tau}{2h^2}) + N_{\alpha,i}^{\frac{1}{2}} (10 + \frac{12\tau}{2h^2}) + N_{\alpha,i-1}^{\frac{1}{2}} (1 - \frac{6\tau}{2h^2})$$

$$= (N_{\alpha,i+1}^{n} + N_{\alpha,i-1}^{n})(1 + \frac{6\tau}{2h^2}) + N_{\alpha,i}^{n}(10 + \frac{12\tau}{2h^2}) + I_{i+1}^{o} + I_{i-1}^{o} + 10 I_i^{o} \tag{25}$$

2) compute $N_{\alpha,i}^{1}$ using (21) but where $I_i^{\frac{1}{2}}$ are calculated using $N_{\alpha,i}^{\frac{1}{2}}$.

THE BI-DIMENSIONAL PROBLEM

The technique is different for solving the two-dimensional non linear equations. If one wants to solve simple sets of linear equations one is led to use splitting up or alternating direction methods. Both families of methods need the computation of the values of the unknowns at some intermediate time step, which can be used with the 'initial' values (at $n\tau$) to extrapolate the 'final' value [at $(n + 1)\tau$]. An ADI method will be preferred because the intermediate step is consistent with the original equation, which is important when one wants to use it for extrapolation. The same requirement of consistency prevents us to use the same technique as above for improving the accuracy of the scheme [Mitchell (1970)]. Moreover, the ADI method is more accurate [$O(\tau^2)$] in the case where no or only linear interactions take place and therefore is expected to be better than any splitting up method with non linear terms.

We have thought it wiser to use as less extrapolated values as possible because the error is greater for these than for any other. That is why, to account for the special form of the non linear terms, we have introduced the following desintegrations of the interactions :

$$k_1 N_1 - k_2 N_1 N_2 = k_1 N_1 (1 - \frac{k_2 N_2}{k_1}) \tag{26a}$$

$$- k_3 N_2 + k_4 N_1 N_2 = - k_3 N_2 (1 - \frac{k_4 N_1}{k_3}) \tag{26b}$$

The reason for introducing these forms will be made clear later.

The intermediate values of the unknowns are computed in the first two steps which are independant from each other

$$N_{1,i,j}^{n+\frac{1}{2}} - N_{1,i,j}^{n} = \frac{\tau}{2h^2} (N_{1,i+1,j}^{n+\frac{1}{2}} + N_{1,i-1,j}^{n+\frac{1}{2}} - 2 N_{1,i,j}^{n+\frac{1}{2}}) \tag{27}$$

$$+ \frac{\tau}{2h^2} (N_{1,i,j+1}^{n} + N_{1,i,j-1}^{n} - 2 N_{1,i,j}^{n}) + k_1 N_1^{n} (1 - \frac{k_2 N_2^{n}}{k_1})$$

and the analoguous formula for $N_2^{n+\frac{1}{2}}$.

For the second step, if one does not intend to solve non linear equations, one must use extrapolated values :

$$N_{2,i,j}^{*} = 2 N_{2,i,j}^{n+\frac{1}{2}} - N_{2,i,j}^{n} \tag{28}$$

The values of N_1 are thus computed in a third step using (28).

$$N_{1,i,j}^{n+1} - N_{1,i,j}^{n+\frac{1}{2}} = \frac{\tau}{2h^2} (N_{1,i+1,j}^{n+\frac{1}{2}} + N_{1,i-1,j}^{n+\frac{1}{2}} - 2 N_{1,i,j}^{n+\frac{1}{2}}) \tag{29}$$

$$+ \frac{\tau}{2h^2} (N_{1,i,j+1}^{n+1} + N_{1,i,j-1}^{n+1} - 2 N_{1,i,j}^{n+1}) + k_1 N_{1,i,j}^{n+1} (1 - \frac{k_2}{k_1} N_{2,i,j}^{*})$$

Now that we have got $N_{1,i,j}^{n+1}$, nothing prevents us from using this value in calculating $N_{2,i,j}^{n+1}$ (fourth step)

$$N_{2,i,j}^{n+1} - N_{2,i,j}^{n+\frac{1}{2}} = \frac{\tau}{2h^2} (N_{2,i+1,j}^{n+\frac{1}{2}} + N_{2,i-1,j}^{n+\frac{1}{2}} - 2 N_{2,i,j}^{n+\frac{1}{2}})$$

(30)

$$+ \frac{\tau}{2h^2} (N_{2,i,j+1}^{n+1} + N_{2,i,j-1}^{n+1} - 2 N_{2,i,j}^{n+1}) - k_3 N_{2,i,j}^{n+1} (1 - \frac{k_4}{k_3} N_{1,i,j}^{n+1})$$

Of course, both sets of unknowns are not computed in the same way, but one can make this algorithm symmetric by permuting the roles of N_1 and N_2 every time that n is even; when n is odd, one follows the above described procedure and when n is even, the first two steps remain the same, while when one extrapolates for N_1^*:

$$N_{1,i,j}^* = 2 N_{1,i,j}^n - N_{1,i,j}^n$$

(31)

the fourth step then takes the place of the third one with $N_{1,i,j}^{n+1}$ replaced by $N_{1,i,j}^*$ and the third one becomes the fourth one with $N_{2,i,j}^*$ replaced by $N_{2,i,j}^{n+1}$.

The whole algorithm is then symmetric in N_1 and N_2 (as far as the digital approximation are concerned) every two complete time steps. It is well known that such a symmetrization is favourable to accuracy.

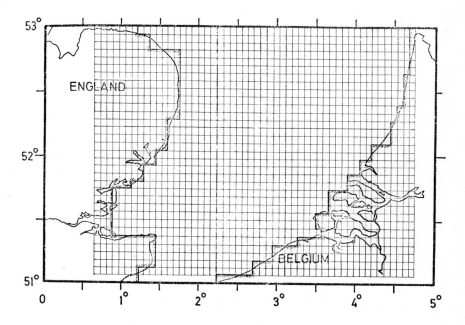

Fig. 3. Numerical grid (33 x 53 points)

BOUNDARY AND INITIAL CONDITIONS

        The two-dimensional problem has been run on a numerical grid covering the
Southern Bight (fig. 3). Both populations are assumed to vanish at all boundaries
(coasts and open sea). These conditions are invalid when the plankton patches
reach (because of residual currents) the northern boundary. The simulation is thus
limited by the residence time of the water masses in the Southern Bight. As initial condition, we assume the existence of a small phytoplankton spike near the
southern boundary (as if it came from the Channel) with associated traces of zooplankton.

COMPUTER IMPLEMENTATION

        Both algorithms are very fast and need less than 200 Fortran IV instruc-
tions. To give an idea of the computational speed, let us assume the two-dimensional problem : to compute a daily evolution (with a time step of 0.1 day) of
prey-predator populations, on the above mentioned grid, the program takes less
than 8 s, including printout on an IBM 370/158 working under OS/VS2.

        This feature is specially useful when one wants to simulate a wide range
of theoretical situations.

CONCLUSIONS

        Numerical integrations of a theoretical model of prey-predator relation-
ships have simulated the behaviour of plankton populations in the Southern Bight.
Plankton wave propagation and structuration of patches have been shown off ; they
match observations previously made while following patches. Further computer experiments are run to test the influence of nutrient limitation, available light
and temperature on the behaviour of patches.

ACKNOWLEDGEMENTS

        The study was part of the Belgian National Program on Physical and Biolo-
gical Environment. The authors are grateful to the Ministry for Science Policy for
the support of this research.

REFERENCES

Adam, Y., (1975). A hermitian finite difference method for the solution of parabo-
        lic equations, Comp. Math. Appl. (to be published).

Collatz, L., (1960). The numerical treatment of differential equations, Springer-
        Verlag, Berlin.

Dubois, D.M., (1975a). The influence of the quality of water on ecological systems,
        IFIP Working Conference on Modeling and Simulation of Water Resources
        Systems, Ghent, Publ. by North Holland, Amsterdam, ed. G.C. Vansteenkiste,
        pp. 535-543.

Dubois, D.M., (1975b). Simulation of the spatial structuration of a patch of prey-
        predator plankton populations in the Southern Bight of the North Sea,
        Proceedings of the Sixth Liège Colloquium on Ocean Hydrodynamics, Univ.
        of Liège, April 1974, Mém. Soc. Roy. Sci. Liège, 6ième Série, tome VII,
        pp. 75-82.

Dubois, D.M., (1975c). A model of patchiness for prey-predator plankton popula-
        tions, Ecological Modeling, 1 : 67-80.

Dubois, D.M., (1975d). Hydrodynamic aspects in environmental and ecological en-
        hancement, Proceedings of the Second World Congress on Water Resources,
        New Delhi, India (in press).

Dubois, D.M., (1975e). Modeling and simulation of the mesoscale mosaic structure of the lower marine trophic levels, VIIth IFIP Conference, Nice, 7-13th September, (in press).

Fasham, M.J.R., Angel, M.V. and ROE, H.S.J., (1974). An investigation of the spatial pattern of zooplankton using the Longhurst-Hardy plankton recorder, J. Exp. Mar. Biol. Ecol., 16, 93-112.

IVLEV, V.S., (1945). The biological productivity of waters, Usp. Sovrem. Biol., 19 (1), 88-120.

Kierstead, H. and Slobodkin, L.B., (1953). The size of water masses containing plankton blooms, J. of Marine Research, XII, 1, 141.

Lees, M., (1970). An extrapolated Crank-Nielson difference scheme for quasi-linear parabolic equations, in Non-linear partial differential equations, (ed. W.F. Ames), Academic Press, New York.

Mitchell, A.R., (1970). Computational Methods in Partial Differential Equations, J. Wiley and Son Ltd., London.

Nihoul, J.C.J. and Ronday, F., (1975). The influence of the tidal stress on the residual circulation, Tellus, 27, 5.

O'Connor, D.J., Di Toro, D.M., Mancini, J.L., (1973). Mathematical model of phytoplankton population dynamics in the Sacramento San Joaquin Bay Delta, Working paper, Modeling of Marine Systems, Ofir, Portugal.

Parsons, T.R., Le Brasseur, R.J. and Fulton, J.D., (1967). Some observations on the dependence of zooplankton grazing on cell size and concentration of phytoplankton blooms. J. Oceanogr. Soc. Japan, 23 (1), 10-17.

Pielou, E.C., (1969). An introduction to mathematical ecology, Wiley, New York.

Platt, T. and Denman, K.L., (1975). Spectral analysis in ecology, Ann. Rev. of Ecol. and Syst., 6, (in press).

Riley, G.A., (1963). On the theory of food chain relations in the sea, in The Sea, Vol. 2, ed. M.N. Hill, N.Y., Interscience Publ., 438-463.

Steele, J.H., (1974). Spatial heterogeneity and population stability, Nature, 248, 5443, 83.

Wyatt, T., (1973). The biology of Oikopleura dioica and Fritillaria borealis in the Southern Bight, Marine Biology, 22, 137.

DISCUSSION

*It is of course very unlikely that the temperature of the whole North Sea
would increase 5 degrees by the activity of man.
It is quite possible that some 5 kilometers of the coast at Zeebrugge, for instance
400 Mwatt or more would be put in the sea. Do you think that such a local discharge
propagates and influences the phenomena you describe ?
As I understand, the plankton comes in from the south ; at a certain moment it must
have been heated. (WAJC)*

I can simulate the dynamics of a patch of plankton with a local increase
of temperature. This increase of temperature produces a local disturbance of the
ecological reactions rates. The disturbance in plankton concentrations propagates
with a velocity depending on diffusive and advective processes. The velocity of
propagation is about 5 km/day which is the velocity of the ring waves. Moreover,
the plankton patches drift to the north-east direction and cross the Southern
Bight with a time corresponding to two months. (DUBOIS)

*How did you compute - or measure - the velocity distribution of the sea
currents ? (FRIED)*

The velocity distribution of the North Sea currents were computed from a
mathematical model (National Program). The currents values are averaged on a few
days. Indeed the time constant of interactions between phytoplankton and zooplankton is about 5 days. The length scale of the numerical grid is about 5 kilometers.
(DUBOIS)

What were the boundary conditions ? (FRIED)

On the coasts and open sea, they are given by a concentration which is
zero for phytoplankton and zooplankton. The simulation is thus limited to the residence time of plankton patches in the Southern Bight. (DUBOIS)

System Simulation in Water Resources, ed. G.C. VANSTEENKISTE
1976, North-Holland Publishing Company

A MOVING CELL SIMULATION MODEL OF THE DYNAMICS
OF DISSOLVED OXYGEN AND RELATED QUALITY VARIABLES
IN RIVERS AND BROOKS

B. de Boer
Provincial Waterboard of Gelderland
Arnhem, The Netherlands

ABSTRACT

This paper describes a dynamic, one-dimensional model of the behaviour
of dissolved oxygen and BOD in a river or brook. The incorporated
processes are waste discharges, extractions, advection, dispersion,
biological oxidation of organical matters, distributed reaeration and
reaeration at weirs. When the oxygen concentration becomes zero, the
biological oxidation rate is constrained to the oxygen supply rate.
Extensions of the model with nitrification and photosynthesis are in
progress.

Stress is laid upon the numerical solution method, a simple explicit
method of characteristics, in order to prevent numerical dispersion.
The place nodes move along the river axis with the stream velocity.
The dispersion coefficient and the velocity may vary with time and
place and may be zero, though the velocity may change but slowly. In
most cases this approximation is expected to be accurate enough.
Nevertheless, improvements of the algorithm are in preparation.

A simple application will be shown. It turns out that combined
parameter identification must be avoided.

INTRODUCTION

The many opposed interests involved in the water management system at
present and in the future make the decision-making process in water resources
systems very complex and difficult. A multidisciplinary study of the water
resources system and its environment is therefore necessary. Application of
mathematical modeling to water resources policy planning is not new; what is new,
however, is our present capability to analyse more complex systems. Models add
new possibilities to the decision-making process by making the system in
consideration better understood, by broadening of the information base, by
predicting the consequences of several alternative courses of action and by
selecting a suitable course of action which will accomplish a prescribed result.
The Committee on Study of the Water Management of Gelderland is developping a
hierarchical model structure, consisting of hydrological and economic models for
the prediction of water demand and supply and for the choice of the best course
of action (Colenbrander and Van de Nes, 1974; Van de Nes, 1975).

The physical aspects of water supply are described by water quantity and
water quality models. The model described here is intended to become the base of
the Committee's surface water quality model. It is restricted tentatively to the
dynamics of oxygen and related quality variables, such as biological oxygen
demand (BOD). The purpose of the model is to predict these variables as functions
of time and place, for given water management measures like waste discharges and
weirs and under given natural circumstances such as discharge, temperature and

biological state of the river. Thus, the model can establish where and when the oxygen concentration becomes lower than a minimum limit value or, if necessary, where and when the BOD exceeds an upper bound. Consequently, waste discharges and other water management measures can be located, dimensioned and, if possible, timed in such a way that these constraints are met.

CONTINUOUS MODEL

As can be gathered from literature (Bella and Dobbins, 1968; Smith and Morris, 1969), a fairly general form of the one-dimensional transport reaction equation for one dissolved matter is

$$\frac{\partial}{\partial t}(AC) = \frac{\partial}{\partial x}\left(AD \frac{\partial C}{\partial x}\right) + \frac{\partial}{\partial x}(AvC) + Ar + S \tag{1}$$

with (units between brackets):

t : time (hr)
x : place coordinate in stream direction (m)
A : wet cross-sectional area (m^2)
C : concentration of the considered matter ($g.m^{-3}$)
D : dispersion coefficient ($m^2.hr^{-1}$)
v : velocity ($m.hr^{-1}$)
r : total (chemical plus biological) reaction rate of the considered matter ($g.m^{-3}.hr^{-1}$)
S : total ("mechanical", i.e. non-reactive) sources and sinks of the considered matter ($g.hr^{-1}.m^{-1}$)

C, D, v and r are averages over A. In general, A, D, v, r and S are functions of place and time, like C. The wet cross-section, A, is left in the equation because it has influence when it varies quickly. The total sources and sinks term must be split up:

$$S = S_Q + S_R + As_r \tag{2}$$

where:

S_Q: advective sources and sinks, caused by water flows into respectively out of the river (influents, effluents) ($g.hr^{-1}.m^{-1}$)
S_R: remaining sources and sinks, caused by other transport mechanisms ($g.hr^{-1}.m^{-1}$)
s_r: as S_R, but treated per unit volume, averaged over A ($g.m^{-3}.hr^{-1}$)

S_Q and S_R must be divided into local and distributed sources and sinks, which is shown here for S_Q only:

$$S_Q = \underset{\{x_I\}}{\Sigma} Q_I(x_I,t).C_L(x_I,t).\delta(x-x_I) +$$

$$- \underset{\{x_E\}}{\Sigma} Q_E(x_E,t).C(x_E,t).\delta(x-x_E) + q_I(x,t).C_I(x,t) - q_E(x,t).C_E(x,t) \tag{3}$$

where:

$Q_I(x_I,t)$: volume discharge of the local influent or point source located at x_I ($m^3.hr^{-1}$)
$C_L(x_I,t)$: concentration in the local influent at x_I ($g.m^{-3}$)
$Q_E(x_E,t)$: volume discharge of the local effluent at x_E ($m^3.hr^{-1}$)
$C(x_E,t)$: concentration in the local effluent at x_E, equal to the concentration in the river at x_E ($g.m^{-3}$)
$q_I(x,t)$: distributed volume discharge of the distributed influent ($m^2.hr^{-1}$)
$C_I(x,t)$: concentration in the distributed influent ($g.m^{-3}$)

$q_E(x,t)$: distributed volume discharge of the distributed effluent, which can only be the seepage to the groundwater ($m^2.hr^{-1}$)

$C_E(x,t)$: concentration in q_E, which is not necessarily equal to the river concentration, $C(x,t)$ ($g.m^{-3}$)

The impulse functions δ are needed to incorporate local sources and sinks in a summation of distributed sources and sinks, the former being concentrated mass flows, the latter mass flows per unit lenght. The impulse functions have the unit m^{-1}. Examples of the various types of sources and sinks are:

S_Q: local influents   : tributaries, waste discharges
     local effluents   : branches, extractions
     distributed influents: sub-surface runoff, seepage from the groundwater
     distributed effluent : seepage to the groundwater

S_R: local sources   : aeration at weirs
     distributed sources : resuspension of benthos matters, whirling of benthos matters into the water by "scour"

s_r : distributed source   : "normal" reaeration
     distributed sink   : sedimentation, adsorption to the benthos

The cross-section of the river bed is assumed to be trapezoidal, in order to simplify the computation of the wet cross-sectional area to

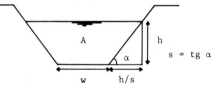

$$A = h (w + h/s) \quad (4)$$

where

$s = tg\ \alpha$

$h(x,t)$: water level
$w(x)$: width of the bottom of the river bed
$s(x)$: slope of the walls of the river bed

Figure 1. Approximation of the cross-section

In this study, (1) is applied to oxygen:

$$\frac{\partial}{\partial t}(AC_{OX}) = \frac{\partial}{\partial x}(AD\frac{\partial C_{OX}}{\partial x}) - \frac{\partial}{\partial x}(AvC_{OX}) + A(r_{OX} + s_{r,OX}) + S_{R,OX} + S_{Q,OX} \quad (5)$$

A similar balance is needed for BOD, because it supplies the biological oxydation rate for the oxygen balance, as will be shown below. The BOD balance is:

$$\frac{\partial}{\partial t}(AC_{BO}) = \frac{\partial}{\partial x}(AD\frac{\partial C_{BO}}{\partial x}) - \frac{\partial}{\partial x}(AvC_{BO}) + A(r_{BO} + s_{r,BO}) + S_{R,BO} + S_{Q,BO} \quad (6)$$

Several tentative simplifications had to be made in order to enable the author to develop a numerical method and a computer program of sufficient generality, in which the improvements of the model can be incorporated easily. The simplifications are as follow.

- The reaction rates comprise only the biological oxidation of organic matter, i.e. of BOD:

$$r_{OX} = r_{BO} = r_{BO,B} \quad (7)$$

- The non-advective oxygen sources consist only of the distributed (re)aeration rate $s_{r,OX,A}$ and the (re)aeration at weirs, while the non-advective oxygen sinks are zero:

$$s_{r,OX} = s_{r,OX,A} \quad (8)$$

$$S_{R,OX} = \sum_{\{x_W\}} F_{OX,A}(x_W,t)\ \delta(x-x_W) \tag{9}$$

where $F_{OX,A}(x_W,t)$ is the oxygen mass flow in $g.hr^{-1}$ of the weir located at x_W.
- The non-advective sources and sinks of BOD are zero:

$$s_{r,BO} = 0 \tag{10}$$

$$S_{R,BO} = 0 \tag{11}$$

The biological oxidation rate is asumed to be linearly dependent of C_{BO} but is constrained to the oxygen supply rate when C_{OX} becomes zero:

$$r_{BO,B} \begin{cases} = -\ (\text{right member of (5) without } r_{BO,B}) \\ \quad \text{if } C_{OX} = 0 \\ \quad \text{and } K_D C_{BO} > (\text{right member of (5) without } r_{BO,B}) \\ = -\ K_D C_{BO}\ ,\ \text{else} \end{cases} \tag{12}$$

This is a sufficient approximation of the real decrease of $r_{BO,B}$ at diminishing C_{OX}, and prevents C_{OX} from becoming negative. C_{OX} stays zero untill $K_D C_{BO}$ becomes smaller than the oxygen supply rate.
The distributed (re)aeration rate is approximated by

$$s_{r,OX,A} = K_A\ (C_{OX,S} - C_{OX}) \tag{13}$$

K_A, the reaeration coefficient, cannot be measured directly. Therefore, it is approximated by the formula of O'Connor and Dobbins (1958):

$$K_A = 0.00273\ \frac{1}{h}\ \sqrt{\frac{v}{h}}\ (1,0241)^{T-20}$$

$$\text{with } K_A \text{ in } hr^{-1},\ v \text{ in } m.hr^{-1},\ h \text{ in } m$$

$$\text{and the water temperature T in } {}^{\circ}C \tag{14}$$

$C_{OX,S}$, the oxygen saturation concentration, is calculated from the water temperature.

Extensions of the reaction terms and the non-advective sources and sinks terms, for instance with photosynthesis, nitrification and sedimentation are in preparation at the Division of Process Control and Environmental Management, Department of Chemical Engineering, Twente University of Technology in Enschede, the Netherlands. One of the questions to be answered is, if extension of the model with algal population and nutrient balances is necessary to predict photosynthesis correctly.

It should be noted that the one-dimensional model is only valid if the lateral mixing is sufficiently fast compared to the dispersion and the reaction. Fisher (1968) and Lau (1972) give suitable conditions.

NUMERICAL METHOD

The continuous model cannot be solved analytically but under unrealistic conditions. For instance, the reaction terms would have to be linear, which is impossible on account of the non-linear relation between the biological oxidation rate and the oxygen concentration. Non-linear kinetics are also encountered with the incorporation of algal population dynamics. Therefore, the numerical solution method must generally not be a numerical approximation of an analytical solution, but a finite difference or finite element method.

The time base points are chosen equidistantly with timestep T:

$$t_n = t_1 + (n-1)T\ ,\quad n = 1,\ldots,N \tag{15}$$

The place axis is divided in cells numbered i = 1,...,J . Their lengths L_i don't need to be equal to each other. The between the cells i and i+1 is called $x_{i+\frac{1}{2}}$, the middle of cell i is the place base point (place node) x_i . See fig. 2.

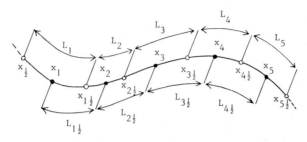

Figure 2. Allocating a place base to the length-axis of a stream; upstream end of the considered reach.
  ● place node, x_i
  ○ cell boundary, $x_{i+\frac{1}{2}}$

Rectangulair grid

A rectangulair grid of nodal points (x_i, t_n) is defined by choosing the place and time base points indepently of each other (fig.3). Both explicit and implicit methods can be defined on this base. A simple explicit method is derived from (1) by approximating all derivatives with respect to the place by the first central difference formula and the derivative with respect to the time by the first forward difference formula:

$$\frac{A_{i,n+1}C_{i,n+1} - A_{i,n}C_{i,n}}{T} = \frac{A_{i+\frac{1}{2},n}D_{i+\frac{1}{2},n}\frac{C_{i+1,n}-C_{i,n}}{L_{i+\frac{1}{2}}} - A_{i-\frac{1}{2},n}D_{i-\frac{1}{2},n}\frac{C_{i,n}-C_{i-1,n}}{L_{i-\frac{1}{2}}}}{L_i} +$$

$$- \frac{A_{i+\frac{1}{2},n}v_{i+\frac{1}{2},n}C_{i+\frac{1}{2},n} - A_{i-\frac{1}{2},n}v_{i-\frac{1}{2},n}C_{i-\frac{1}{2},n}}{L_i} + A_{i,n}r_{i,n} + S_{i,n} \qquad (16)$$

where the concentration on the cell-boundary $x_{i+\frac{1}{2}}$ must be interpolated between C_i and C_{i+1}:

$$C_{i+\frac{1}{2},n} = (L_i C_{i+1,n} + L_{i+1}C_{i,n}) / (L_i + L_{i+1}) \qquad (17a)$$

or be equal to the upstream concentration:

$$C_{i+\frac{1}{2},n} = C_{i,n} \qquad (17b)$$

The same formula must be applied to $C_{i-\frac{1}{2},n}$.

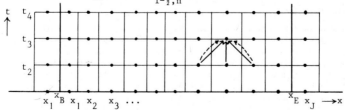

Figure 3. Rectangular grid. The arrows show the information flows for one execution of (16),(17a). The dash arrows symbolise the dispersion term.

In the model discussed here, these equations have to be applied to dissolved oxygen and BOD, corresponding with the partial differential equations (5) and (6). Consequently, (2), (3) and (10)-(14) have to be expressed in the discrete place and time, x_i and t_n.

As this scheme uses a rectangular place time grid, it has to calculate the advection by means of mass flows crossing the cell boundaries. These flows are

$$A_{i-\frac{1}{2},n} v_{i-\frac{1}{2},n} C_{i-\frac{1}{2},n} \quad \text{entering cell i at } x_{i-\frac{1}{2}}$$

and

$$A_{i+\frac{1}{2},n} v_{i+\frac{1}{2},n} C_{i+\frac{1}{2},n} \quad \text{leaving cell i at } x_{i+\frac{1}{2}} .$$

Therefore, the scheme is not able to describe the transfer of a concentration peak with a length less than L_i over a distance less than $L_{i+\frac{1}{2}}$: the model cannot reconstruct the place and the shape of the peak if the latter is between two nodes. Instead, the model divides the peak over the two adjacent nodes according to its position between the nodes. So the peak is spreaded spatially, which goes on as time goes by. The error acts as an extra dispersion and it is called numerical dispersion, consequently. For larger values of D, the numerical dispersion (16),(17b) can largely be reduced by correcting the dispersion coefficient with the amount of expected numerical dispersion, or by using (17a) instead of (17b). However, both improved methods impose restrictions on the step sizes in order to avoid the remaining numerical dispersion, instabilities and other errors. For small values of D, these restrictions amount

for method (16),(17a) to: for method (16),(17b)
                                         with corrected D to:

$$L \leq \frac{2D}{v} \qquad (18a) \qquad\qquad L \leq \frac{2D}{v} + vT \qquad (18b)$$

$$T \leq \frac{L}{3v} \qquad (19a) \qquad\qquad T \leq \frac{L}{v} \qquad (19b)$$

and for both methods to:

$$L \geq 2\sqrt{DT} \qquad (20)$$

$$T \leq 1/K \qquad (21)$$

$$T \leq \frac{2D}{v^2} \qquad (22)$$

It can be concluded from (18), (19) and (22) that L and T can become very small if D decreases. This means that neither of these methods can simulate a river with "small" dispersion and "fastly varying" waste discharges, without numerical dispersion, instability or another error, except at the cost of a very large number of place and time steps. This situation was encountered with the modeling of the Groenlose Slinge, a small river in the east of the Netherlands. A very short reach of this river, namely with a length of only 4 km, could only be described accurately by model (16),(17a or b) if 2,000 place steps and at least 10,000 time steps were used (v = 100 m/hr, D = 300 m^2/hr, $L_i \equiv 2$ m, T = 20 sec).

Some implicit and higher order explicit methods are less restrictive, but they cannot handle low values of D either, without errors or very small place and time steps.

Curvilinear grid: method of characteristics or moving cells

Numerical dispersion is caused by the description of advection by means of mass flows crossing cell boundaries, which is necessary if a rectangular grid is used, as explained above. Numerical dispersion can be eliminated by representing the advection by the movement of the cells with the stream velocity of its own time and place, thus eliminating the advective mass flows accross the cell boundaries. This means that all cells must "flow with the stream". The movement of a cell boundary is a solution of

$$\frac{dx}{dt} = v(x,t) \qquad\qquad\qquad (23)$$

Again, both explicit and implicit methods can be defined on this curvilinear grid. The choice will depend on the concentration gradients, encountered and to be expected in practice. Owing to the elimination of numerical dispersion, D may be smaller than $\frac{1}{2}vL$ or even be zero in all cases. Implicit methods of characteristics are generally less restrictive to the parameter values and the step sizes (L and T) for the sake of a certain accuracy than the explicit methods of characteristics are. However, for small values of D and rapidly changing waste discharges or other inputs, high concentration gradients may occur. In these cases, explicit methods of characteristics take far less computer time than the implicit ones do, provided that both types of schemes have the same accuracy. This is the result of the relatively large step sizes which the explicit schemes may maintain at high concentration gradients. The step sizes may even be chosen such that they suit well to the highest expected v, D and the reaction rate coefficients, and to the lowest accuracy accepted. In the case of oxygen and BOD, which cannot be measured with errors less than 10 %, the numerical errors do not need to be smaller than, say, 5 %.

The situation of low dispersion coefficient values, **rapidly changing waste discharges and a high photosynthesis activity,** with the resulting high concentration gradients, is often encountered in the small rivers of Eastern Gelderland. An example of low dispersion only is the Groenlose Slinge, mentioned above. In these cases, explicit methods of characteristics are to be preferred.

Similar reasoning is followed by Pandolfi (1975), who quotes Moretti on this point.

A simple, explicit method of characteristics is chosen. Every cell boundary $x_{i-\frac{1}{2}}$ moves along an approximation of (23), obtained by lowest order or "rectangular" integration:

$$x_{i-\frac{1}{2},n} = x_{i-\frac{1}{2},n-1} + T\, v_{i-\frac{1}{2},n-1}$$

The nodes are evaluated at each time step as the middles of the cells:

$$x_{i,n} = \frac{1}{2}\,(x_{i-\frac{1}{2},n} + x_{i+\frac{1}{2},n})$$

So, each node is shifted over a distance of about $v_{i,n-1}.T$ during each time step (fig.4).

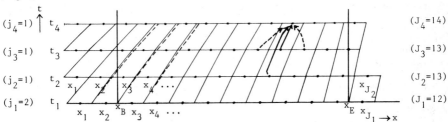

Figure 4. The curvilinear grid of the explicit method of characteristics or moving cells chosen here.
----- characteristic curve of cell boundary
——— its approximation
The arrows have the same significance as in fig. 3.
To the left: j_n, number of new upstream cells.
To the right: J_n, total number of cells.

This approximation of (23) is only accurate enough if v changes only slowly with place and time. On account of the shifting of the cells, a new cell must be added at the upstream side of the reach regularly, in order to keep the whole reach covered with cells and to maintain two cells outside the upstream boundary. This number of upstream boundary cells is chosen to permit the velocity to exceed L/T. When one or two upstream boundary cells are added, the place indices are increased with the same number, j_n, in order to keep the index of the first cell at the value 1. So j_n is a function of time and assumes the values 0, 1 and 2. The correct formulas for the movement of the cells are

$$x_{i-\frac{1}{2}+j_n,n} = x_{i-\frac{1}{2},n-1} + T\, v_{i-\frac{1}{2},n-1} \qquad \text{(cell boundaries)}$$

$$x_{i,n} = \tfrac{1}{2}\,(x_{i-\frac{1}{2},n} + x_{i+\frac{1}{2},n}) \qquad \text{(place nodes)}$$

$$L_{i,n} = x_{i+\frac{1}{2},n} - x_{i-\frac{1}{2},n} \qquad \text{(cell lengths)}$$

$$L_{i+\frac{1}{2},n} = x_{i+1,n} - x_{i,n} \qquad \text{(place steps)}$$

$$(24)$$

After this shifting of the cells, the concentrations are advected with them by simply adding j_n to its place indices.

Next the dispersion, reactions, sources and sinks are calculated in essentially the same way as in (16). An exception is made for the reaction terms, which seem to be of dominant importance. These terms are integrated trapezoidally instead of rectangularly, except at $t = t_1$ (initial conditions) and $t = t_2$ (rectangular integration).

The adding of the right amount of mass to a cell which passes a point source is approximated tentatively by distributing the source over a length of three average cell lengths, 3L. The same treatment is given to the point sinks. The result is, that spatial concentration steps do not occur at the point sources and the non-advective point sinks, though they should. This computational step will be improved in future.

The upstream boundary conditions are only put in in the newly added boundary cells. A downstream boundary condition can be imposed on cell number J_n, if it is desired. It is only necessary if the river has a high dispersion and ends in a lake, see or other surface water body which can not be described by the same one-dimensional dispersion-advection-reaction equation. Otherwise the model can provide its own downstream boundary condition, which is the most accurate in that case.

All inputs and outputs are defined on their own, rectangular place-time-grids. Information transfer to and from the moving cell grid is achieved by linear interpolation.

The tentative character of this difference scheme must be emphasized. Improvements of several computational steps are in preparation, such as the advection of the cells and the mass transfer between the steady point sources and sinks and the moving cells. However, the model is expected to suit sufficiently well to practical purposes in this form already.

PROGRAM

The FORTRAN IV(G) program is set up modularly, in order to provide for easy modifications of the simulated case. In particular, extensions with rivers of the same basin or with processes like photosynthesis and nitrification must be possible.

A SIMPLE EXAMPLE: IDENTIFICATION WITH A STATIC SITUATION

     The model is applied to the situation in the Groenlose Slinge on October 11th and 12th, 1972, as measured by Van Gennip and Uunk (1973). During those days all measured processes were rather constant. The point x=0 is located at the only waste discharge, that of the sewage purification plant of Groenlo. Therefore, the upstream end of the considered reach is located at x = - 153 m, the downstream end at x = 4140 m ; a rather short reach. The dispersion coefficient is supposed to assume the values which are measured by Van den Oever (1972) in May 1972. This assumption is not harmfull because the dispersion will appear to be less important. All inputs are constant in time; the next are also constant in place:

    dimensions of the river bed:
       width of the bottom: $w = 5.8$ m
       slope of the walls: $s = 0.25$
   water level: $h = 1.05$ m
   velocity: $v = 100$ m/hr
   biological oxidation coefficient*: $K_D = 0.08$ hr^{-1}
   waste discharge (point source) at x = 0 m:
       volume discharge: Q_I $= 186$ m^3/hr
       BOD (carbon stage) concentration*: $C_{BO,L} = 100$ mg/l
       oxygen concentration $C_{OX,L} = 5.3$ mg/l
   reaeration at weirs:

location x of weir (m)	aerated oxygen mass flow (g/hr)	resulting step discontinuity in oxygen concentration vs. place (mg/l)
450	1050	1.
1040	3517	3.35
2140	1470	1.4
3140	1470	1.4
4140	1260	1.2

The following inputs are functions of the place:

place x (m)	dispersion coefficient D (m^2/hr)	water temperature T ($^{\circ}$C)	initial conditions (at t = t$_1$) BOD concentr.* (mg/l)	oxygen concentr. (mg/l)	upstream boundary conditions (at all t) BOD concentr. (mg/l)	oxygen concentr. (mg/l)
-153.	300.	11.	3.	12.25	3.	12.25
0.	300.	12.2	15.	10.7	3.	9.
140.	300.	12.2	16.5	10.1		
300.	300.	10.2	15.6	10.3		
499.9	300.	10.9	13.5	6.4		
450.1	410.	10.9	13.5	7.4		
840.	410.	10.7	9.4	4.6		
1039.9	410.	10.	7.5	2.8		
1040.1	410.	10.	7.5	6.15		
1640.	410.	9.5	4.2	2.5		
2139.9	410.	11.	2.5	1.85		
2140.1	410.	11.	2.5	3.25		
3139.9	410.	10.5	0.95	3.9		
3140.1	410.	10.5	0.95	5.3		
4140.	410.	14.	0.36	3.8		

     The variables indicated with an asterisk (*) had to be "adjusted" to other values than measured. The study of Van Gennip and Uunk (1973) pointed out that nitrification and photosynthesis could be neglected in this situation, and that sedimentation played an important role. The latter could be concluded from the steep descent of the BOD concentration after its immission in the river, that did not cause a corresponding decrease of the oxygen concentration. As sedimentation is not yet included in the model, the BOD (carbon stage) concentration in the waste discharge (x) had to be decreased from 620 to 100 mg/l. The initial BOD concentration profile (x) had to be diminished with an amount that approximated the otherwise sedimentated part. This part was a function of time and could only be estimated roughly, because sedimentation and oxidation influence each other's BOD consuming rate. The initial oxygen concentration profile got the measured values.

After 48 hours of simulated time, the differences between the initial conditions and the static solution of the model had flowed out of the river reach, so that the static situation was reached (fig.5). To fit the computed, static oxygen profile to the measured one, the biological oxidation coefficient (x) had to be "adjusted" to 0.01 hr^{-1}, in contrary to the value it has when sedimentation is included, namely 0.025 hr^{-1}.

The jumps in the measured oxygen concentration profile at the weirs and in the measured BOD concentration profile at the waste discharge were represented by smooth curves in the computed static profiles. This is due to the input/output interpolation procedure and to the representation of the local sources by short distributed sources. It will be remembered that the latter, most important error source will be eliminated in due time. The dispersion coefficient could equally well be made zero without affecting the results, so dispersion had no influence.

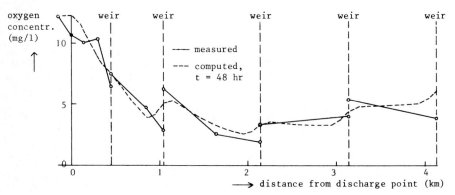

Figure 5. Measured and computed static oxygen profiles.

The good correspondence between the measured and the computed oxygen profile shows what happens when a too simple model is fitted to data that are too scarce. For sedimentation was not included in the model and only the oxygen concentration was used, while the knowledge about the BOD concentrations in the waste discharge and in the river was ignored.

A DYNAMIC EXAMPLE

A test of the numerical accuracy of the dynamic response was carried out with the assumed decrease of the stream velocity that is shown in fig. 6. The change was started after the static situation that is discussed above, had been reached.

This change of v is not only hypothetical, it is also unrealistic, because v(x,t) is constant in x, changing everywhere in the same way at the same moments, further because v(t) is too abrupt, because the water level remains constant in x and t, and because the reaeration at the weirs remains constant. However, the assumption is only made for the sake of the example.

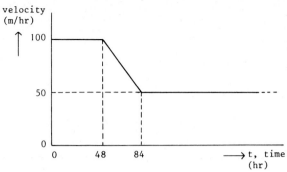

Figure 6. Assumed decrease of the stream velocity.

The decrease of the velocity has the following direct effects.
- As h remains constant, the flow discharge increases proportionally to v, thus diminishing the dilution of the BOD at the discharge point and of the reaerated oxygen at the weirs. At these points, the concentration jumps become higher.
- The reaeration coefficient decreases with v (h remains constant).
- As long as the oxygen concentration does not become zero, the BOD-decay is "displayed" over a shorter distance than before.

In turn, these changes have the following effects.
- The increased BOD concentration and the lower reaeration coefficient cause the oxygen concentration to become zero, particularly in the new static situation (t = 192 hr). The weirs give only a local relief of this oxygen shortage (fig. 8).
- Due to (12), the biological oxidation rate is decreased to the oxygen supply rate when the oxygen concentration becomes zero. The slope of the BOD concentration vs. distance diminishes there (fig. 7, t = 192 hr).
- The static situation of t = 48 hr streams out of the river reach before t = 192 hr (fig. 7 and 8, t = 96 hr).

These changes are right within the unnatural assumptions concerning the change of the velocity, so they do not indicate numerical errors. However, the approximation of the local sources mentioned already under the static example, is also smoothing the concentration jumps at those sources in this case and, besides, adding a small ripple to the concentrations downstream when v does not equal L/T (L being the average of the $L_{i,n}$). This error source will be eliminated in due time.

CONCLUSIONS

The continuous model shows several lacks, such as photosynthesis, nitrification, sedimentation and the velocity dependence of the reaeration at weirs.

The numerical approximation can be improved on some non-vital points, among which the movement of the cells (advection) and the inflow off mass at point sources (waste discharges, weirs). However, the model shows no numerical dispersion, and the calculation of advection and dispersion is sufficiently accurate.

Being defined by these transport processes, the structure of the numerical model and the program prove to be correct and are fit for extensions which eliminate the errors mentioned above. The main improvements of the model are in preparation.

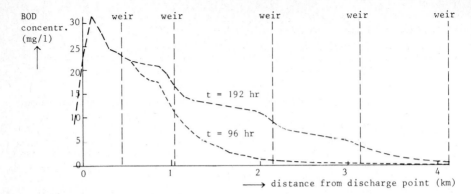

Figure 7. Computed instantaneous BOD profiles during transition (t = 96 hr) and the new static situation (t = 192 hr).

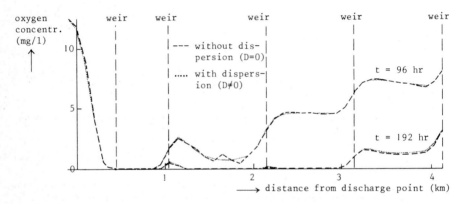

Figure 8. Computed instantaneous oxygen profiles during transition (t = 96 hr) and the new static situation (t = 192 hr).

REFERENCES

Bella, D.A. and Dobbins, W.E. (1968). Difference modeling of stream pollution. J.San. Eng. Div., Proc. ASCE, 94, SA5, 995.

Boer, B. de (1974). Simulatiemodel van de zuurstofhuishouding in beken en rivieren. Verslag, handl., bijl.. Twente University of Technology. Inform.: Provincial Waterboard of Gelderland, Arnhem.

Colenbrander, H.J. and Nes, Th. J. van de (1974). Waterhuishouding vroeger, nu en in de toekomst. H_2O, 7, 10.

Fisher, H.B. (1968). Dispersion prediction in natural streams. J. San. Eng. Div., Proc. ASCE, 94, SA5, 927.

Gennip, R. van and Uunk, E. (1973). Reaktiepatronen in de Groenlose Slinge. Div. of Process Contr. and Environm. Managem., Dept. Chem. Eng., Twente University of Technology, Enschede.

Lau, J.L. (1972). A note on the prediction of BOD profiles due to a source of effluent discharged in a uniformly flowing stream. Water Research, 6, 749-757.

Moretti, G. (1972). Thoughts and afterthoughts about shock computations.
Polytechnic Institute of Brooklyn, PIBAL report nr. 72-37.

Nes, Th. J. van de (1975). Modelonderzoek 1971-1975 ten behoeve van de waterhuishouding in Gelderland. Deel 1 : Onderzoek in relatie tot beleidsvoorbereiding.
Commissie Bestudering Waterhuishouding Gelderland. Werkgroep-rapport nr. 1. Arnhem.

O'Connor, D.J. and Dobbins, W.E. (1958). Trans. ASCE, 123, 641.

Oever, M.L. van den (1972). Het ontwikkelen van een meetmethode om mengpatronen in
beken te bepalen. Div. of Process Contr. and Environm. Managem., Dept. of Chem.
Eng., Twente University of Technology, Enschede.

Pandolfi, M. (1975). Numerical experiments on free surface water motion with bores.
In : G.C. Vansteenkiste, ed. (1975). Computer simulation of water resources sys-
tems, 157. Proceedings IFIP. North Holland Publ. Comp., Amsterdam, Oxford.
American Elsevier Publ. Comp., Inc., New York.

Smith, E.T. and Morris, A.R. (1969). Systems analysis for optimal water quality
management. J. Water Poll. Control Fed., 41, 1635.

DISCUSSION

What do you think is the value of using partial differential equations over a lot of parameters ? (BECK)

You can see what happens in the river in rather good detail, as the model describes it. (DE BOER)

But you only have to know what the BOD and DO are in discrete points, and not in the continuum. (BECK)

Of course, but one often wants to know where a concentration exceeds a maximum limit value or where it becomes smaller than a minimum limit value. There-fore, the concentrations must not only be known at the beginning and the end of a long river reach, but also at several points in between.
Another disadvantage of an input-output type model for a long river reach is, that mostly the equations have to be linearized. In this case, where we have rather complicated reactions, the disadvantage would be insurmountable. We have tried the input-output approach, but it proved to be either wrong or more elaborate than the partial differential equations approach. (DE BOER)

This is a very interesting question, because I would ask you what is the differential equation as used ? It is really a material balance equation. If you are applying it in microscale, what you are doing is apply material balance to boxes, a sequence of boxes. Is your question : why not to use a single box instead of using 5 boxes ? (NEUMAN)

*Not really. It was just in control engineering terms.
For this partial differential equation you have two continuous independent vari-ables, space and time.
Here we are using a lumped system. In some sense it is using a lot of these lumped parameter box models, which can simulate the dispersion characteristics, which appear in your distributed parameter model. Perhaps we have been lazy in our work at Cambridge. We always used a nonparametric approach and we have in practice*

found it to be quite adequate. (BECK)

Are you interested specially in the variations of concentrations because of purification plants ? (DE BOER)

No. (BECK)

The Committee for which I work is interested in effects of water quality control measures as purification plants as well as the effects of water quantity control measures such as weirs (additional reaeration, decrease of stream velocity) on the oxygen dynamics of the river. In that case it is best to look at the whole river reach at once, after each time step. (DE BOER)

You talked in your abstract about the estimation of parameters, and the evaluation of these parameters was done by the empirical relationships and the O'Connor-Dobbins reaeration rate constant. And have you estimated the BOD-decay rate constant ? (BECK)

We estimated it from the slope of the BOD concentration profile.

From the actual data taken in the river ? (BECK)

Yes. (DE BOER)

Did you predict or did you calibrate ? (NEUMAN)

This was no prediction. The parameters were calibrated one by one : we tried to find their values out of the measurements one by one.
So the measurements must relate to the parameters closely. The parameters were not calibrated all together in an automatic procedure. But the example is still a calibration, not a prediction. (DE BOER)

Note of the author : It is our intention to use a more realistic version of the model for predictions, after a satisfying parameter identification and validation.

System Simulation in Water Resources, ed. G.C. VANSTEENKISTE
1976, North-Holland Publishing Company

OPTIMIZATION OF P- AND N- UPTAKE
BY SCENEDESMUS 276 - 3a

H.R. Paelinck and J. De Maeseneer
Fakulteit van de Landbouwwetenschappen
Rijksuniversiteit Gent
Gent, Belgium

ABSTRACT

The N and P requirements of the Scenedesmus strain 276 - 3a were investigated in semi-continuous laboratory cultures. For various NO_3 and PO_4 concentrations the growth rate, biomass increase (dry weight) and the assimilated quantity of these nutrients was determined. From these data the yield could be deduced as a function of the initial concentration as well as the growth and the residual quantity of these elements.
From these figures it could be determined how much dry weight has to be produced in order to achieve a complete elimination of the growth-limiting substances N and P from the solution. By taking into account the accumulation of these elements in the cell it also could be deduced for which N/P ratios N as well as P can be removed from the solution.

INTRODUCTION

In practice eutrophication producing elements can be removed from domestic sewage by means of growing algae. For a complete elimination of certain nutrients and the optimization of it a more profound knowledge af the nutritive requirements of the algae is necessary.
Attention is to be given especially to the major elements N and P besides CO_2, which is also important for the pH of the culture. Of both elements N is quantitatively the most important nutrient. Owing to the fact that N-fixation is possible by bluegreen algae P is the element determining growth in most natural habitats. The removal of P from the effluents to be discharged is therefore compulsory but sufficient in order to prevent limnophilic waters from being eutrophicated. For this purpose use can be made of the "luxury uptake" of PO_4 (Borchardt & Azad, 1968). In the tertiary treatment of domestic sewage N is therefore to be considered in relation to the PO_4 removal.

PO_4 UPTAKE

The PO_4 uptake was investigated within the range of 0.05 - 30 mg/l PO_4. At 0.05 - 0.10 - 0.25 - 0.50 - 1 - 2.5 - 5 - 7.5 - 10 - 12.5 - 15 - 20 - 25 and 30 mg/l PO_4 the growth rate, the biomass increase and the assimilated PO_4 were investigated. The experiments were done twice in order to prevent the elimination of a certain concentration due to experimental error. Therefore all concentrations could not be considered at the same time. In a first run the values of 0.05 to 5 mg/l PO_4 were investigated; a second run consisted of the 5 - 30 mg/l range. Al all concentrations 4 replicates were carried out. Because at 5 mg/l PO_4 the growth rates in both runs did not differ significantly the observations in both runs could be considered as belonging to one series. The results are graphically presented in Figure 1.

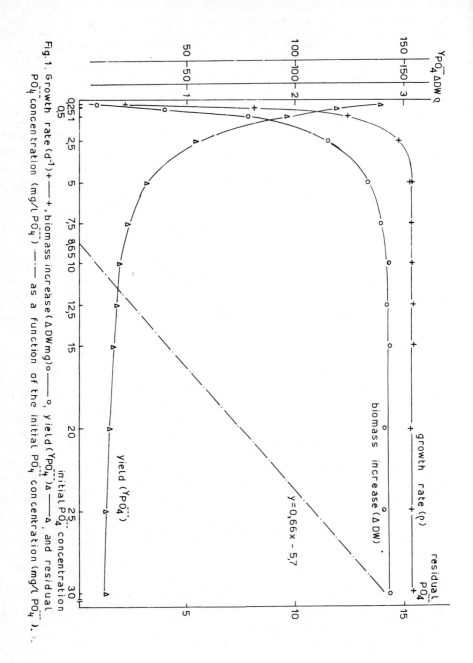

Fig. 1. Growth rate (d⁻¹) + —— +, biomass increase (ΔDW mg) o —— o, yield (Y_{PO_4})Δ —— Δ, and residual PO_4 concentration (mg/l PO_4^{--}) — · — as a function of the initial PO_4^{--} concentration (mg/l PO_4^{--}).

At initial PO_4^{---} concentrations below 0.25 mg/l semi-continuous culturing was impossible. Although at higher concentrations the growth rate and the DW-production increased rapidly the cultures remained chlorotic under 1 mg/l. From this value onwards the cenobia remained fairly well suspended whereby culturing was easy. Up to 5 mg/l the growth rate increases furtheron. From 5 to 30 mg/l the growth rate remained steady. Although the maximum growth rate was obtained at 5 mg/l PO_4^{---} soluted PO_4^{---} could only be detected in the effluent from 10 mg/l onwards. At higher initial concentrations the concentrations found in the effluent increased but not proportionally to the initial concentration. Only at 25 and 30 mg/l the PO_4^{---} increase in the effluent was proportional to the increase in the effluent. At the different concentrations the yield (YPO_4^{---}) is not constant. In static cultures a maximum of 318 mg DW could be produced per mg PO_4^{---} ($Y_{PO_4^{---}}$ = 318). This value could not be obtained in semi-continuous cultures. At the lowest PO_4^{---} concentration (0.25 mg/l) the yield was 140. At higher concentrations the PO_4^{---} efficiency decreased rapidly. At 1 mg/l the $Y_{PO_4^{---}}$ was 35. From $Y_{PO_4^{---}}$ = 40 onwards the maximum growth rate was attained, yet without any trace of PO_4^{---} in the effluent. Up to $Y_{PO_4^{---}}$ = 20 (corresponding with 8.65 mg/l PO_4^{---}) no PO_4^{---} appeared in the effluent. At higher phosphate concentrations the yield kept on diminishing and stabilized at a value of about $Y_{PO_4^{---}}$ = 11.
In order to remove a given amount of PO_4^{---} by growing algae it is therefore compulsory to produce at least 20 mg DW per mg PO_4^{---} ($Y_{PO_4^{---}}$ = 20).
Higher DW productions without growth inhibition are possible. Only at $Y_{PO_4^{---}}$ values over 80 serious growth inhibition is apparent. Basing on the luxury uptake phenomenon PO_4^{---} (as growth limiting nutrient !) can be removed under favourable conditions. In practice $Y_{PO_4^{---}}$ = 40 can be considered at as a good working figure. Dry weight productions oscillating between half and the double of this figure still allow for complete PO_4^{---} removal without seriously affecting the growth rate.

NO_3^- UPTAKE

The NO_3^- uptake was investigated at the following concentrations : 5 - 10 - 15 - 20 - 30 - 75 - 90 - 100 - 125 - 150 - 200 and 300 mg/l NO_3^-. As for the PO_4^{---} uptake the same parameters were considered. The experiments were also carried out in duplo and with four replicates. In a first run the concentrations between 5 and 100 mg/l NO_3^- (with the exception of 90 mg/l) were considered. The second run contained all concentrations from 90 mg/l onwards. Since no significant difference between the growth rates in both runs at 100 mg/l could be evaluated the results of both runs can be regarded as belonging to one series. Figure 2 gives the graphical presentation of these results.
At initial concentrations under 10 mg/l NO_3^- semi-continuous culturing apparently was impossible. From 10 to 50 mg/l the growth rate increased considerably; at higher concentrations it continued to do so but at a slower pace and reached a maximum value at about 150 mg/l NO_3^-. At higher concentrations the growth rate apparently went down again. Although at 90 mg/l NO_3^- the maximum growth rate was not yet attained NO_3^- became apparent in the effluent. At higher concentrations the residual NO_3^- concentrations increased but now proportionally to the initial amounts of NO_3^- .
Taking into account the results of static cultures, the yield ($Y_{NO_3^-}$) apparently oscillated between 7.7 and 1.8. At 10 mg/l the available N was used most efficiently ($Y_{NO_3^-}$ = 6.6). At increasing amounts of NO_3^- the efficiency diminished very rapidly. Up to 75 mg/l NO_3^- - being the highest value at which all NO_3^- was taken up - the $Y_{NO_3^-}$ decreased to 2.3. At this value an almost optimum growth rate was obtained. At higher concentrations the available NO_3^- was no more used up completely. Up to 200 mg/l the $Y_{NO_3^-}$ remained constant ($Y_{NO_3^-}$ = 2.1). At still higher concentrations (300 mg/l NO_3^-) the yield decreased again ($Y_{NO_3^-}$=1.8).

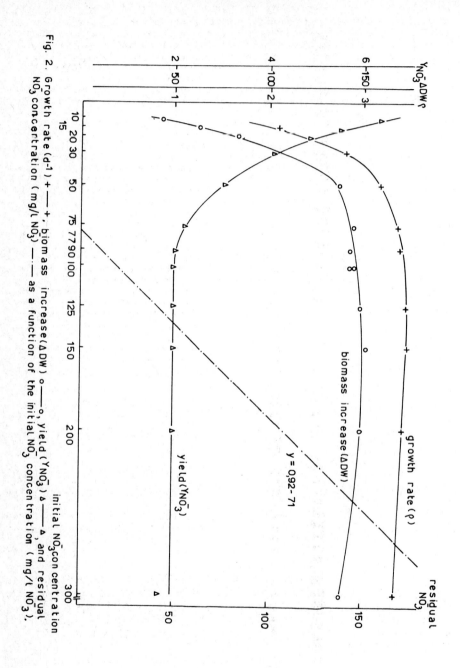

Fig. 2. Growth rate(d^{-1}) + —— +, biomass increase(ΔDW) o ——o, yield(Y$_{NO_3^-}$) ▵ —— ▵, and residual NO$_3^-$ concentration (mg/l NO$_3^-$) —·—· as a function of the initial NO$_3^-$ concentration (mg/l NO$_3^-$).

Since luxury uptake apparently is unexistant the removal of NO_3^- strictly depends
on a certain DW - production. Yet the NO_3^- use is still flexible enough in order
to eliminate the NO_3^- (as a growth compound) by biological extraction. Therefore
at least 2.3 mg DW has to be produced for each mg of NO_3^-. In practice $Y_{NO_3^-} = 3.2$
can be regarded as a fairly satisfactory mean. For DW productions between
$Y_{NO_3^-} = 4$ and 2.3 total NO_3^- removal is guaranteed under optimum growing conditions.

UPTAKE OF PO_4^{---} AND NO_3^- AS NON-GROWTH-LIMITING SUBSTANCES

From the foregoing observations it is apparent that the cell takes up more
nutrients than is strictly necessary for the biomass build-up. Therefore it must
be possible, within certain limits, to take up completely the non-growth-limiting
element. In order to get a better insight into this problem it was investigated
how the yield of the non-growth-limiting element is influenced by the available
nutrient amount.
The PO_4^{---} and NO_3^- yields were evaluated at the following NO_3^-/PO_4^{---} ratios : 20/7.5
30/7.5, 40/7.5, 50/7.5, 75/7.5, 100/7.5 (NO_3^- limitation) and 75/1, 75/1.5,
75/2.5, 75/5, 75/7.5, 75/12.5 (PO_4^{---} limitation).
In order to investigate the effect of a supplementary amount of non-growth-limiting
element the following ratios were inserted : 30/12.5, 40/12.5, 50/12.5, 75/12.5
(NO_3^- limitation) and 100/2.5, 100/5, and 100/7.5 (PO_4^{---} limitation). As in the
previous experiments the same parameters were used.
Since all ratios could be treated simultaneously it was impossible to run the
experiments in duplo. Yet the experiments were replicated five times. The results
are presented in graphical form in Figure 3 (PO_4^{---} limitation) and Figure 4 (NO_3^-
limitation).
The conclusions from the previous experiments were confirmed by the new observations. Moreover it could be seen that the Y-values of the growth-limiting element
are determined solely by the very growth-limiting element. With the data from
the previous experiments and disregarding the concentration of the non-growth-
limiting nutrient, it can therefore be deduced what amount of dry weight has to
be grown in order to remove a given amount of growth-limiting element. In contrast
to the uptake of the growth-limiting nutrient the uptake of the non-growth-limiting
indeed seems to be influenced by the available amount of growth-limiting nutrient.
At decreasing PO_4^{---} uptake the NO_3^- uptake seemed to diminish as well (Fig. 3).
Yet, then the amount of residual NO_3^- increased. The same phenomenon could be observed when the initial NO_3^- concentration was increased from 75 to 100 mg/l. Yet
for the same PO_4^{---} concentration the $Y_{NO_3^-}$ value was lower. Apparently the NO_3^-
uptake is moreover influenced by the amount of available NO_3^-. Up to $Y_{PO_4^{---}} = 40$
(which is the upper limit of the luxury uptake) the $Y_{NO_3^-}$ value remains virtually
constant at 2.2. At $Y_{PO_4^{---}} = 60$ the $Y_{NO_3^-}$ value is enhanced to 2.4. At $Y_{PO_4^{---}} = 80$
(presented previously as the upper limit for PO_4^{---} removal) a $Y_{NO_3^-}$ value of 2.6
was already attained. Yet at the latter value the residual NO_3^- concentration
was quite high. When the growth is only slightly inhibited, the influence of the
PO_4^{---} concentration upon the NO_3^- uptake is negligible. The NO_3^- uptake is only
considerably and the more affected at increasing PO_4^{---} deficiency. In contrast
the NO_3^- uptake the uptake of PO_4^{---} as non-growth-limiting nutrient was only to a
limited extent affected by the available amount of NO_3^- (Figure 4). This is
obvious from the diverging of the curves representing the evolution of $Y_{NO_3^-}$ and
$Y_{PO_4^{---}}$. With higher residual PO_4^{---} concentrations lower $Y_{PO_4^{---}}$ values correspond.
Yet the uptake of PO_4^{---} was not completely independant of the NO_3^- amount. Indeed,
the $Y_{PO_4^{---}}$ curve corresponding with an initial PO_4^{---} concentration of 12.5 mg
showed a slight increase instead of a decrease, which could be expected at increasing residual PO_4^{---} concentration. Also the $Y_{PO_4^{---}}$ value, obtained at the
NO_3^-/PO_4^{---} ratio 75/12.5 was lower than at the ratio of 20/7.5 although in both
cases the same amount of PO_4^{---} was found in the effluent.

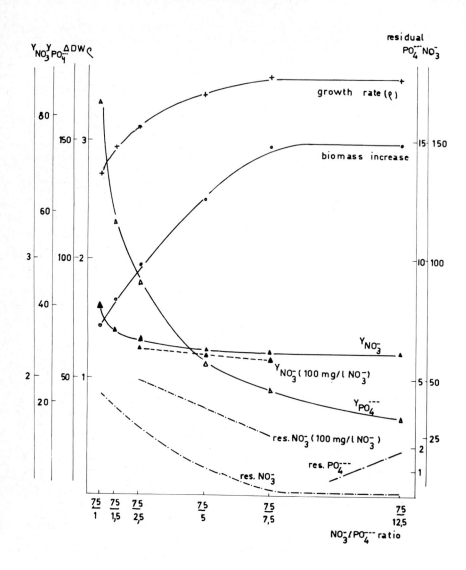

Fig.3. Growth rate(d⁻¹), biomass increase (ΔDWmg), yield, residual PO₄⁻⁻⁻
and NO₃⁻ (mg/l) as a function of the NO₃⁻/PO₄⁻⁻⁻ ratio.
part: PO₄⁻⁻⁻ limitation

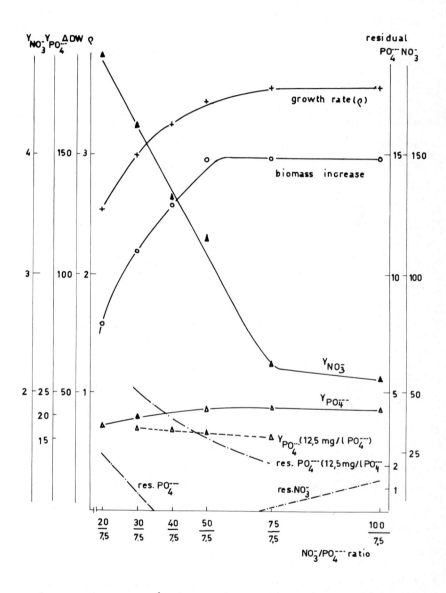

Fig. 4. Growth rate (d^{-1}), biomass increase (ΔDW), yield, residual PO_4^{---} and NO_3^- (mg/l) as a function of the NO_3^-/PO_4^{---} ratio. part, NO_3^- limitation

For the NO_3^-/PO_4^{---} ratios investigated however the influence is limited. If NO_3^- is limiting growth, the PO_4^{---} uptake can be considered as being unaffected, especially considering the fact that extreme N-deficiency is not likely to occur. Aquantitative evaluation of the NO_3^- and PO_4^{---} uptake as non-growth-limiting nutrients seemed to be impossible. Therefore a threedimensional diagram is needed in which on the x- and y-axes the initial concentrations of NO_3^- and PO_4^{---} are drawn and on the z-axis the different parameters. Since also other nutrients (n) are likely to interfere a (n+1) order diagram is to be drawn for a complete quantitative evaluation.

RELATION OF YIELD TO N/P RATIO

Taking into account the above data it can be deduced at which NO_3^-/PO_4^- ratios both nutrients can be taken up completely. For a complete NO_3^- and PO_4^{---} exhaustion 2.3 respectively 20 mg DW has to be produced. When the amount of NO_3^- corresponds with PO_4^{---} as 20 to 2.3 ($NO_3^-/PO_4^{---} = Y_{PO_4^{--}}/Y_{NO_3^-} = 20/2.3 = 8.8$) all NO_3^- and PO_4^{---} will be removed from the solution at a minimum DW production (Fig. 5). Since NH_4 is taken up by preference (Hattori, 1957; Syrett & Morris, 1963; Pribil & Marvan, 1971) the NO_3^- fraction will be taken up last at total N-depletion. This justifies the use of the recalculated Y_P, Y_N and N/P values when besides NO_3^- also NH_4 has to be removed : the NO_3^-/PO_4^{---} ratio = 8.8 becomes N/P = 6.

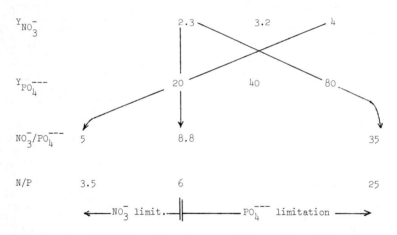

Figure 5 - Utmost limiting N/P ratios at which total N and P removal can be
             achieved. Data obtained from the yield studies.

For lower NO_3^-/PO_4^{---} ratios NO_3^- is growth-limiting.
Since the PO_4^{---} uptake is almost unaffected by the available amount of NO_3^- the lowest NO_3^-/PO_4^{---} ratio at which under fabourable conditions NO_3^- as well as PO_4^{---} can be removed is the one at which a growth with the highest possible yield ($Y_{NO_3} = 4$) is capable of just taking up all PO_4^{---} ($Y_{PO_4^{--}} = 20$). So $NO_3^-/PO_4^{---} = Y_{PO_4^{--}}/Y_{NO_3} = 5$ (N/P = 3.5).
In order to remove both nutrients between the NO_3^-/PO_4^{---} ratios of 5 and 8.8 it is sufficient to determine the biomass which is necessary to remove the PO_4^{---}. Therein $Y_{NO_3^-}$ can be chosen freely. For the lower NO_3^-/PO_4^{---} ratios the $Y_{PO_4^{---}}$ will

have to come close to the lowest limit for total PO_4^{---} uptake in order to keep a growth with an acceptable $Y_{NO_3^-}$.
At NO_3^-/PO_4^{---} ratios above 8.8 PO_4^{---} is growth-limiting. If the NO_3^- uptake were un-affected by P-deficiency the highest NO_3^-/PO_4^{---} ratio at which both elements can be removed is to be determined from the quotient of the highest desirable $Y_{PO_4^{---}}$ value (= 80) and the lowest possible $Y_{NO_3^-}$ value at which still all NO_3^- is taken up. (= 2.3). This gives a NO_3^-/PO_4^{---} ratio of 35 (N/P = 25). However since the NO_3^- uptake diminishes at increasing P-deficiency more biomass will have to be produced. Owing to the pronounced P-deficiency which is to be expected at such a growth this is undesirable. The last-mentioned values seem therefore to be too high as the upper limits. Since within the region of "luxury uptake" of PO_4^{---} ($Y_{PO_4^{---}}$ = 40) the NO_3^- uptake is almost unaffected by PO_4^{---} up to the NO_3^-/PO_4^{---} ratio = 20 (N/P = 15), the necessary algae biomass is to be determined from the data of Figure 5. If the maximum $Y_{PO_4^{---}}$ value is not exceeded $Y_{NO_3^-}$ can be choosen freely. Yet at progressively increasing P = deficiency more biomass will have to be produced than the calculated amounts.

PRACTICAL APPLICATIONS
───────────────────

Theoretically for each NO_3^-/PO_4^{---} ratio between 5 and 35 all NO_3^- and PO_4^{---} can be removed from an effluent. The algae biomass required to achieve this aim can be calculated from the yield and from the concentrations in the effluent. At the practical application, when one will have to work outdoors, the use of algae productions per m^2 are prererable. Indeed in the open algal growth is chiefly a function of the radiant solar energy (per m^2). By taking into account average daily productions differences in illumination and in temperature can be met. These data are well known for our regions among others by the Trebon-reports. Since domestic sewage seems to produce an effluent suitable for the growth of algae the calculated daily averages can be used as a reliable source of information. Fromm the necessary DW production per liter and from the expected DW production per m^2 the depth of the culture can be calculated.
Accepting a retention time of 1 day and knowing the volume of the effluent to be treated the necessary surface for tertiary treatment by means of algae can be calculated.

REFERENCES
──────────

Borchardt, J.A., and Azad, H.S. (1968). JWPCF. 40, 1739.

Hattori, A. (1957). J. Biochem. 44, 253.

Pribil, S., and Marvan, P. (1971). Arch. Hydrobiol./Suppl. 39, Algological studies 5, 334.

Syrett, P.J. and Morris, J. (1963). Biochem. Biophys. Acta 67, 566.

DISCUSSION

What happens when the water is containing toxic elements such as heavy metals ? (PECK)

After secondary purification the presence of toxic elements, at least in domestic sewage, is unlikely. Heavy metals are indeed very toxic for algae, but during the secondary purification, they are removed together with the sludge. We determined heavy metals, but toxic concentrations have not been found. (PAELINCK)

How could your model be put into practice ? (BECK)

It is possible as soon as sufficient high dry weight concentrations under natural circonstances can be obtained. In our countries it is only possible in summertime, not in winter. Tertiary purification by means of algae is especially favourable in countries with high temperatures all the year round. (PAELINCK)

If a certain amount of toxic metals would kill the algae, how long would it take to regrow them ? (BECK)

When part of the culture is undamaged it will take not more than a few days. When, however, all the cells are killed and there is no inoculum available, the regeneration will depend on the number of algae cells present into the secondary effluent. In these circumstances it is not impossible that another species will temporarily become dominant. Because of the continuity it would be preferable to have a second culture, e.g. in an artificial medium, which can be used as inoculum when necessary. (PAELINCK)

You say tertiary treatment by algae is not possible in winter. What temperature is needed for the growth of this algae ? (PECK)

Not only temperature but also illumination is important. If working with different kinds of algae, more importance should be attached to the illumination. So in our latitudes diatoms can cause waterbloom in February, when however the temperature of the water is still very low, but illumination is considerably increased. With Scenedesmus we can work from the beginning of April till October. By using other kinds of algae, e.g. diatoms in Spring, this period can be extended substantially. (PAELINCK)

PART SIX

WATER RESOURCES SIMULATION FOR CONTROL

System Simulation in Water Resources, ed. G.C. VANSTEENKISTE
1976, North-Holland Publishing Company

A COMPUTER CONTROLLED STRATEGY
FOR AN OPEN CHANNEL WASTE WATER SYSTEM

K. Rennicke (Germany), E. Polak (The Netherlands)

ABSTRACT

For an open channel waste water system a control strategy
is proposed and tested in a simulation study before its
implementation. The aim of the channel control consists
in taking a maximum utilization of channel storage capacity
and of giving the customer the opportunity to choose the
location of unavoidable water overflows up to a certain
degree.

INTRODUCTION

The pollution of receiving waters by overflows from sewers
is a serious problem. To reduce the possibility of these overflows
one has either to treat the largest overflow expected or to build
auxiliary storage sufficient to hold peak flows for later release
and treatment. The storage alternative seems the most feasible and
it suggests the necessity for developing control strategies which
are able to minimize overflows or discharges of pollutants and to
take maximum utilizations of treatment equipment.

This concept of an automated control system has been subject
of investigations in several cities of the world. In contrast to
those proposals where a mathematical optimization by means of a
linear programming technique is tried (e.g. Labadie et al. (1975)),
taking different constraints for mass, flow and storage into account
and assuming known input variables for rainfall, we are trying here
more "classical" control methods. Because in our case input disturbance variables as for example rainfall are unknown quantities
which will not be measured.

In a waste water channel system it is economic to design
the capacity of the treatment plant for an average load of the
waste water flow, and to damp out peaks of the inflow rate by a
special buffer reservoir.

This buffer can be the free capacity of the open channel
system itself. It is efficient to separate the channels into different sections, whose water levels are controlled by one single
process computer.

Such a channel system has been built near Eindhoven/The
Netherlands. It consists of a main channel of approximately 30 km
length and tributaries coming from industry and municipalities
(Fig. 1).

Each section of the main channel having a rectangular or
circular cross section area is connected to the neighbourchannels
by a flow control station, being governed by a central process

computer. An overflow of waste water into a river near the channel
is possible in each channel section at specially assigned locations.

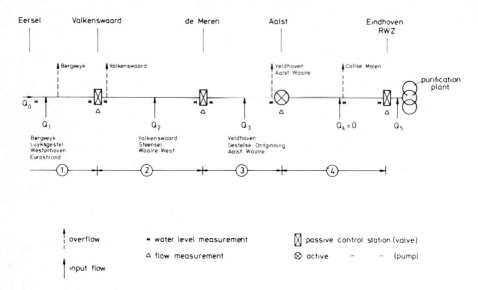

Fig. 1: Measuring points at the Dommel main Channel system

        The dynamic behaviour of the channel system in connection
with the process computer control had been simulated. The special
aim was to investigate and to test the behaviour of a control
strategy before setting the whole system into operation. Both a
continuous channel model, solving the hyperbolic wave equation
and a simplified lumped model with discrete elements as inte-
grators, delay times and other function blocks were tried.

        One problem for the implementation of the control strategy
on a process computer is the exact determination of the water volume in different channel sections, because only a few measurement
points for the height are available and because the channel geometry consists of irregular circular and cascadic structures. By
linearizing this cascadic geometry and by considering the hydrodynamic friction at the channel walls, more simplified relations
between measured water height and stored water volume could be
reached.

THE DOMMEL WASTE WATER CHANNEL SYSTEM

        The task of the installed process computer consists besides
of general monitoring and documentation work in controlling the
water levels in the different channel sections. The first aim of
this process control is to prevent overflow from a channel section
if there is any free capacity in the neighboured channels. That
means that the computer has to balance the water levels belonging
to different sections.

The second aim of the computer control consists in deciding
at which channel section an unavoidable overflow e.g. into a river
may happen. Here the customer has the possibility to choose
priorities.

It is clear that not in any case the control will work
satisfactory, because the possible variation of flows in a valve
or a pump are limited and the input waste water flows may exceed
for a short time these limits.

Nevertheless we believe that for most cases a balance of
water volumes belonging to different channel sections may be
reached.

Measuring points at the main channel

Fig. 1 shows the main channel separated into 4 different
sections by active and passive control stations. A purification
plant at the end of the channel takes up the total water volumes.

At each passive control station the flow may be measured
by means of an ultrasonic flow measurement device. The measured
flow values are converted to telemetric signals and transmitted
to the central process computer.

Water level measurements, also transmitted to the process
computer, are available only at a few points (marked with an
asterix in Fig. 1).

Generally there exists more than one overflow point in a
channel section. In our simulation we only take one overflow into
account. A similar restriction is made with lateral input flows:
Only one input flow is regarded in the simulation procedure, but
this one represents a weighted combination of all inputs, available in a channel.

Underlying flow control

A passive control station is divided into two actuators
(Fig. 2). The first one, the main slide valve is open if the waterlevel in front of the station remains under a prescribed critical
value. In this case the second control slide valve is completely
closed. If the waterlevel exceeds this critical value the main
slide valve closes and the control slide valve may be actuated.
The position of the control slide valve is determined by the output of a three-point-step control regulator, switching an asyn-
chronous motor on and off and reversing its phase sequence. The
desired value of this regulator is chosen by the process computer
according to the control strategy, transmitted to the regulator
device and compared with the actual value of the water flow in
this control pipe. As the regulator combined with the motor drive
works like a switched PI-controller, no static error arises between measured actual flow and desired flow in the pipe. That means
that the characteristic curve of the valve and the influence of the
pressure difference on the flow are eliminated. However, an error
between desired and actual flow value will remain, depending on the
quality of the flow measurement device.

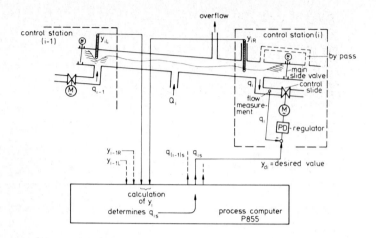

Fig. 2: Structure of the i-th channel-section

A CONTINUOUS ONE DIMENSIONAL MODEL

In order to get some impression of wave propagation effects and water level distributions computations were made describing one dimensional unsteady water flows in open channels in conjunction with control valve operation.

The governing equations of unsteady flow through a straight open channel with uniform properties are the equation of continuity and the equation of momentum. These are nonlinear partial differential equations. They were solved by methods of characteristics.

Dynamic behaviour of a level controlled channel section

One part of the whole channel system – channel section 3 –, has been regarded in a closed loop mode. As actuator only the downstream control station was used (Fig. 3). The two measured level values y_L and y_R were weighted in this case by 0.5 and the sum $y = (y_L + y_R)/2$ was regarded as the actual value of the water level which is proportional to the water volume in this channel section if a rectangular cross section area exists and if the water depth y changes linearly with the horizontal coordinate x. The flow rate Q_3 was set by a proportional control loop. The different modes of the control station (main slide valve in action or control slide valve, saturation of flow Q_3 when the slide valve stands at its limits) were

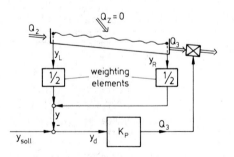

Fig. 3: Open channel water level control with downstream valve actuator

neglected, assuming absolutely linear relations between the actual flow and the set point flow of Q_3.

The program starts with a pair of initial values $v(0,0)$ for velocity and $y(0,0)$ for water level and computes for $t = 0$ the spatial distribution $y(0,x)$ (backwater curve) (Fig. 4). From this initial values $y(x)$ the stationary distribution in reaction with the control loop will be reached after a transient time of about 50 min.

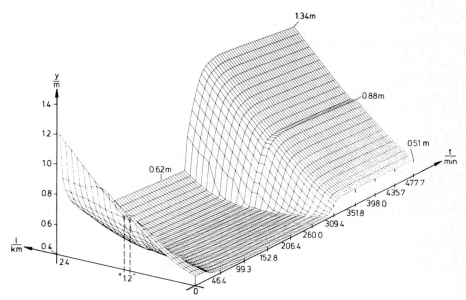

Fig. 4: Transient response for set point variation

Fig. 4 is showing the temporal water level distribution $y(x,t)$ (water level drawn versus channel length and time) after changing the desired value from $y_{soll} = 0.41$ m to 0.82 m at $t = 260$ min. The response is characterized by a monotoneous rising water level without any periodic variation. The reaction starts at the downstream control station propagating upstream. The difference y_d is independent from a set point variation caused by the integral relation between total input flow rates and water volume.

As the average stationary value $y = 0.92$ exceeds the water level in the middle of the channel (0.88 m) because of the rising level inclination $\delta y/\delta x > 0$ the weighting of the measured value (Fig. 3) does not lead to a quite correct average value y. Therefore the weighting of y_L and y_R should be done by a factor about 5% smaller than 0.5.

Exchanging the place of the control valve actuator from the downstream end to the upstream end (Fig. 5), the response of the water depth may become now more nervous, showing now a $\lambda/2$ oscillation of the water level in the channel (Fig. 6).

The reason for this oscillatory
transient behaviour in contrast
to Fig. 4 consists in the location of the actuator. The upstream located actuator produces
disturbances which propagate downstream and which are less damped
than the disturbance waves resulting from a downstream located actuator, moving into the
opposite direction.

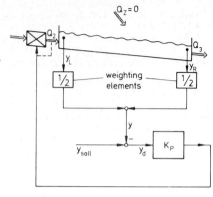

The oscillation depends
on the average water level distribution. It will vanish if the
setpoint has been diminished
sufficiently. That is a consequence of the nonlinear behaviour of the channel.

Fig. 5: Open channel water
level control with upstream
valve actuator.

Wave oscillation may be a very annoying phenomenon at the
measuring points of water level, installed at both ends of the
channel because the period of the waves lies in the order of
0.7 hours for channel section 3 and a smoothing of these low frequent oscillations must slow down the dynamic behaviour of the
controlled channel system. On the other hand, without filtering,
complications within the whole computer controlled system cannot
be avoided.

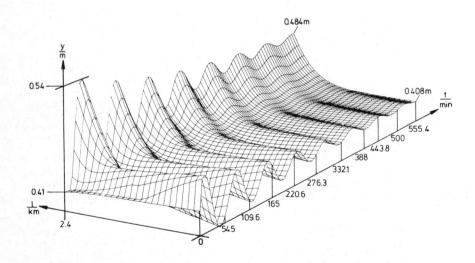

Fig. 6: Response from a given initial distribution

As the numerical value of the proportional regulator should not be reduced, damping may be improved by smoothing the measuring signal with a low pass filter time constant of about 10 min.

A LUMPED MODEL FOR THE CHANNEL SYSTEM

The continuous channel model for one channel section proved to be too complex to be used for the total computer controlled system in a lucid way. Therefore a more simplified model was chosen, consisting of lumped elements (Fig. 7). The control logic and the DDC-part inherent in this model is implemented on the process computer controlling the Dommel channel system.

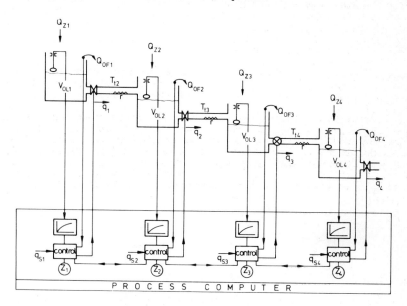

Fig. 7: A physical lumped model for the channel system

Each channel section has been represented by

a water basin containing the channel volume,
a water pipe symbolizing a delay and a friction,
a valve actuator or a pump.

These elements are interacting with the process computer receiving from it set point values for the flow rate and supplying water level measurements as actual values.

The input signals to the process computer from a keyboard or a teletype are priority values $z_1 \ldots z_4$ for the channel overflows or set points for maximal flow rates q_s. The number $z_1 \ldots z_4$ correspond to the weight by which an overflow shall be punished.

In the simulation the model takes the following properties into account:

- constraints for water volume in the different channel sections,
- constraints for maximal flow rate determined by channel geometry and pumping stations,
- the logic for control stations for main- and control-slide valve and cascadic pumping configuration,
- DDC-operation in connection with the process computer and the control stations, influencing each channel section in a control loop structure like Fig. 5,
- a logic deciding the priority of overflows, and adapting control parameters to these priorities,
- approximated channel laws combining water level and flow rate in a nonlinear manner, depending on friction and channel geometry,
- delay, damping and filtering of propagating disturbances in the channel.

In Fig. 8 an example of the results obtained by this model is given. The vertical scale is in units of 10^4 m^3 for volumes and 1 m^3/sec for flow rates, the horizontal scale in units of 10^4 sec. Beginning from the top of the picture, the filtered water volumes, listed as YY1-YY4 are drawn. The zero coordinates have an offset of a multiple of 2 units. The computation starts with zero volume. Next listed as QZ1 and QZ3, two of the four disturbing inflows are plotted (zero coordinates corresponding to the drawing). After the four different flow rates Q11 - Q44 (defined with negative signs) the overflowed volumes OF1 - OF4 follow.

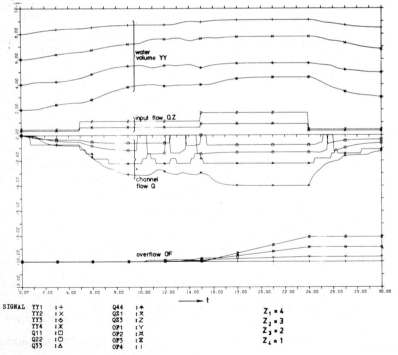

SIGNAL	YY1	:+	Q44	:*		$Z_1 = 4$
	YY2	:×	QZ1	:X		$Z_2 = 3$
	YY3	:◇	QZ3	:Z		$Z_3 = 2$
	YY4	:X	OF1	:Y		$Z_4 = 1$
	Q11	:□	OF2	:H		
	Q22	:◉	OF3	:X		
	Q33	:△	OF4	:I		

Fig. 8: Water volume and flow rate transient response

The amplitudes of the disturbing inflows are set at time
t = 0 to their stationary value and are increased at t = 15 up to
their maximum rainfall amount. At t = 24 the amplitude is decreased
again to the stationary value.

The priorities chosen for unavoidable overflows are set in
this case so that channel 1 gets the highest $(z_1 = 4)$ and channel 4
the lowest priority $(z_4 = 1)$. The overflows which appear after increasing input flows correspond in their amount and their location
to the chosen priorities.

CONCLUSION

By means of the introduction of control stations in the
channel, thus dividing the channel into sections, the storage
performance of the channel is improved. As soon as this storage
capacity has been exploited completely, an overflow of water will
occur. The simulation proved that the amount of overflowing water
from the different sections can be influenced according to predetermined priorities and that a balancing water level distribution at the different sections may be reached.

ACKNOWLEDGEMENT

Thanks are going to Prof. Pandolfi and Ing. grad. Bünz for
their support to program waterflow in open channel systems.

REFERENCES

Labradie, W., Grigg, S., and Bradford, H. (1975). Automatic Control
        of Large-Scale combined Sewer Systems. Journal of the
        Environmental Engineering Division.
Pandolfi, M. (1973). Numerical computation of one-dimensional un-
        steady flow in channels. Meccanica No. 4 (Vol. VIII).

DISCUSSION

*I'm not sure if I got it but I saw a kind of instability when you used the
distributed model for the river. (DE BOER)*

The continuous channel model represents a nonlinear process depending on
nonlinear partial differential equations. Badly damped wave oscillations as in
Fig. 6 may therefore disappear if other setpoints for the water level are chosen
or if control parameters are changed.
The lumped model discussed in the second part of the paper contains also nonlinear
elements as for example switching characteristics. Oscillations of this model are
also possible. But in this case they would show the total water volume in one
channel and not the water level distribution. The lumped model is a very rough one.
It is easier to handle than the continuous channel model but some effects as water
level oscillations cannot be simulated. (RENNICKE)

System Simulation in Water Resources, ed. G.C. VANSTEENKISTE
1976, North-Holland Publishing Company

ON THE OPTIMIZATION OF WATER RESOURCES SYSTEMS WITH STATISTICAL INPUTS[1]

M. Jamshidi[2] and M. Mohseni
Department of Electrical Engineering
School of Engineering
Pahlavi University
Shiraz, Iran

ABSTRACT

The optimization of water resources systems has been the subject of several investigations throughout the world. Methods
of optimization such as linear, nonlinear and dynamic programming are considered by many workers in the field. The
linear programming is limited to static models while the non-
linear programming method requires nonlinear forms of the
cost functionals. The dynamic programming, on the other hand,
has been one of the most widely used methods due to its natural characteristics of being able to deal with discrete
dynamic models and no limitations on the types of equations
governing the system, constraints, or cost functional. The
dynamic programming, although very useful, has its shortcomings in the amount of storage and time consumed in a digital computer simulation. In an attempt to use dynamic programming, several approximation schemes have been proposed.
The "successive approximation", "incremental dynamic programming" and "corridoring" are only three such proposals.
The primary concern of the last approach, used in this study,
is that in each iteration a corridor is formed around a previously defined trajectory and a new trajectory is obtained

---

This work was supported by Iranian National Research Council of
Ministry of Science and Higher Education, Teheran, Iran, June, 73.

Presently on leave with the Institut für Verfahrenstechnik und
Dampfkesselwesen, Universität Stuttgart, W. Germany, on the Vi-
siting Professor' Program of Deutscher Akademischer Austauschdienst (DAAD), Bonn.

by applying the discrete differential dynamic programming
within the present corridor, hence reducing the computer
time and memory requirements.

In this paper a four reservoir water resources system with
four power plants, two input rivers and an irrigation area is
considered. Optimum trajectories are obtained for the reservoirs' water storages and releases assuming statistical data
for the rivers' inflows.

INTRODUCTION

The efficient and optimum use of natural resources in a new era of
severe shortage of energy is an absolute necessity for any nation's
industrial and economic planning and growth to keep their pace. This
is of course very much so for the developing countries who need to
make extended long-range economic planning and their future demands
for energy would become relatively higher than in an already industrialized nation. After oil and natural gas, water has been the
instrumental factor in nations' sectors of economy such as agriculture, urban planning, electric utility and tourist industry to name
a few.

One of the fundamental problems in water resources systems is their
operation and management. Such systems models are often linear discrete and their actual operating data are mostly in tabulated form
and statistical in nature. Moreover, besides system constraints in
discrete form, nonlinearities of objective functions and stochastic
nature of inputs makes the choice of an appropriate optimization
technique a delicate decision. There are several practical optimization methods such as the conjugate gradient, Fletcher and Powell
(1963), second variation, Bryson and Ho (1969), linear programming,
Hays (1968), nonlinear programming, Martos (1975), and dynamic programming, Bellman (1957). The application of every one of the above
methods to water resources requires modifications. Among them, dynamic programming (DP) has been the most suitable considering the
system characteristics into account. Unfortunately, the application
of DP as stated by the Principle of Optimality, Bellman (1957), requires an excessive amount of computer time and storage. It can, in
fact, be demonstrated that the computer requirements go up exponentially as the system's order increases. For this very reason, several
investigators have tried to come up with approximate techniques to

curb the difficulties involved in computer simulation. Among the approximations, the early works of Mayne (1966) in second-order gradient method, Larson and Keckler (1969) in successive approximation, Jacobson (1968) in second variation, Lee (1968) in quasilinearization, Heidari, et.al. (1971a) in a corridoring technique, Chow, et.al. (1974) and Maidment, et.al. (1974) in computer time and memory reductions must all be mentioned. Although all investigators have tried to reduce computational limitations of DP, its application to water resources systems has been made only by Larson (1968), Larson and Keckler (1969), Heidari, et.al. (1971a), Chow, et.al. (1974), Maidment, et.al. (1974), Jamshidi and Heidari (1975).

In this paper, a four-reservoir system considered by Larson and Keckler (1969) and Heidari, et.al. (1971a) is used with statistical observations on the incoming water flows and the corridoring technique of Heidari, et.al. (1971a) to find the optimum trajectories. The simulations were made on an IBM-370/135 computer with 48k-32 bit words memory.

SYSTEM MODEL

The water resources system considered in this paper is presented in Figure 1. As shown, there are four reservoirs, four hydro-power plants, two input streams, and an irrigation area. The variables expressed in this figure are defined as follows:

$y_i(n)$ = inflow into ith reservoir during the month (period or stage) n, i=1,2, in normalized units.

$u_i(n)$ = outflow from ith reservoir during month n, i=1,...,4 in normalized units, also called decision or policy.

$s_i(n)$ = storage of the ith reservoir during the month n, i=1,...,4 in normalized units, also called state.

$e_i(n)$ = evaporating water of the ith reservoir during the month n, i=1,...,4. Table 1 shows the numerical data on the evaporation.

The $y_i(n)$ and $e_i(n)$ variables can be considered to be statistical. The entire outflow of the fourth reservoir is used to irrigate land as shown in figure 1. The system's state equations, after considering the continuity principle would be

$$s_1(n+1) = s_1(n)+y_1(n)-u_1(n)-e_1(n) \qquad (1)$$

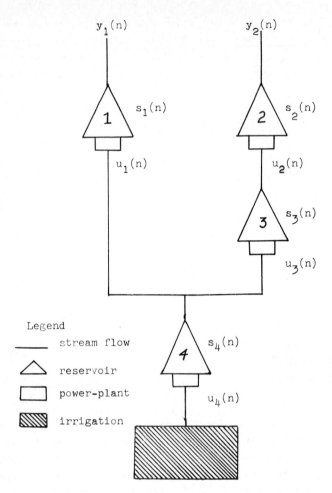

Figure 1: A four-reservoir water resources system

$$s_2(n+1) = s_2(n)+y_2(n)-u_2(n)-e_2(n) \qquad (2)$$

$$s_3(n+1) = s_3(n)+u_2(n)-u_3(n)-e_3(n) \qquad (3)$$

$$s_4(n+1) = s_4(n)+u_1(n)+u_3(n)-u_4(n)-e_4(n) \qquad (4)$$

with n=1,2,3,...,12. There are four primary activities in the system. These are hydro-power generation, irrigation, recreation and flood control. The recreation activity is guaranted by assuming a minimum allowable storage for each reservoir. This minimum is chosen to be zero in normalized units. The maximum value, on the other hand, gives a safeguard for preventing flood. Based on this discussion the follo-wing constraints on the system states is assumed, Larson and Keckler

n	$e_1(n)$	$e_2(n)$	$e_3(n)$	$e_4(n)$
0	.35	.25	.30	.20
1	.40	.30	.30	.25
2	.35	.25	.20	.20
3	.15	.10	.15	.15
4	.10	.08	.10	.10
5	.05	.05	.08	.08
6	.03	.04	.05	.07
7	.09	.08	.06	.07
8	.12	.15	.10	.12
9	.20	.18	.13	.15
10	.32	.22	.18	.16
11	.40	.30	.20	.25

Table 1: Evaporation Functions

(1969),

$$0 \leq s_1(n) \leq 10$$
$$0 \leq s_2(n) \leq 10$$
$$0 \leq s_3(n) \leq 10$$
$$0 \leq s_4(n) \leq 15$$

(5)

In a similar argument, a pre-specified minimum for the normalized decision variables would serve the municipal, industrial and conservation purposes while the rated output power of hydro-generators give a maximum for the water outflows, Larson and Keckler (1969). Based on this discussion, the following constraints are assumed for the normalized decision variables, Larson and Keckler (1969),

$$0 \leq u_1(n) \leq 3$$
$$0 \leq u_2(n) \leq 4$$
$$0 \leq u_3(n) \leq 4$$
$$0 \leq u_4(n) \leq 7$$

(6)

The optimization problem for the system shown in Figure1 can now be stated. Find a sequence of decision variables $u_i(n)$, $i=1,\ldots,4$ and $n=0,1,2,\ldots,11$ such that equations (1) through (6) are satisfied and the following benefit function is maximized,

$$F = \sum_{n=0}^{11} \sum_{i=1}^{4} b_i(n) \cdot u_i(n) + \sum_{n=0}^{11} r(n) \cdot u_4(n) + \sum_{i=1}^{4} g_i(s_i(N), a_i(N)) \quad (7)$$

where

i = number of reservoirs

$a_i(N)$ = final or target value of ith reservoir

$b_i(n)$ = return from the hydro-power generation due to ith reservoir during stage n which depends on power curves and their values are given in Table 2.

n	$b_1(n)$	$b_2(n)$	$b_3(n)$	$b_4(n)$	$r(n)$
0	1.1	1.4	1.0	1.0	1.6
1	1.0	1.1	1.0	1.2	1.7
2	1.0	1.0	1.2	1.8	1.8
3	1.2	1.0	1.8	2.5	1.9
4	1.8	1.2	2.5	2.2	2.0
5	2.5	1.8	2.2	2.0	2.0
6	2.2	2.5	2.0	1.8	2.0
7	2.0	2.2	1.8	2.2	1.9
8	1.8	2.0	2.2	1.8	1.8
9	2.2	1.8	1.8	1.4	1.7
10	1.8	2.2	1.4	1.1	1.6
11	1.4	1.8	1.1	1.0	1.5

Table 2: Coefficients of the Benefit Functions

$g_i(.)$ = a penalty function introduced so that the final reservoirs' states satisfy the desired target values. It is defined as follows, Larson and Keckler (1969),

$$g_i(.) = \begin{cases} -40(s_i(N)-a_i(N))^2, & s_i(N) \leq a_i \\ 0 & \text{otherwise} \end{cases}$$

DISCRETE DIFFERENTIAL DYNAMIC PROGRAMMING TECHNIQUE

The discrete differential dynamic programming (DDDP) is an iterative technique in which the recursive formula of DP is used about a trial trajectory to improve upon the discrete states and decisions. Consider the state difference equation of a system,

$$s(n) = h(s(n-1),u(n-1),n-1), \quad n=1,2,\ldots,N \tag{8}$$

where s and u are m-dimensional state and p-dimensional decision vectors, respectively. The system constraints may be defined as,

$$s(n)\epsilon S(n) , \quad u(n)\epsilon U(n) \tag{9}$$

where $S(n)$ and $U(n)$ are the states and decisions admissible domains, respectively. The optimization problem is to obtain the sequence of decisions $u_i(n)$, $i=1,2,\ldots,p$ which satisfies (8) - (9) while maximizing (or minimizing) an objective function,

$$F = \sum_{n=1}^{N} R(s(n-1), u(n-1), n-1) \qquad (10)$$

where F is the sum of returns R obtained as the result of applying decision $u(n-1)$ for one stage when the system is at state $s(n-1)$. Using DP's forward algorithm,

$$F^*(s(n),n) = \max_{u(n-1)\epsilon U(n-1)} (R(s(n-1),u(n-1),n-1)+F(s(n-1),n-1)) \qquad (11)$$

where $F^*(s(n),n)$ is the maximum of the total returns from stage 0 to stage n. Solving (8) for $s(n-1)$, assuming that the system is invertible, Heidari, et.al. (1971a), one obtains,

$$s(n-1) = k(s(n),u(n-1),n-1). \qquad (12)$$

Substituting (12) into (11), the following recursive equation results

$$F^*(s(n),n) = \max_{u(n-1)\epsilon U(n-1)} (R(k,u(n-1),n-1)+F^*(s(n-1),n-1)) \qquad (13)$$

which can be solved for every state $s(n)\epsilon S(n)$, as a function of $u(n-1)$ only. Now assume that the optimization problem formulated by (8) - (10) has a pre-specified end condition on the state,

$$s(0) = a(0) , s(N) = a(N) . \qquad (14)$$

In the "corridoring technique" of Heidari, et.al. (1971a), a sequence of trial initial decision variables $\bar{u}_i(n)$, $i=1,\ldots,p$ and $n=0,1,2,\ldots,N-1$ which results in a sequence of trial states $\bar{s}_j(n)$, $j=1,2,\ldots,m$ and $n=1,2,\ldots,N$, is assumed. Consider a set of m-dimensional incremental state vectors,

$$\Delta s_i(n) = (\delta s_{i1}(n) \ \delta s_{i2}(n) \ \ldots \ \delta s_{1m}(n))' \qquad (15)$$

for $n=0,1,2,\ldots,N$ and $i=1,2,\ldots,M^m$ whose jth component $\delta s_{ij}(n)$, $j=1,2,\ldots,m$ can take on any value $\sigma_{i,k}$, $i=1,2,\ldots,m$ and $k=1,2,\ldots,M^m$ within the admissible state domain when the incremental state vectors (15) are added to trial state trajectory $\bar{s}(n)$, a sub-domain called $D(n)$ is obtained

$$D(n): \bar{s}_i(n)+\Delta s_i(n), \ i=1,2,3,\ldots,M^m. \qquad (16)$$

Figure 2 shows a sub-domain $D(n)$ corresponding to $m=1$, $M=3$ and $N=12$. All the lattice points in $D(n)$ are called "corridor" by Heidari, et.al.

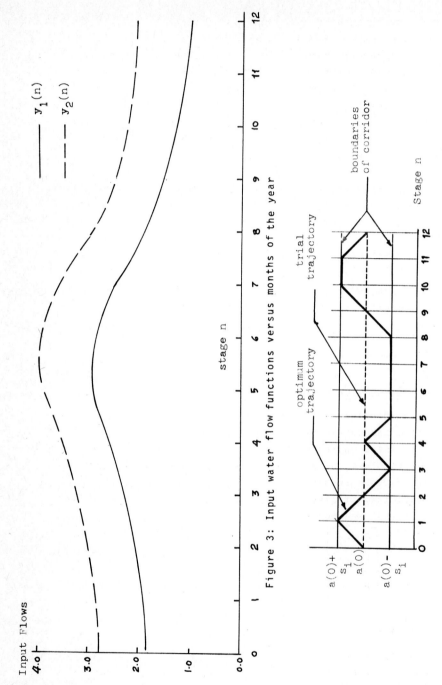

Figure 3: Input water flow functions versus months of the year

Figure 2: A corridor showing the trial and optimal trajectories with m=1, M=3 and N=12

(1971a), designated by C. In the application of DDDP, at the kth iteration, the domain (9) is reduced to the kth corridor C_k. Hence using the recursive formula (13) a new value for the objective function is obtained. This value F_k is compared with the previous one F_{k-1} and if an improvement is attained the present trajectory will be used as the trial trajectory for the (k+1)th iteration an so on. The computational steps of the corridoring technique are now briefly summarized. For greater detail and a flow chart the interested reader may refer to Heidari, et.al. (1971a, 1971b) or Mohseni (1975).

Step 1: Use the (k-1)st trajectories as the trial trajectories for the kth-iteration, $(\bar{s}(n))_k = (s^*(n))_{k-1}$, $(\bar{u}(n))_k = (u^*(n))_{k-1}$.

Step 2: Select $\sigma_{i,k}$, $i=1,2,\ldots,M^m$ to define corridor C_k and use (13) to maximize F subject to $s(n) \epsilon C_k$.

Step 3: Trace and obtain the optimum trajectory satisfying boundary conditions (14), i.e. $(s^*(n))_k$, $(u^*(n))_k$ and F_k^*.

Step 4: If $F_k^* > F_{k-1}^*$ then go to Step 1.

Step 5: Stop

COMPUTER SIMULATION

Using the numerical values defined by Tables 1 and 2 and equations (5) - (7), the corridoring technique was simulated on an IBM 370/135 computer. The computer simulation, coded in FORTRAN IV, consists of seven subroutines and a main program. The detail functions and listing of these programs may be found in Mohseni (1975). As initial trial trajectories, the following was assumed, Larson and Keckler (1969) and Mohseni (1975),

$$
\bar{s}(n) = \begin{bmatrix} \bar{s}_1(n) \\ \bar{s}_2(n) \\ \bar{s}_3(n) \\ \bar{s}_4(n) \end{bmatrix} = \begin{bmatrix} 5 \\ 5 \\ 5 \\ 5 \end{bmatrix} \qquad \bar{u}(n) = \begin{bmatrix} \bar{u}_1(n) \\ \bar{u}_2(n) \\ \bar{u}_3(n) \\ \bar{u}_4(n) \end{bmatrix} = \begin{bmatrix} 2 \\ 3 \\ 3 \\ 5 \end{bmatrix} \qquad (17)
$$

for $n=0,1,2,\ldots,12$.

The input functions $y_i(n)$, $i=1,2$ were obtained by applying the linear regression on observed data for each reservoir's past ten-years history. A special program was written for this purpose, Mohseni (1975).

Iteration 1 Corridor 1

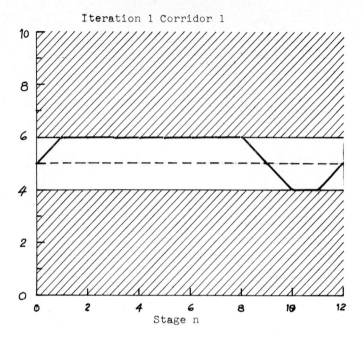

Stage n

Part a

Iteration 2 Corridor 1

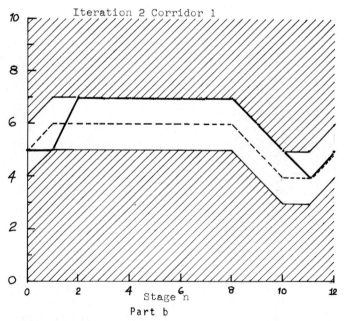

Stage n

Part b

Figure 4: Reservoir one normalized storage capacity for a
         twelve-month period

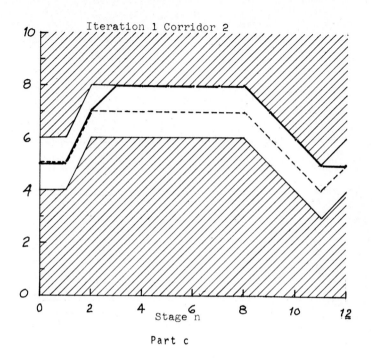

Part c

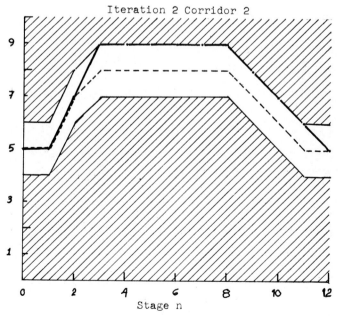

Figure 4   Part d

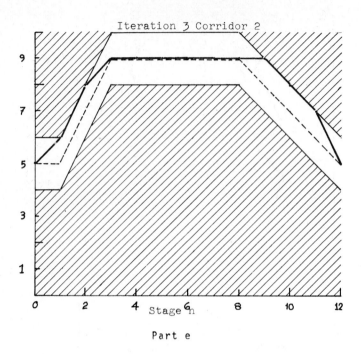

Part e

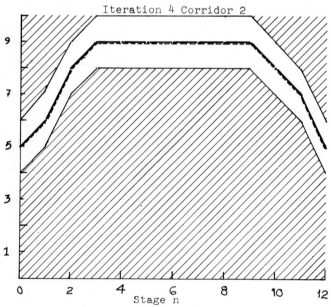

Part f - Optimum Trajectory

Figure 4

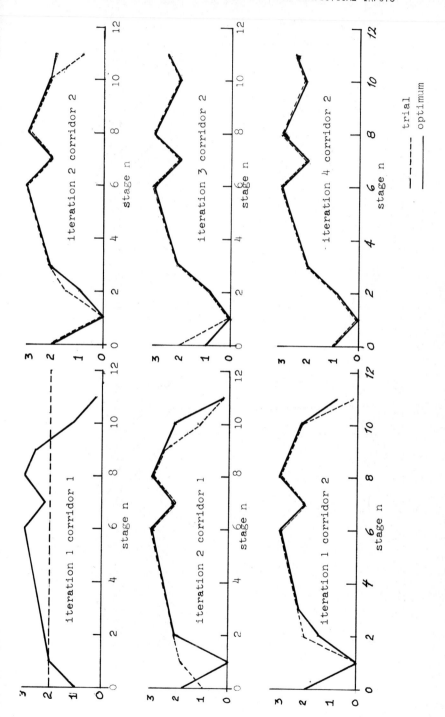

Figure 5: Optimum trajectory of reservoir one water release after six iterations

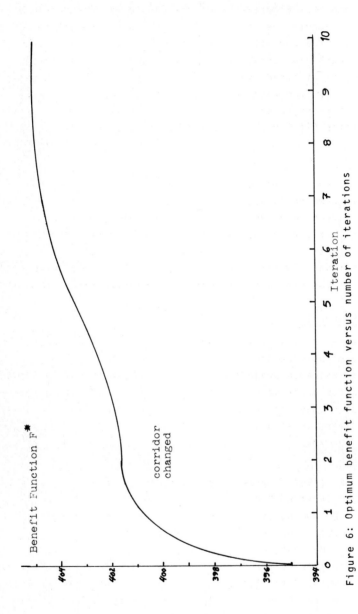

Figure 6: Optimum benefit function versus number of iterations

Figure 3 shows the resulting input water flows $y_1(n)$ and $y_2(n)$. Based on the initial trial trajectories given by (17), the benefit function (10) became 395. Figure 4 shows the resulting reservoir one storage in a twelve-month period. Note that in each case the corridor is clearly shown along with the current trial trajectory. In most cases going through two corridors and a maximum of three iterations a convergence was attained. Figure 5 shows the corresponding optimum water outflow from reservoir one as a function of time. The convergence of the trajectories can also be demonstrated by a plot of benefit function $F^*(.)$ vs. the number of iterations as shown in Figure 6.

CONCLUSIONS

In this paper, a corridoring technique for discrete differential dynamic programming is used to optimize the reservoir hold-up and release waters throughout an operational twelve-month period. The data on incoming river flows over a ten-year history was gathered and linear regression was used to obtain the coefficients of the approximate functions. In almost all cases, for the four reservoirs of the system, convergence was attained in about six iterations.

ACKNOWLEDGEMENTS

The authors are thankful to the Iranian National Research Council, Ministry of Science and Higher Education, Teheran, Iran, for supporting this research project. The financial backing of the Deutscher Akademischer Austauschdienst (DAAD), Bonn, F.R.G., is also sincerely appreciated. The services of Computer Center of Pahlavi University, Shiraz, Iran, is also acknowledged.

REFERENCES

Bellman, R. (1957). Dynamic Programming. (Princeton University Press, Princeton, N.J.).

Bryson, A.E. and Ho, Y.C. (1969). Applied Optimal Control. Blaisdell Publishing Co., Waltham, Mass., pp. 131-141.

Chow, V.T., Maiment, D.R. and Tauxe, G.W. (1974). Computer Time Requirements for DP and DDDP in Water Resources Systems Analysis. Proc. 55th Annual AGU Conf., Washington, D.C.

Fletcher, R. and Powell, M.J.D. (1963). A Rapidly Convergent Descent Method for Minimization. The Computer Journal 6, pp.163-168.

Heidari, M., Chow, V.T., Kokotović and Meredith, D.D. (1971a). The
    Discrete Differential Dynamic Programming Approach to Water
    Resources Systems Optimization. Water Resources Research 7,
    pp. 273-282.
Heidari, M., Chow, V.T. and Meredith, D.D. (1971b). Water Resources
    System Analysis by Discrete Differential Dynamic Program-
    ming. Civil Engr. Studies Hydraulic Series No. 24, Univer-
    sity of Illinois, Urbana, Illinois.
Jacobson, D.H. (1968). New Second-Order and First-Order Algorithms
    for Determining Optimal Control: A Differential Dynamic
    Programming Approach. J. Optimization Theory and Applica-
    tion 2.
Jamshidi, M. and Heidari, M. (1975). Modelling and Optimization of
    Khuzestan Water Resources System. Proc. 6th IFAC Congress,
    Boston, Mass.
Larson, R.E. (1968). State Increment Dynamic Programming. American
    Elsevier Publishing Co. Inc., New York.
Larson, R.E. and Keckler, W.G. (1969). Application of Dynamic Pro-
    gramming to Control of Water Resources Systems. IFAC J.
    Automatica 5, pp. 15-26
Lee, S.E. (1968). Dynamic Programming, Quasilinearization and the
    Dimensionality Difficulty. J. Math. Anal. Appl. 27, pp.
    303-322.
Maidment, D.R., Chow, V.T. and Tauxe, G.W. (1974). Computer Memory
    Requirements for DP and DDDP in Water Resources Systems
    Analysis. Proc. 55th Annual AGU Conf., Washington, D.C.
Martos, B. (1975). Nonlinear Programming. (North Holland Publishing
    Co., Amsterdam, Holland).
Mayne, D. (1966). A Second-Order Gradient Method for Determining Op-
    timal Trajectory of Nonlinear Discrete-Time Systems. Int.
    J. Control 3, pp. 85-95.
Mohseni, M. (1975). Stochastic Analysis of Water Resources Systems.
    Internal Report, Dept. of Electrical Engineering, Pahlavi
    University, Shiraz, Iran.
Orchard-Hays. (1968). Advanced Linear Programming-Computing Techniques.
    (Mc Graw Hill Book Co., New York, N.Y.)

M.B. BECK
  *Control Engineering Group, Department of Engineering, University of Cambridge,
  Mill Lane, Cambridge CB2 1RX, England.*

B. CAUSSADE
  *INP-ENSEEIHT, Institut de Mécanique des Fluides, 2 rue Ch. Camichel,
  31071 Toulouse-Cedex, France.*

A. COTTENIE
  *Laboratorium voor Analytische en Agrochemie, Rijksuniversiteit Gent,
  Coupure Links 533, 9000 Gent, Belgium.*

L.W. DE BACKER
  *Faculté des Sciences Agronomique, Université Catholique de Louvain,
  Département de Génie Rural, Place Croix du Sud 3, 1348 Louvain-la-Neuve,
  Belgium.*

B. DE BOER
  *Provinciale Waterstaat van Gelderland, Provinciehuis, Marktstraat 1, Arnhem,
  The Netherlands.*

J. DE MAESENEER
  *Fakulteit van de Landbouwwetenschappen, Rijksuniversiteit Gent, Coupure
  Links 533, 9000 Gent, Belgium.*

G. DE MARSILY
  *Centre d'Informatique Géologique, Ecole des Mines de Paris, 35 rue St.Honore,
  77305 Fontainebleau, France.*

H. DIESTEL
  *Leichtweiss-Institute for Water Research, Technical University Braunschweig,
  Postfach 3329, 33 Braunschweig, Germany.*

D.M. DUBOIS
  *Institut de Mathématique, Université de Liège, 15 avenue des Tilleuls,
  4000 Liège, Belgium.*

W. EHLERS
  *Institut für Pflanzenbau und Pflanzenzüchtung, Georg-August University,
  34 Goettingen, West Germany.*

J.J. FRIED
  *Institut de Mécanique des Fluides, Université Louis Pasteur, 2 rue Boussing-
  ault, 67000 Strasbourg, France.*

M. JAMSHIDI
Department of Electrical Engineering, Pahlavi University, Shiraz, Iran.

W.J. KARPLUS
Computer Science Dept., School of Engineering and Applied Science, University of California, Los Angeles, California 90024, U.S.A.

D.O. LOMEN
Department of Mathematics, University of Arizona, Tucson, Arizona 85721, U.S.A.

S.P. NEUMAN
Institute of Soil and Water, Agricultural Research Organization, P.O. Box 6, Bet Dagan, Israel.
presently on leave at Department of Hydrology and Water Resources, University of Arizona, Tucson, Arizona 85721, U.S.A.

J.C.J. NIHOUL
Conseil Scientifique de L'Environnement, Université de Liège, 15 avenue des Tilleuls, 4000 Liège, Belgium.

A.J. PECK
CSIRO, Division of Land Resources Management, Private Bag, P.O., Wembley, W.A. 6014, Australia.

E. PERSOONS
Departement de Genie Rural, Kardinaal Mercierlaan 92, 3030 Heverlee, Belgium.

H. PROPFE
Leichtweiss-Institute for Water Research, Technical University Braunschweig, Postfach 3329, 33 Braunschweig, Germany.

K. RENNICKE
Philips Forschungslabor, 2 Hamburg 54, Vogt-Kölnn-Strasse 30, Germany.

J.R. ROGERS
Department of Civil Engineering, Cullen College of Engineering, University of Houston, Houston, Texas 77004, U.S.A.

T.M. SIMUNDICH
Computer Science Dept., School of Engineering and Applied Science, University of California, 3732 Boelter Hall, Los Angeles, California 90024, U.S.A.

E. TODINI
Centro Scientifico IBM, Via S. Maria 67, 56100 Pisa, Italy.

G. VACHAUD
Institut de Mécanique, U.S.M.G., Université de Grenoble, B.P. 53, 38041 Grenoble Cedex, France.

R.R. VAN DER PLOEG
Institute of Soil Science and Forest Nutrition, Georg-August University, 2 Buesgenweg, 34 Goettingen, West Germany.

M.TH. VAN GENUCHTEN
Water Resources Program, Engineering Quadrangle, Princeton University, Princeton, N.J. 08540, U.S.A.

G.C. VANSTEENKISTE
Seminarie voor Toegepaste Wiskunde en Biometrie, Rijksuniversiteit Gent, Coupure Links 533, 9000 Gent, Belgium.

W. VERSTRAETE
Laboratorium voor algemene en industriële microbiologie, Rijksuniversiteit Gent, Coupure Links 533, 9000 Gent, Belgium.

S.J. WAJC
Dienst voor Chemische Ingenieurstechniek en Industriële Scheikunde, Vrije Universiteit Brussel, Adolf Buyllaan 105, 1050 Brussel, Belgium.

A.W. WARRICK
Department of Hydrology and Water Resources, University of Arizona, Tucson, Arizona 85721, U.S.A.

P.G. WHITEHEAD
Control Engineering Group, Department of Engineering, University of Cambridge, Mill Lane, Cambridge CB2 1RX, England.

P.J. WIERENGA
Department of Agronomy, New Mexico State University, Las Cruces, N.M. 88003, U.S.A.
presently on leave at Institut de Mécanique, CNRS, Grenoble, France.

AUTHOR INDEX

CONFERENCE PARTICIPANTS

M. AYYILDIZ, College of Agriculture, Agricultural Engineering Department, University of Ankara, Ankara, Turkey.

K. BAKKER, Ingenieursbureau Dwars, Heederik en Verhey, Laan 1914, Amersfoort, Holland.

G. BARON, Dienst voor Chemische Ingenieurstechniek en Industriële Scheikunde, Vrije Universiteit Brussel, Adolf Buyllaan 105, 1050 Brussel, Belgium.

G. BAZIER, Département de Génie Rural, U.C.L., 1348 Louvain-la-Neuve, Belgium.

M.B. BECK, Control Engineering Group, Department of Engineering, University of Cambridge, Mill Lane, Cambridge CB2 1RX, England.

C. BELMANS, Fakulteit der Landbouwwetenschappen, Afdeling Landelijk Genie, K.U.L., Kardinaal Mercierlaan 92, Heverlee, Belgium.

D. BOUILLOT, ENSIMAG, Ecole d'Ingénieurs, Domaine Universitaire, Grenoble 38, France.

M. BRUYNEEL, Ministerie voor Volkgezondheid, Rijksadministratief Centrum, Arcade Gebouw, 1010 Brussel, Belgium.

B. CABIBEL, Institut National de la Recherche Agronomique, Station de Science du Sol, Domaine St. Paul, 84140 Montfavet, France.

B. CAUSSADE, INP-ENSEEIHT, Institut de Mécanique des Fluides, 2 rue Ch. Camichel, 31071 Toulouse-Cedex, France.

O. COGELS, Département de Génie Rural, Université Catholique de Louvain, Place Croix du Sud 3, 1348 Louvain-la-Neuve, Belgium.

A. COTTENIE, Laboratorium voor Analytische en Agrochemie, Rijksuniversiteit Gent, Coupure Links 533, 9000 Gent, Belgium.

R. CROSBIE, Department of Electrical Engineering, University of Salford, M5 4WT, Lancashire, England.

L.W. DE BACKER, Faculté des Sciences Agronomique, Université Catholique de Louvai Département de Génie Rural, Place Croix du Sud 3, 1348 Louvain-la-Neuve, Belgium.

B. DE BOER, Provinciale Waterstaat van Gelderland, Provinciehuis, Marktstraat 1,
   Arnhem, The Netherlands.

M. DE BOODT, Fakulteit van de Landbouwwetenschappen, Rijksuniversiteit Gent,
   Coupure Links 533, 9000 Gent, Belgium.

J. DE MAESENEER, Fakulteit van de Landbouwwetenschappen, Rijksuniversiteit Gent,
   Coupure Links 533, 9000 Gent, Belgium.

G. DE MARSILY, Centre d'Informatique Géologique, Ecole des Mines de Paris,
   35 rue St.Honore, 77305 Fontainebleau, France.

F. DE SMEDT, Instituut voor Wetenschappen van het Leefmilieu, Vrije Universiteit
   Brussel, Adolf Buyllaan 105, 1050 Brussel, Belgium.

H. DIESTEL, Leichtweiss-Institute for Water Research, Technical University
   Braunschweig, Postfach 3329, 33 Braunschweig, Germany.

D.M. DUBOIS, Institut de Mathématique, Université de Liège, 15 avenue des Tilleuls,
   4000 Liège, Belgium.

J.J. FRIED, Institut de Mécanique des Fluides, Université Louis Pasteur,
   2 rue Boussingault, 67000 Strasbourg, France.

R. GUENNELON, Institut National de la recherche Agronomique, Station de Science
   du Sol, Domaine St. Paul, 84140 Montfavet, France.

W.J. KARPLUS, Computer Science Department, School of Engineering and Applied
   Science, University of California, Los Angeles, California 90024, U.S.A.

E. LEDOUX, Ecole des Mines de Paris, 35 rue St.Honore, 77300 Fontainebleau,
   France.

D.O. LOMEN, Department of Mathematics, University of Arizona, Tucson, Arizona
   85721, U.S.A.

S.P. NEUMAN, Institute of Soil and Water, Agricultural Research Organization,
   P.O. Box 6, Bet Dagan, Israel.
   Presently on leave at Department of Hydrology and Water Resources, University
   of Arizona, Tucson, Arizona 85721, U.S.A.

H. PAELINCK, Faculteit van de Landbouwwetenschappen, Rijksuniversiteit Gent,
   Coupure Links 533, 9000 Gent, Belgium.

A.J. PECK, CSIRO, Division of Land Resources Management, Private Bag, P.O.,
   Wembley, W.A. 6014, Australia.

H. PROPFE, Leichtweiss-Institute for Water Research, Technical University
   Braunschweig, Postfach 3329, 33 Braunschweig, Germany.

K. RENNICKE, Philips Forschungslabor, 2 Hamburg 54, Vogt-Kölln-Strasse 30,
   Germany.

J.R. ROGERS, Department of Civil Engineering, Cullen College of Engineering,
University of Houston, Houston, Texas 77004, U.S.A.

A.S. ROGOWSKI, USDA-ARS, Northeast Watershed Research Center, 111 Research
Building A, University Park, Pennsylvania 16802, U.S.A.

T.M. SIMUNDICH, Computer Science Department, School of Engineering and Applied
Science, University of California, 3732 Boelter Hall, Los Angeles, California
90024, U.S.A.

J. SMITZ, Conseil Scientifique de L'Environnement, Université de Liège,
15 avenue des Tilleuls, 4000 Liège, Belgium.

E. TODINI, Centro Scientifico IBM, Via S. Maria 67, 56100 Pisa, Italy.

G. VACHAUD, Institut de Mécanique, U.S.M.G., Université de Grenoble, B.P. 53,
38041 Grenoble Cedex, France.

L. VALADARES TAVARES, Portuguese Engineering Society, Rua Tristao Vaz - N°37 -
2°Esq., Lisbon-3, Portugal.

A. VAN DER BEKEN, Instituut voor Wetenschappen van het Leefmilieu, Vrije Universiteit Brussel, Adolf Buyllaan 105, 1050 Brussel, Belgium.

R.R. VAN DER PLOEG, Institute of Soil Science and Forest Nutrition, Georg-August
University, 2 Buesgenweg, 34 Goettingen, West Germany.

R. VANLOOCKE, Faculteit van de Landbouwwetenschappen, Rijksuniversiteit Gent,
Coupure Links 533, 9000 Gent, Belgium.

P. VAN REMOORTERE, Koninklijke Militaire School, Renaissancelaan, 1040 Brussel,
Belgium.

G.C. VANSTEENKISTE, Seminarie voor Toegepaste Wiskunde en Biometrie, Rijksuniversiteit Gent, Coupure Links 533, 9000 Gent, Belgium.

D. VRIELYNCK, Ministerie van Openbare Werken, Bestuur voor Elektriciteit en
Elektromechanica, Wetstraat, 1040 Brussel, Belgium.

S.J. WAJC, Dienst voor Chemische Ingenieurstechniek en Industriële Scheikunde,
Vrije Universiteit Brussel, Adolf Buyllaan 105, 1050 Brussel, Belgium.

P.G. WHITEHEAD, Control Engineering Group, Department of Engineering, University
of Cambridge, Mill Lane, Cambridge CB2 1RX, England.

P.J. WIERENGA, Department of Agronomy, New Mexico State University, Las Cruces,
N.M. 88003, U.S.A.
Presently on leave at Institut de Mécanique, CNRS, Grenoble, France.